DRIFTING DRAGONS

Taku Kuwabara

3

DRIFTING DRAGONS

Table of Contents

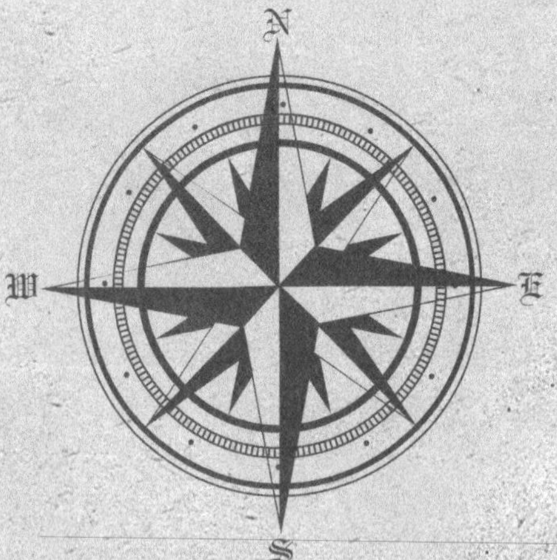

N
W
E
S

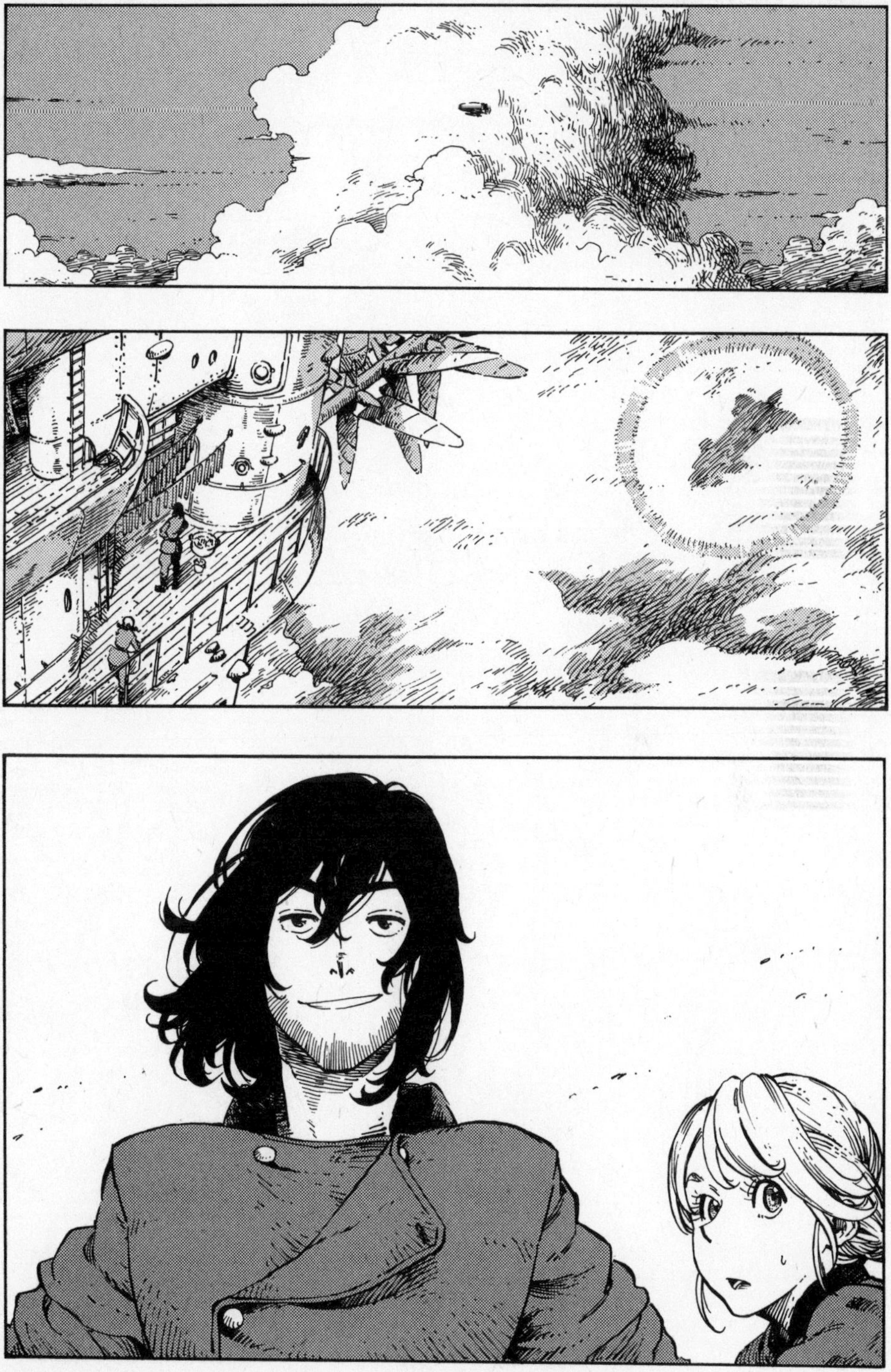

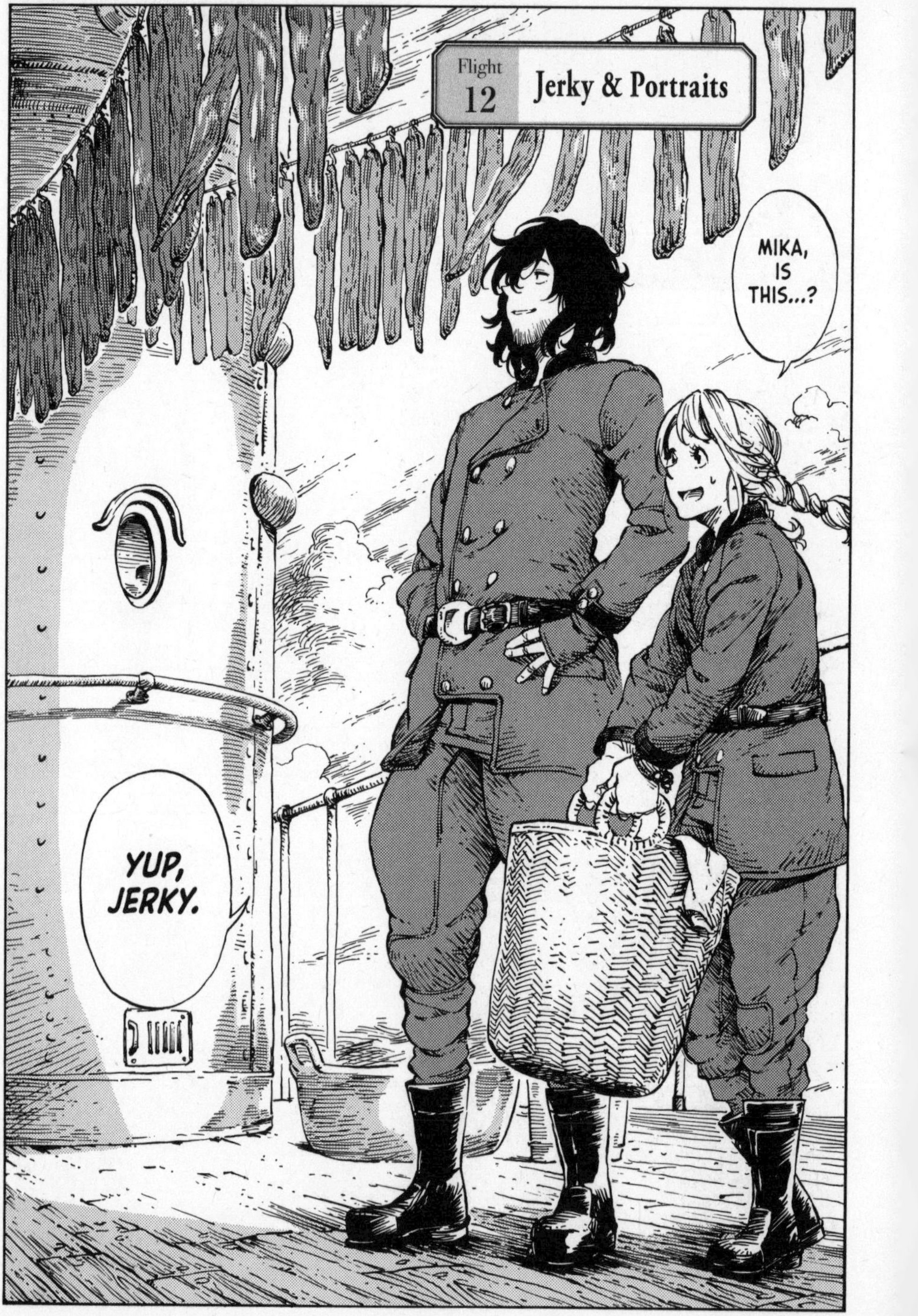
Flight 12
Jerky & Portraits
MIKA, IS THIS...?
YUP, JERKY.

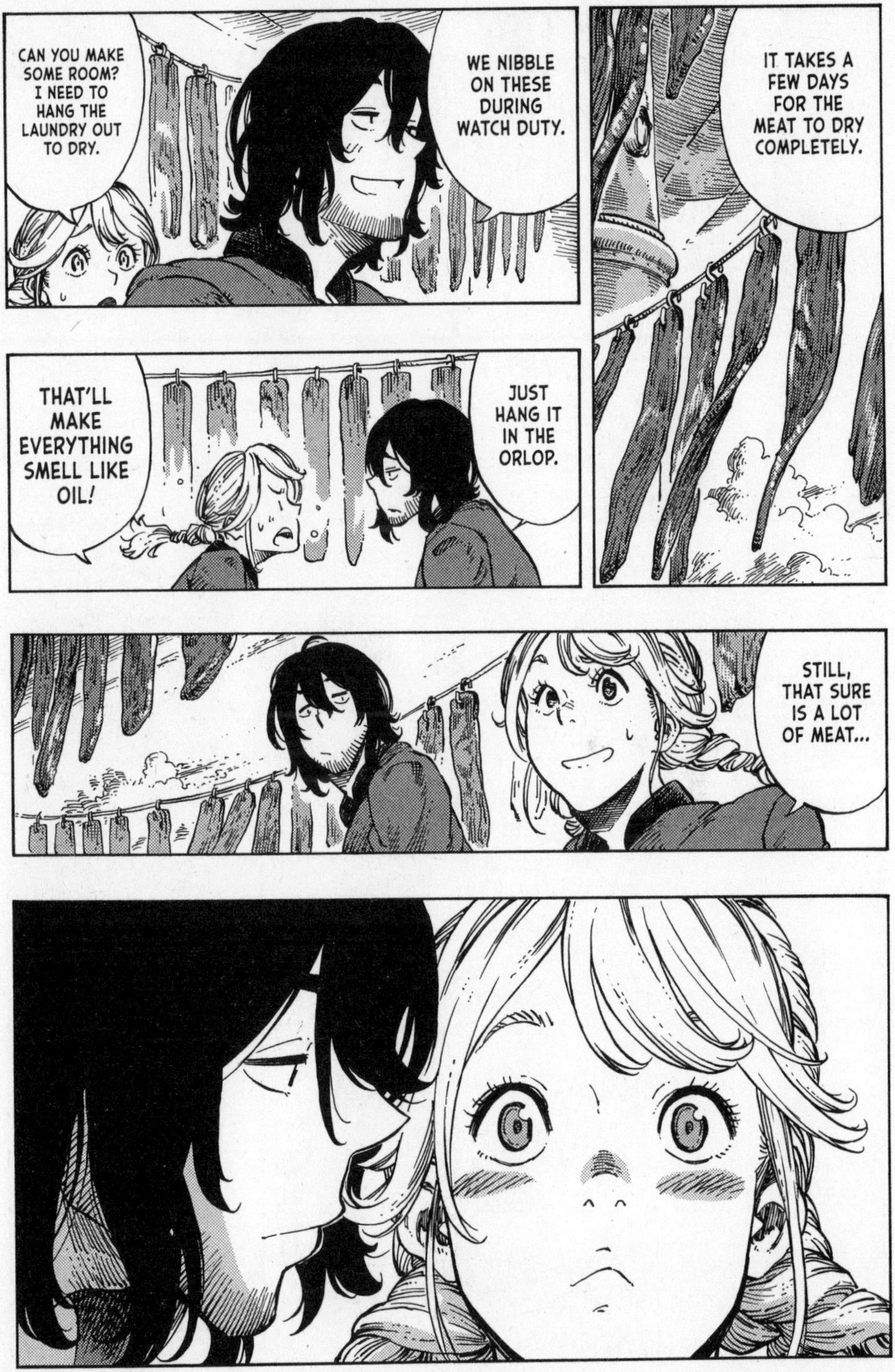
IT TAKES A FEW DAYS FOR THE MEAT TO DRY COMPLETELY.
WE NIBBLE ON THESE DURING WATCH DUTY.
CAN YOU MAKE SOME ROOM? I NEED TO HANG THE LAUNDRY OUT TO DRY.
JUST HANG IT IN THE ORLOP.
THAT'LL MAKE EVERYTHING SMELL LIKE OIL!
STILL, THAT SURE IS A LOT OF MEAT...

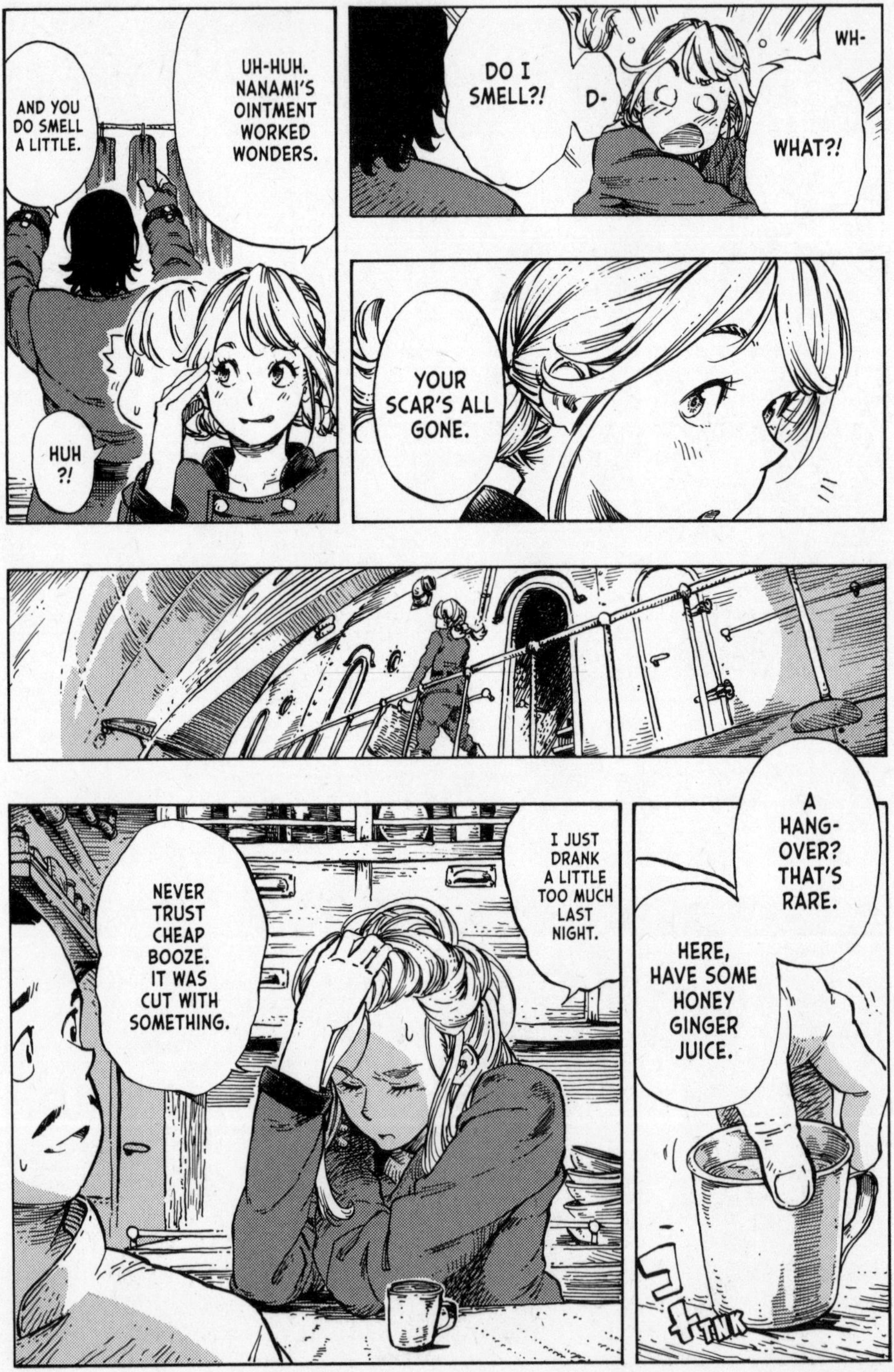
WH-
WHAT?!
D-
DO I SMELL?!
YOUR SCAR'S ALL GONE.
UH-HUH. NANAMI'S OINTMENT WORKED WONDERS.
AND YOU DO SMELL A LITTLE.
HUH ?!
A HANG-OVER? THAT'S RARE.
HERE, HAVE SOME HONEY GINGER JUICE.
TINK
I JUST DRANK A LITTLE TOO MUCH LAST NIGHT.
NEVER TRUST CHEAP BOOZE. IT WAS CUT WITH SOMETHING.

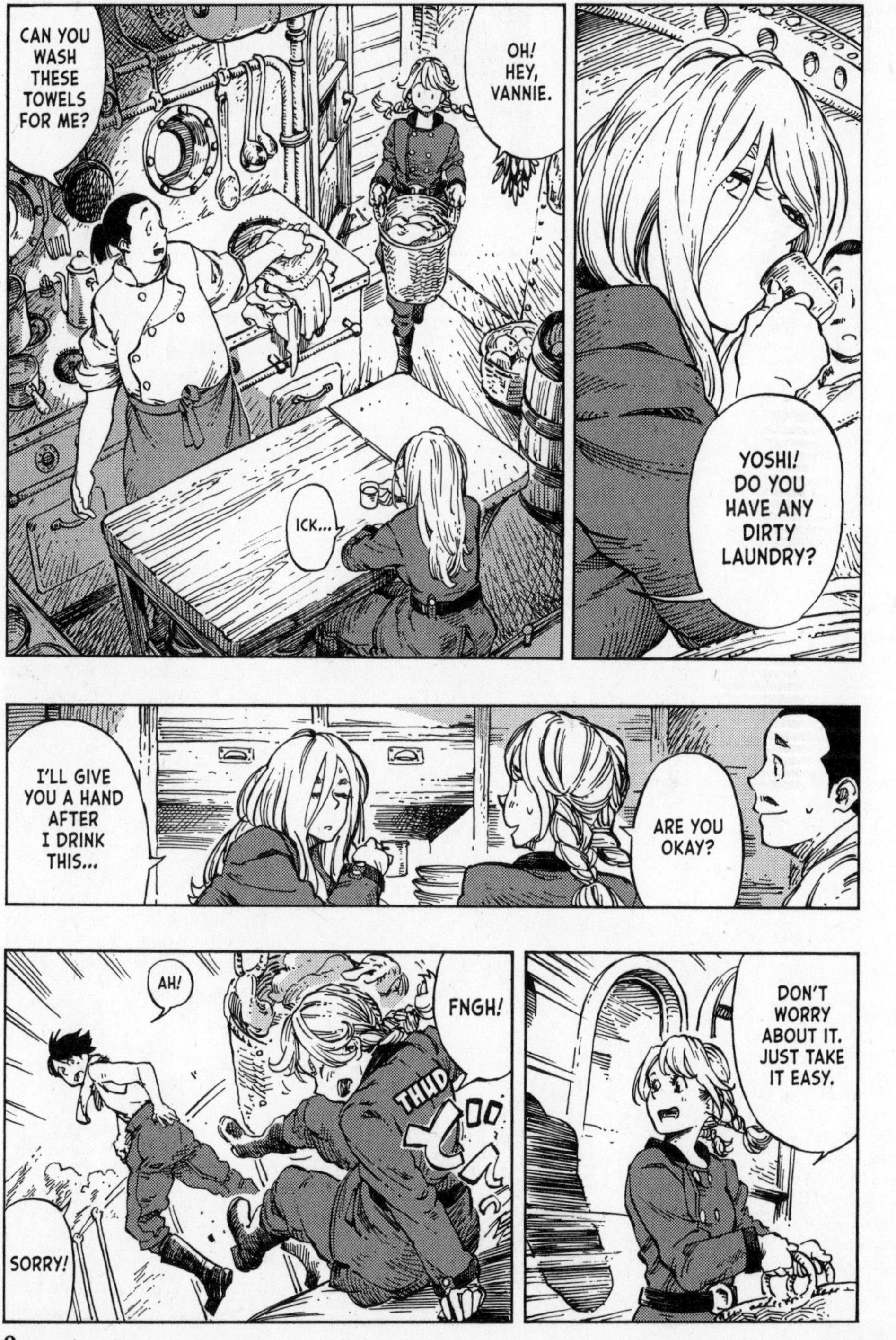
YOSHI! DO YOU HAVE ANY DIRTY LAUNDRY?
OH! HEY, VANNIE.
CAN YOU WASH THESE TOWELS FOR ME?
ICK...
ARE YOU OKAY?
I'LL GIVE YOU A HAND AFTER I DRINK THIS...
DON'T WORRY ABOUT IT. JUST TAKE IT EASY.
FNGH!
THUD
AH!
SORRY!

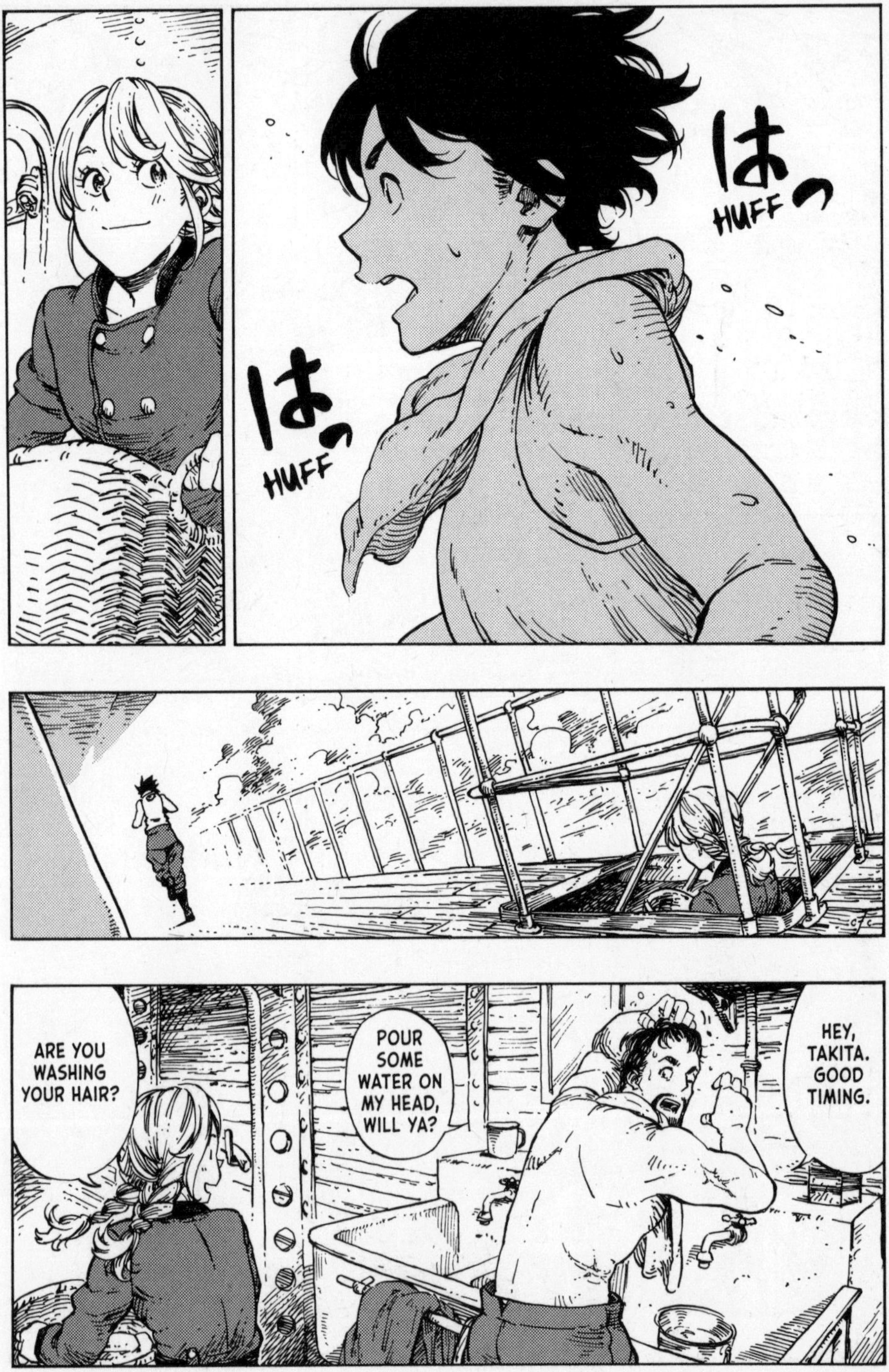
はっ
HUFF
はっ
HUFF
HEY, TAKITA. GOOD TIMING.
POUR SOME WATER ON MY HEAD, WILL YA?
ARE YOU WASHING YOUR HAIR?

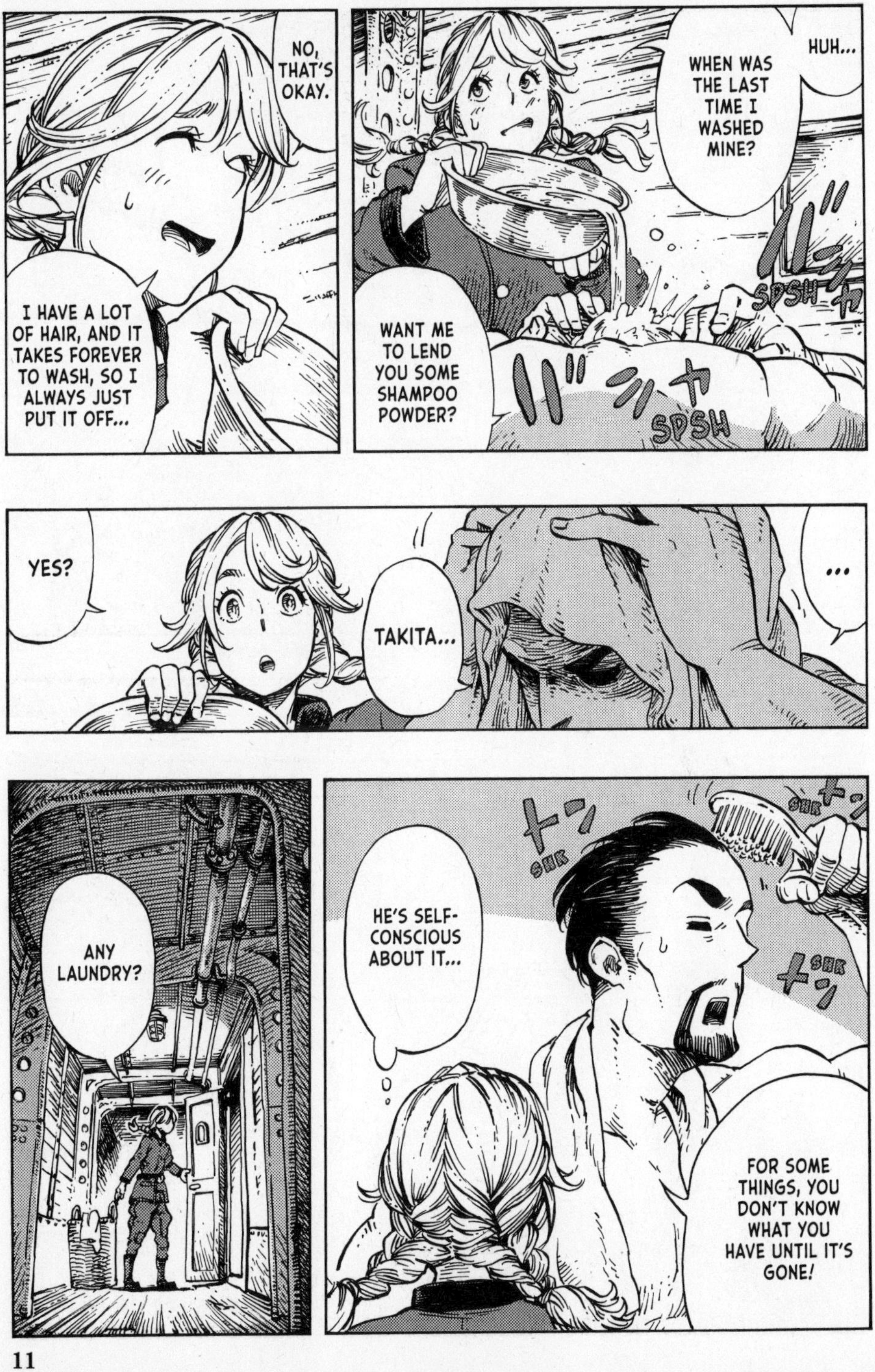
HUH...
WHEN WAS THE LAST TIME I WASHED MINE?
SPSH
WANT ME TO LEND YOU SOME SHAMPOO POWDER?
SPSH
NO, THAT'S OKAY.
I HAVE A LOT OF HAIR, AND IT TAKES FOREVER TO WASH, SO I ALWAYS JUST PUT IT OFF...
...
TAKITA...
YES?
SHK
HE'S SELF-CONSCIOUS ABOUT IT...
SHK
SHK
FOR SOME THINGS, YOU DON'T KNOW WHAT YOU HAVE UNTIL IT'S GONE!
ANY LAUNDRY?

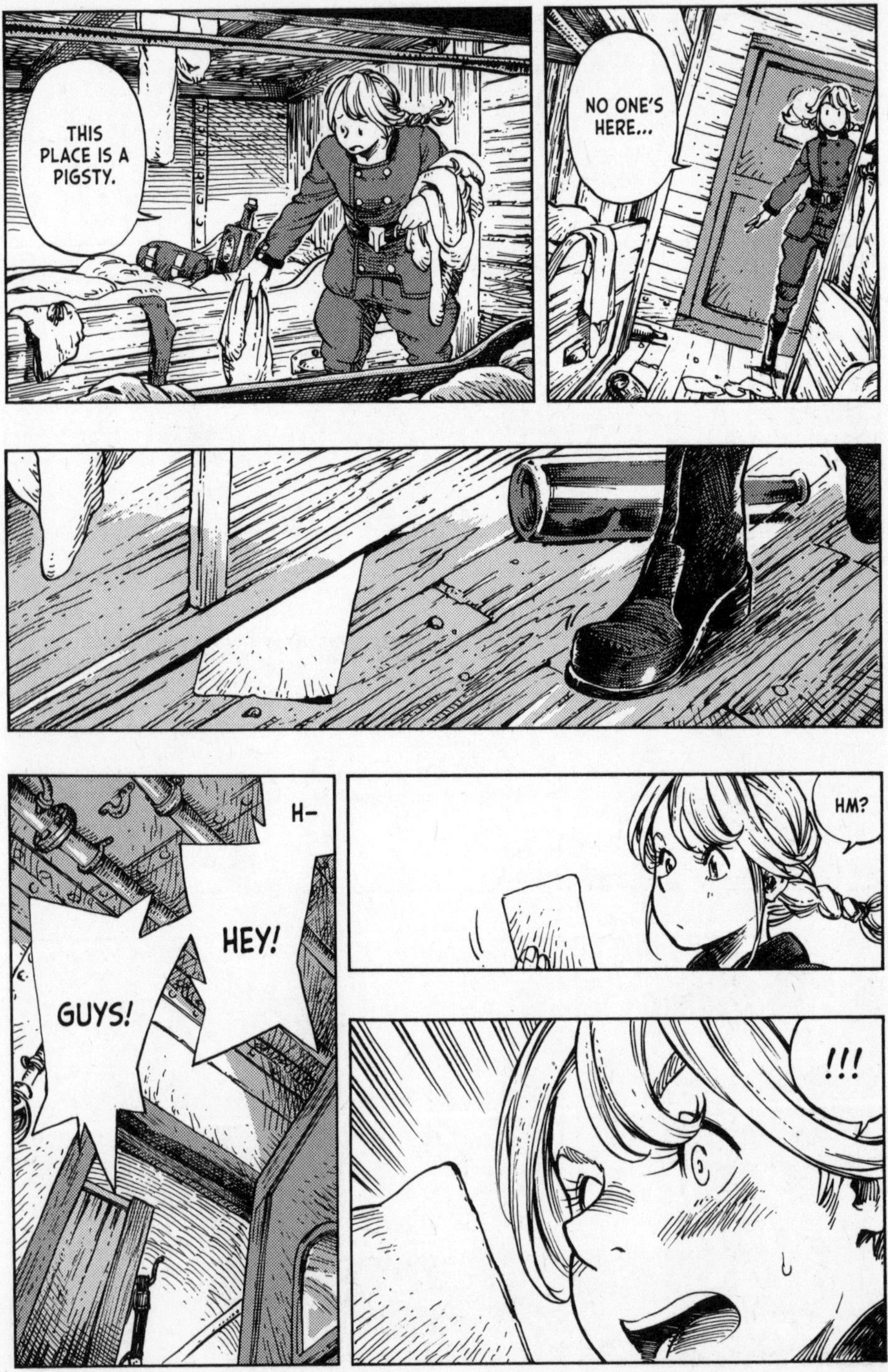
NO ONE'S HERE...
THIS PLACE IS A PIGSTY.
HM?
!!!
H-
HEY!
GUYS!

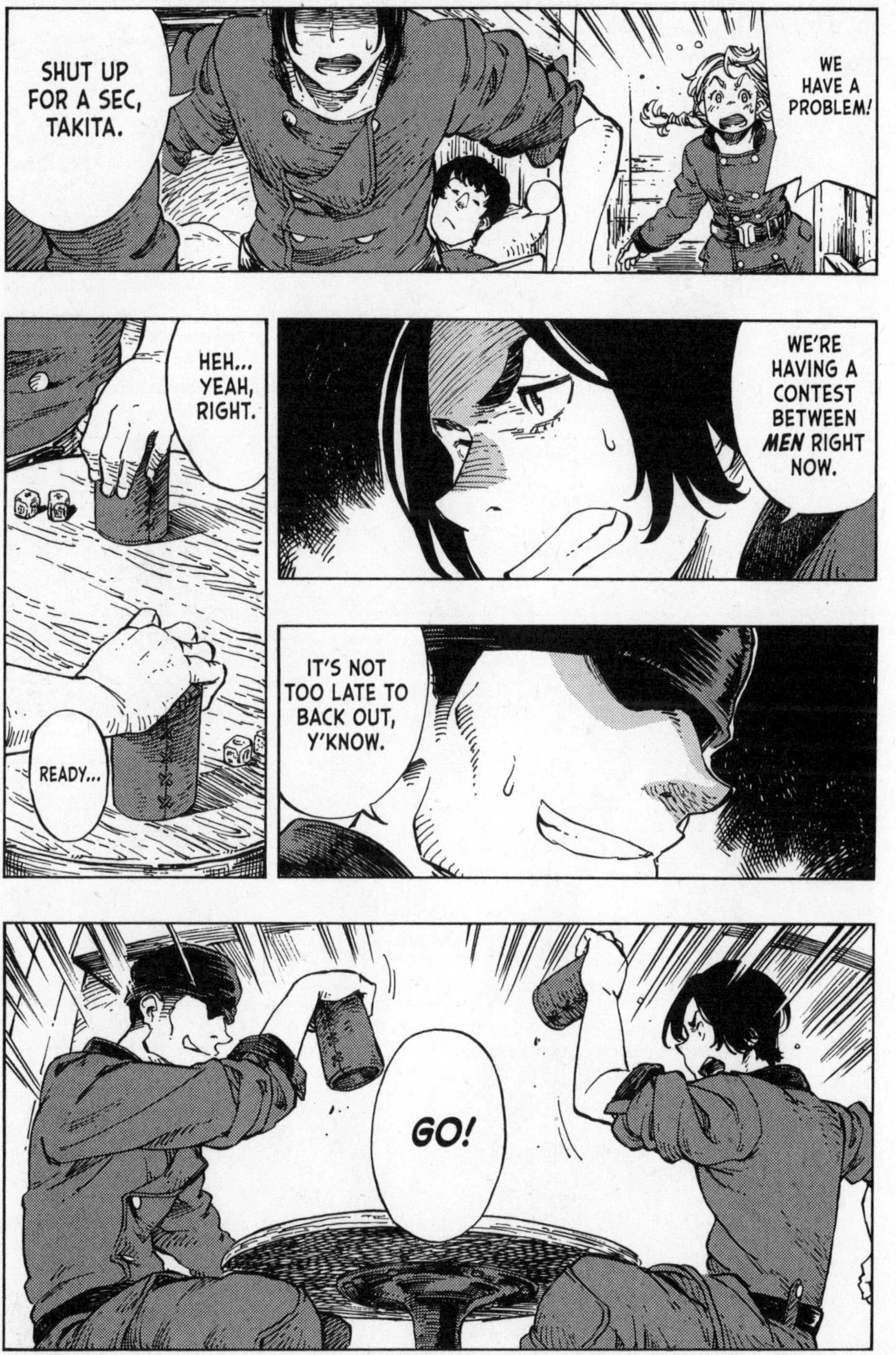
WE HAVE A PROBLEM!
SHUT UP FOR A SEC, TAKITA.
WE'RE HAVING A CONTEST BETWEEN *MEN* RIGHT NOW.
IT'S NOT TOO LATE TO BACK OUT, Y'KNOW.
HEH... YEAH, RIGHT.
READY...
GO!

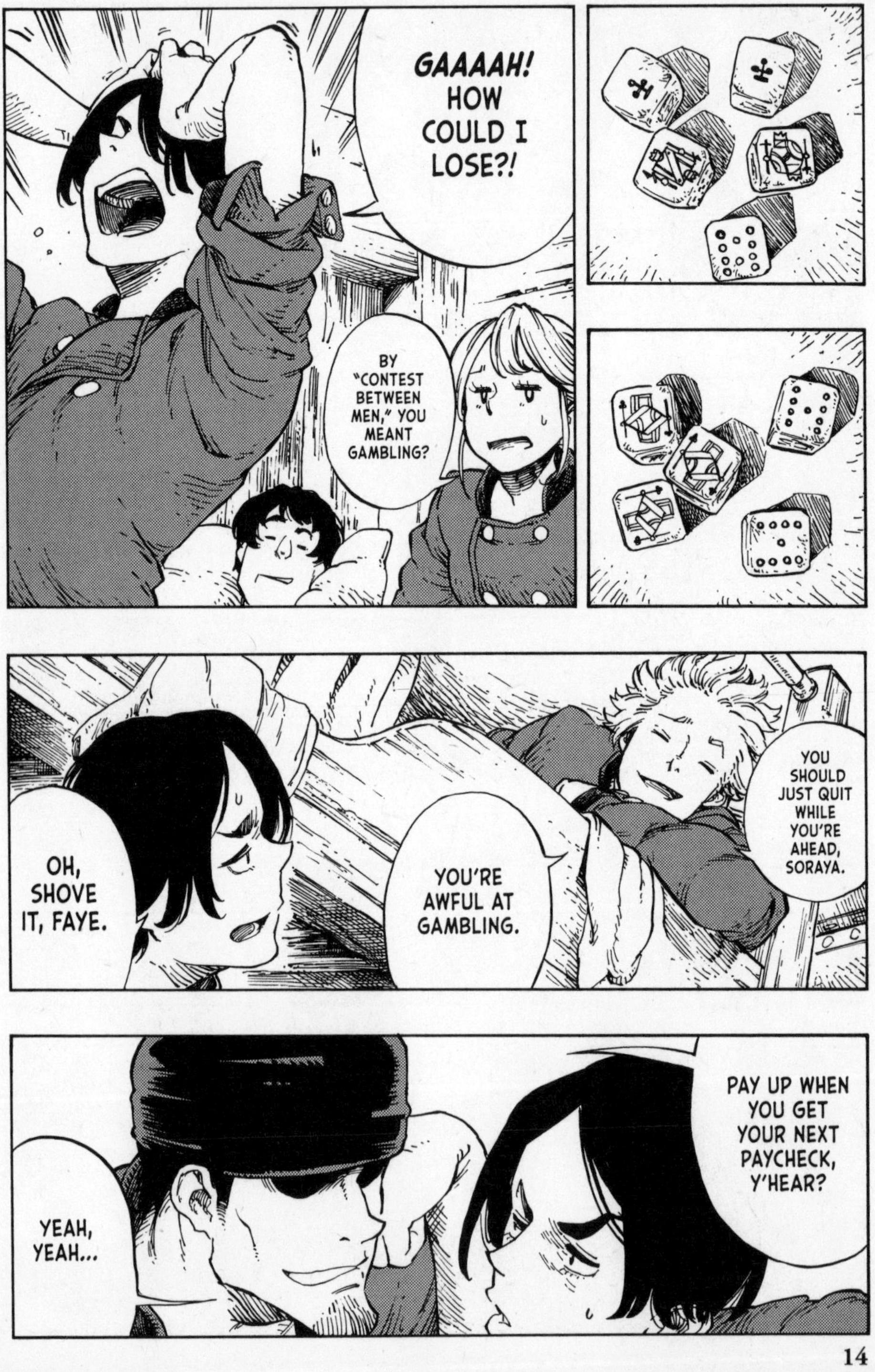
GAAAAH! HOW COULD I LOSE?!
BY "CONTEST BETWEEN MEN," YOU MEANT GAMBLING?
YOU SHOULD JUST QUIT WHILE YOU'RE AHEAD, SORAYA.
YOU'RE AWFUL AT GAMBLING.
OH, SHOVE IT, FAYE.
PAY UP WHEN YOU GET YOUR NEXT PAYCHECK, Y'HEAR?
YEAH, YEAH...

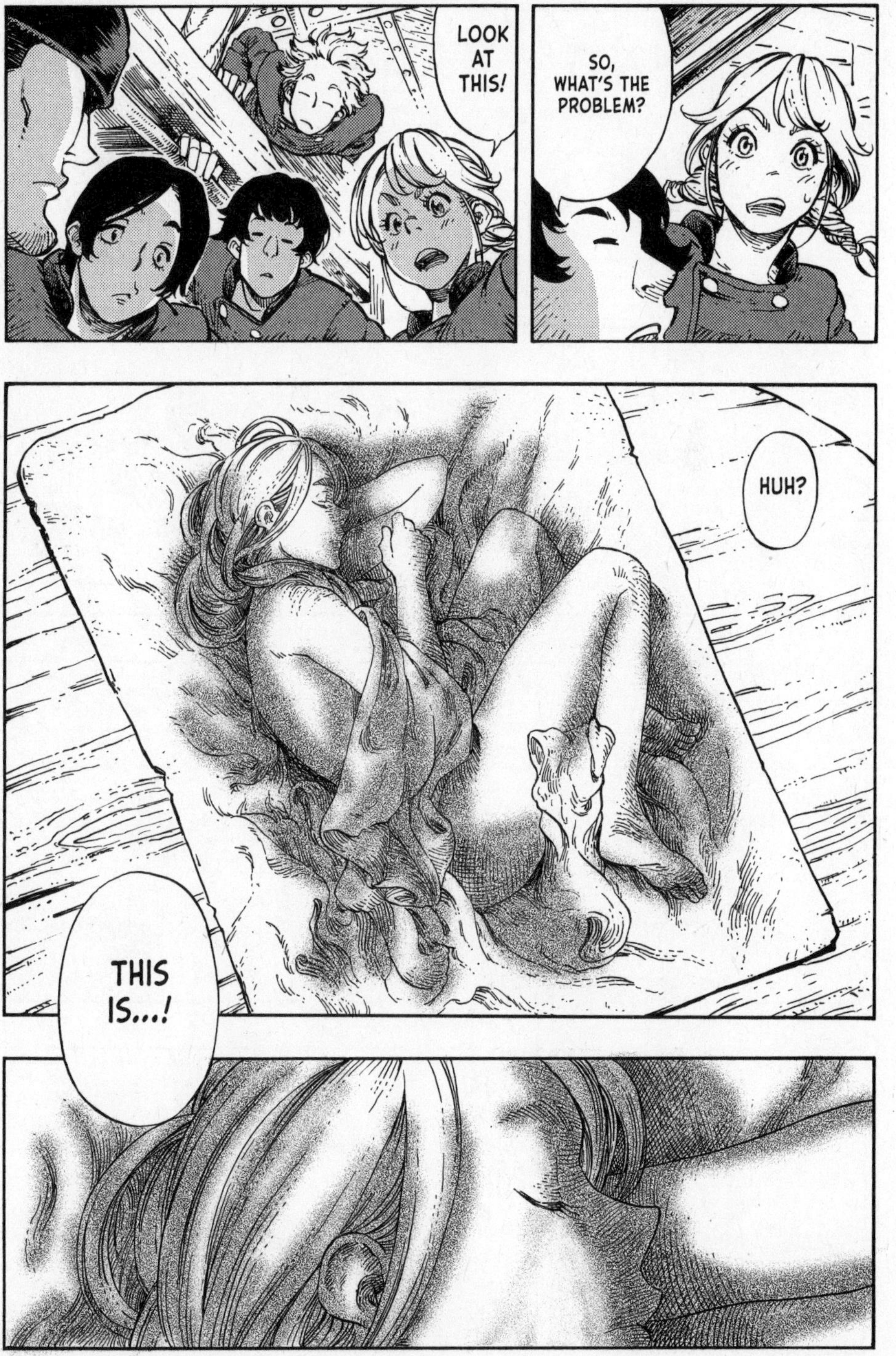
SO, WHAT'S THE PROBLEM?
LOOK AT THIS!
HUH?
THIS IS...!

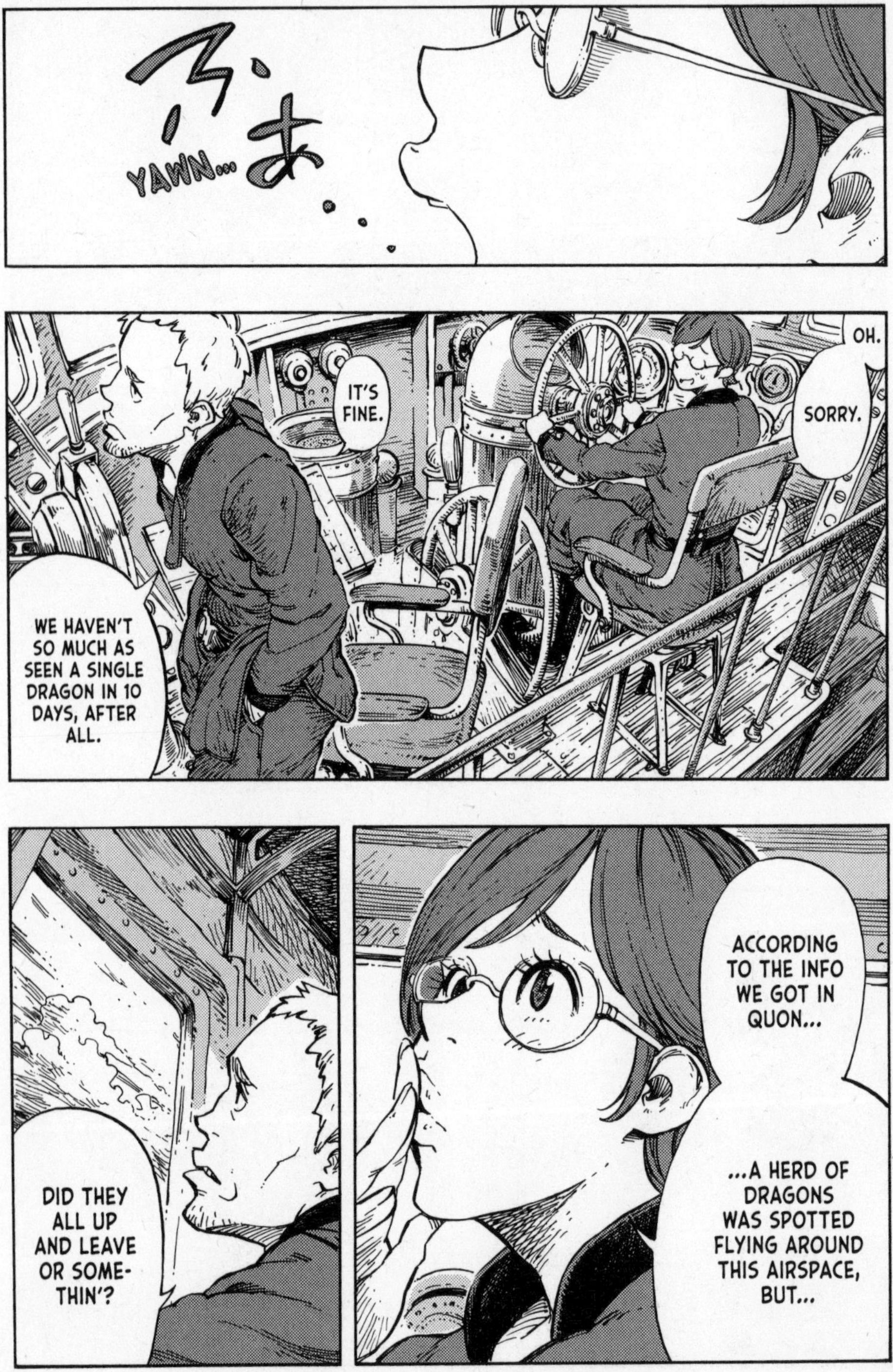
ふあ
YAWN...
OH.
SORRY.
IT'S FINE.
WE HAVEN'T SO MUCH AS SEEN A SINGLE DRAGON IN 10 DAYS, AFTER ALL.
ACCORDING TO THE INFO WE GOT IN QUON...
...A HERD OF DRAGONS WAS SPOTTED FLYING AROUND THIS AIRSPACE, BUT...
DID THEY ALL UP AND LEAVE OR SOME-THIN'?

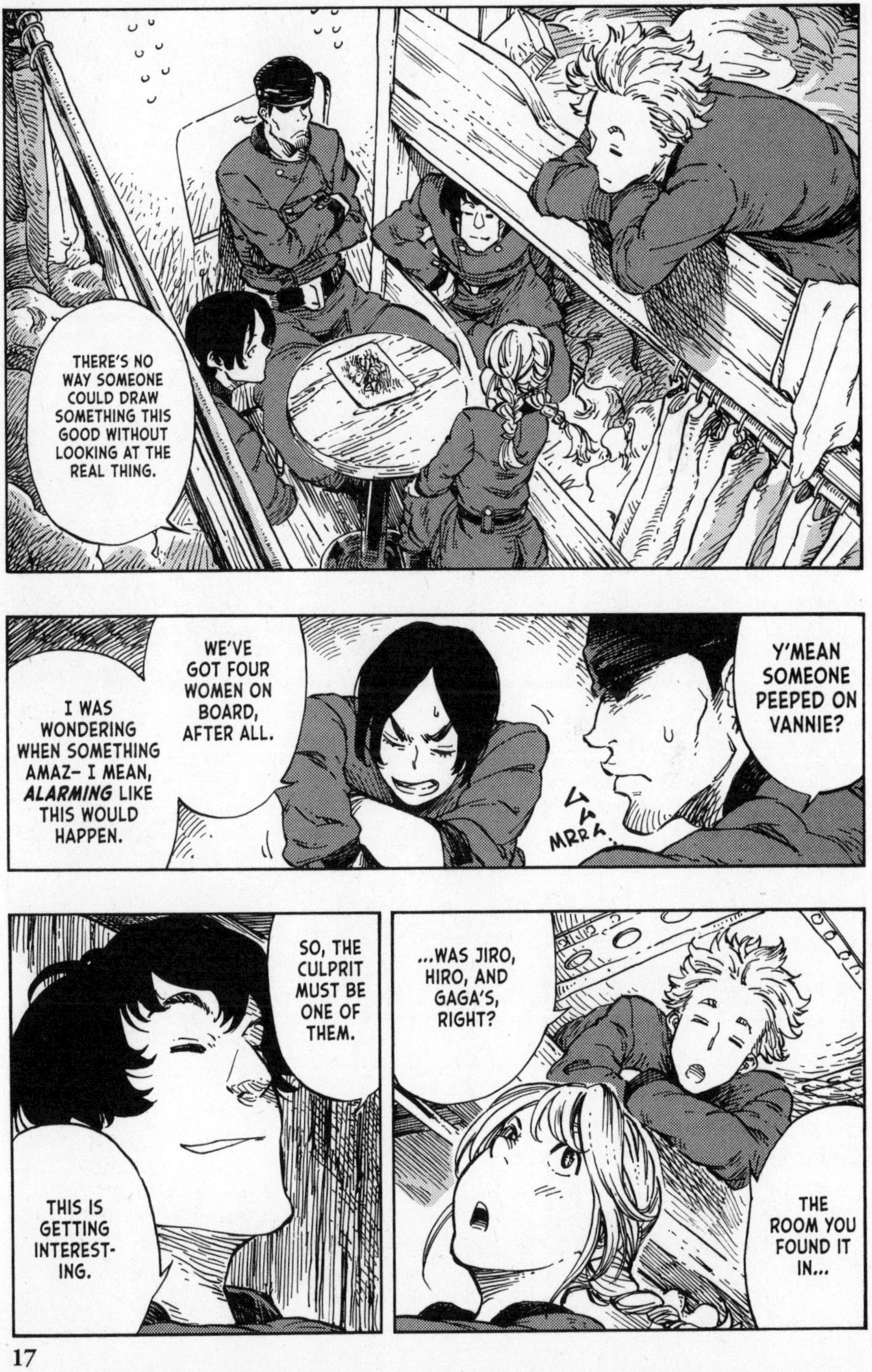
THERE'S NO WAY SOMEONE COULD DRAW SOMETHING THIS GOOD WITHOUT LOOKING AT THE REAL THING.
Y'MEAN SOMEONE PEEPED ON VANNIE?
MRRA...
WE'VE GOT FOUR WOMEN ON BOARD, AFTER ALL.
I WAS WONDERING WHEN SOMETHING AMAZ– I MEAN, *ALARMING* LIKE THIS WOULD HAPPEN.
THE ROOM YOU FOUND IT IN...
...WAS JIRO, HIRO, AND GAGA'S, RIGHT?
SO, THE CULPRIT MUST BE ONE OF THEM.
THIS IS GETTING INTEREST-ING.

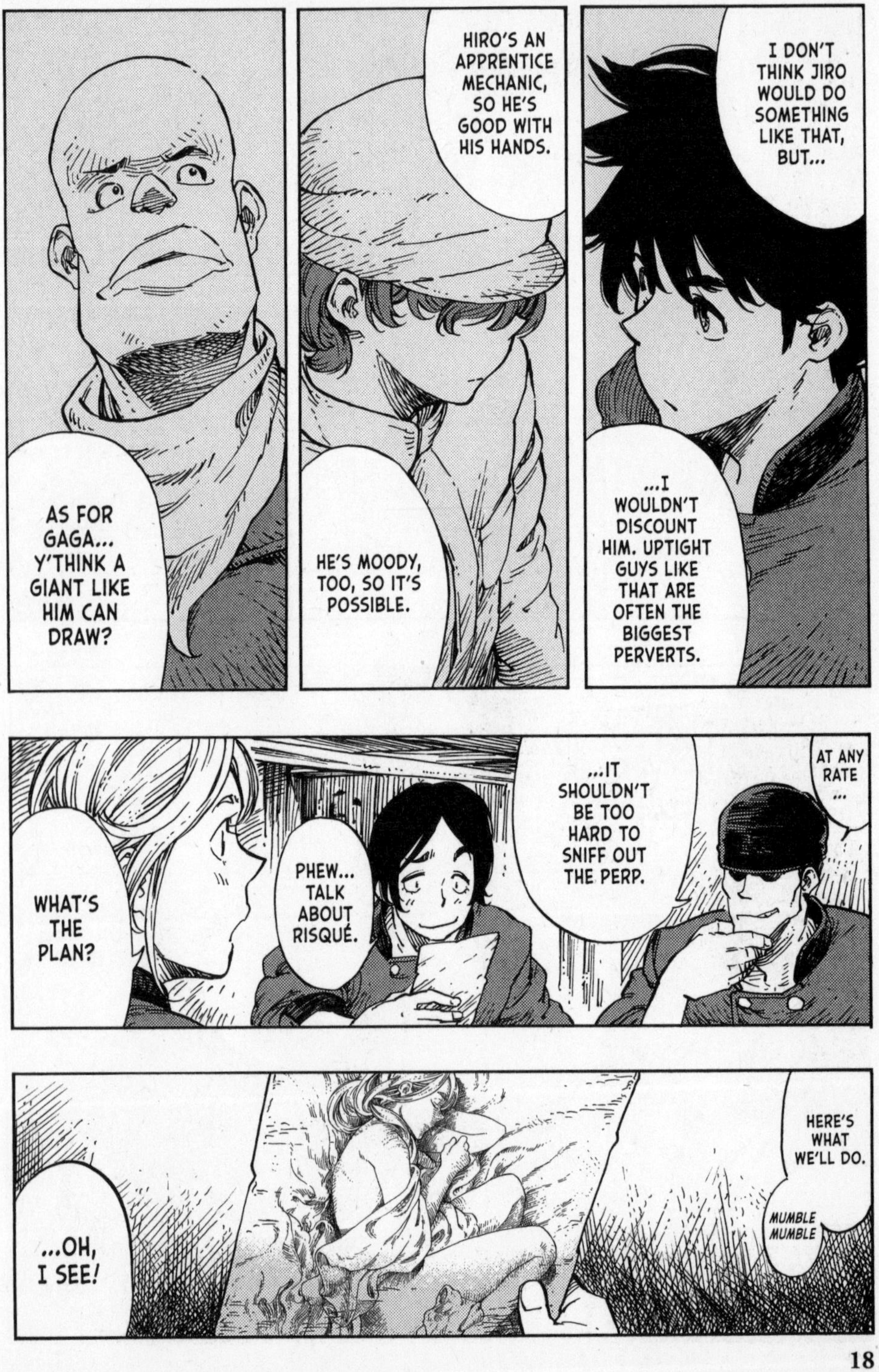
I DON'T THINK JIRO WOULD DO SOMETHING LIKE THAT, BUT...
...I WOULDN'T DISCOUNT HIM. UPTIGHT GUYS LIKE THAT ARE OFTEN THE BIGGEST PERVERTS.
HIRO'S AN APPRENTICE MECHANIC, SO HE'S GOOD WITH HIS HANDS.
HE'S MOODY, TOO, SO IT'S POSSIBLE.
AS FOR GAGA... Y'THINK A GIANT LIKE HIM CAN DRAW?
AT ANY RATE ...
...IT SHOULDN'T BE TOO HARD TO SNIFF OUT THE PERP.
PHEW... TALK ABOUT RISQUÉ.
WHAT'S THE PLAN?
HERE'S WHAT WE'LL DO.
MUMBLE MUMBLE
...OH, I SEE!

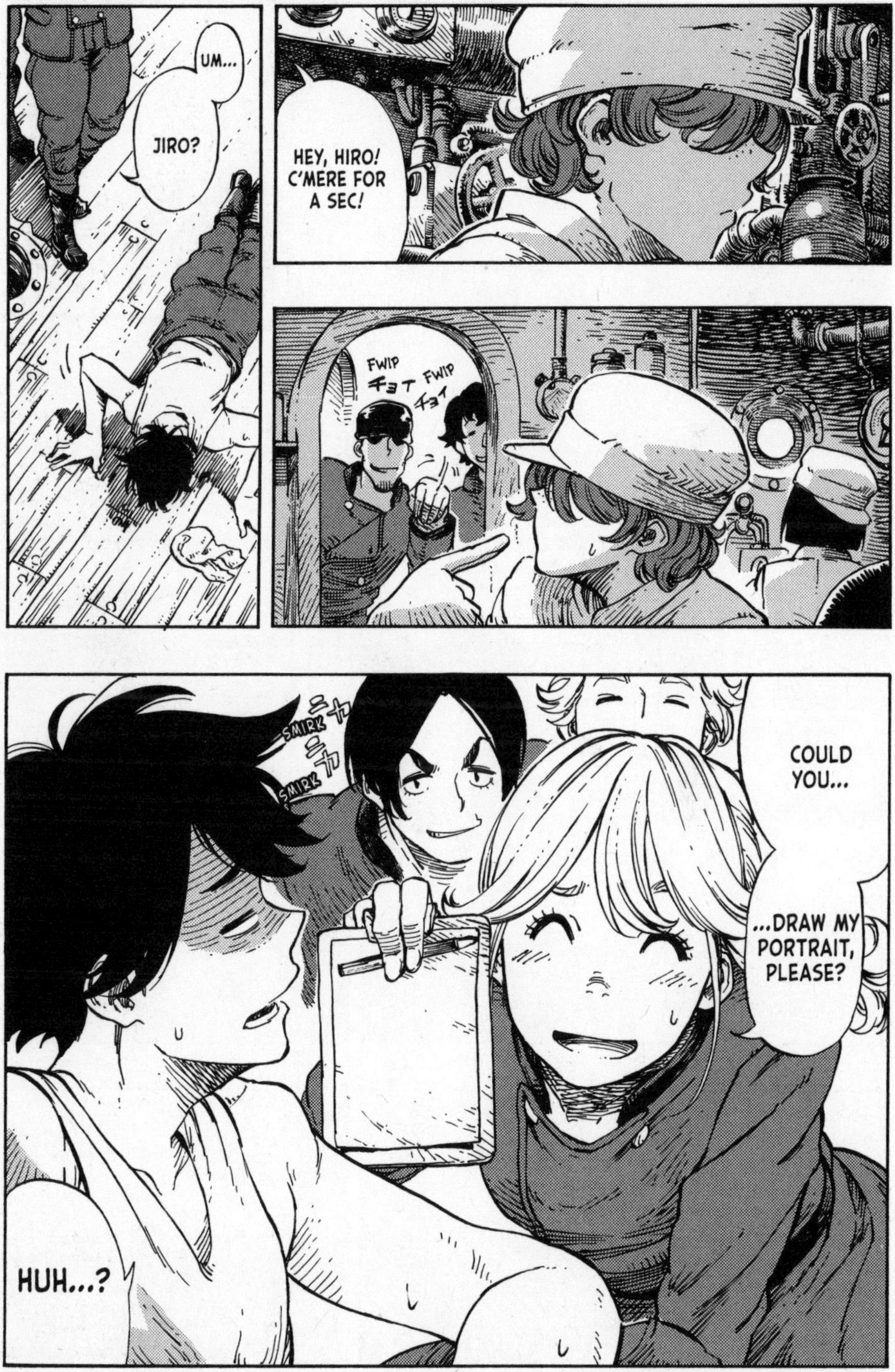
HEY, HIRO! C'MERE FOR A SEC!
FWIP チョイ FWIP チョイ
UM...
JIRO?
COULD YOU...
...DRAW MY PORTRAIT, PLEASE?
SMIRK ニヤ SMIRK ニヤ
HUH...?

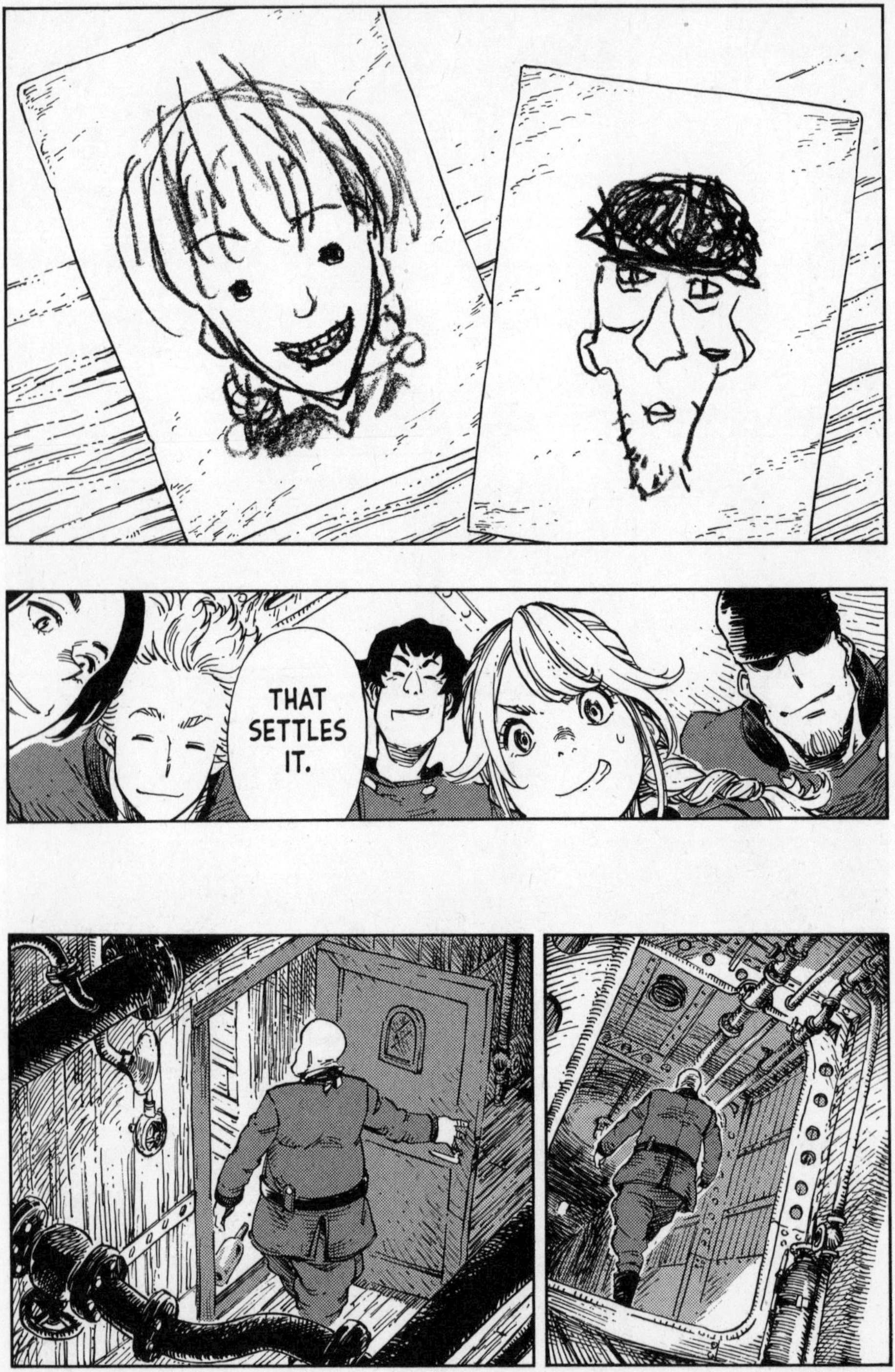
THAT SETTLES IT.

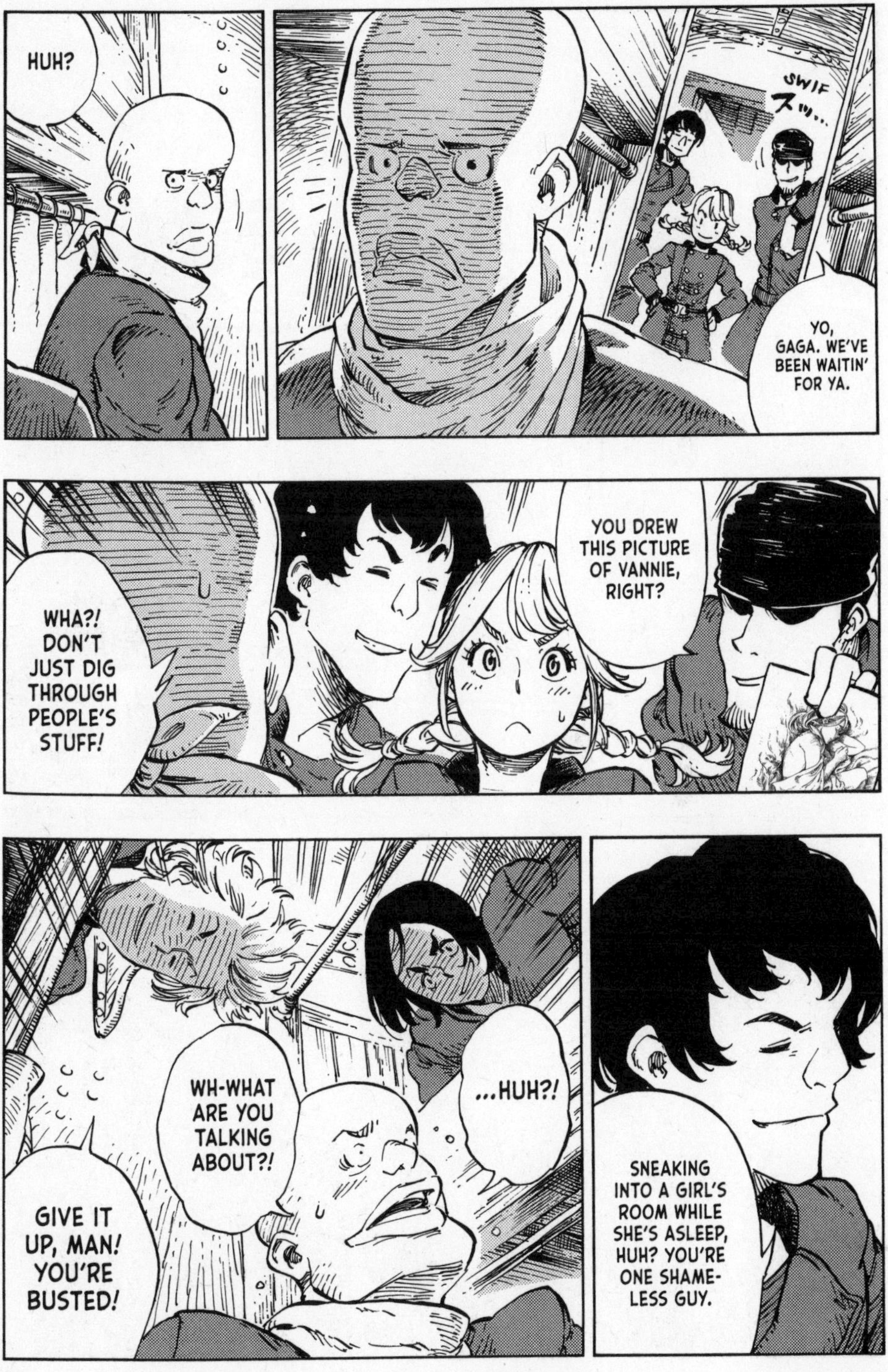
SWIF
スッ…
YO, GAGA. WE'VE BEEN WAITIN' FOR YA.
HUH?
YOU DREW THIS PICTURE OF VANNIE, RIGHT?
WHA?! DON'T JUST DIG THROUGH PEOPLE'S STUFF!
SNEAKING INTO A GIRL'S ROOM WHILE SHE'S ASLEEP, HUH? YOU'RE ONE SHAME-LESS GUY.
...HUH?!
WH-WHAT ARE YOU TALKING ABOUT?!
GIVE IT UP, MAN! YOU'RE BUSTED!

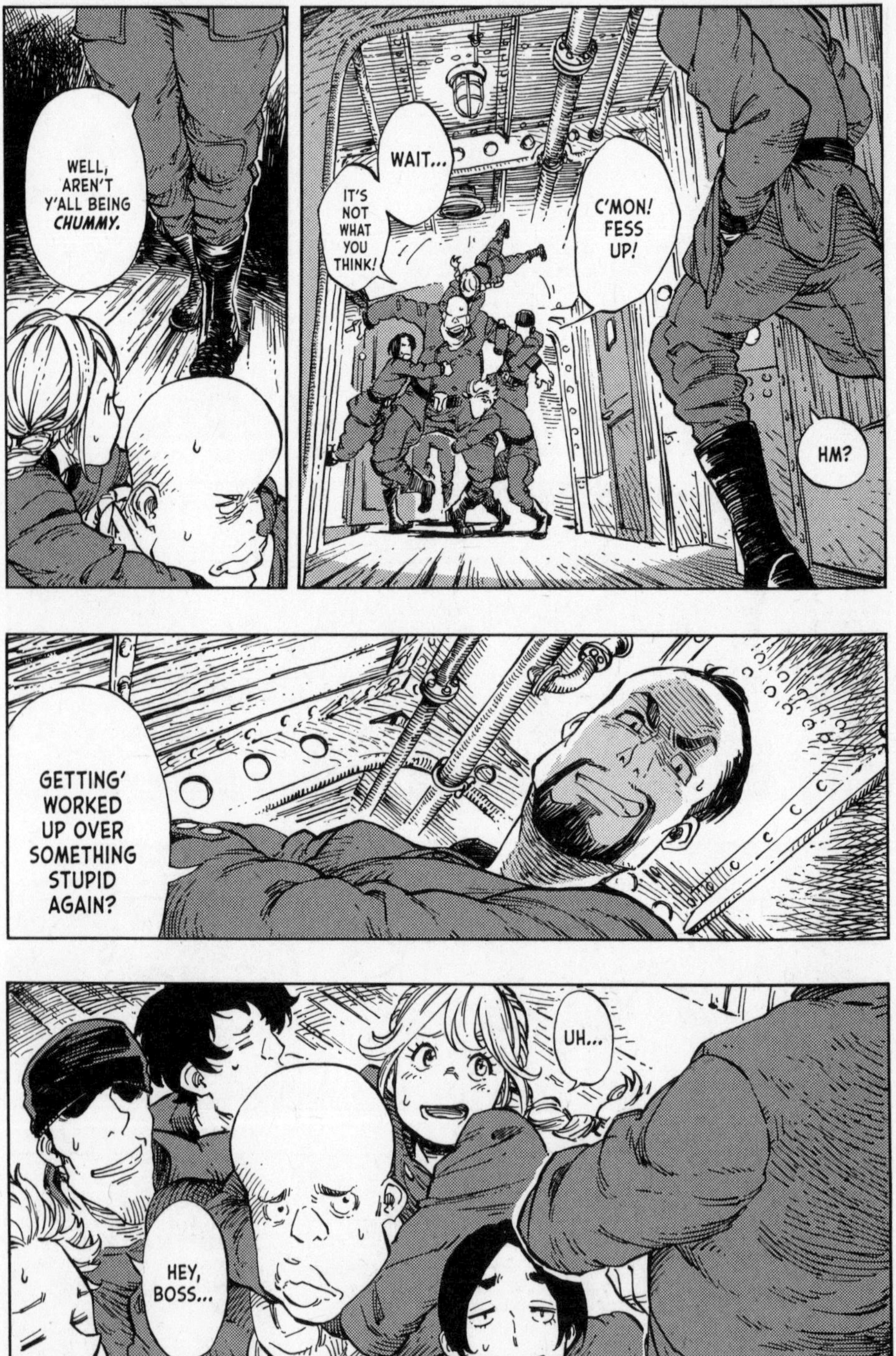
C'MON! FESS UP!
WAIT...
IT'S NOT WHAT YOU THINK!
HM?
WELL, AREN'T Y'ALL BEING *CHUMMY.*
GETTING' WORKED UP OVER SOMETHING STUPID AGAIN?
UH...
HEY, BOSS...

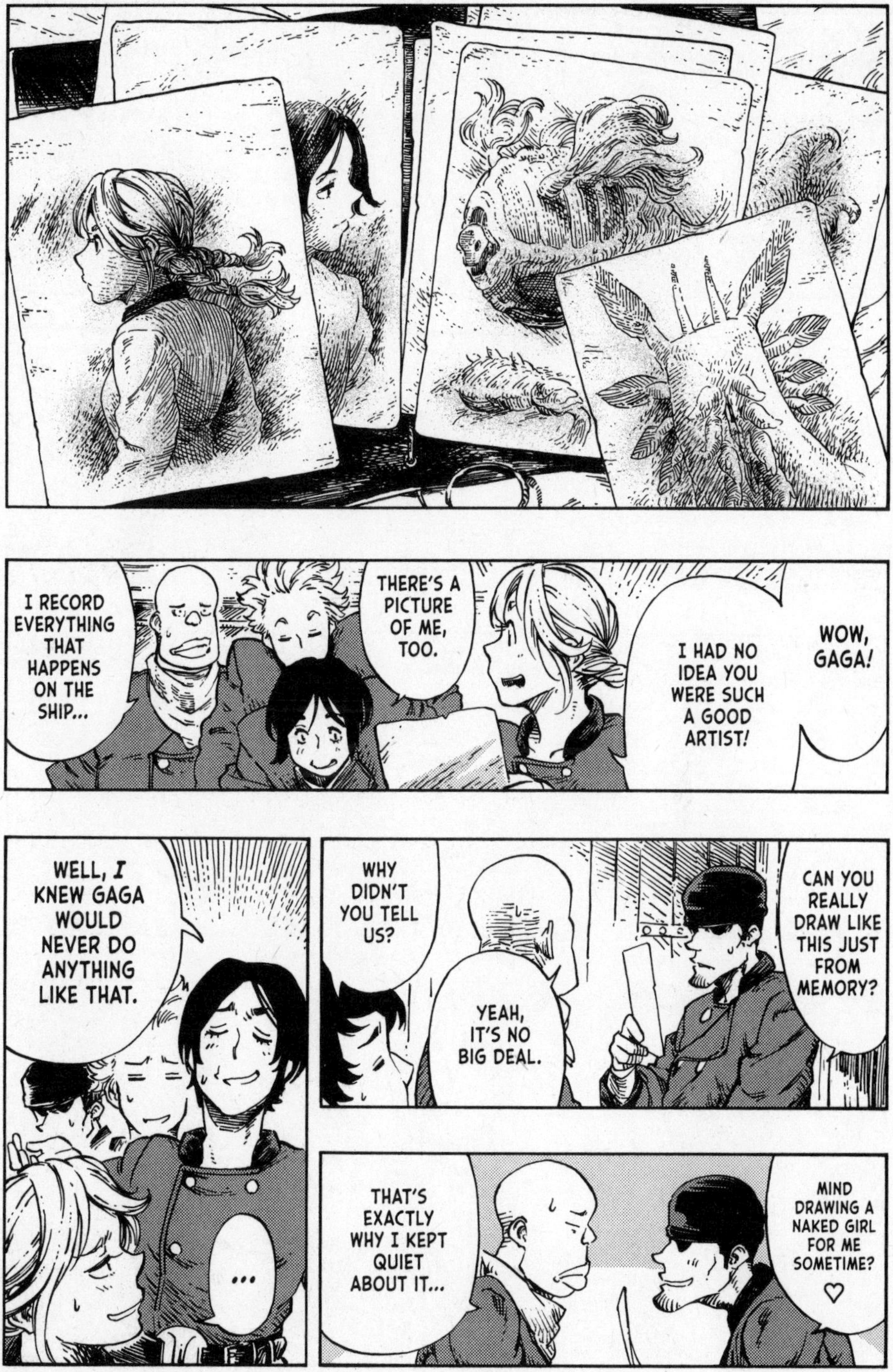
WOW, GAGA!
I HAD NO IDEA YOU WERE SUCH A GOOD ARTIST!
THERE'S A PICTURE OF ME, TOO.
I RECORD EVERYTHING THAT HAPPENS ON THE SHIP...
CAN YOU REALLY DRAW LIKE THIS JUST FROM MEMORY?
WHY DIDN'T YOU TELL US?
YEAH, IT'S NO BIG DEAL.
MIND DRAWING A NAKED GIRL FOR ME SOMETIME? ♥
THAT'S EXACTLY WHY I KEPT QUIET ABOUT IT...
WELL, *I* KNEW GAGA WOULD NEVER DO ANYTHING LIKE THAT.
...

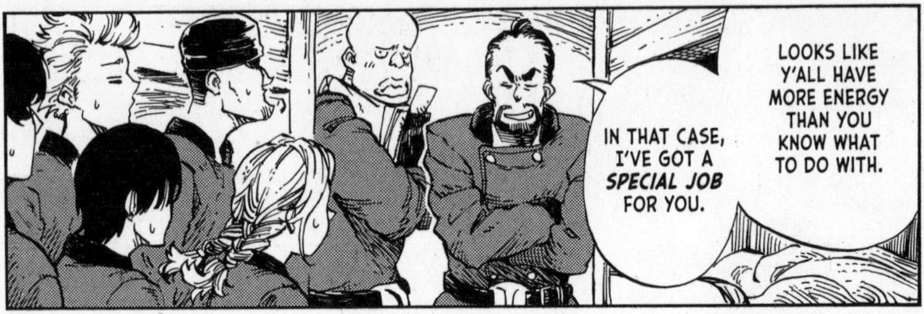
LOOKS LIKE Y'ALL HAVE MORE ENERGY THAN YOU KNOW WHAT TO DO WITH.
IN THAT CASE, I'VE GOT A *SPECIAL JOB* FOR YOU.

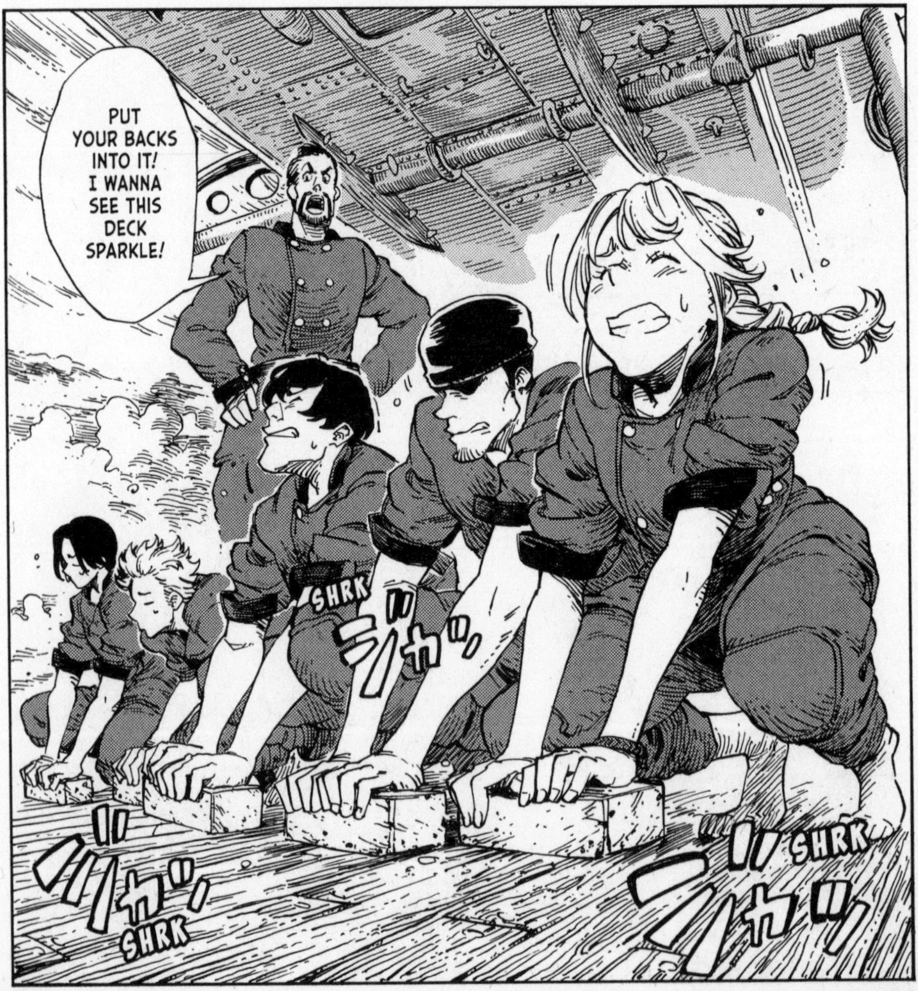
PUT YOUR BACKS INTO IT! I WANNA SEE THIS DECK SPARKLE!
SHRK
SHRK
SHRK

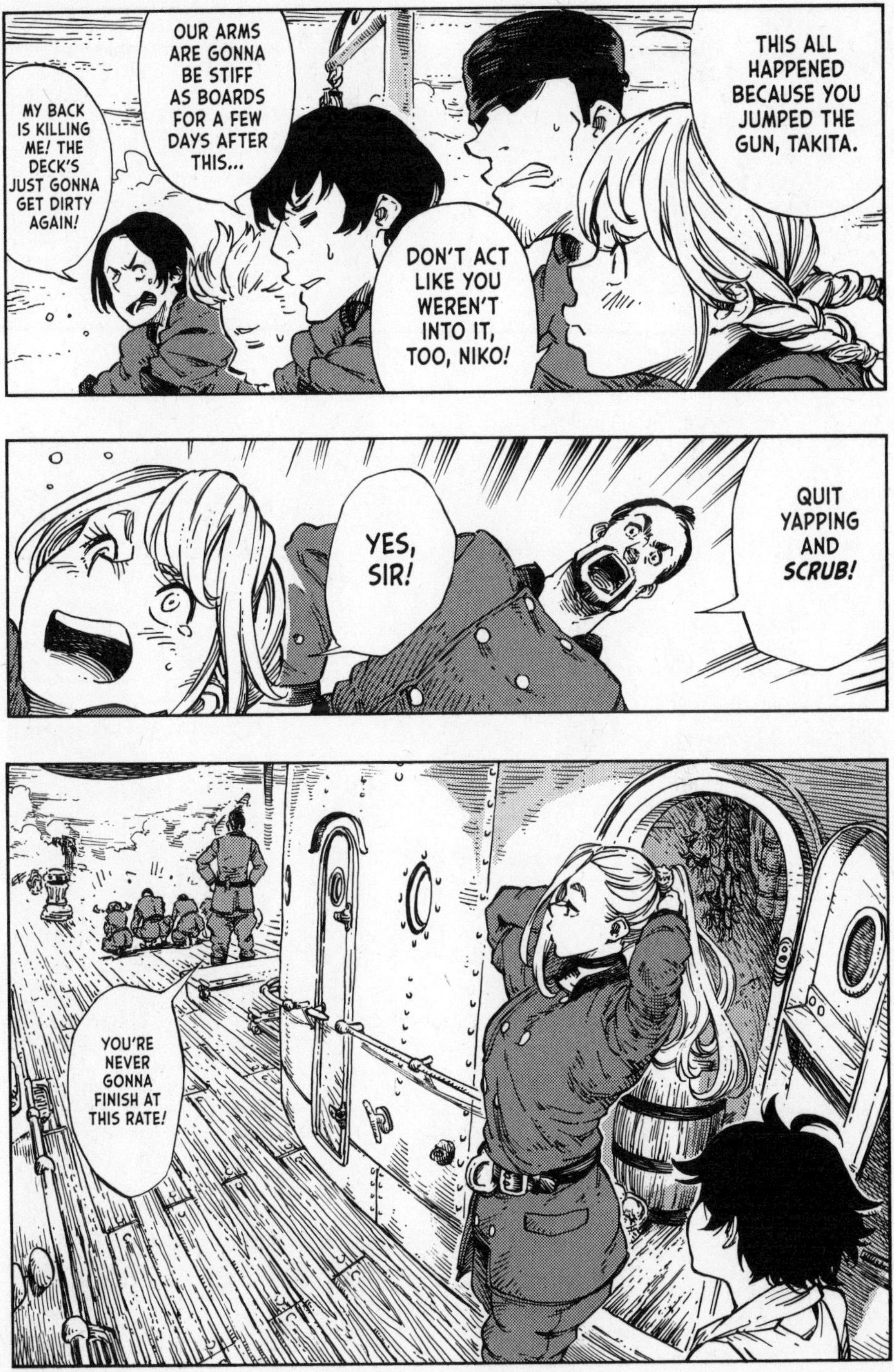
THIS ALL HAPPENED BECAUSE YOU JUMPED THE GUN, TAKITA.
DON'T ACT LIKE YOU WEREN'T INTO IT, TOO, NIKO!
OUR ARMS ARE GONNA BE STIFF AS BOARDS FOR A FEW DAYS AFTER THIS...
MY BACK IS KILLING ME! THE DECK'S JUST GONNA GET DIRTY AGAIN!
QUIT YAPPING AND *SCRUB!*
YES, SIR!
YOU'RE NEVER GONNA FINISH AT THIS RATE!

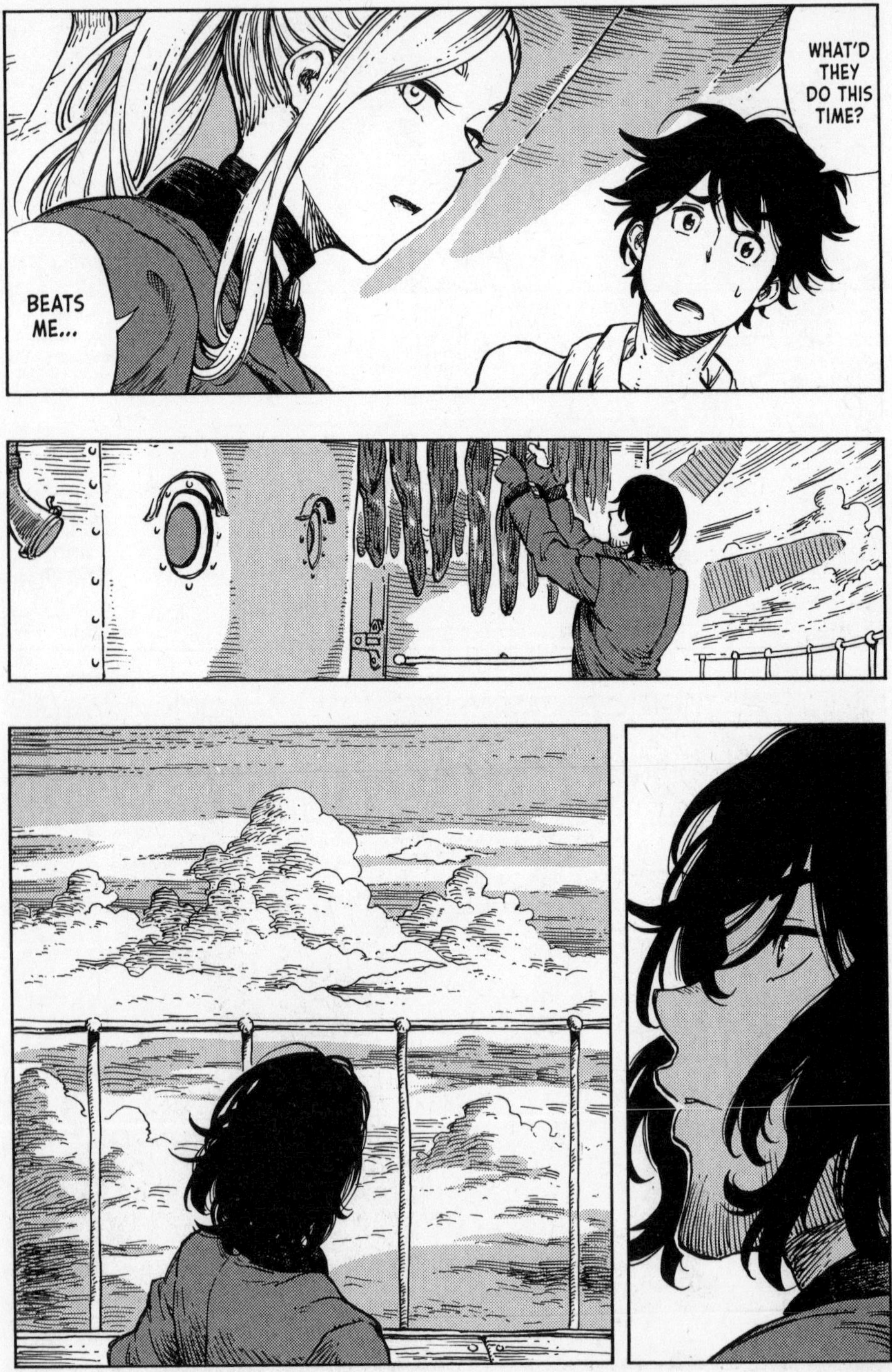
WHAT'D THEY DO THIS TIME?
BEATS ME...

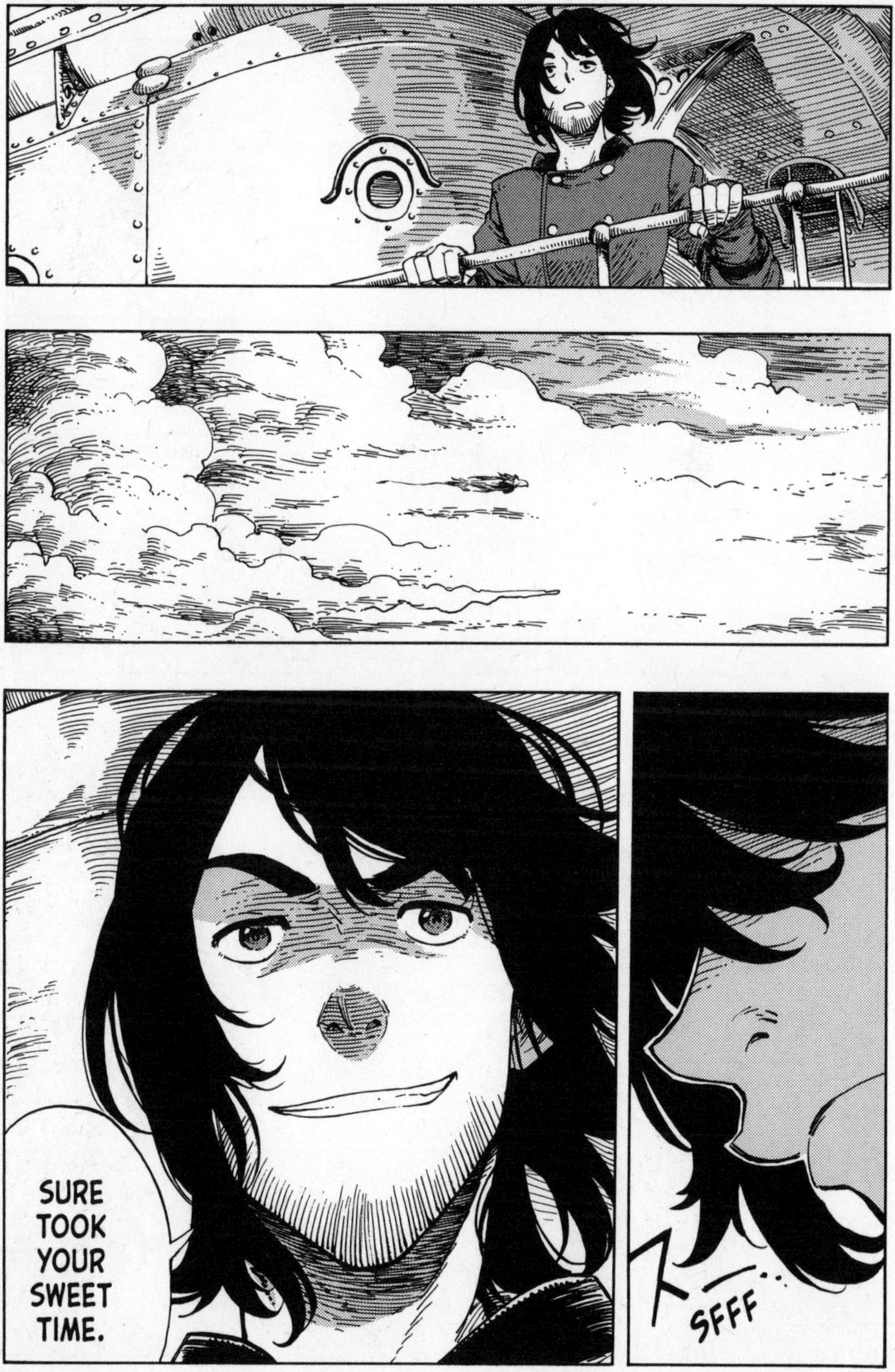
SFFF
SURE TOOK YOUR SWEET TIME.

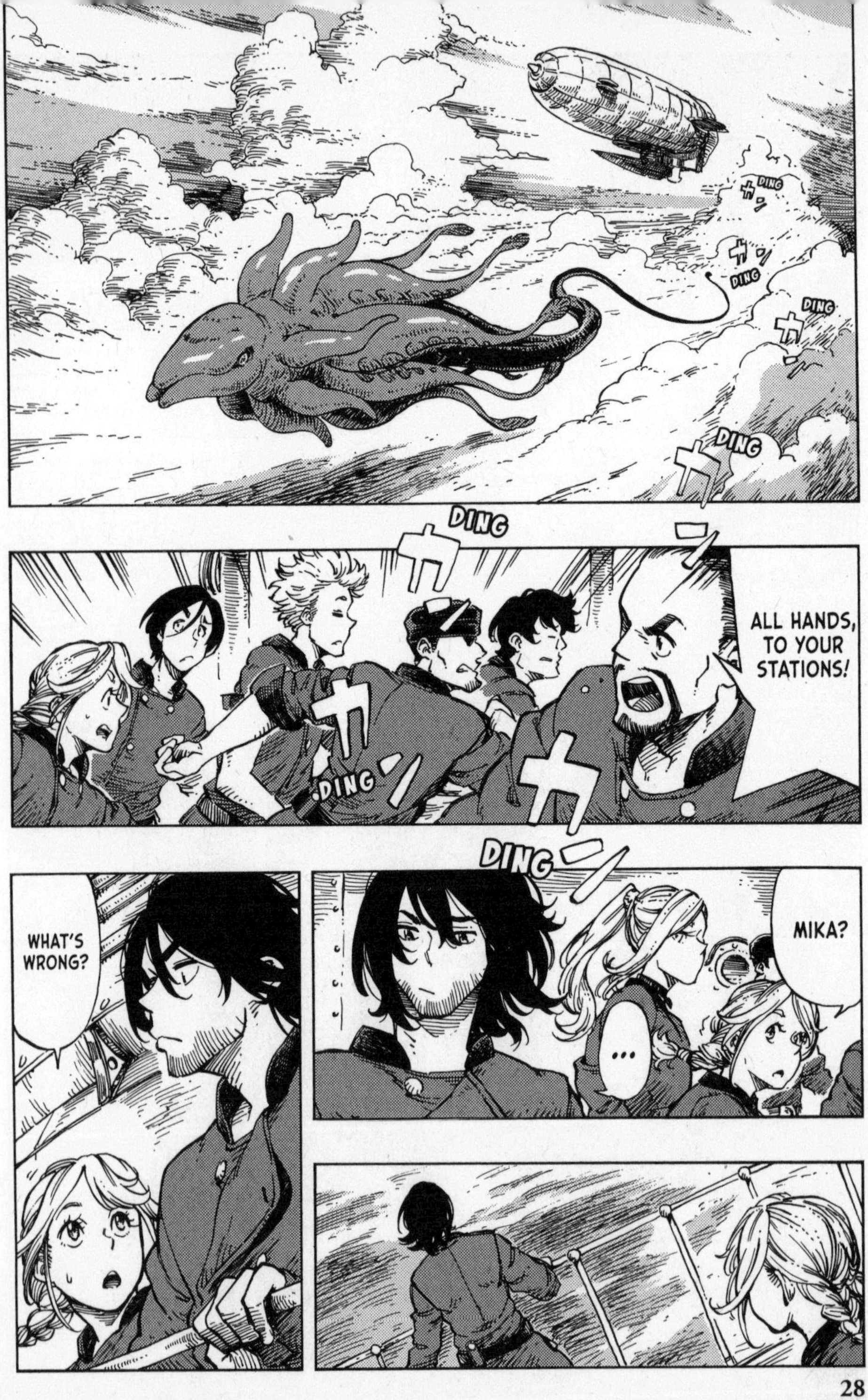
DING
DING
DING
DING
DING
ALL HANDS, TO YOUR STATIONS!
DING
DING
MIKA?
...
WHAT'S WRONG?

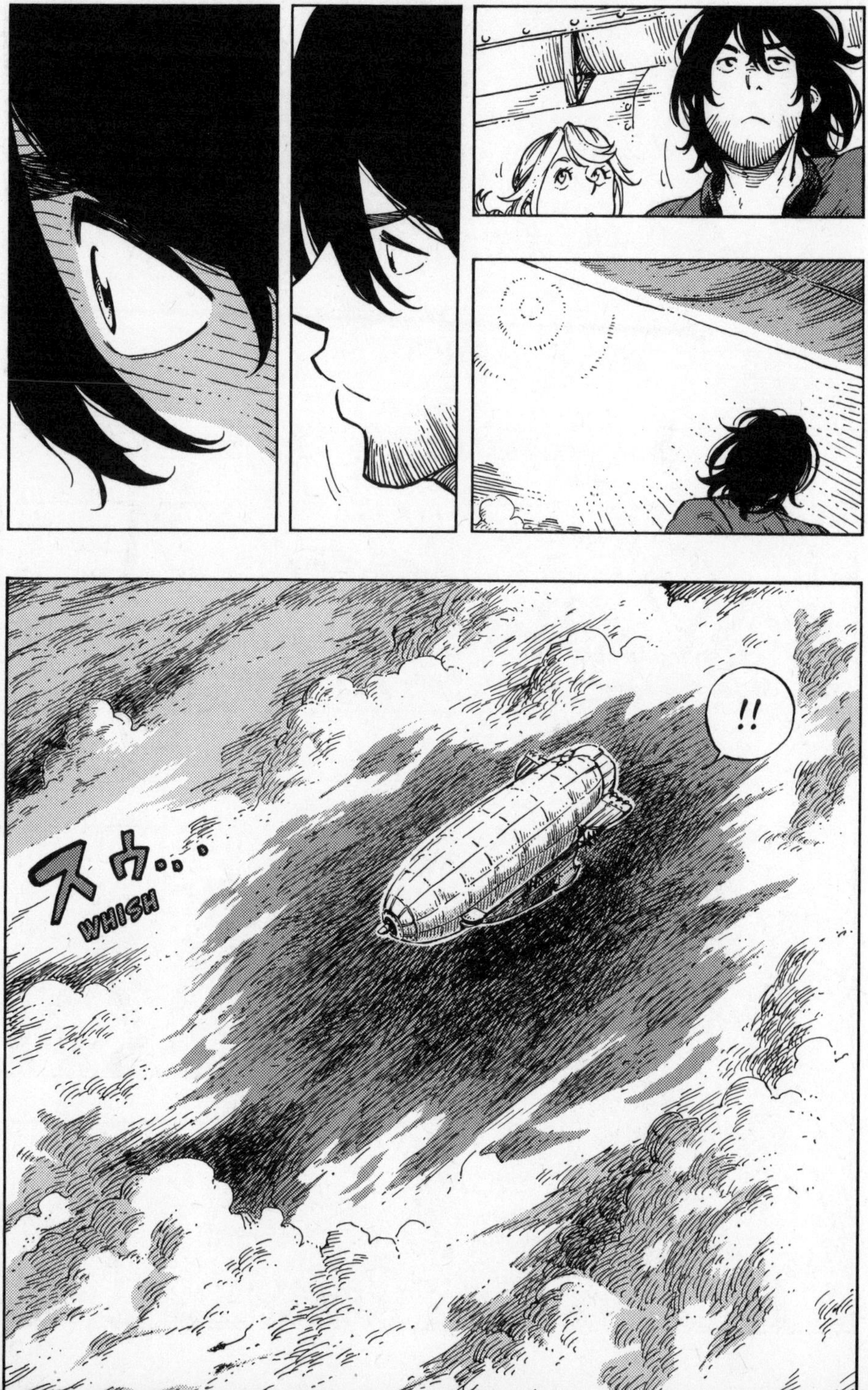
!!
スゥ...
WHISH

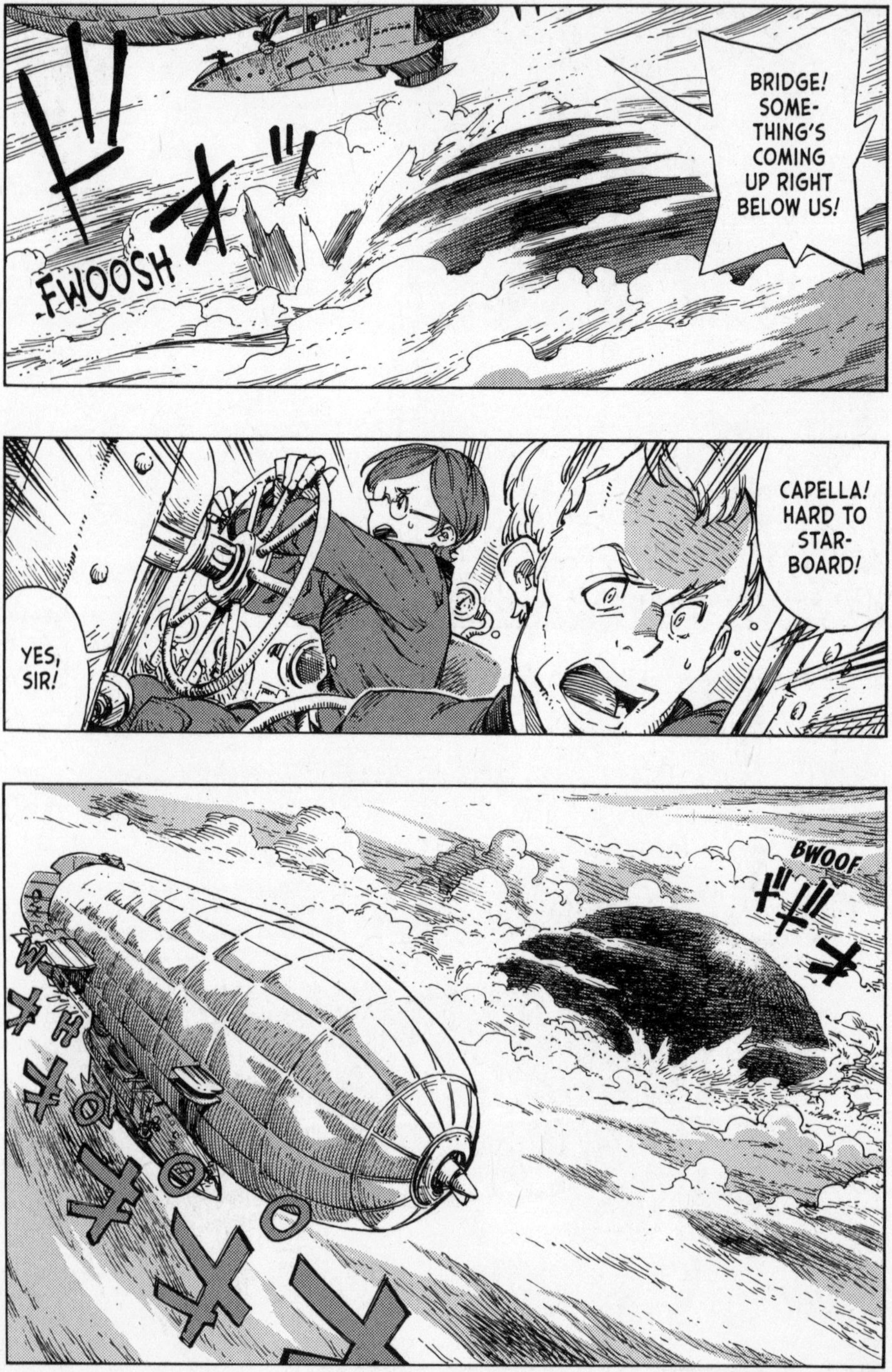
BRIDGE! SOME-THING'S COMING UP RIGHT BELOW US!
FWOOSH
CAPELLA! HARD TO STAR-BOARD!
YES, SIR!
BWOOF

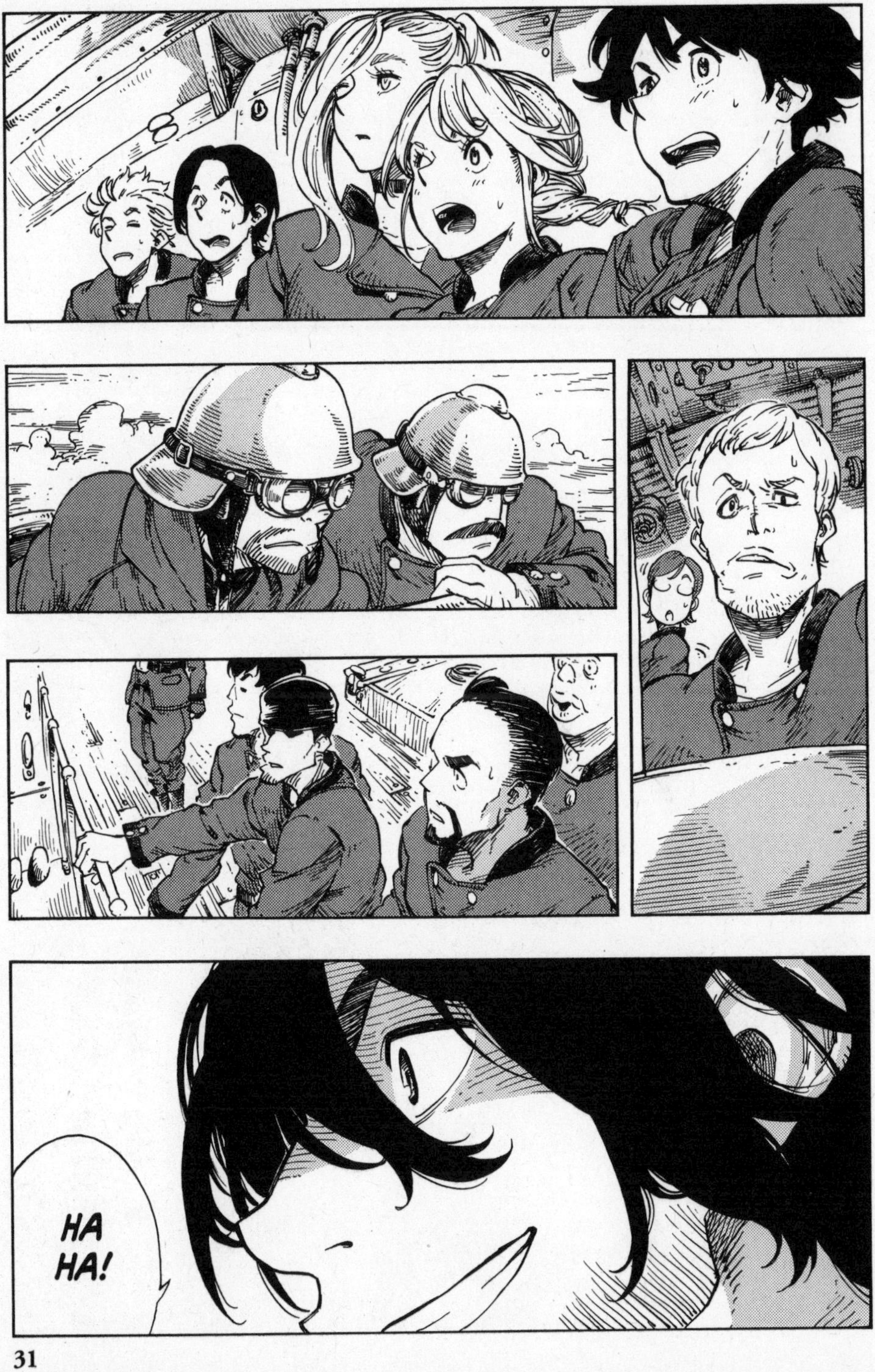
HA
HA!

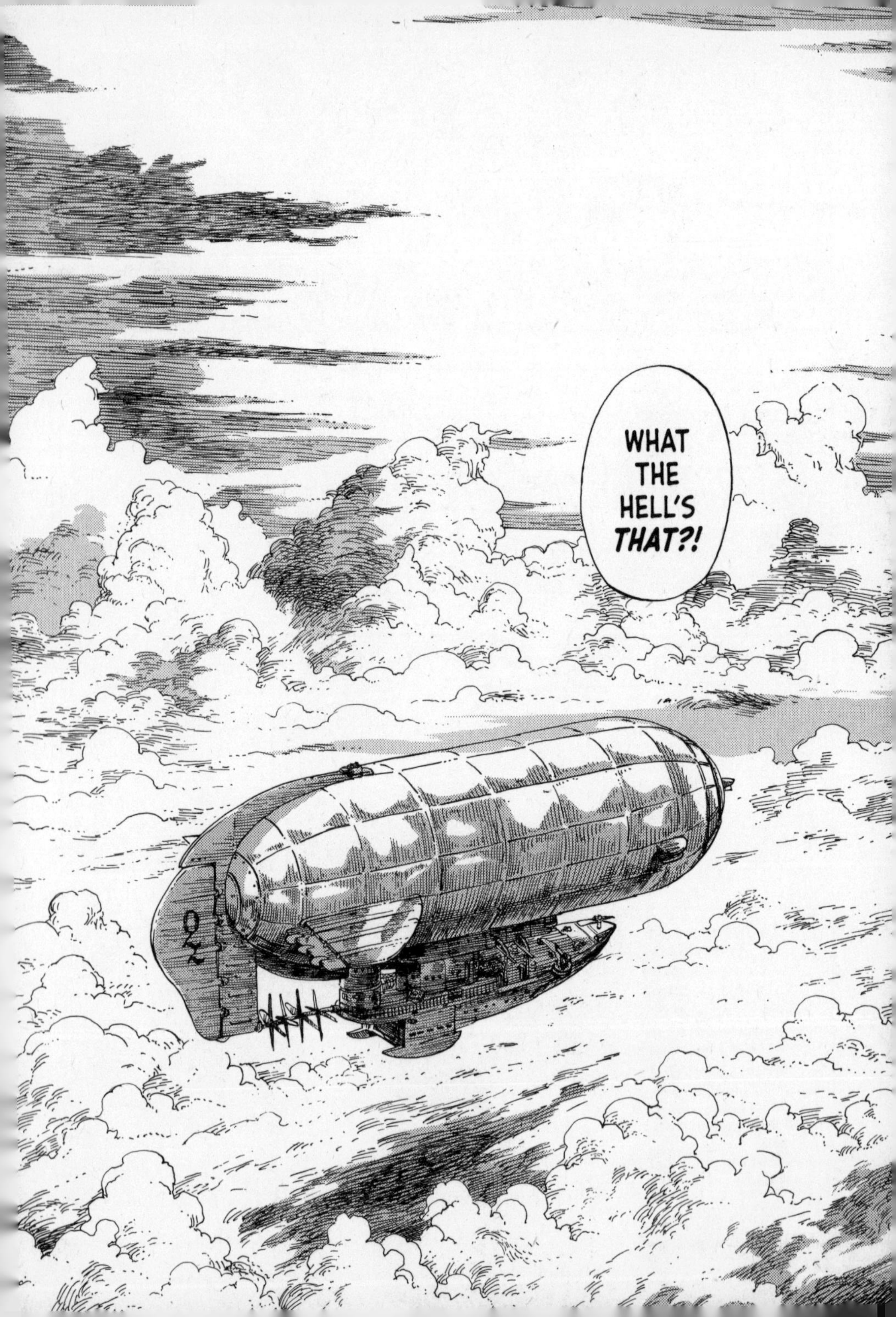
WHAT THE HELL'S *THAT?!*

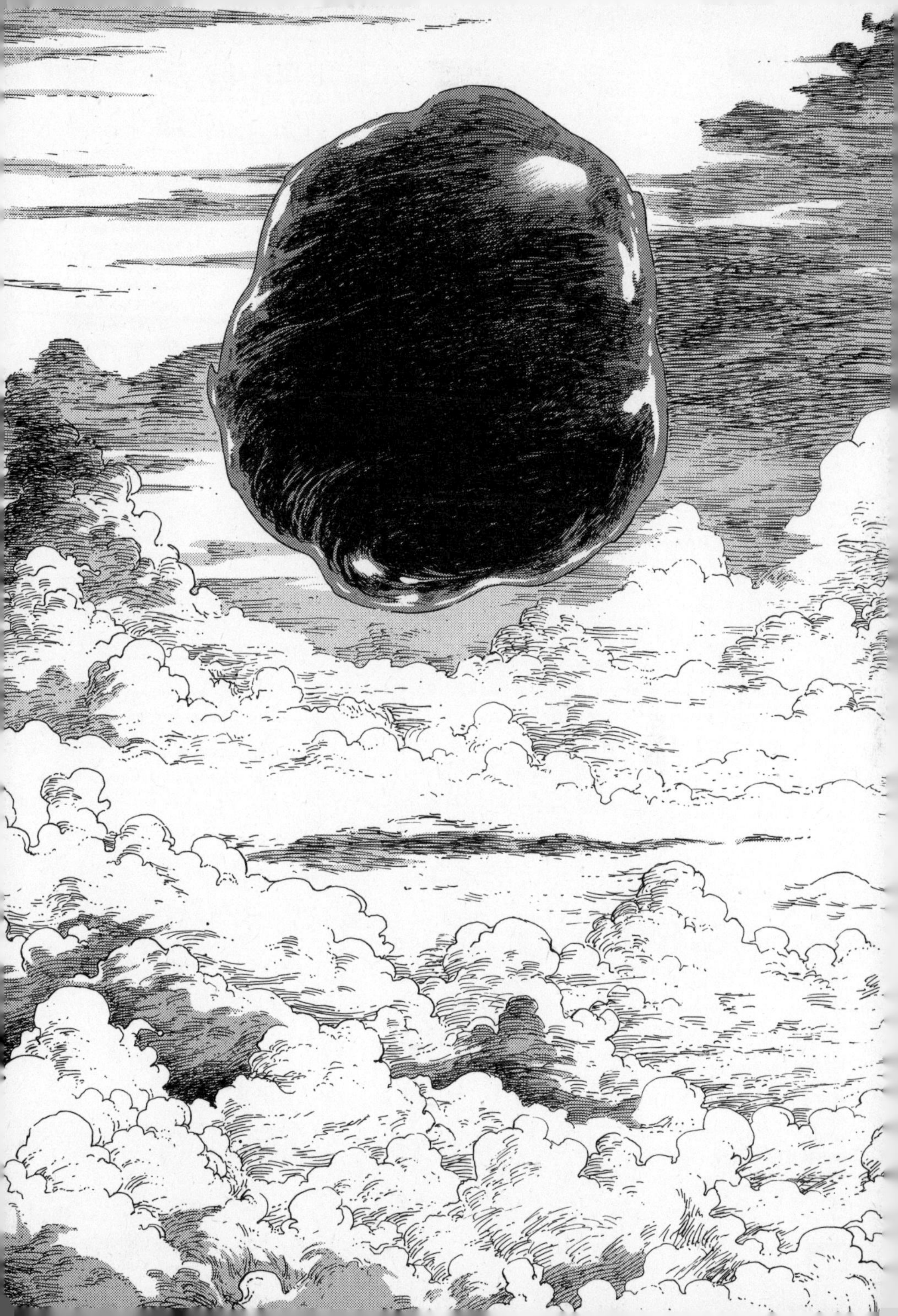

Dragon Jerky

Ingredients

✦ Dragon meat (fatty cuts for juicier jerky, lean cuts for tougher jerky)

✦ Salt: 5-10% the weight of the meat

✦ Five-spice powder to taste

✦ Sugar to taste

01
Slice the meat into 5-10 mm strips and rub with salt, spices, and sugar.

02
Place meat in a basket or net set over a tray and let rest in a cool, dark place for 2-5 days. Discard any liquid from the meat that collects in the tray.

03
Soak the meat in water for about 2 hours to remove excess salt. Change the water once halfway.

04
Run a wire or string through the meat and hang to dry in a well-ventilated area away from direct sunlight. If mold begins to form on the meat during the drying process, wipe away with high-strength alcohol.

05
Once fully dried and rigid, the jerky is done. It can be eaten as-is, grilled, or tossed in a soup.

JERKY TAKES A WHILE TO MAKE, BUT IT'S A MUST-HAVE FOR TRAVELING THROUGH THE SKIES.

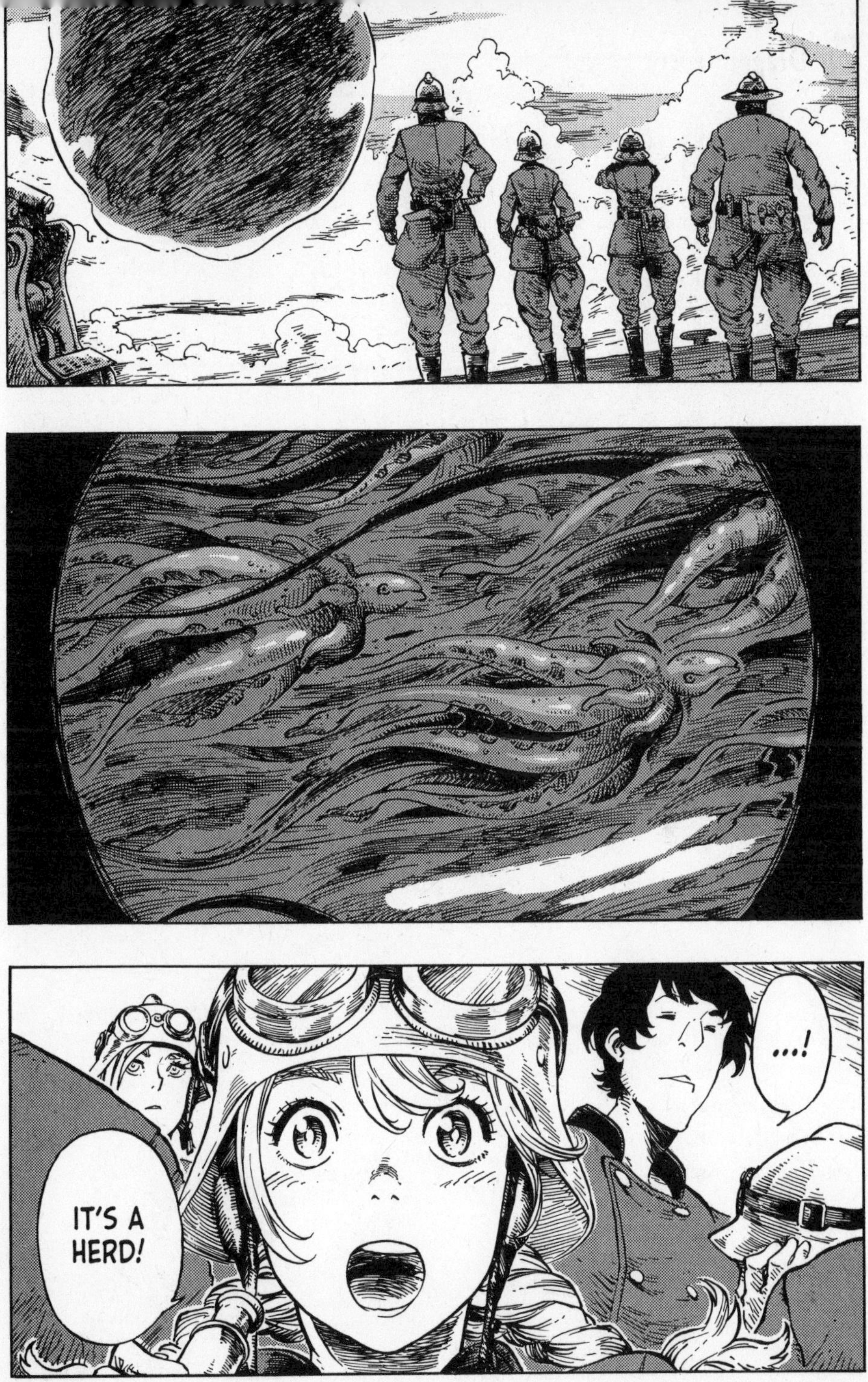
...!
IT'S A HERD!

Flight 13 Migrating Dragons & the Chasm Depths

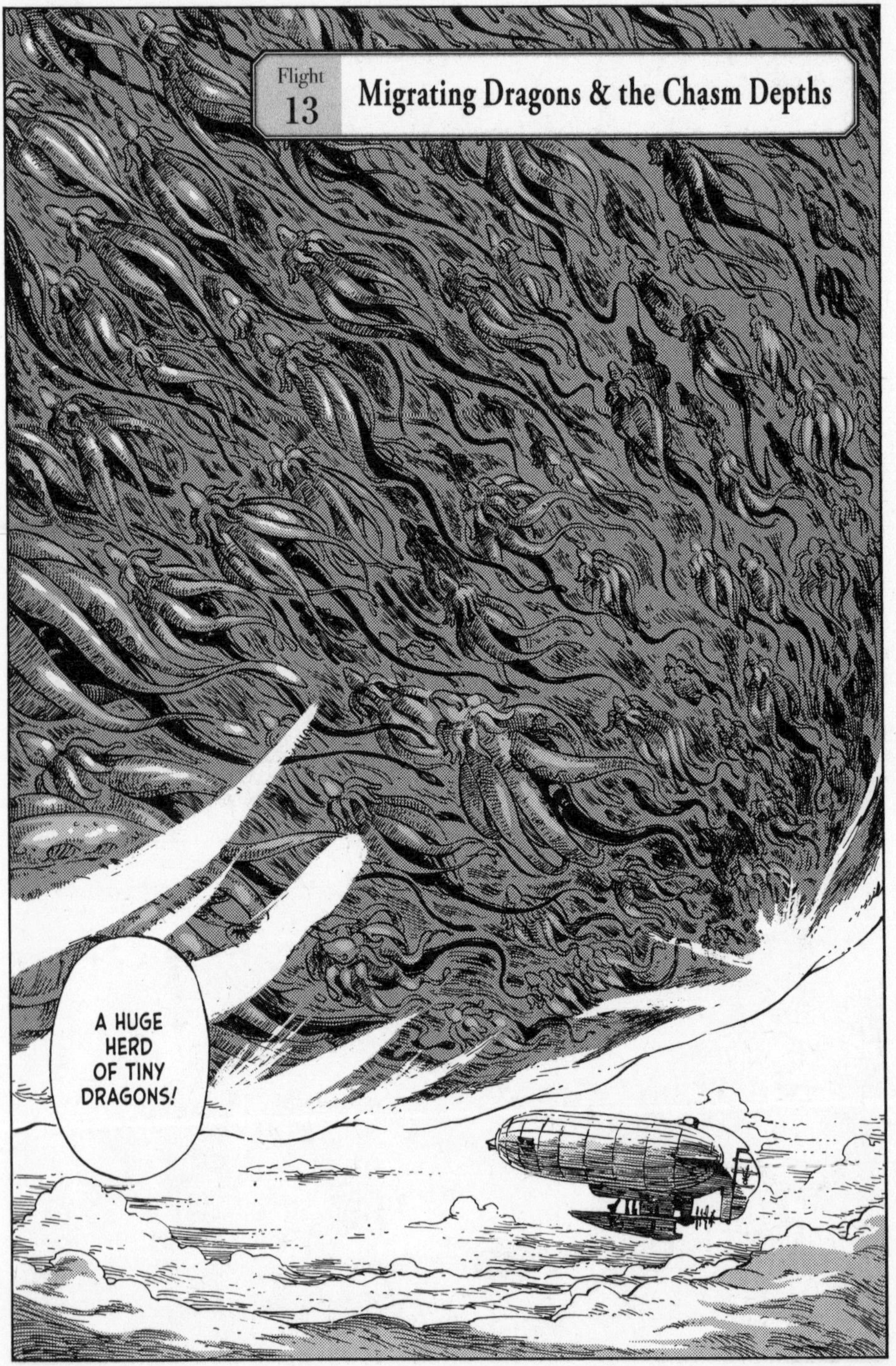
A HUGE HERD OF TINY DRAGONS!

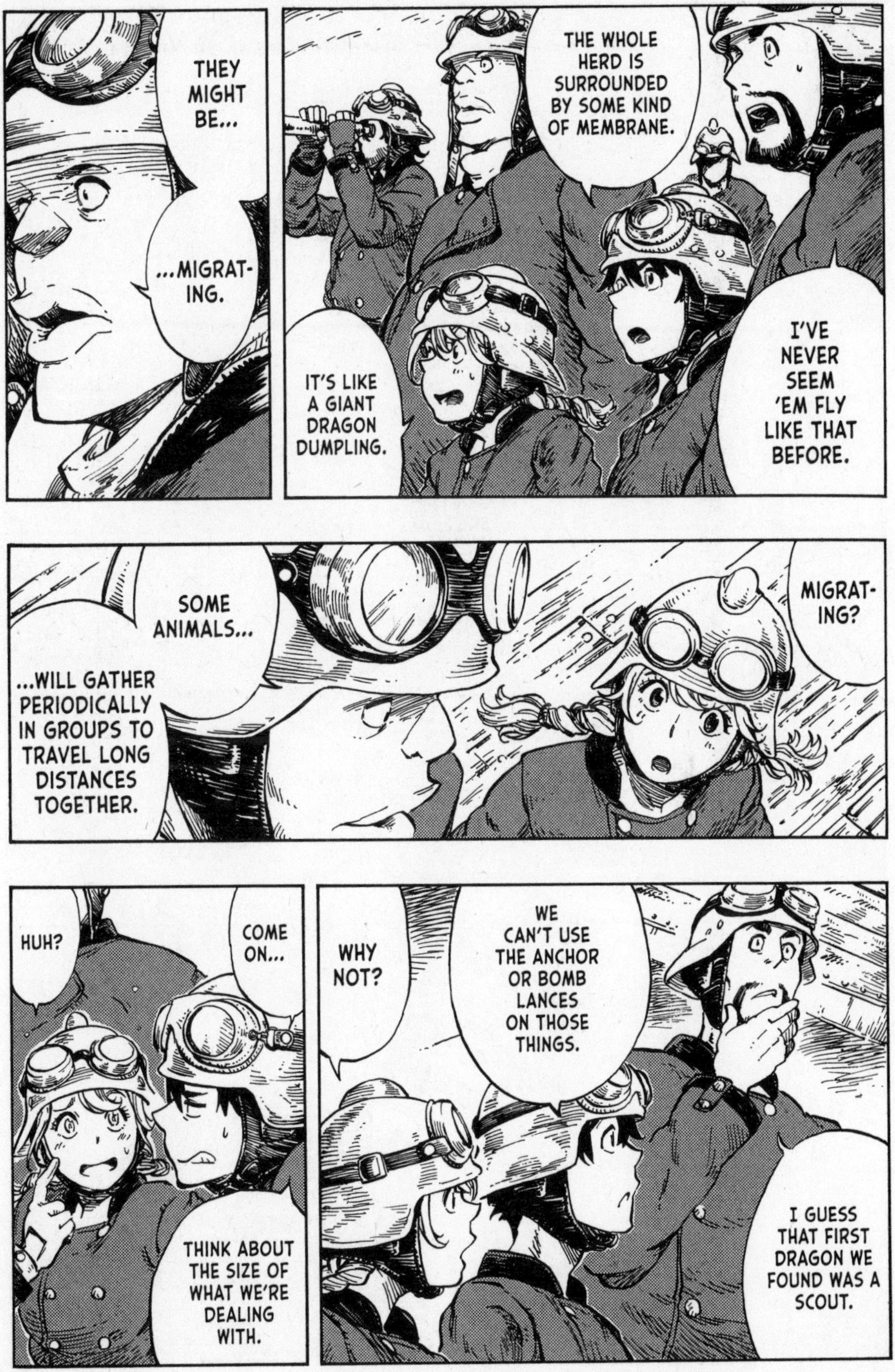
THE WHOLE HERD IS SURROUNDED BY SOME KIND OF MEMBRANE.
I'VE NEVER SEEM 'EM FLY LIKE THAT BEFORE.
IT'S LIKE A GIANT DRAGON DUMPLING.
THEY MIGHT BE...
...MIGRAT-ING.
MIGRAT-ING?
SOME ANIMALS...
...WILL GATHER PERIODICALLY IN GROUPS TO TRAVEL LONG DISTANCES TOGETHER.
WE CAN'T USE THE ANCHOR OR BOMB LANCES ON THOSE THINGS.
WHY NOT?
I GUESS THAT FIRST DRAGON WE FOUND WAS A SCOUT.
COME ON...
HUH?
THINK ABOUT THE SIZE OF WHAT WE'RE DEALING WITH.

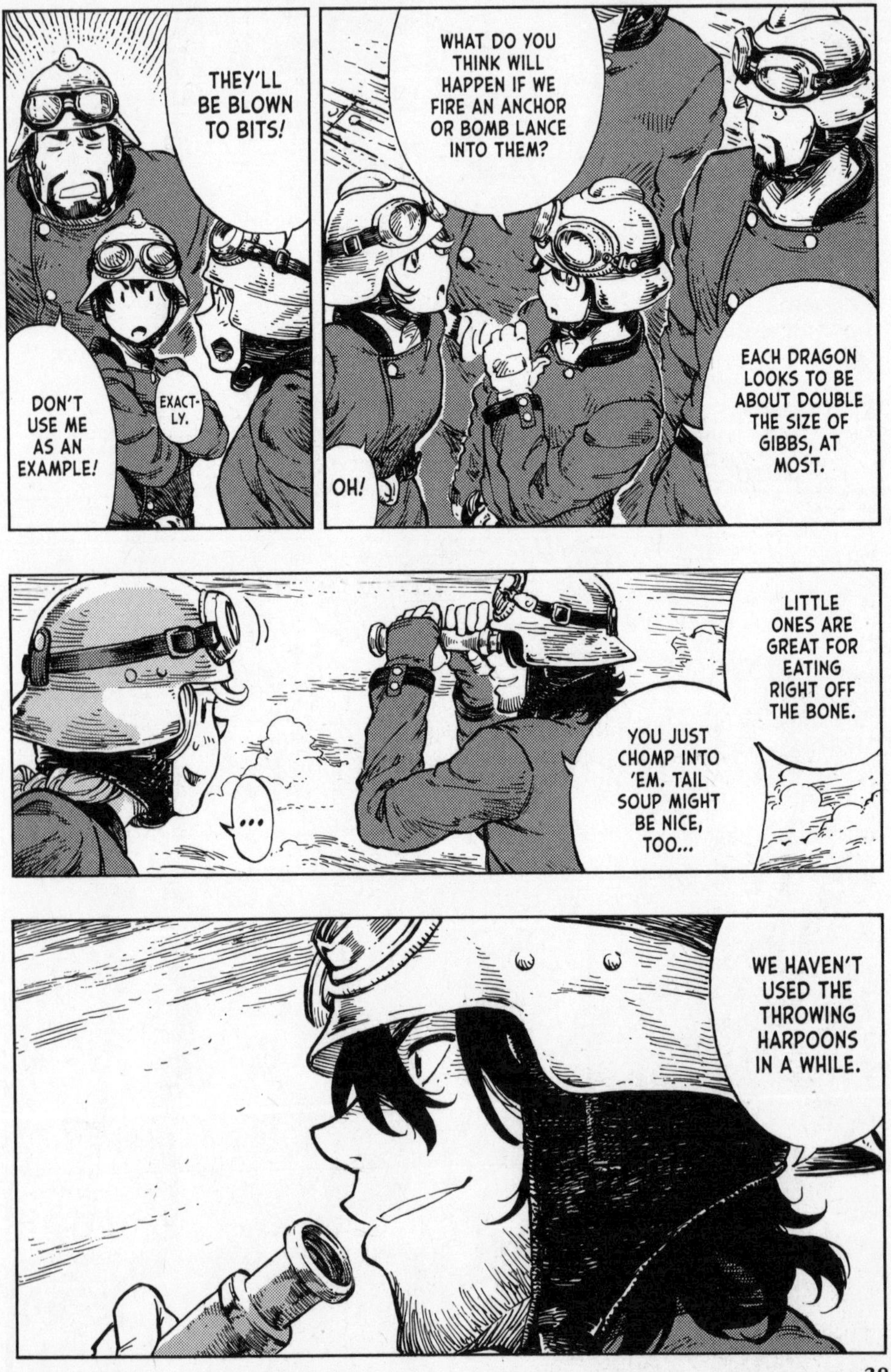
EACH DRAGON LOOKS TO BE ABOUT DOUBLE THE SIZE OF GIBBS, AT MOST.
WHAT DO YOU THINK WILL HAPPEN IF WE FIRE AN ANCHOR OR BOMB LANCE INTO THEM?
OH!
THEY'LL BE BLOWN TO BITS!
EXACT-LY.
DON'T USE ME AS AN EXAMPLE!
LITTLE ONES ARE GREAT FOR EATING RIGHT OFF THE BONE.
YOU JUST CHOMP INTO 'EM. TAIL SOUP MIGHT BE NICE, TOO...
...
WE HAVEN'T USED THE THROWING HARPOONS IN A WHILE.

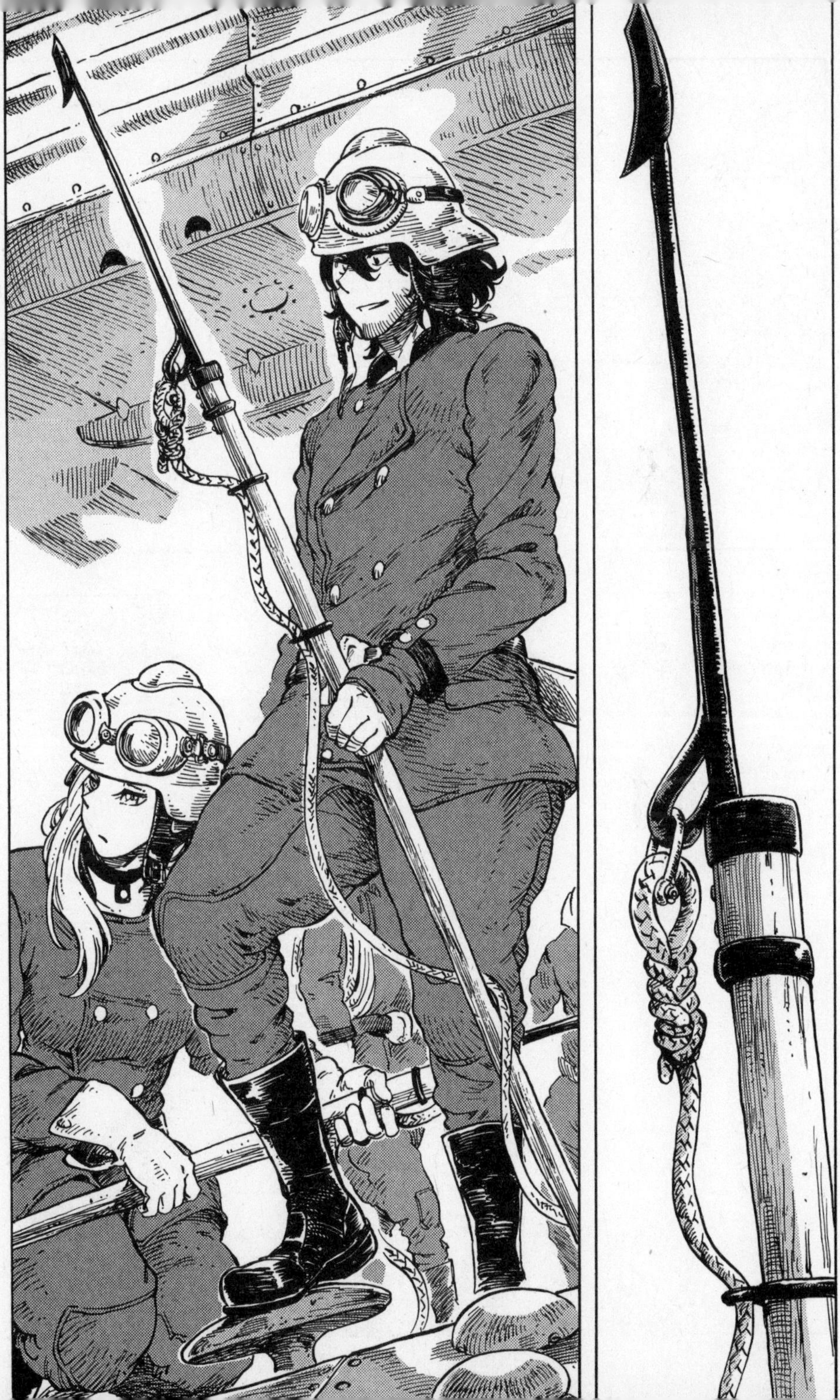

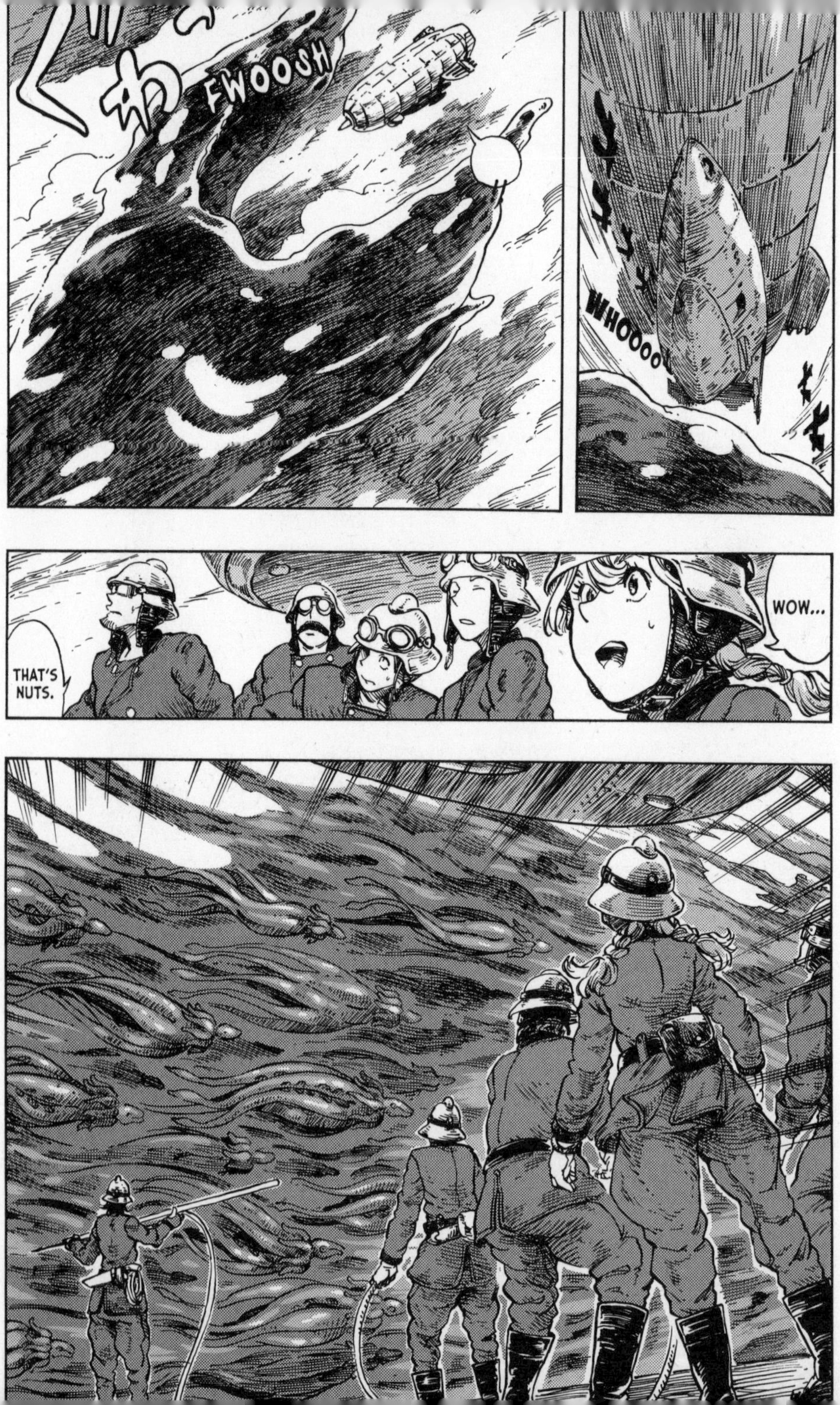
WHOOOO
FWOOSH
WOW...
THAT'S NUTS.

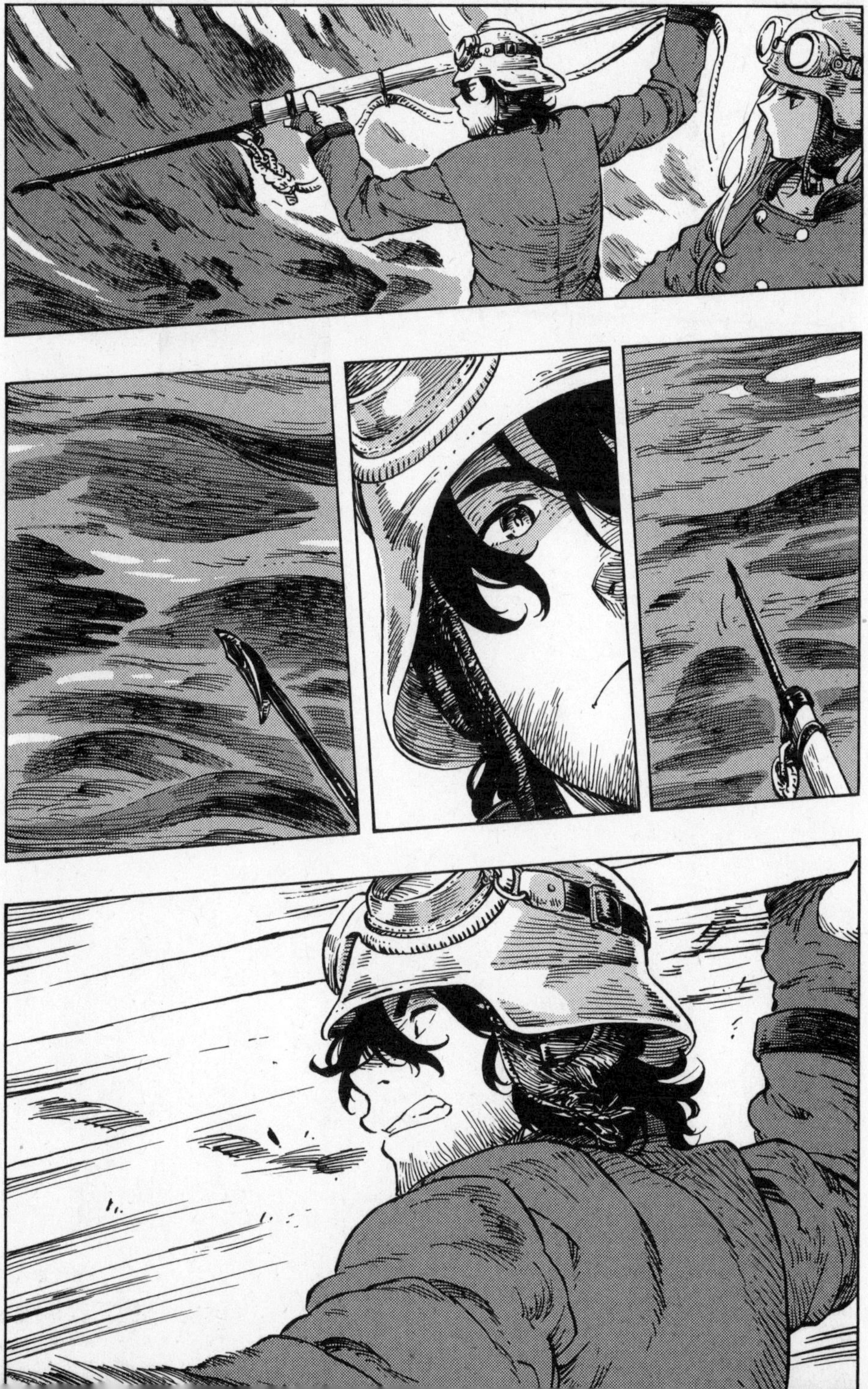

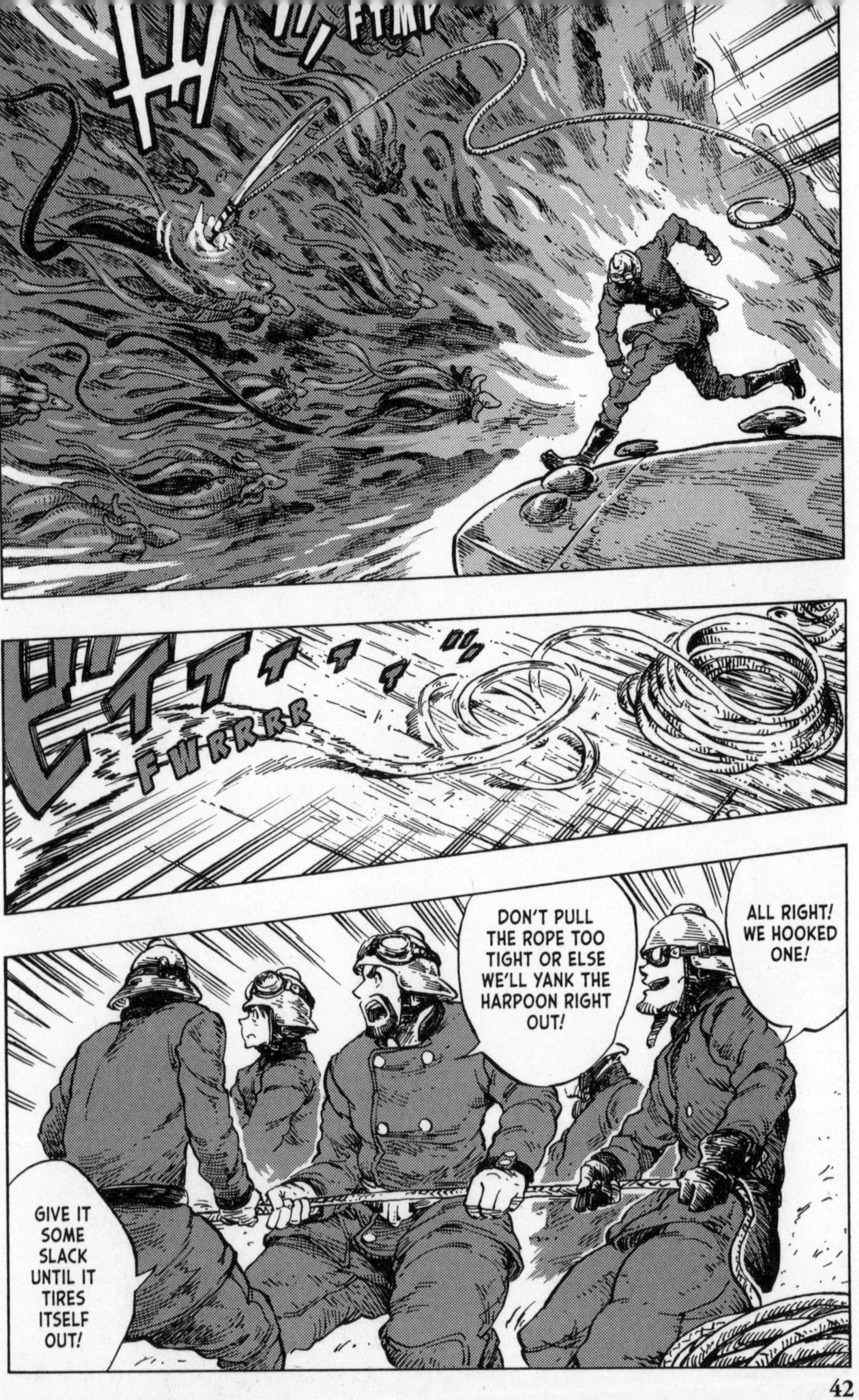
FTMP
FWRRRR
ALL RIGHT! WE HOOKED ONE!
DON'T PULL THE ROPE TOO TIGHT OR ELSE WE'LL YANK THE HARPOON RIGHT OUT!
GIVE IT SOME SLACK UNTIL IT TIRES ITSELF OUT!

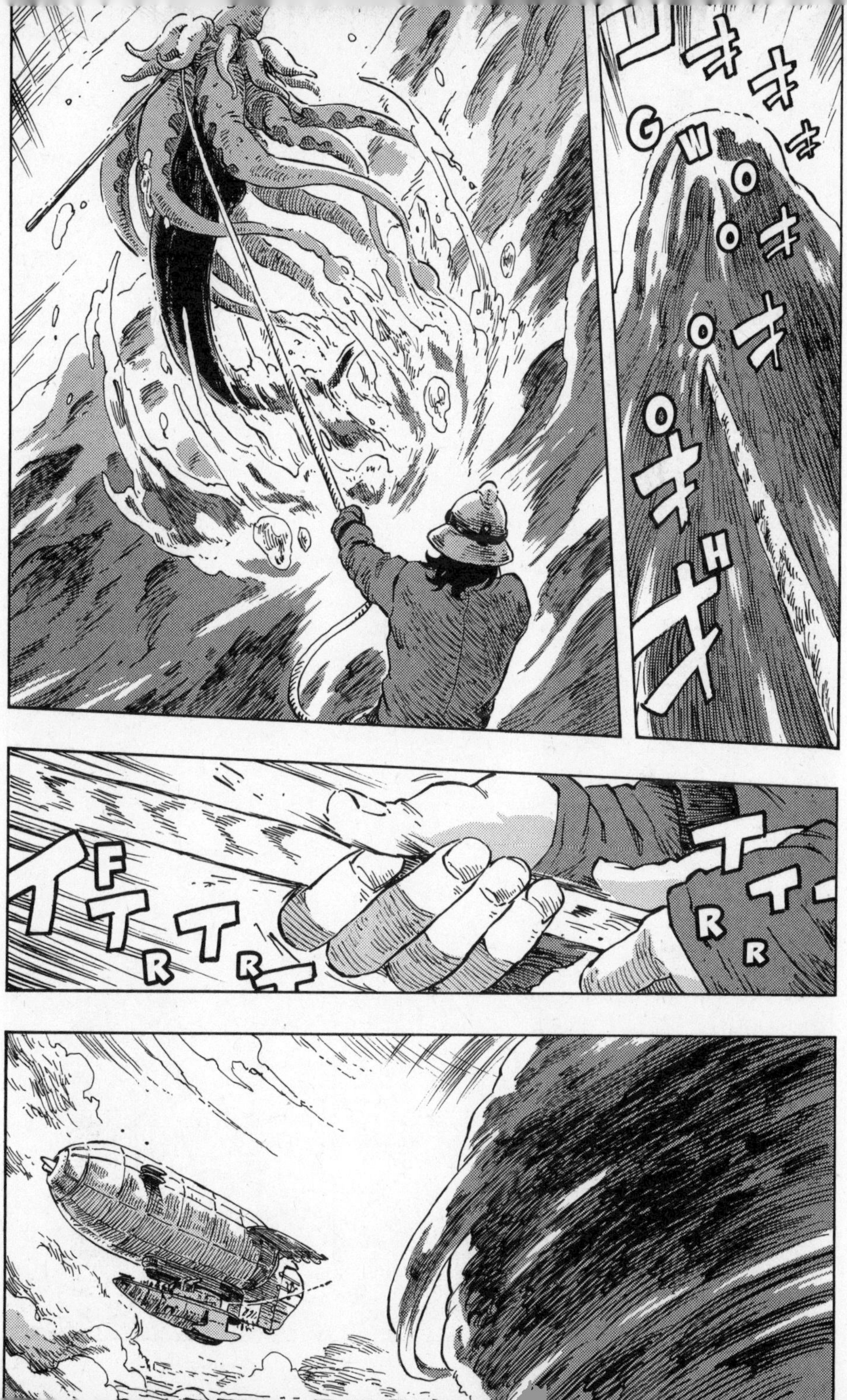
GWOOOOH
FRRRR

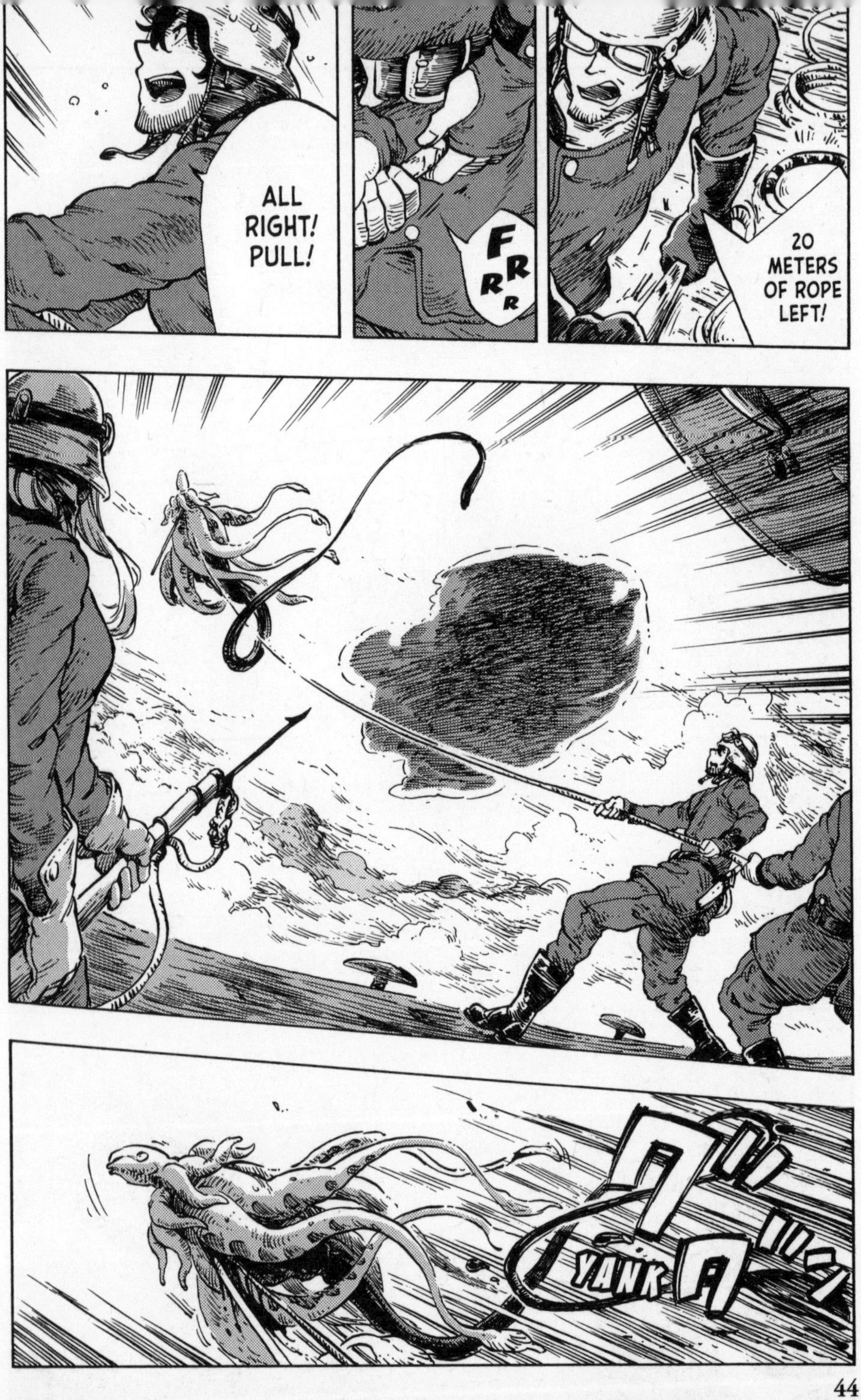
20 METERS OF ROPE LEFT!
FRRRR
ALL RIGHT! PULL!
YANK

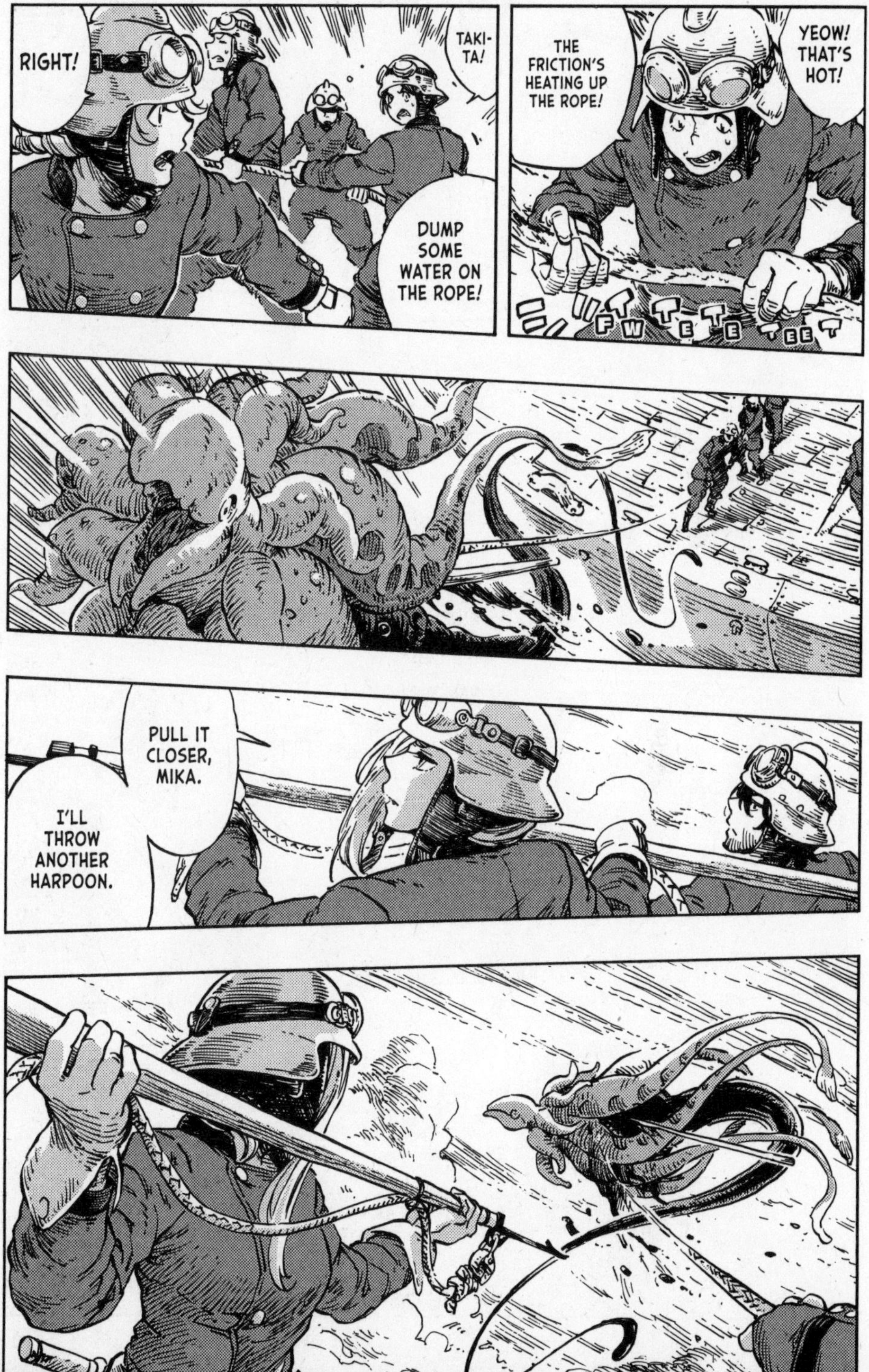
YEOW! THAT'S HOT!
THE FRICTION'S HEATING UP THE ROPE!
FWTETETEET
TAKI-TA!
RIGHT!
DUMP SOME WATER ON THE ROPE!
PULL IT CLOSER, MIKA.
I'LL THROW ANOTHER HARPOON.

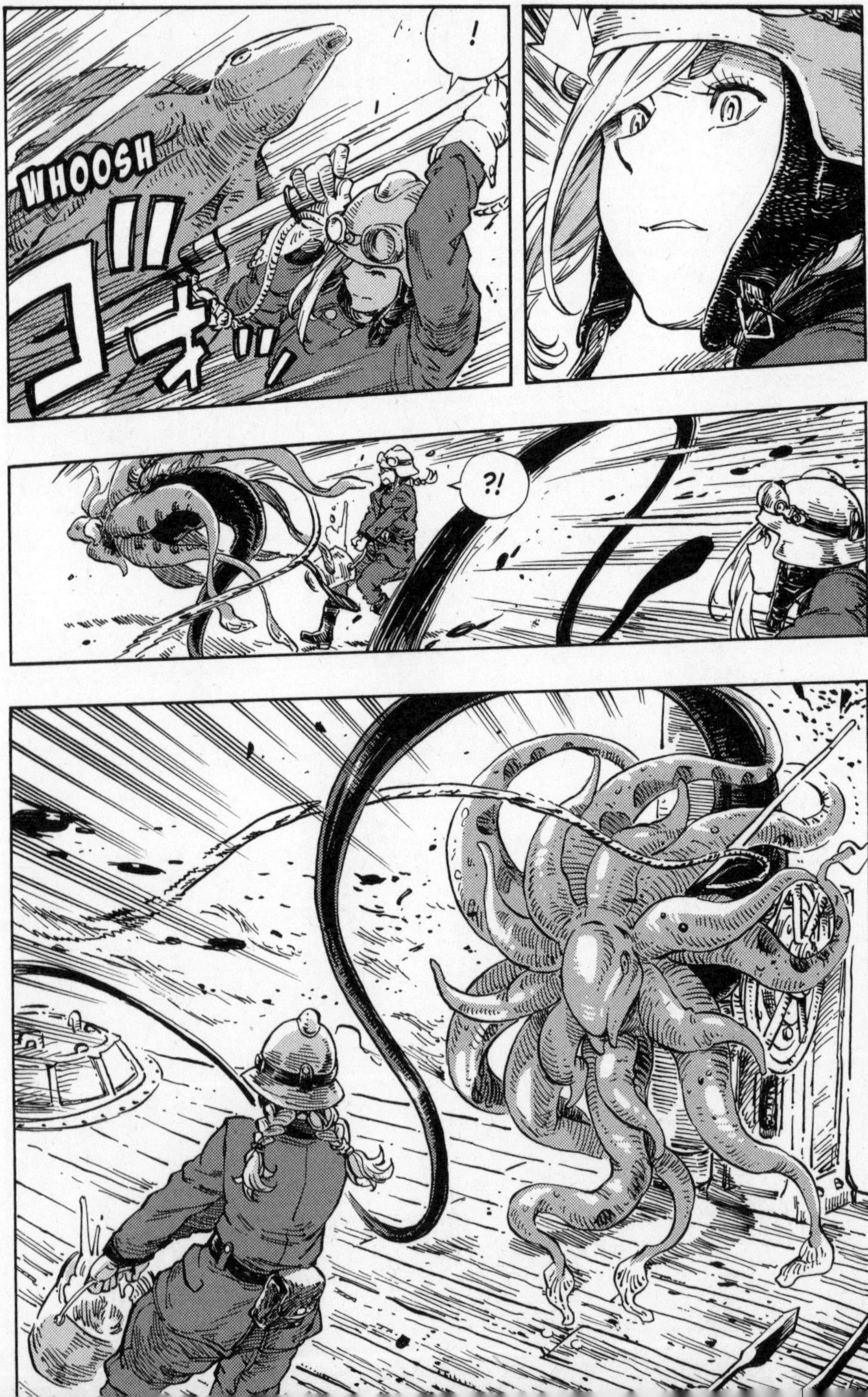
!
WHOOSH
?!

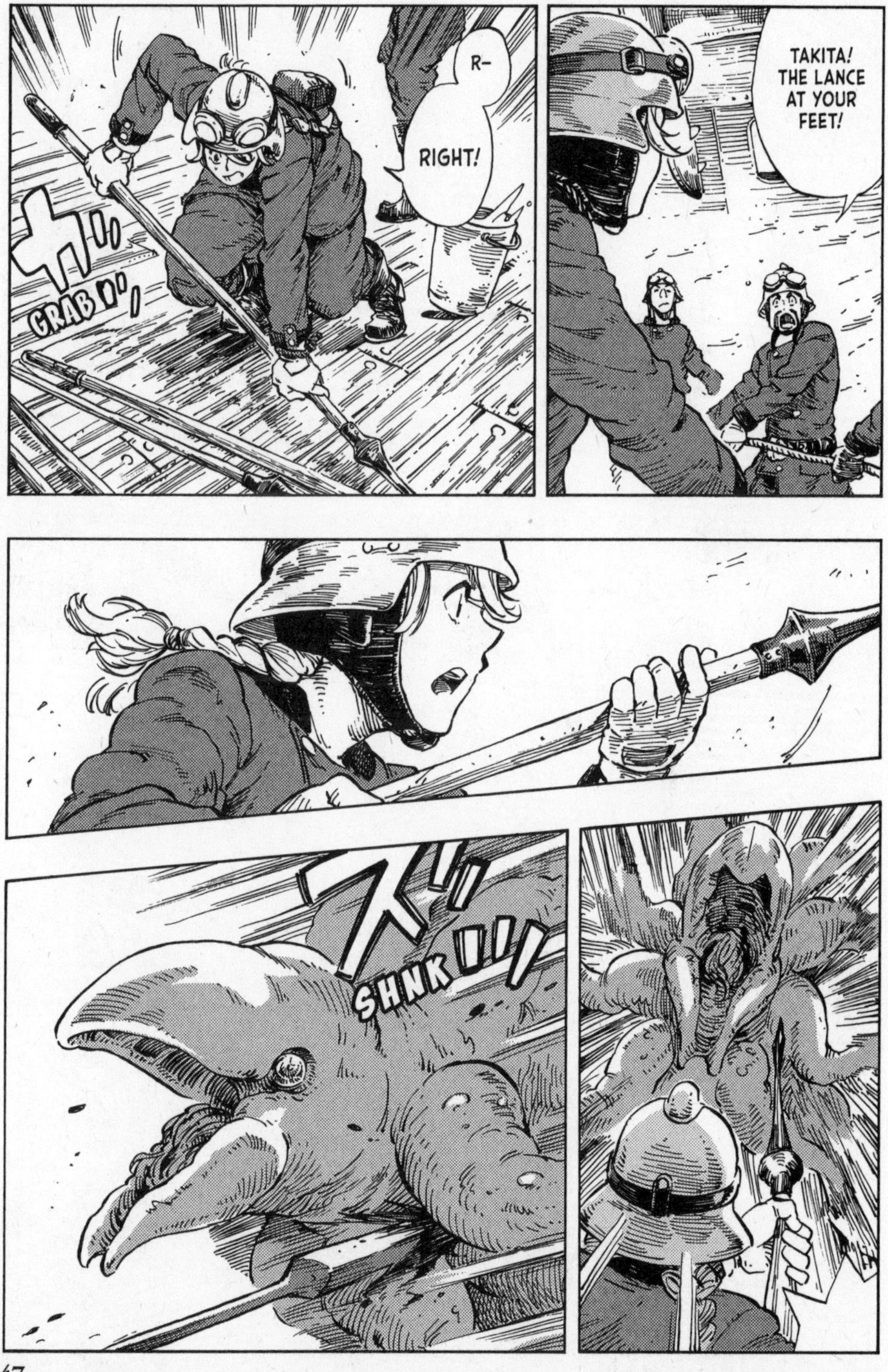
TAKITA! THE LANCE AT YOUR FEET!
R-
RIGHT!
GRAB
SHNK

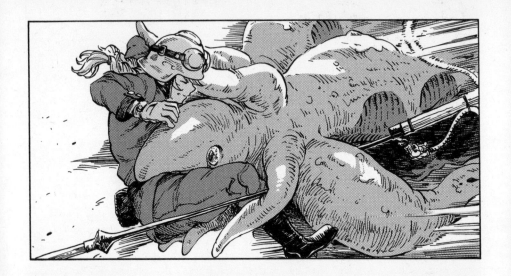

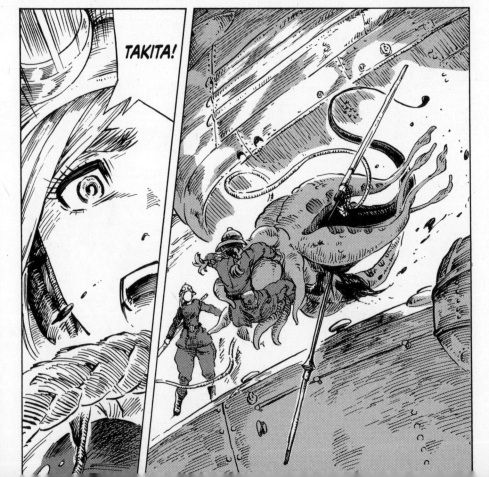

TAKITA!

ズ
ZOOSH
キッ

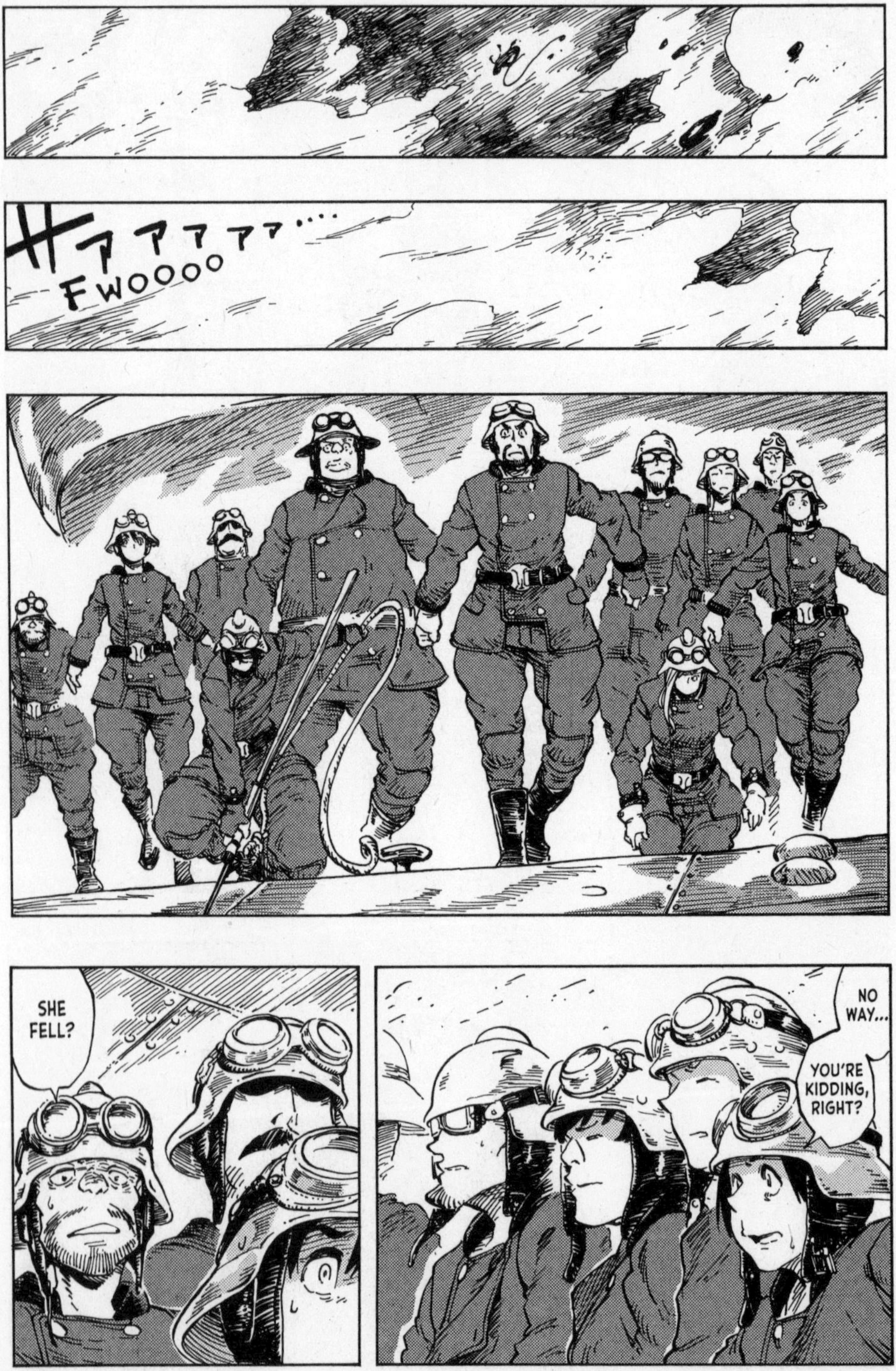
サァァァァァ....
FWOOOO
NO WAY...
YOU'RE KIDDING, RIGHT?
SHE FELL?

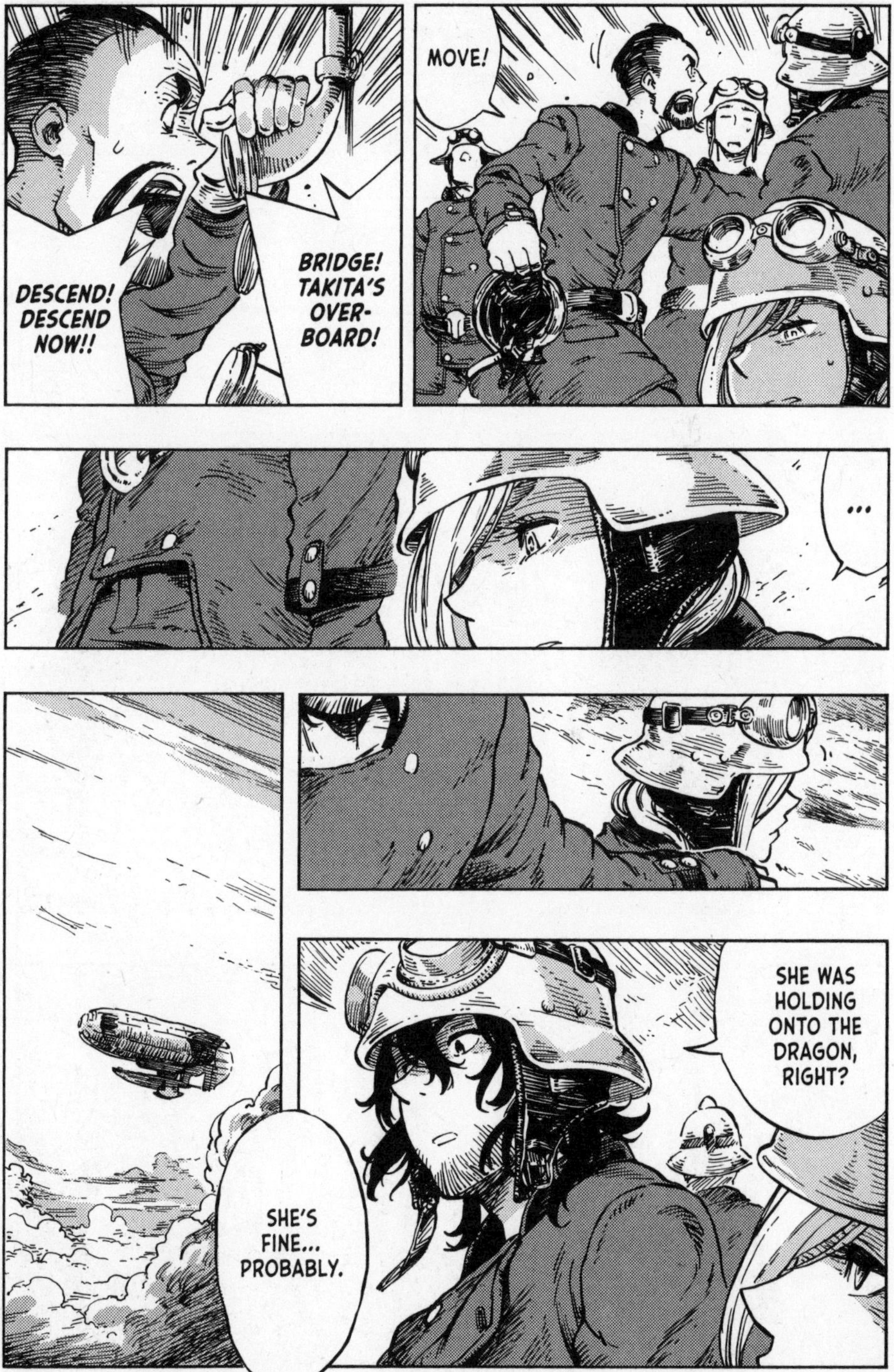
MOVE!
BRIDGE! TAKITA'S OVER-BOARD!
DESCEND! DESCEND NOW!!
...
SHE WAS HOLDING ONTO THE DRAGON, RIGHT?
SHE'S FINE... PROBABLY.

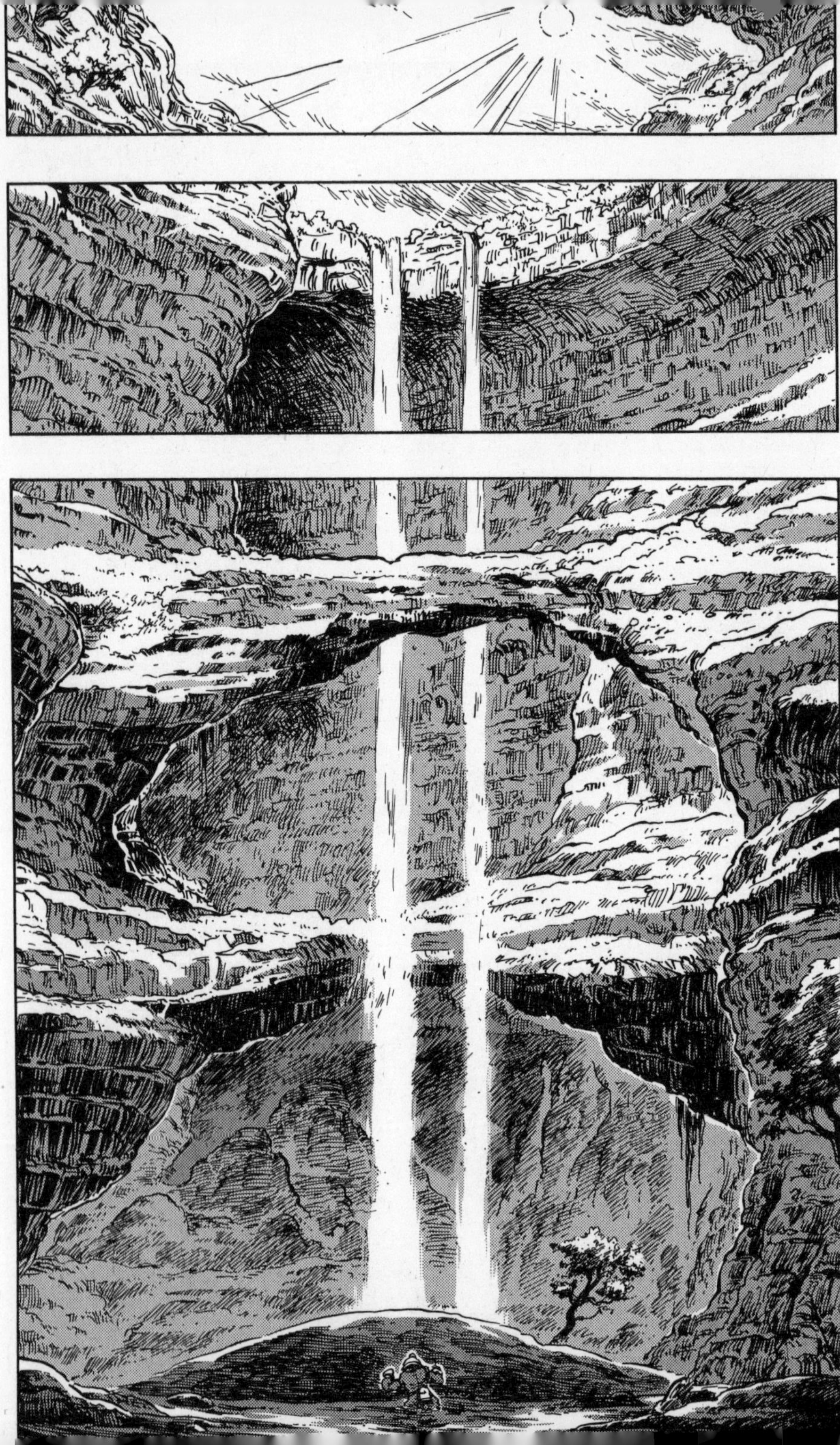

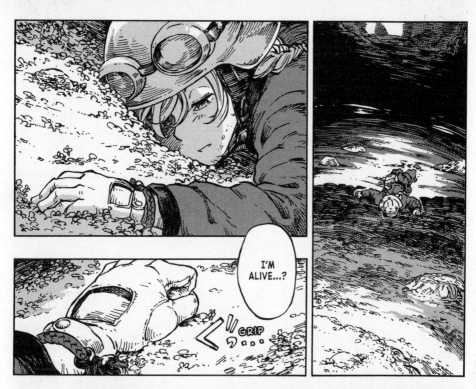

I'M ALIVE...?

GRIP

AH...!

I'VE GOT THAT OINTMENT NANAMI GAVE ME.

OH, YEAH.

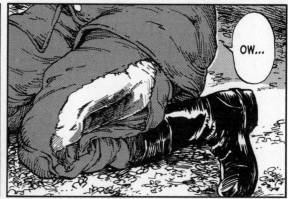

OW...

···

WHERE AM I?

...I HAVE TO SIGNAL THE SHIP.

GLINT

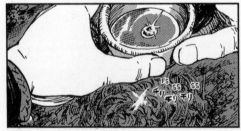

AH!

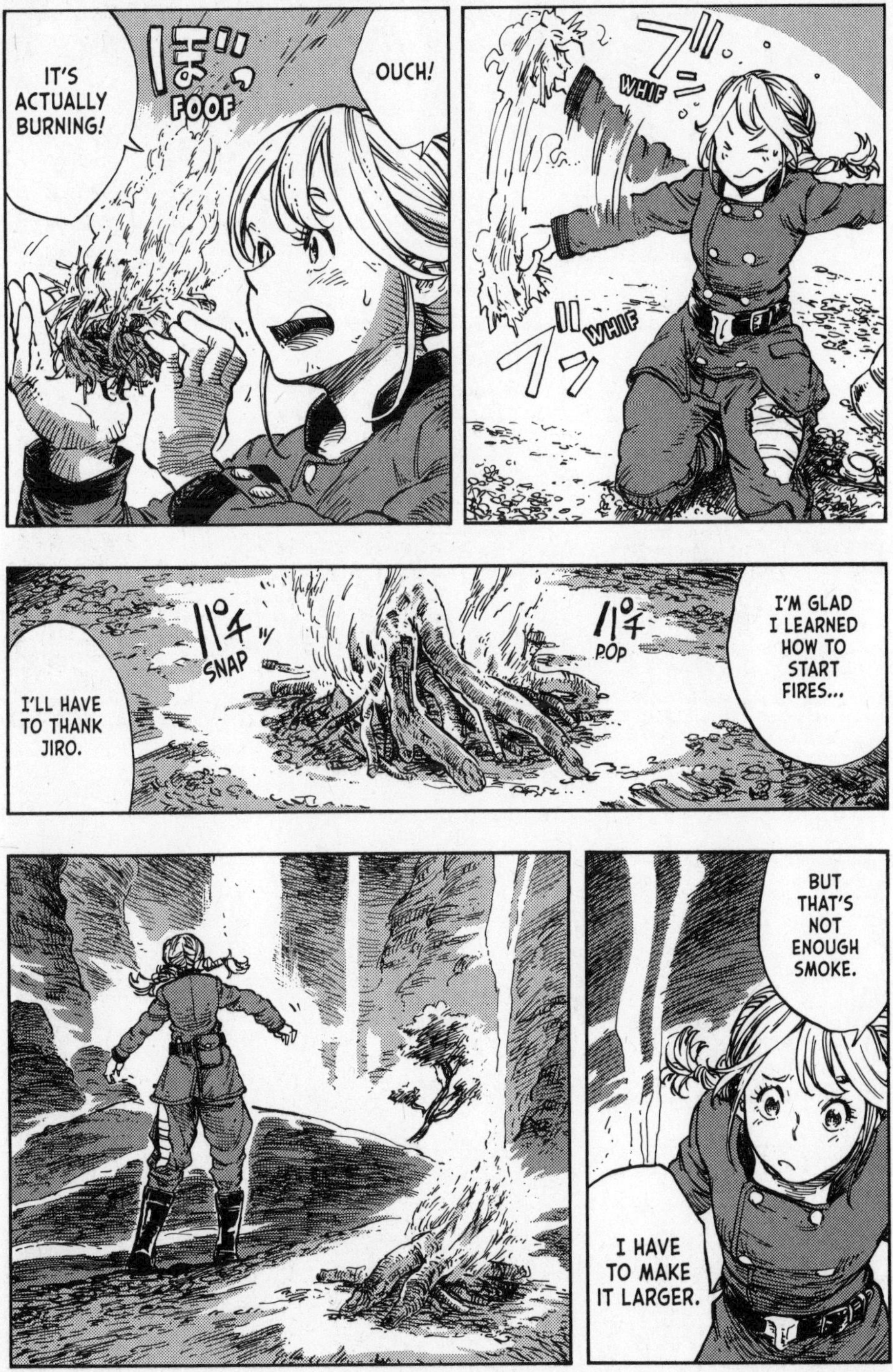
WHIF
WHIF
OUCH!
ぼっ
FOOF
IT'S ACTUALLY BURNING!
I'M GLAD I LEARNED HOW TO START FIRES...
パチ
POP
パチッ
SNAP
I'LL HAVE TO THANK JIRO.
BUT THAT'S NOT ENOUGH SMOKE.
I HAVE TO MAKE IT LARGER.

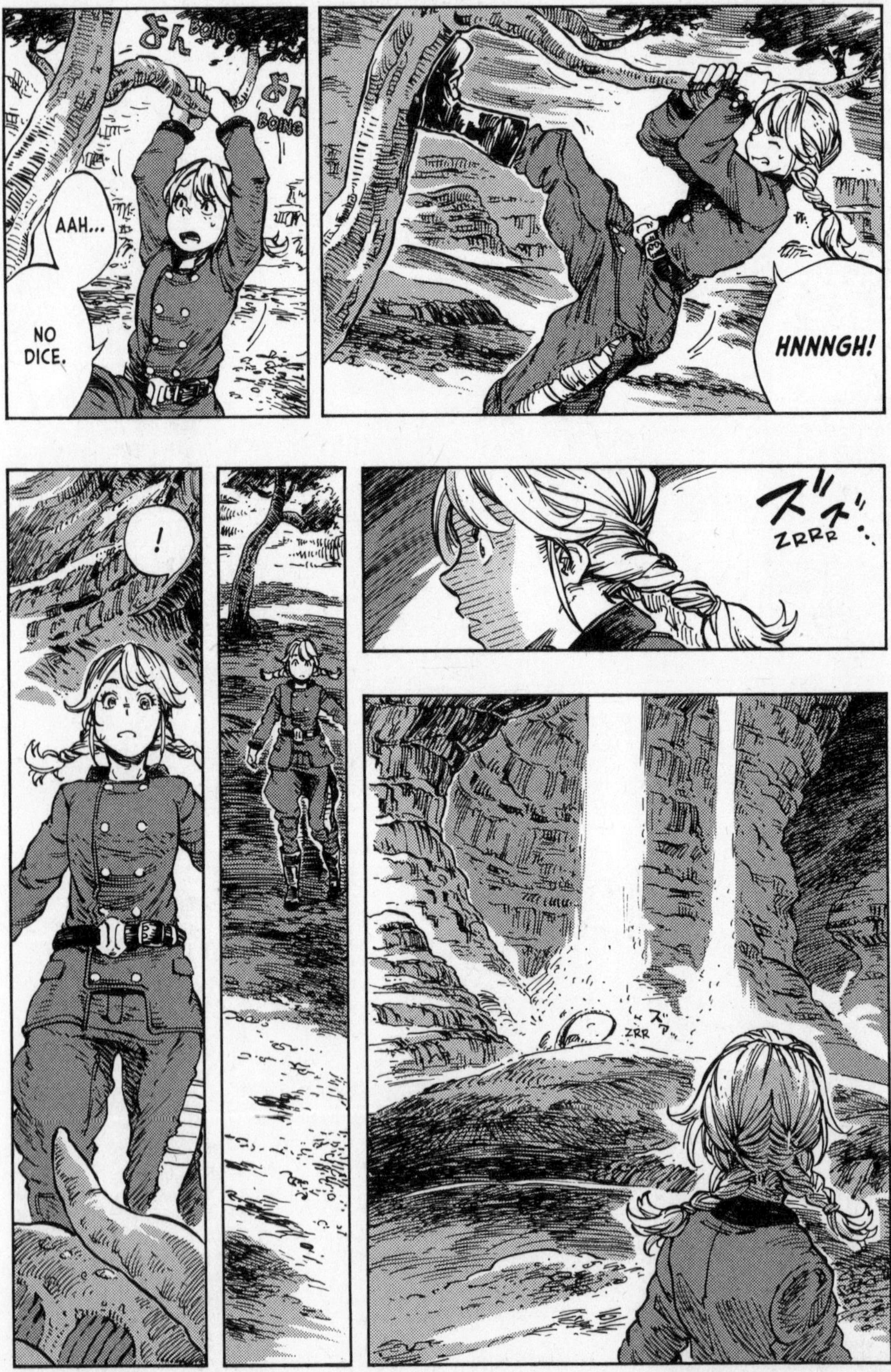
HNNNGH!
ぶん BOING
ぶん BOING
AAH...
NO DICE.
ズズズ... ZRRR
ズア ZRR
!

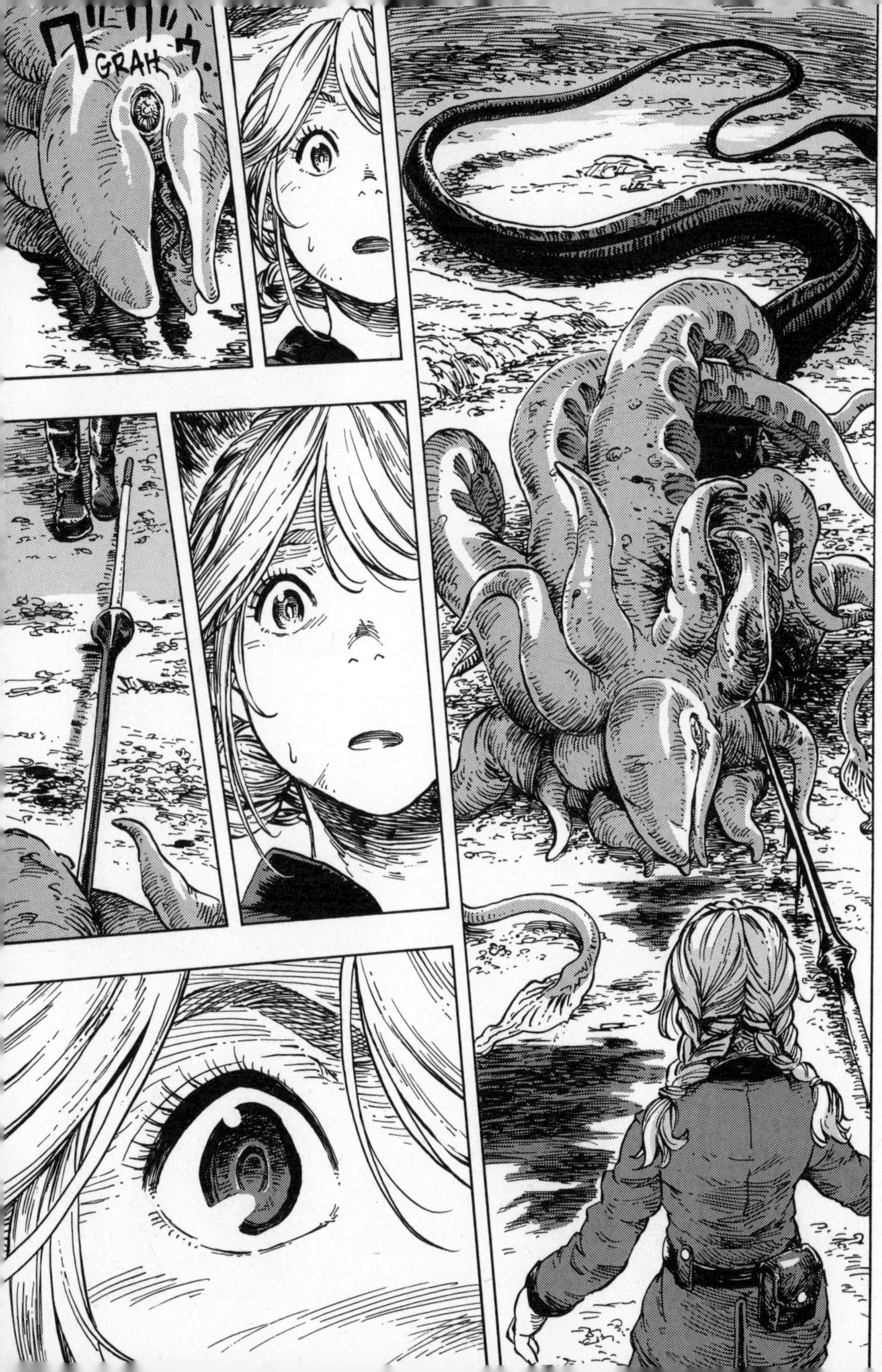
GRAH

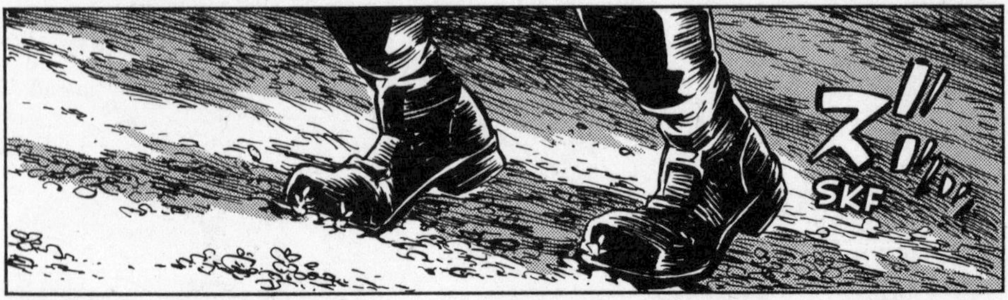
ズリ
SKF

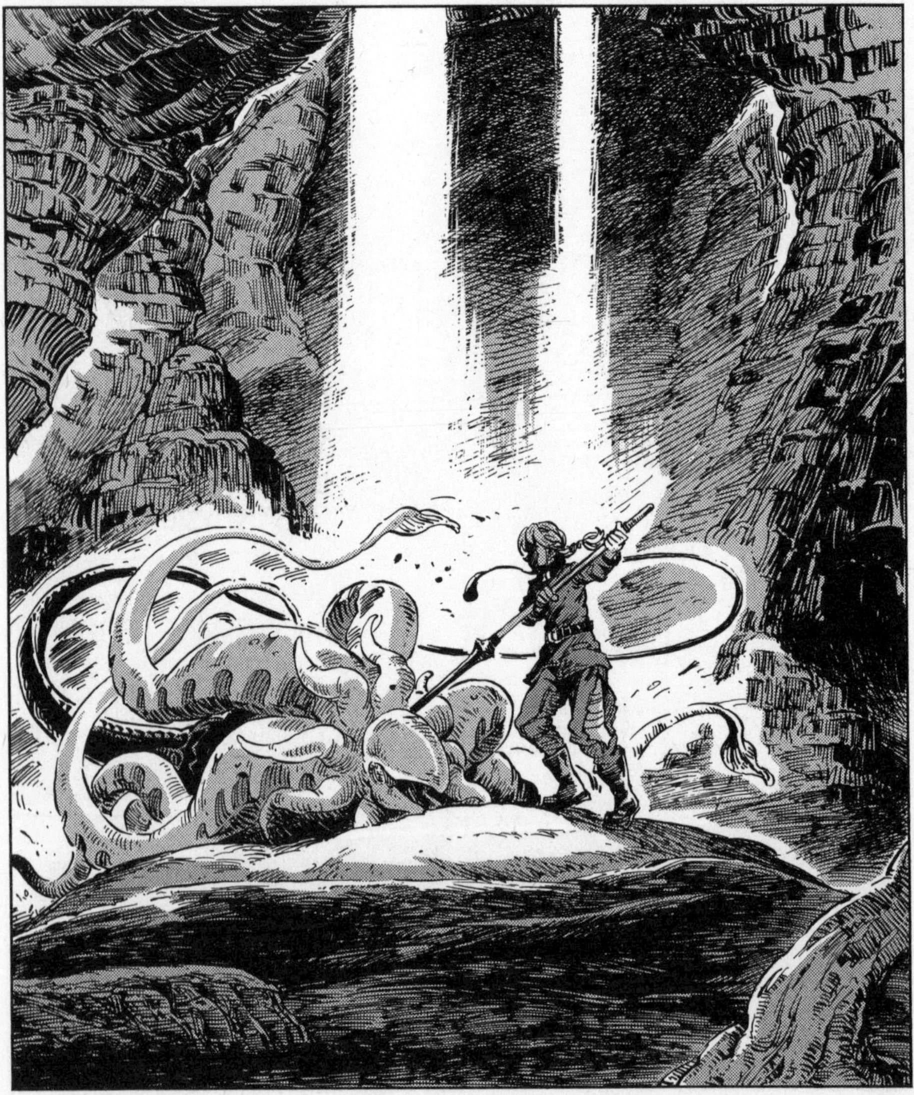

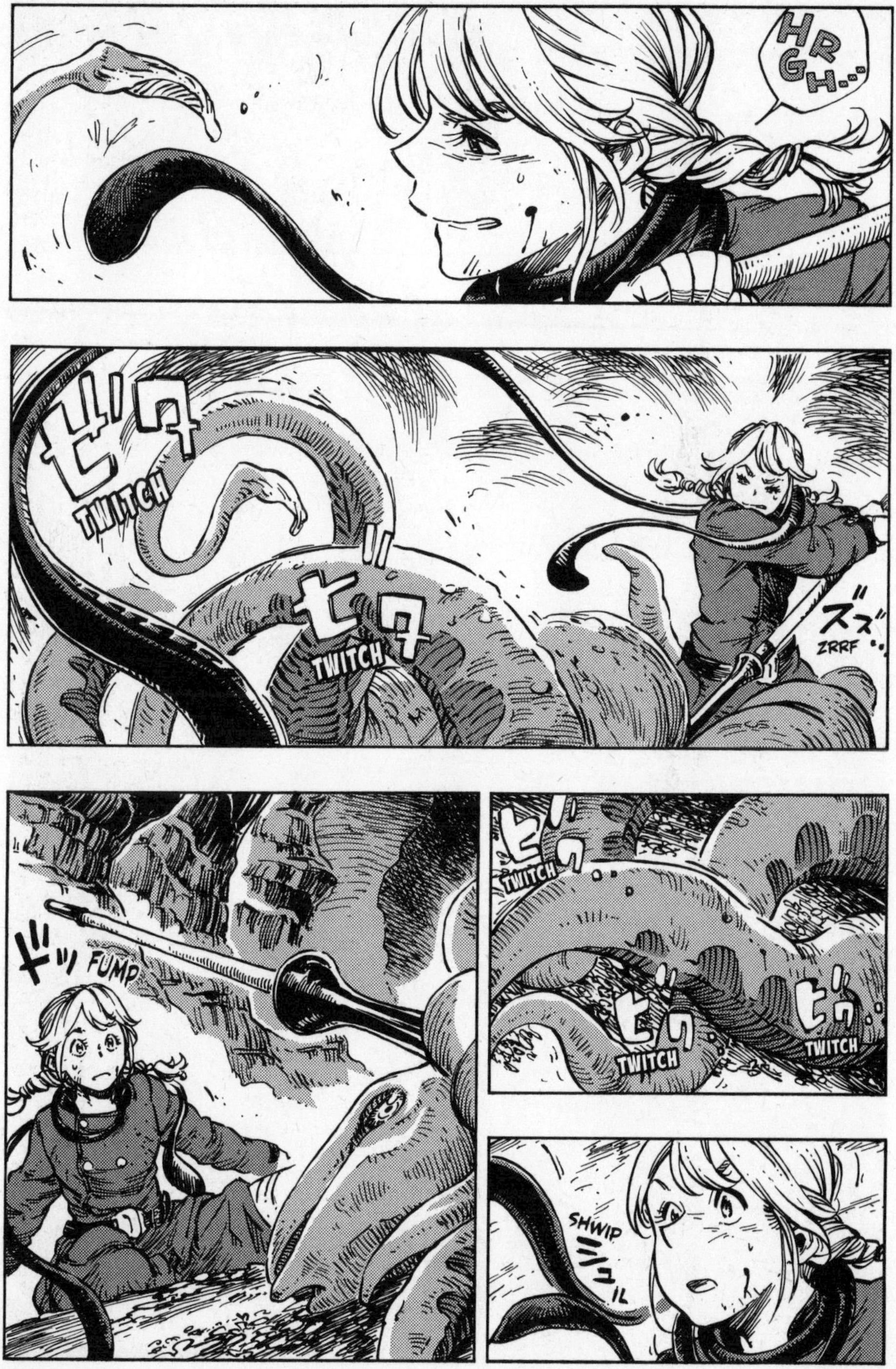
HRGH...
ビクッ
TWITCH
ビクッ
TWITCH
ズズ
ZRRF...
ビクッ
TWITCH
ビクッ
TWITCH
ビクッ
TWITCH
SHWIP
シュル
ドッ
FUMP

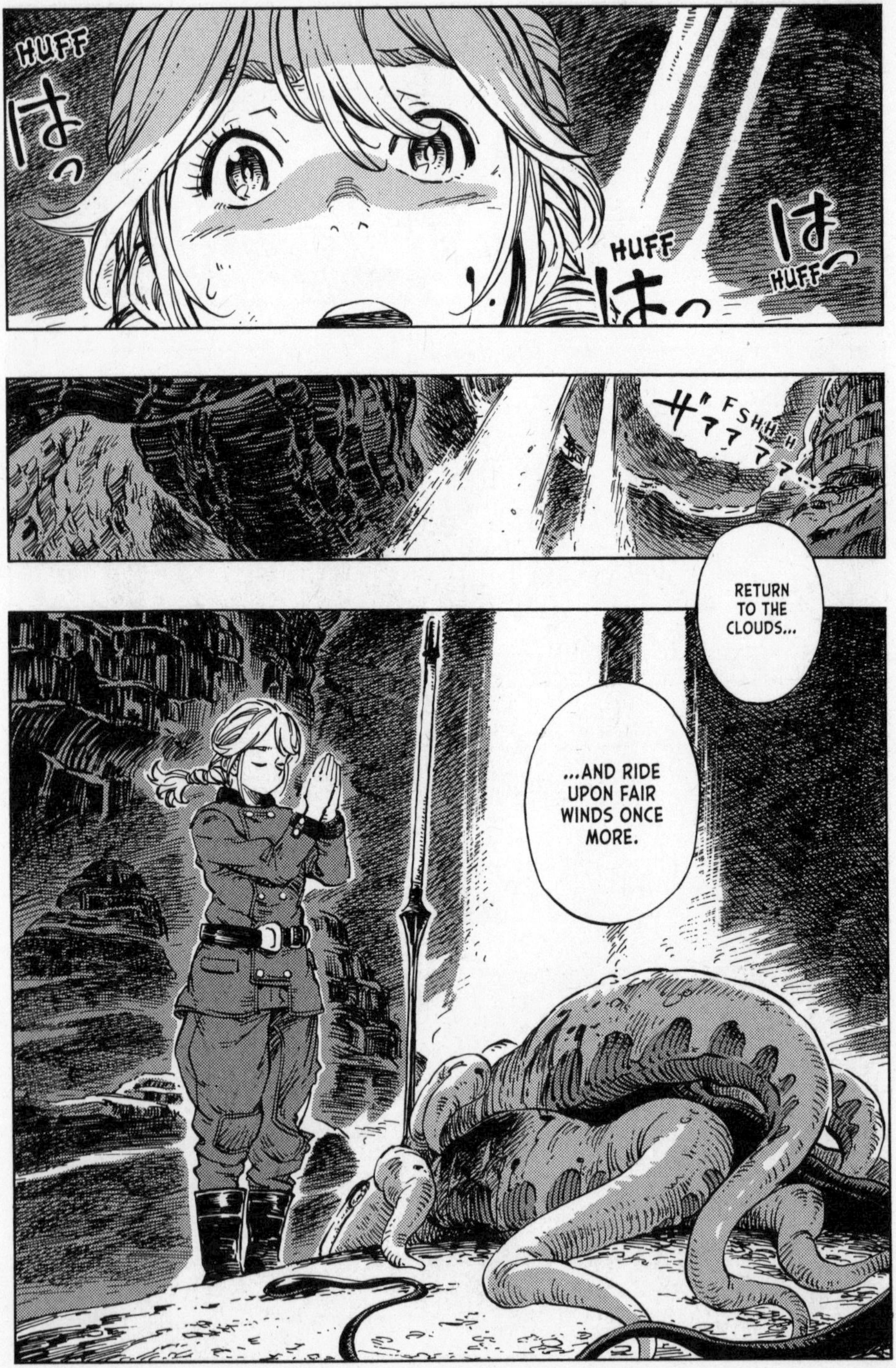
はっ
HUFF
HUFF
はっ
HUFF
はっ
ザァァァァ
FSHHHH
RETURN TO THE CLOUDS...
...AND RIDE UPON FAIR WINDS ONCE MORE.

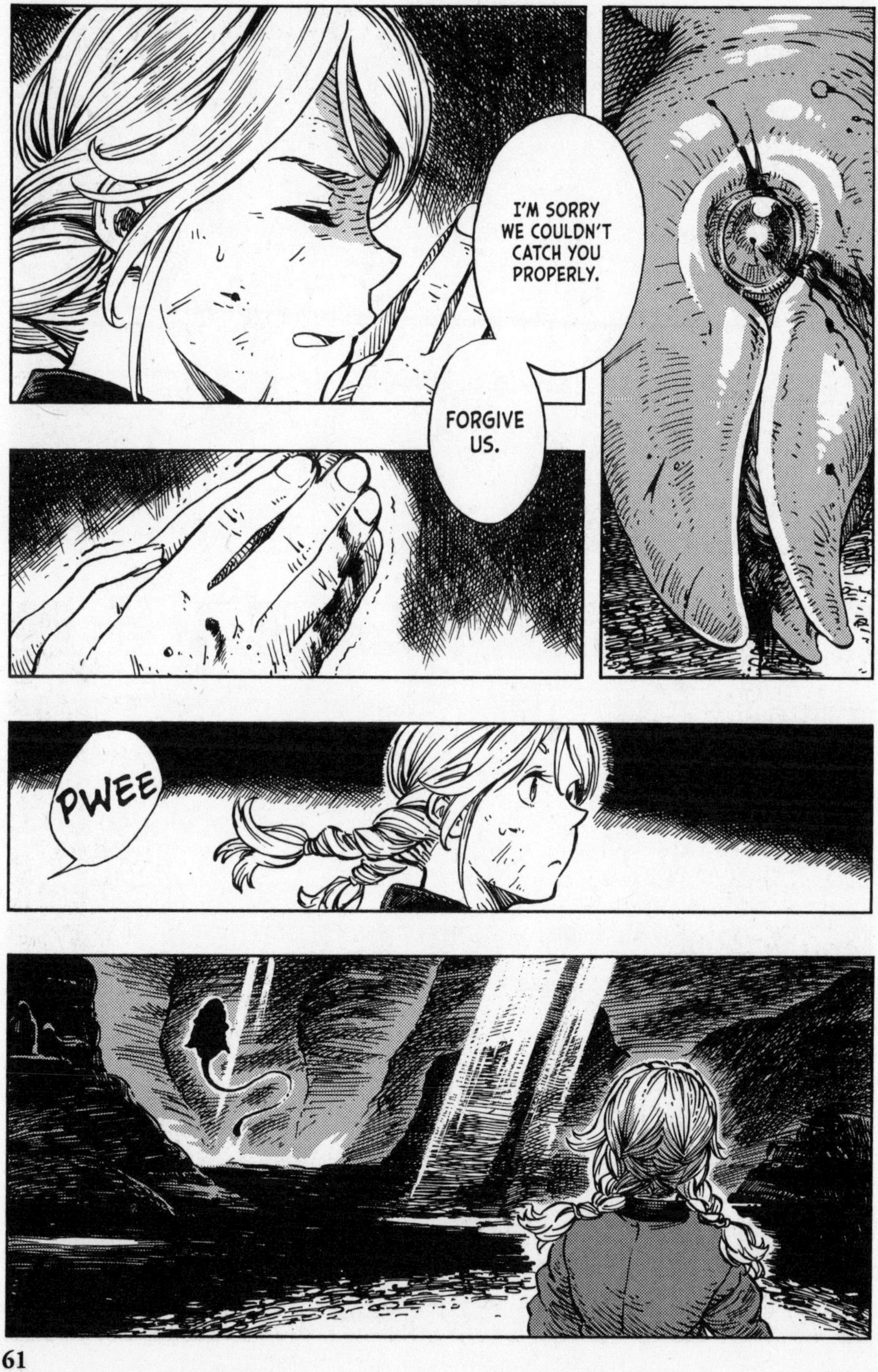
I'M SORRY WE COULDN'T CATCH YOU PROPERLY.
FORGIVE US.
PWEE

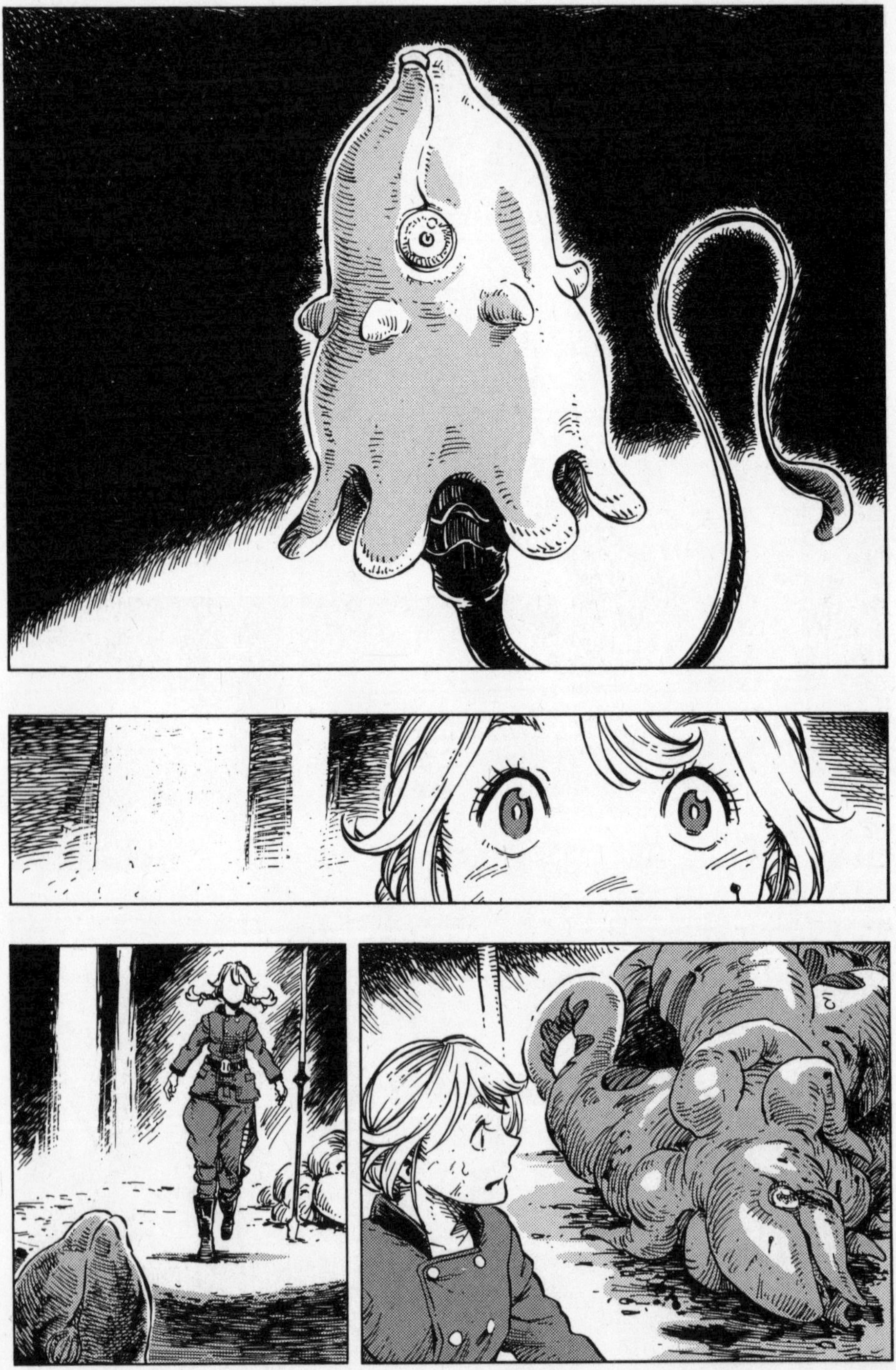

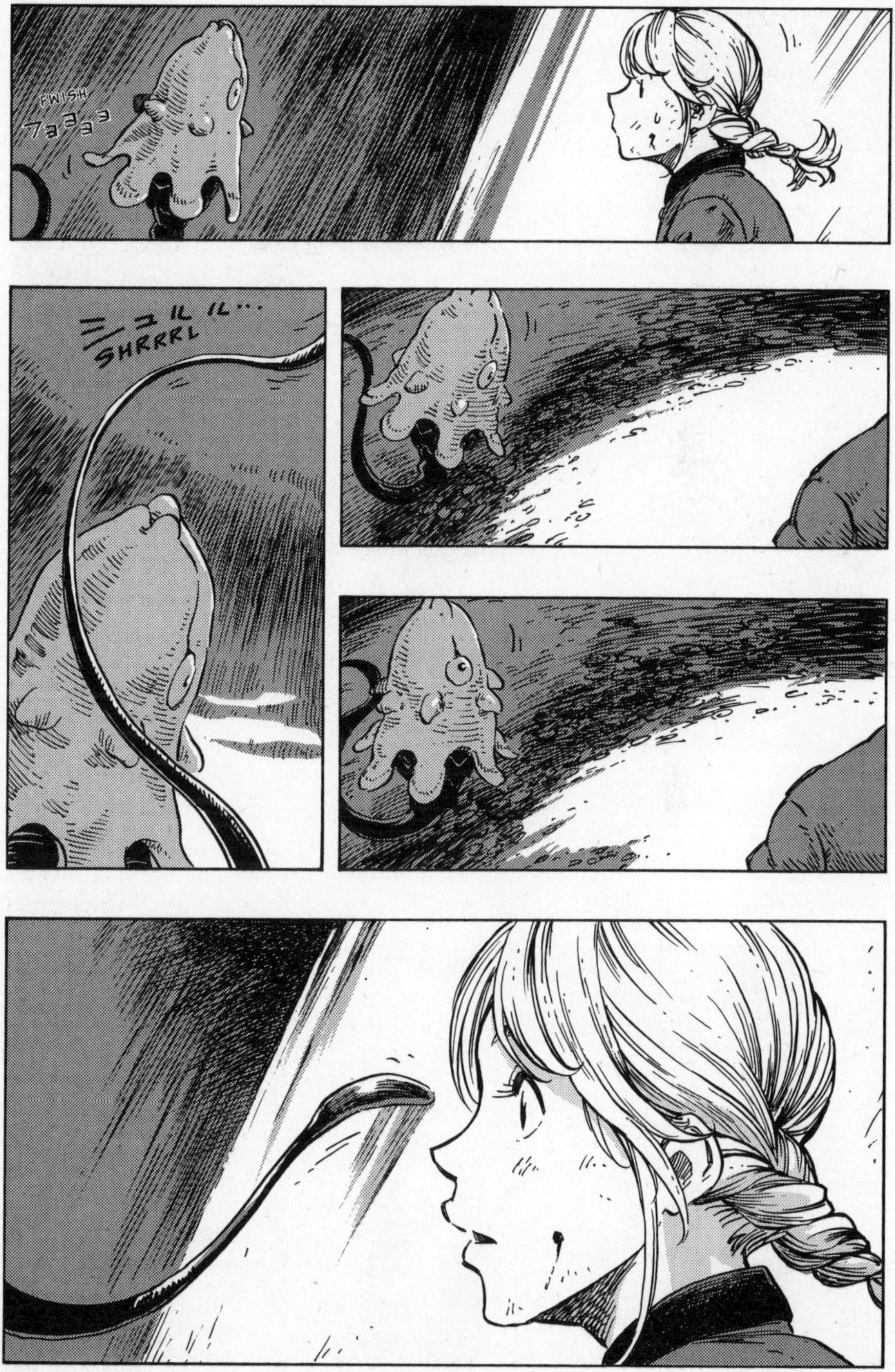
FWISH
フヨヨヨ
シュルル…
SHRRRL

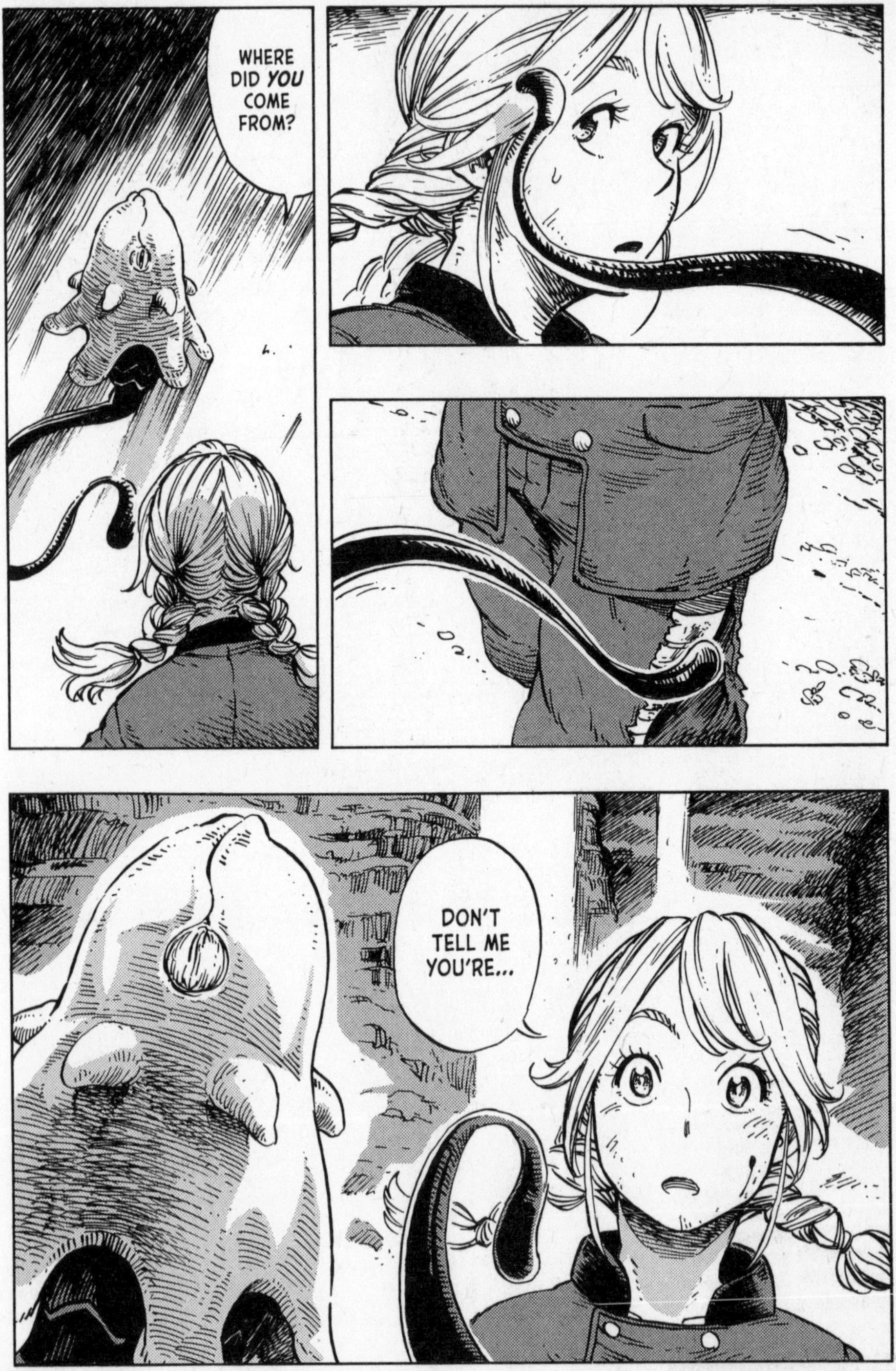
WHERE DID *YOU* COME FROM?
DON'T TELL ME YOU'RE...

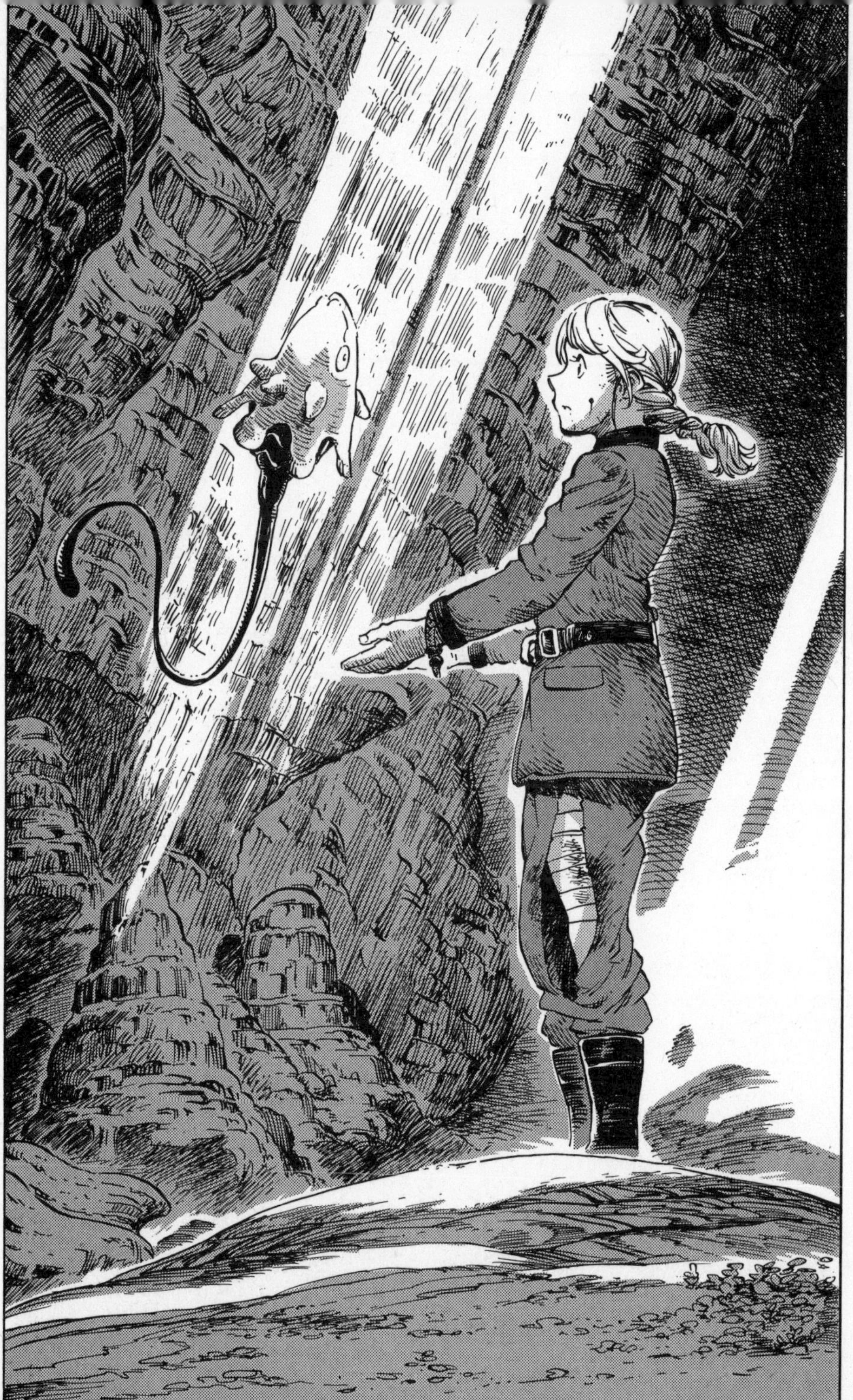

Starting a Fire

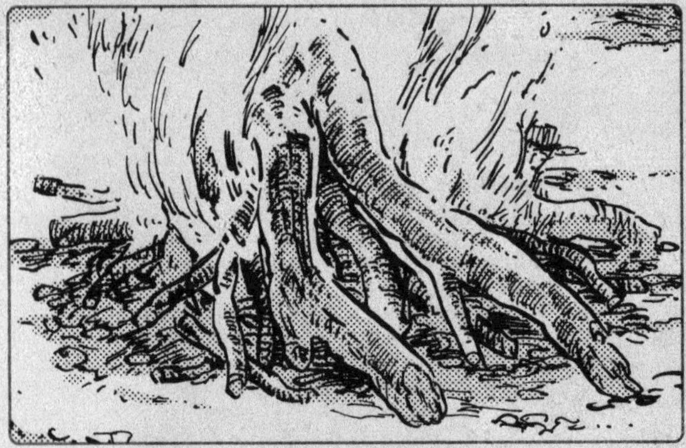

What you'll need:

- ✦ Glasses or a pair of wind goggles
- ✦ Water
- ✦ Dried grass for tinder

01
Rub or grind the grass with a stone to break it into thin strands.

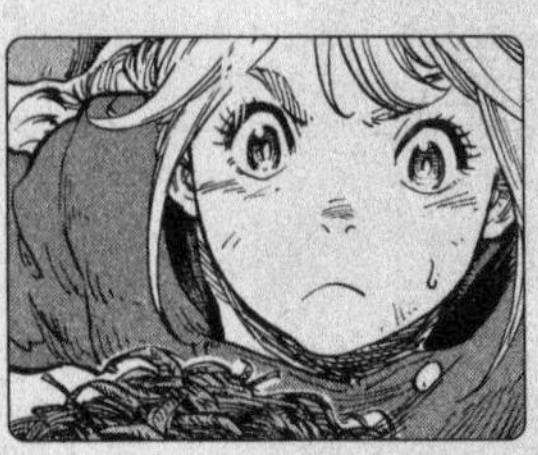

02
Drip a bead of water onto the glass.

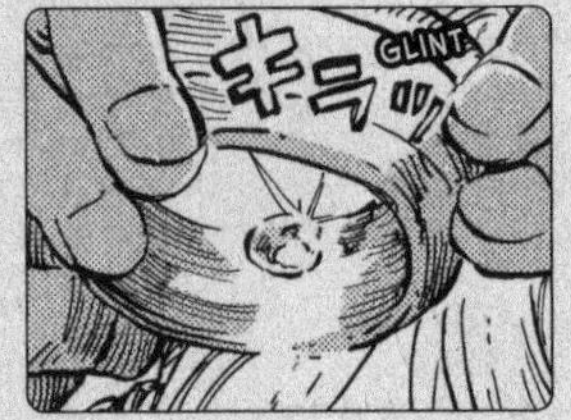
キラ
GLINT

03
Hold the glass so that sunlight shines through the bead, and focus the light on the tinder.

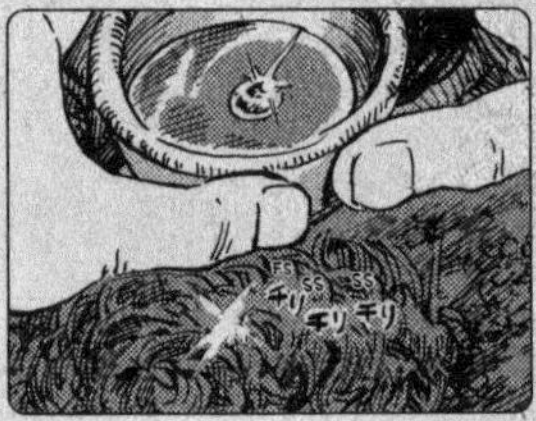

04
Once smoke begins to form, gather up the grass and wave vigorously.

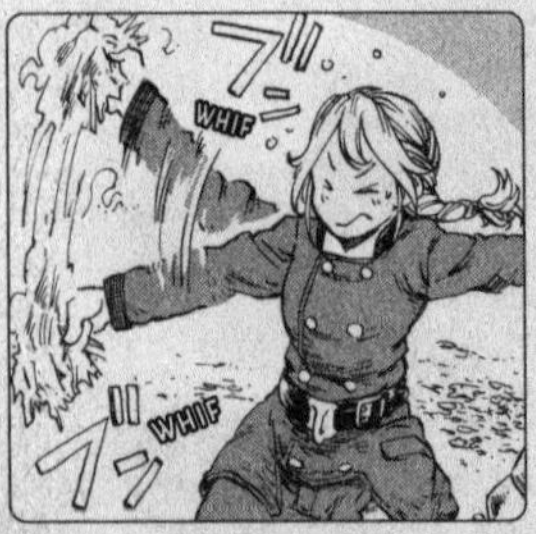
WHIF
WHIF

05
Once it catches fire, transfer the tinder to twigs or other flammable material.

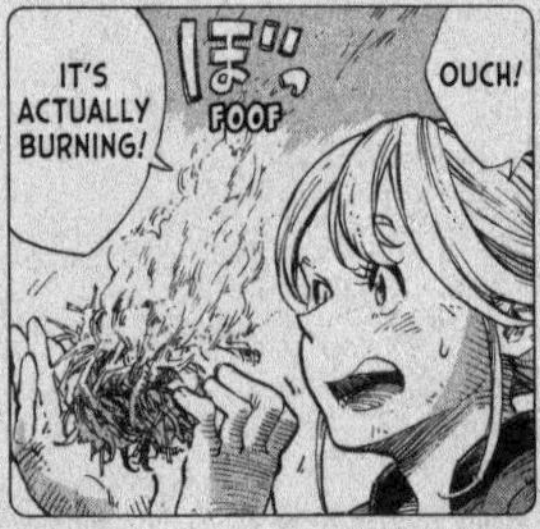
OUCH!
FOOF
IT'S ACTUALLY BURNING!

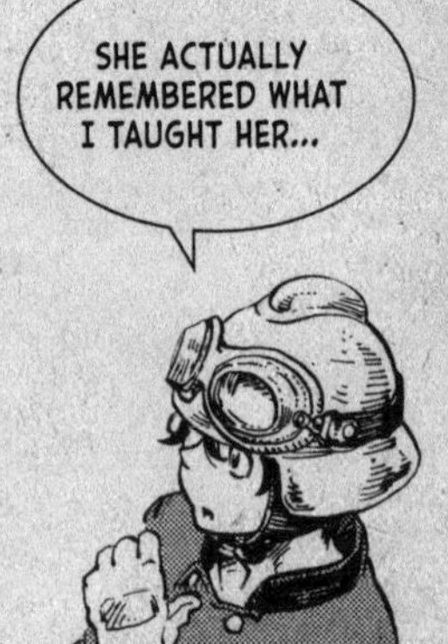
SHE ACTUALLY REMEMBERED WHAT I TAUGHT HER...

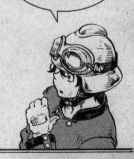

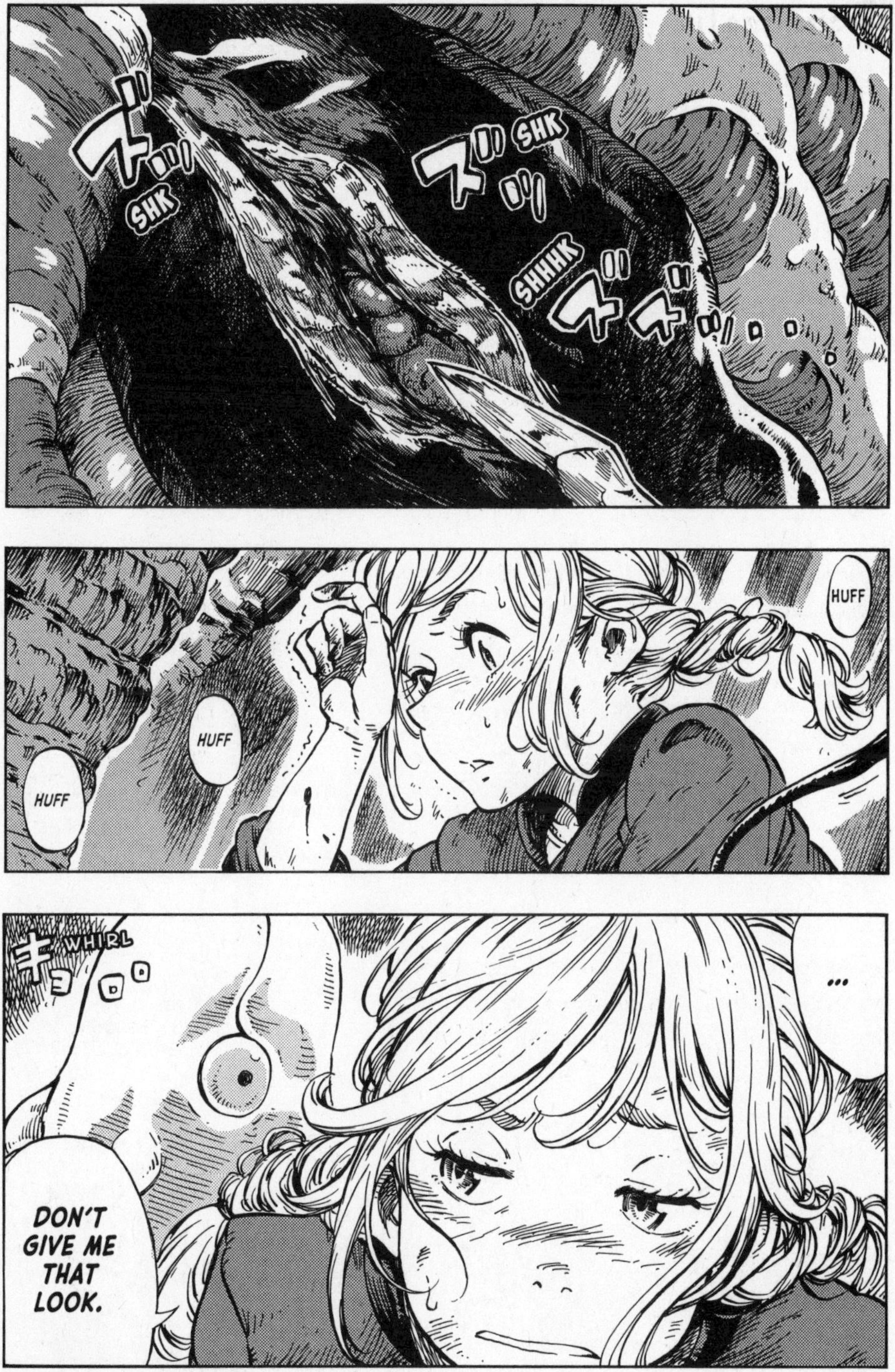
SHK
SHHHK
SHK
HUFF
HUFF
HUFF
...
WHIRL
DON'T GIVE ME THAT LOOK.

Flight 14 Dragonet & Dragon Brain Hunter Stew

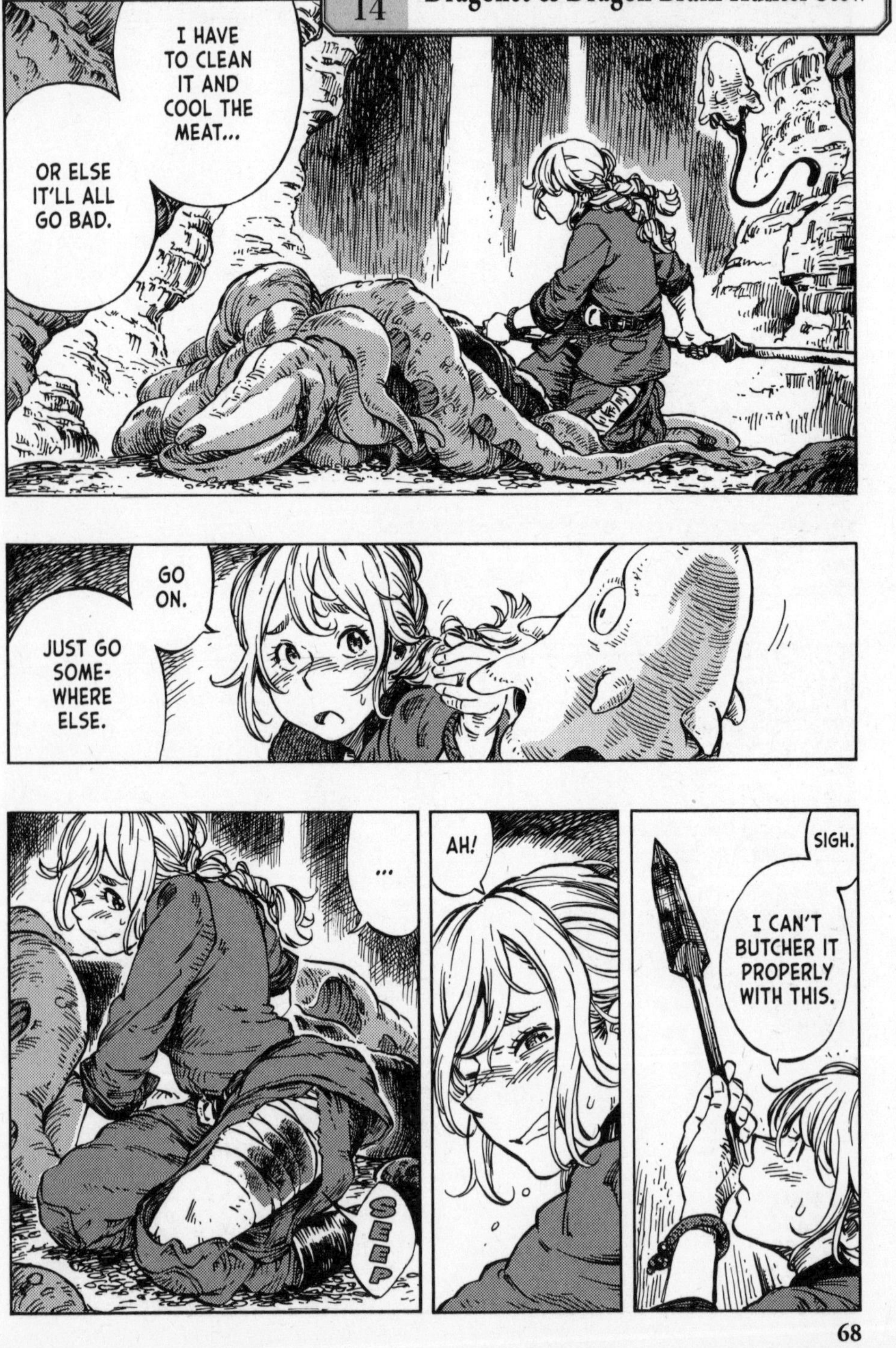
I HAVE TO CLEAN IT AND COOL THE MEAT...
OR ELSE IT'LL ALL GO BAD.
GO ON.
JUST GO SOME-WHERE ELSE.
SIGH.
I CAN'T BUTCHER IT PROPERLY WITH THIS.
AH!
...
SEEP

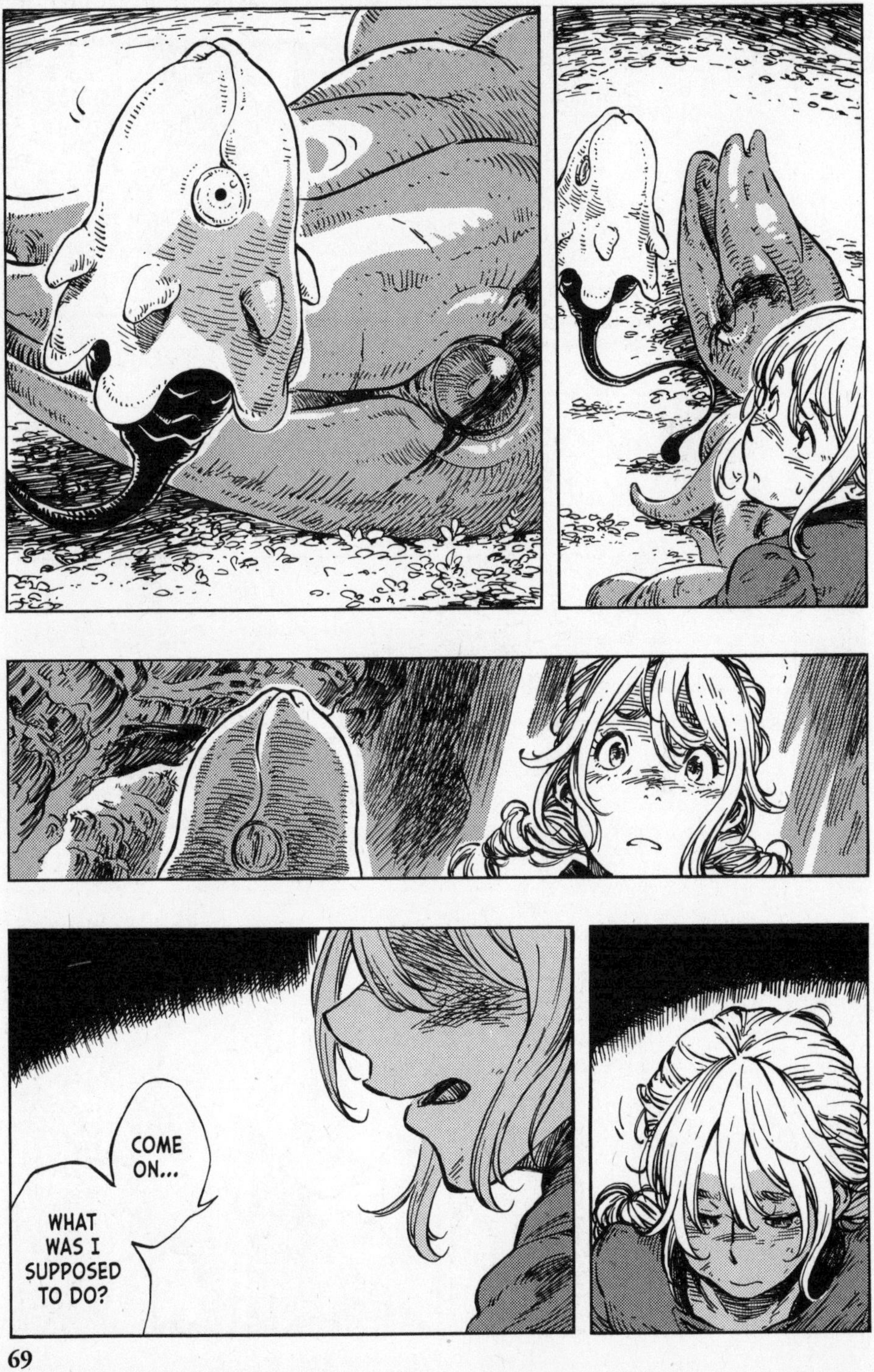
COME ON...
WHAT WAS I SUPPOSED TO DO?

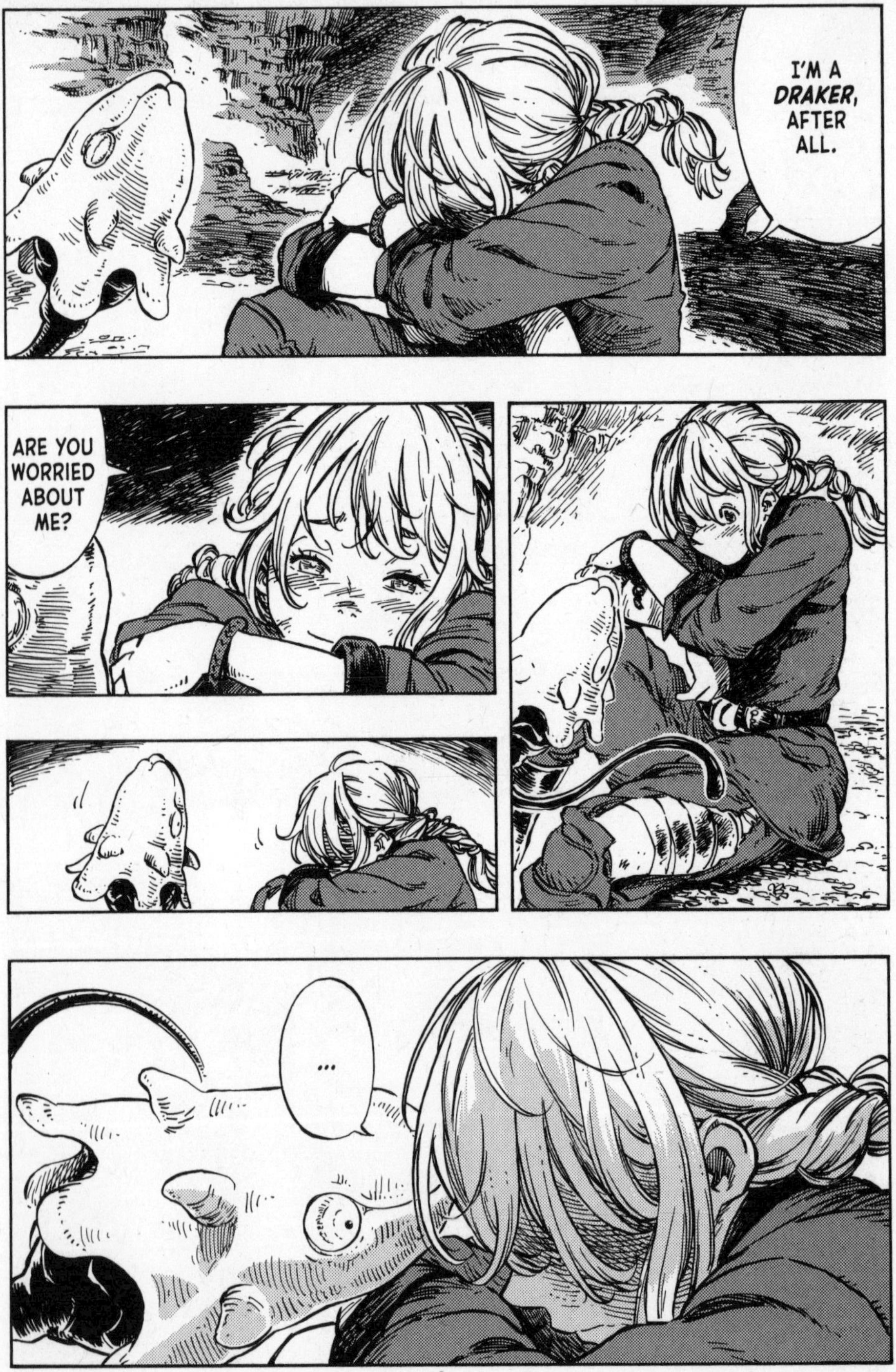
I'M A *DRAKER*, AFTER ALL.
ARE YOU WORRIED ABOUT ME?
...

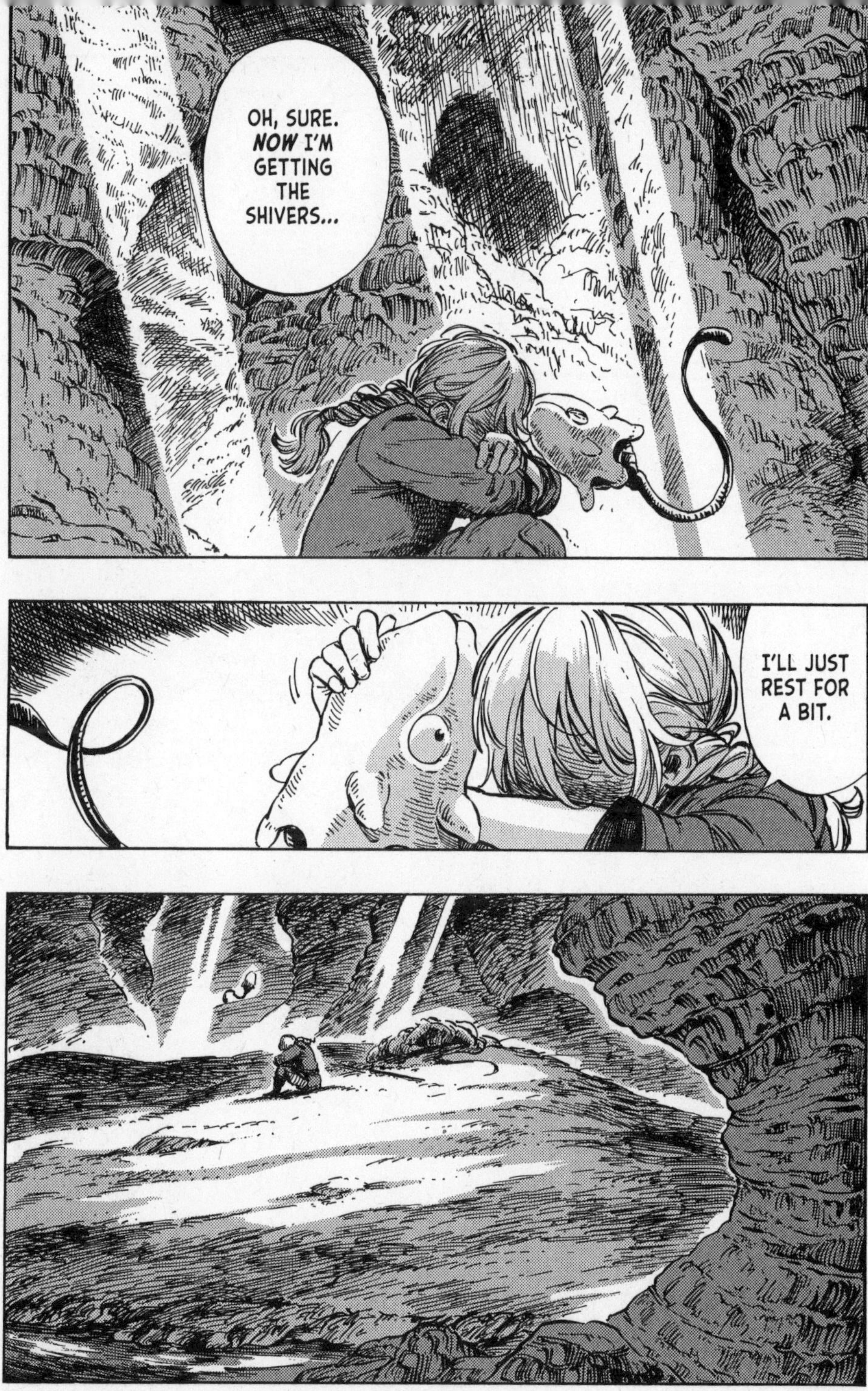
OH, SURE. *NOW* I'M GETTING THE SHIVERS...
I'LL JUST REST FOR A BIT.

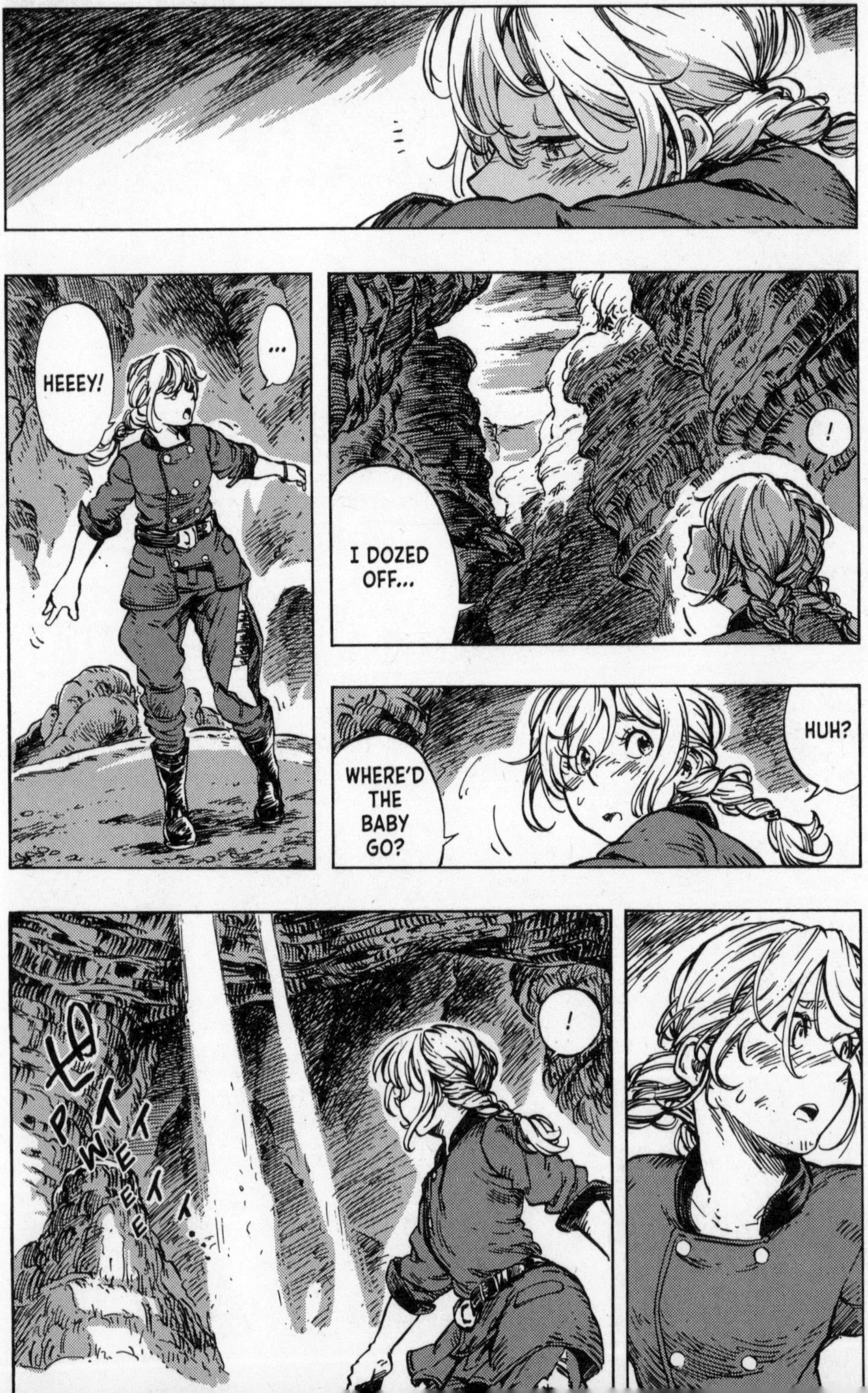
!
I DOZED OFF...
HUH?
WHERE'D THE BABY GO?
...
HEEEY!
!
PWEEE

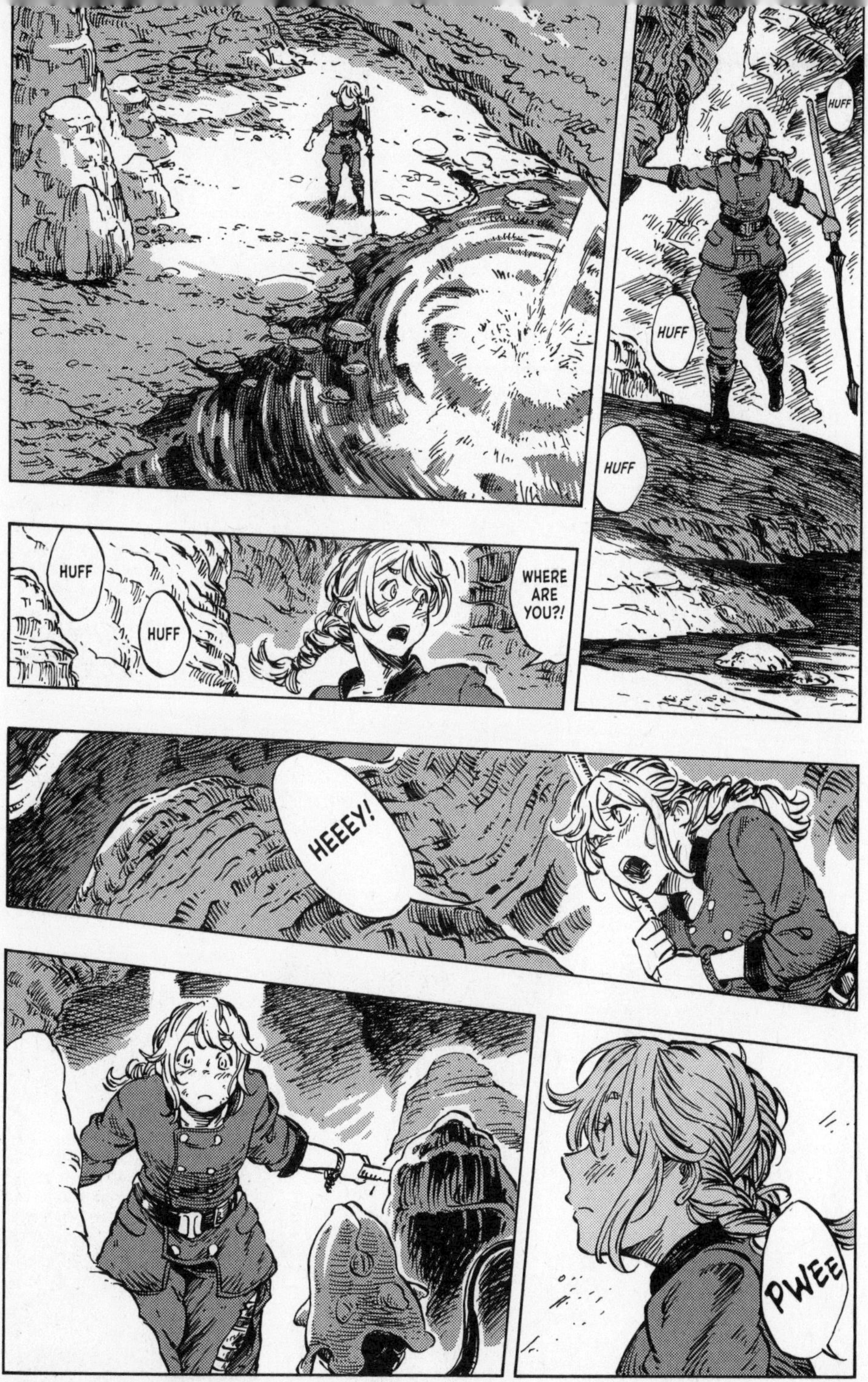
HUFF
HUFF
HUFF
WHERE ARE YOU?!
HUFF
HUFF
HEEEY!
PWEE

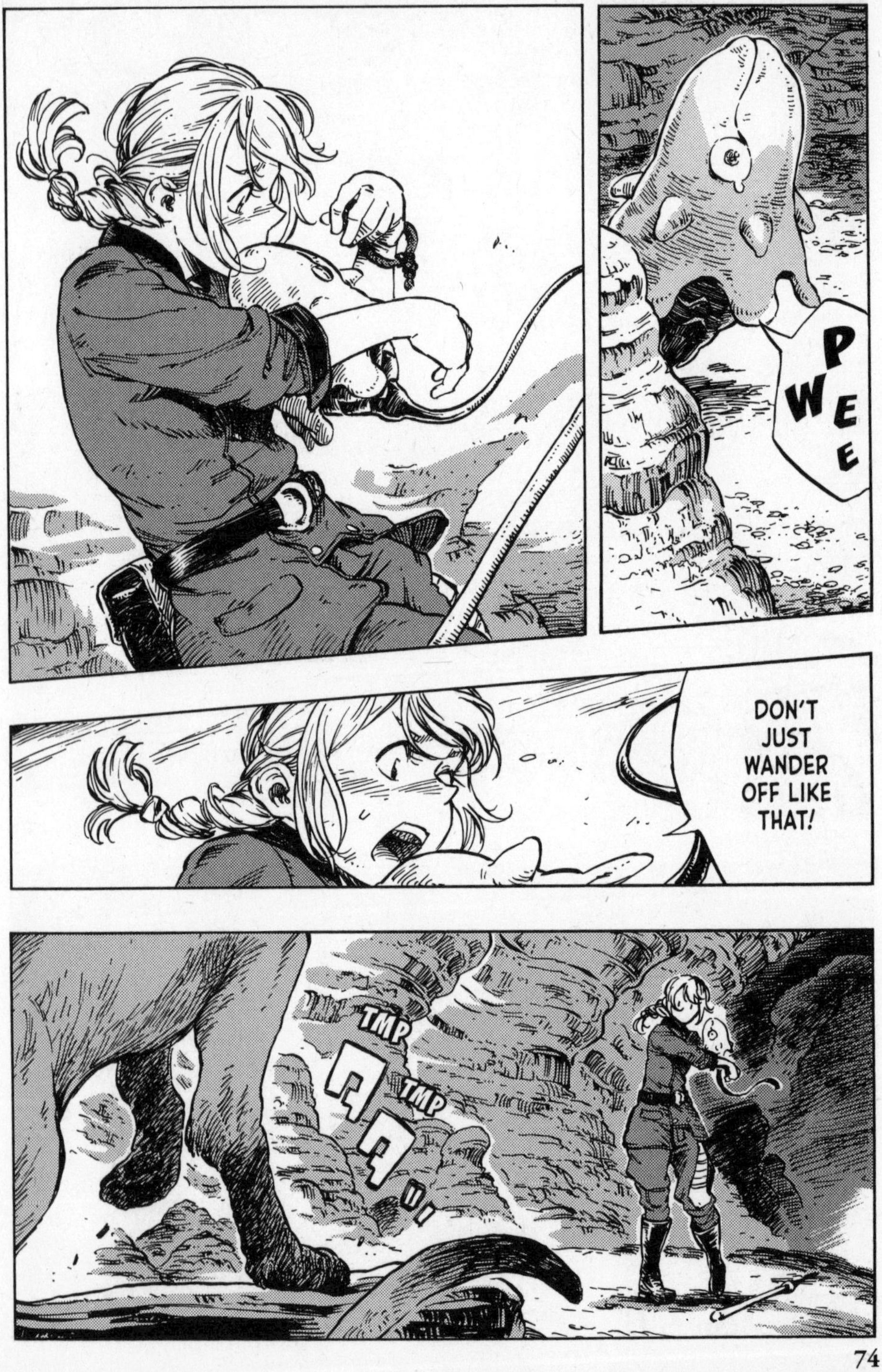
PWEE
DON'T JUST WANDER OFF LIKE THAT!
TMP
TMP

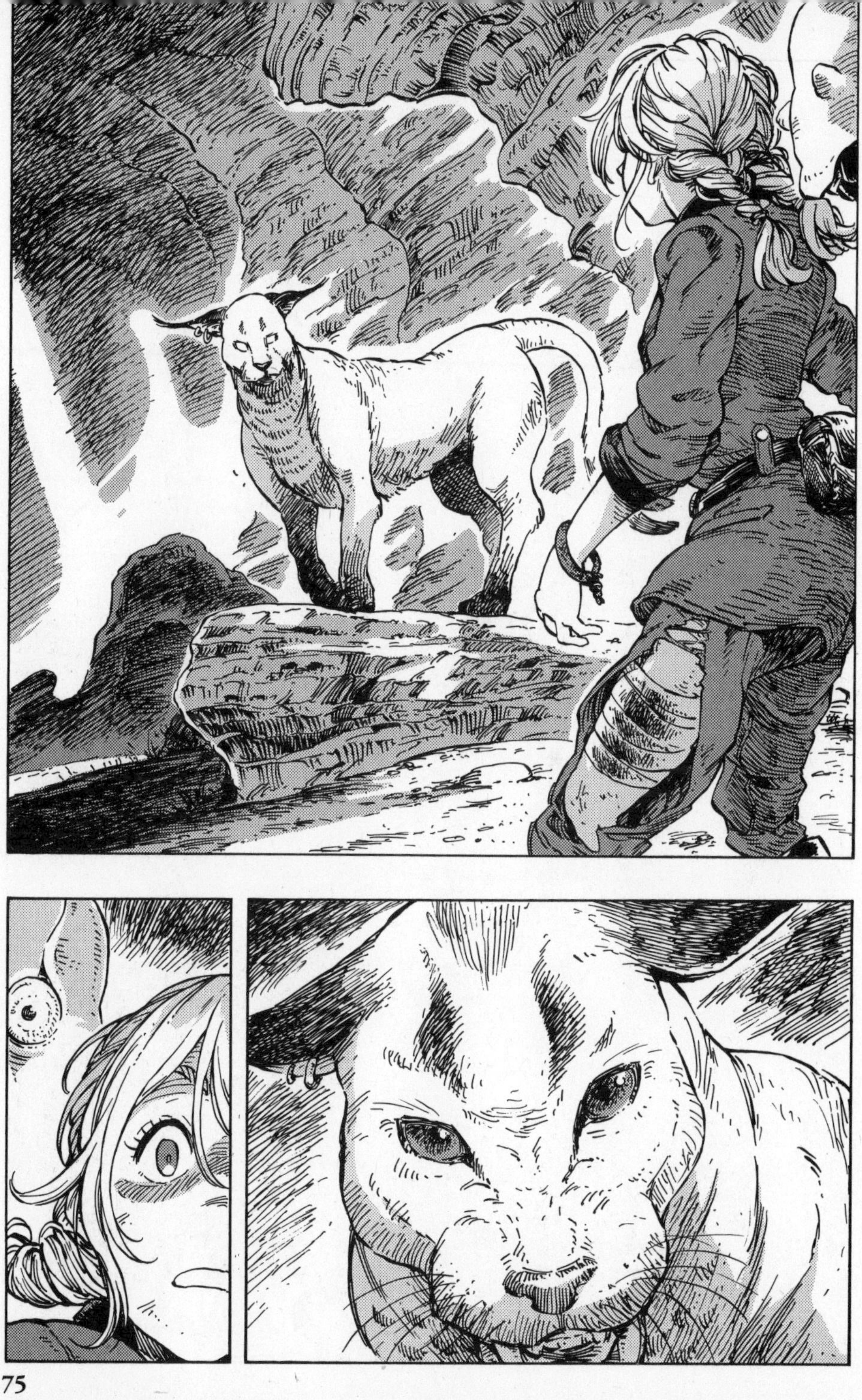

GRRR
ILIL

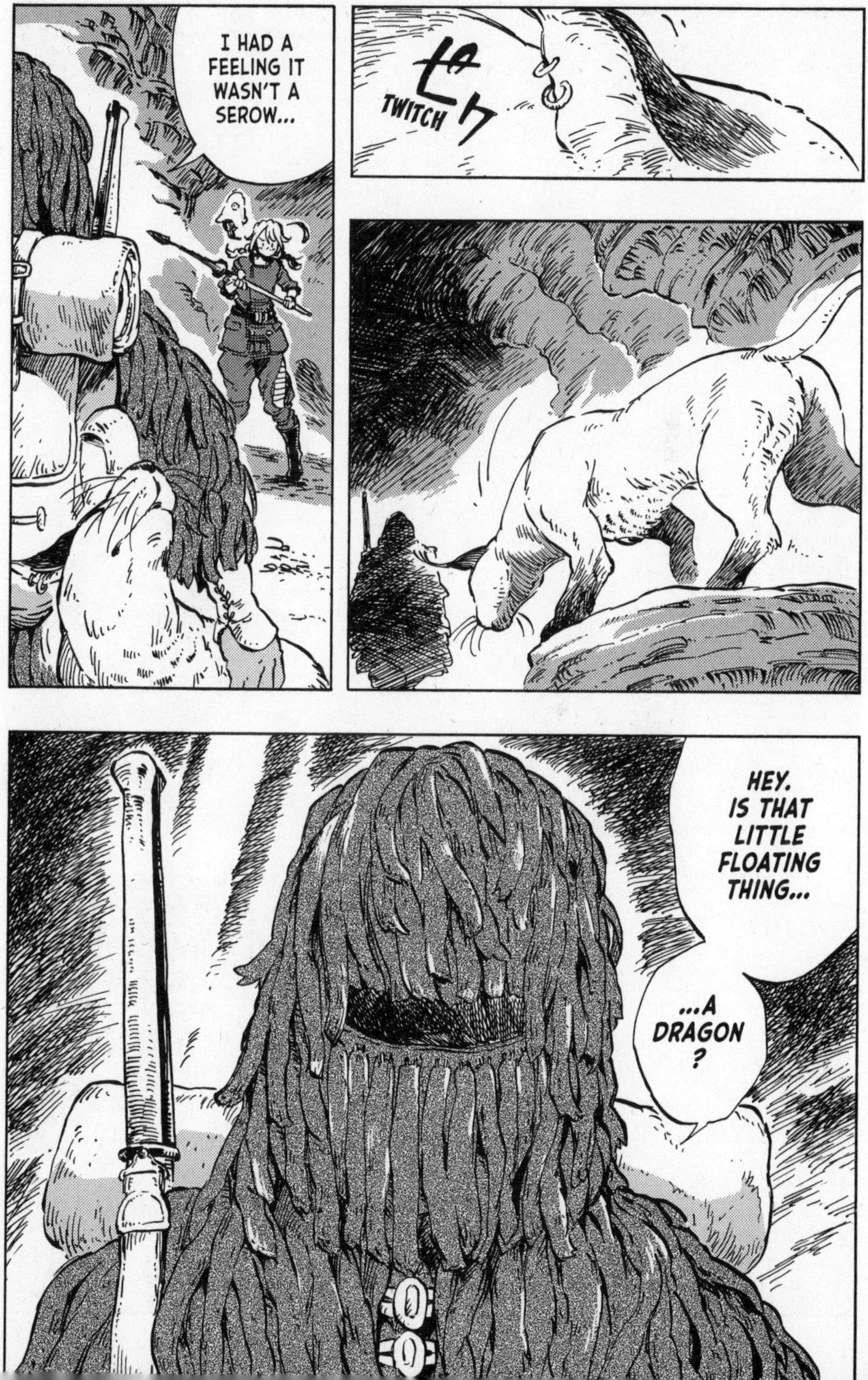
TWITCH
I HAD A FEELING IT WASN'T A SEROW...
HEY. IS THAT LITTLE FLOATING THING...
...A DRAGON ?

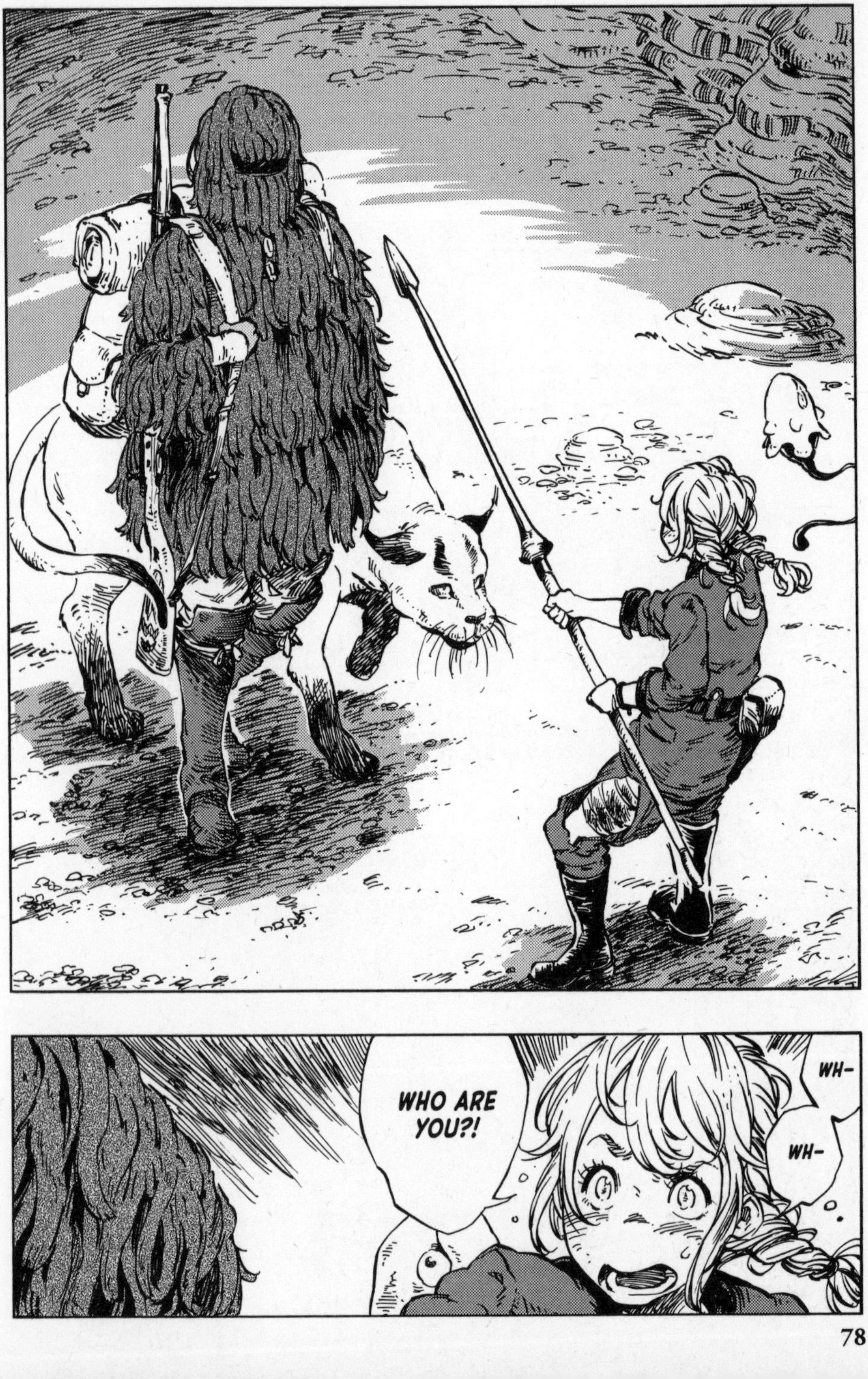
WH-
WH-
WHO ARE YOU?!

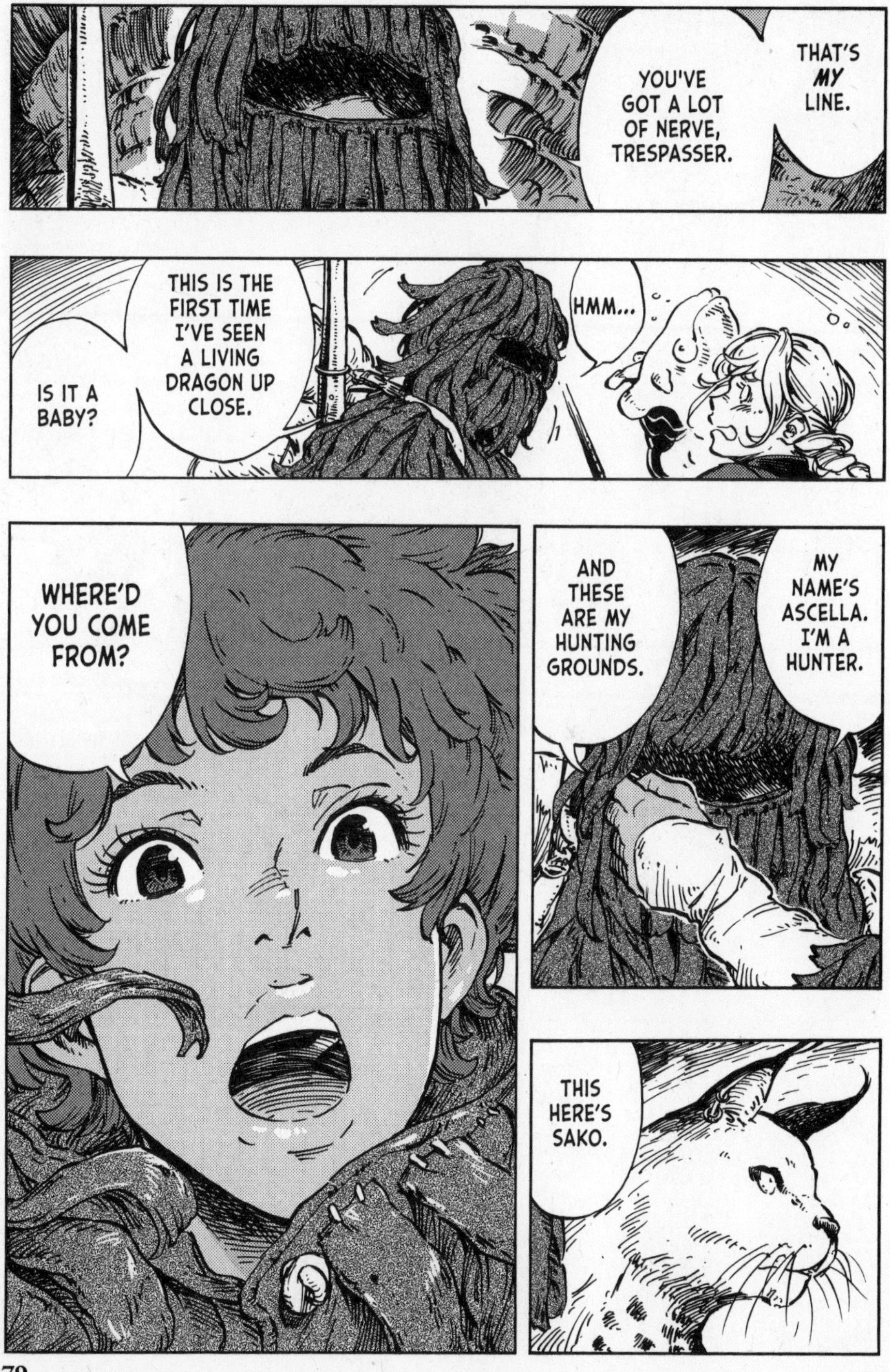
THAT'S MY LINE.
YOU'VE GOT A LOT OF NERVE, TRESPASSER.
HMM...
THIS IS THE FIRST TIME I'VE SEEN A LIVING DRAGON UP CLOSE.
IS IT A BABY?
MY NAME'S ASCELLA. I'M A HUNTER.
AND THESE ARE MY HUNTING GROUNDS.
THIS HERE'S SAKO.
WHERE'D YOU COME FROM?

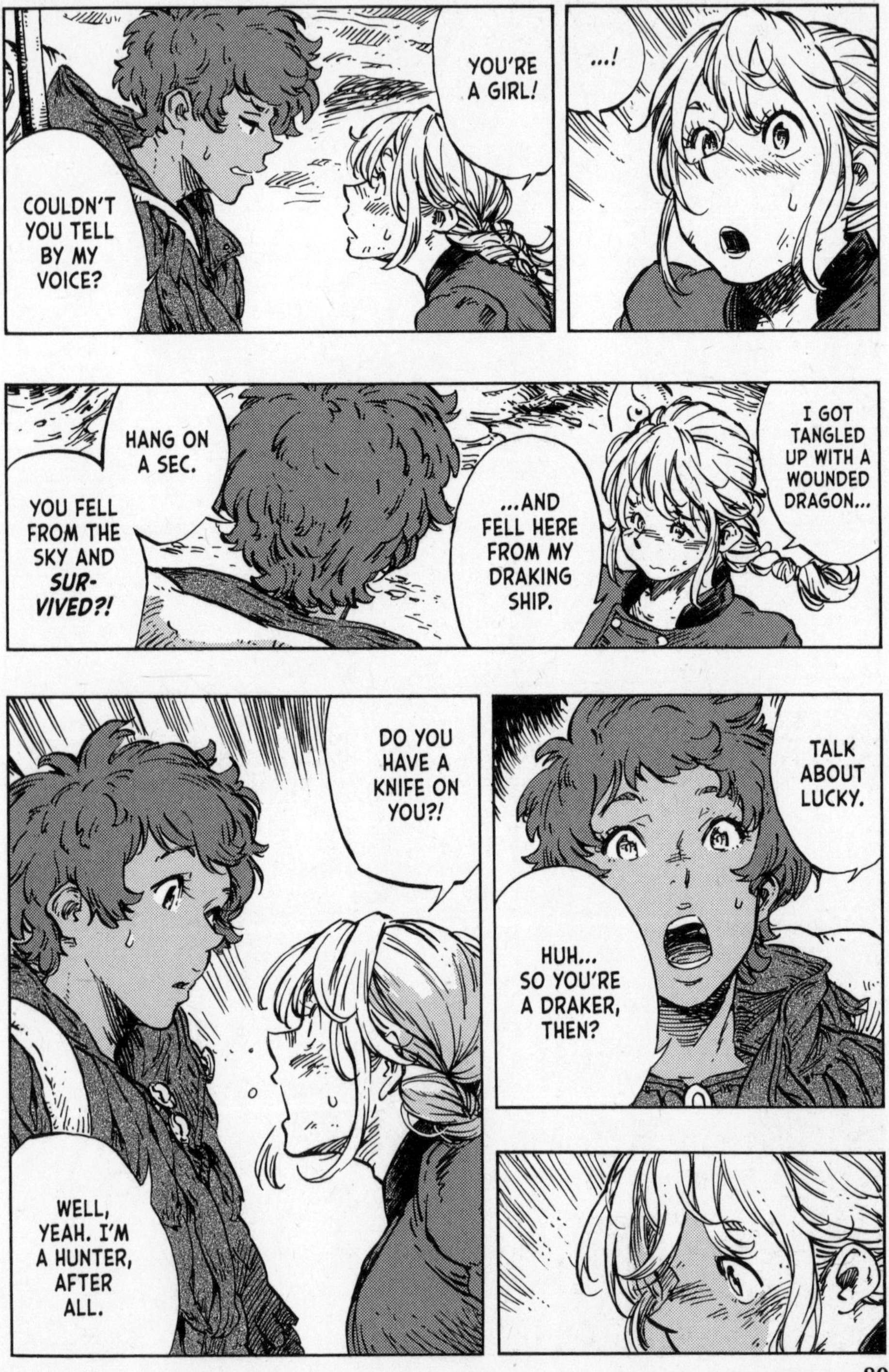
...!
YOU'RE A GIRL!
COULDN'T YOU TELL BY MY VOICE?
I GOT TANGLED UP WITH A WOUNDED DRAGON...
...AND FELL HERE FROM MY DRAKING SHIP.
HANG ON A SEC.
YOU FELL FROM THE SKY AND *SURVIVED?!*
TALK ABOUT LUCKY.
HUH... SO YOU'RE A DRAKER, THEN?
DO YOU HAVE A KNIFE ON YOU?!
WELL, YEAH. I'M A HUNTER, AFTER ALL.

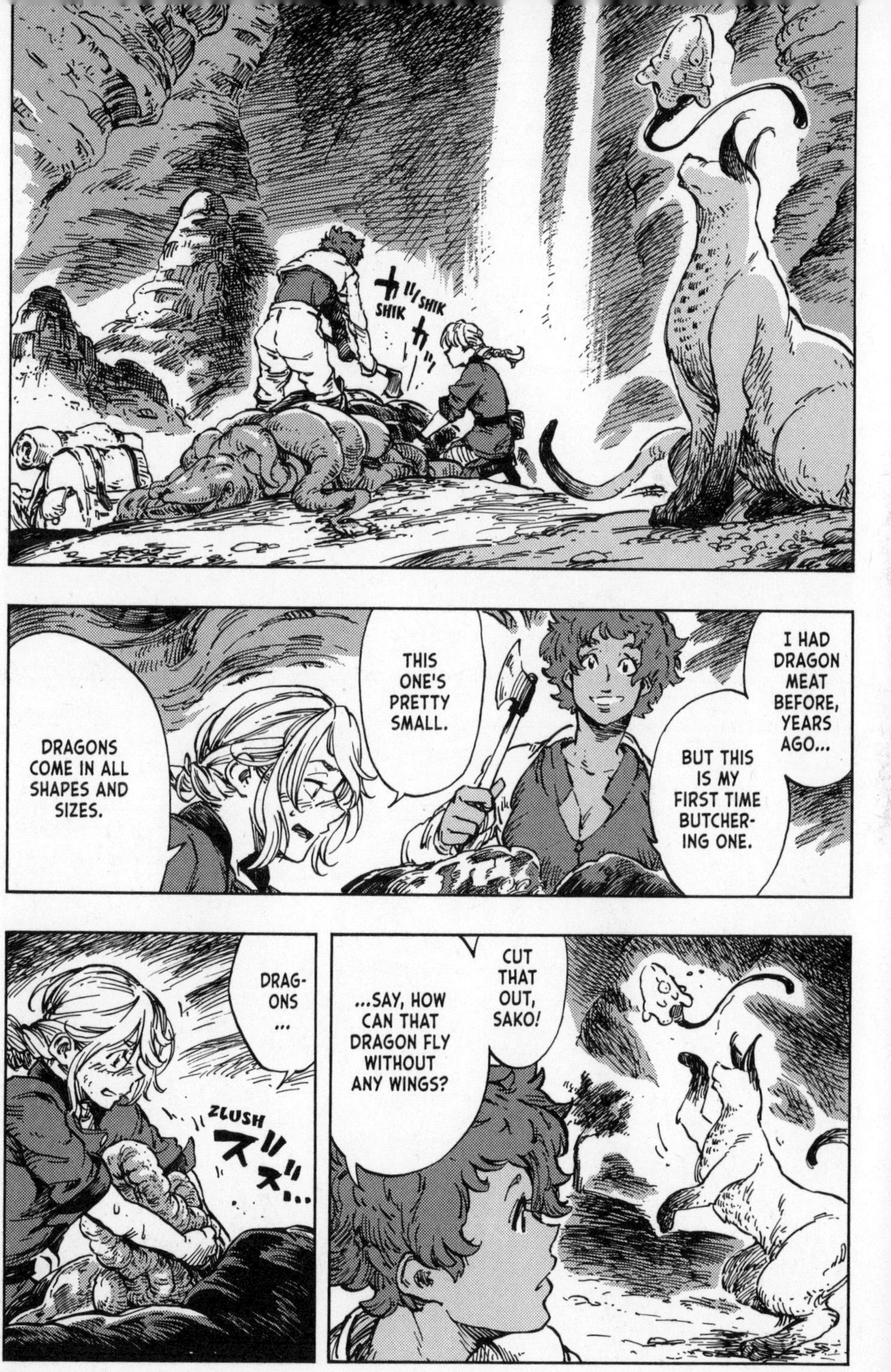
SHIK
SHIK
I HAD DRAGON MEAT BEFORE, YEARS AGO...
BUT THIS IS MY FIRST TIME BUTCHER-ING ONE.
THIS ONE'S PRETTY SMALL.
DRAGONS COME IN ALL SHAPES AND SIZES.
CUT THAT OUT, SAKO!
...SAY, HOW CAN THAT DRAGON FLY WITHOUT ANY WINGS?
DRAG-ONS...
ZLUSH

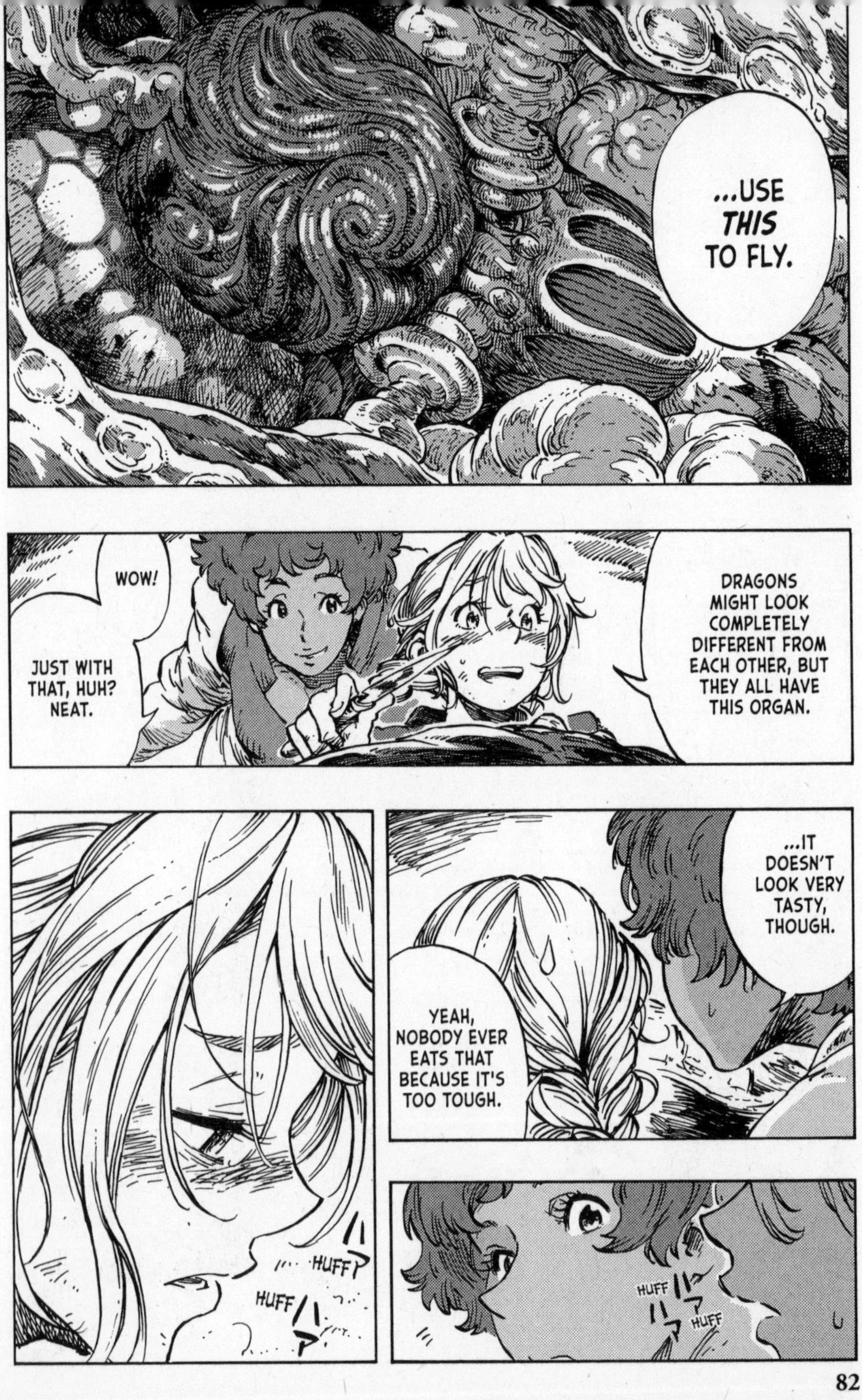
...USE THIS TO FLY.
DRAGONS MIGHT LOOK COMPLETELY DIFFERENT FROM EACH OTHER, BUT THEY ALL HAVE THIS ORGAN.
WOW!
JUST WITH THAT, HUH? NEAT.
...IT DOESN'T LOOK VERY TASTY, THOUGH.
YEAH, NOBODY EVER EATS THAT BECAUSE IT'S TOO TOUGH.
HUFF
HUFF
HUFF
HUFF

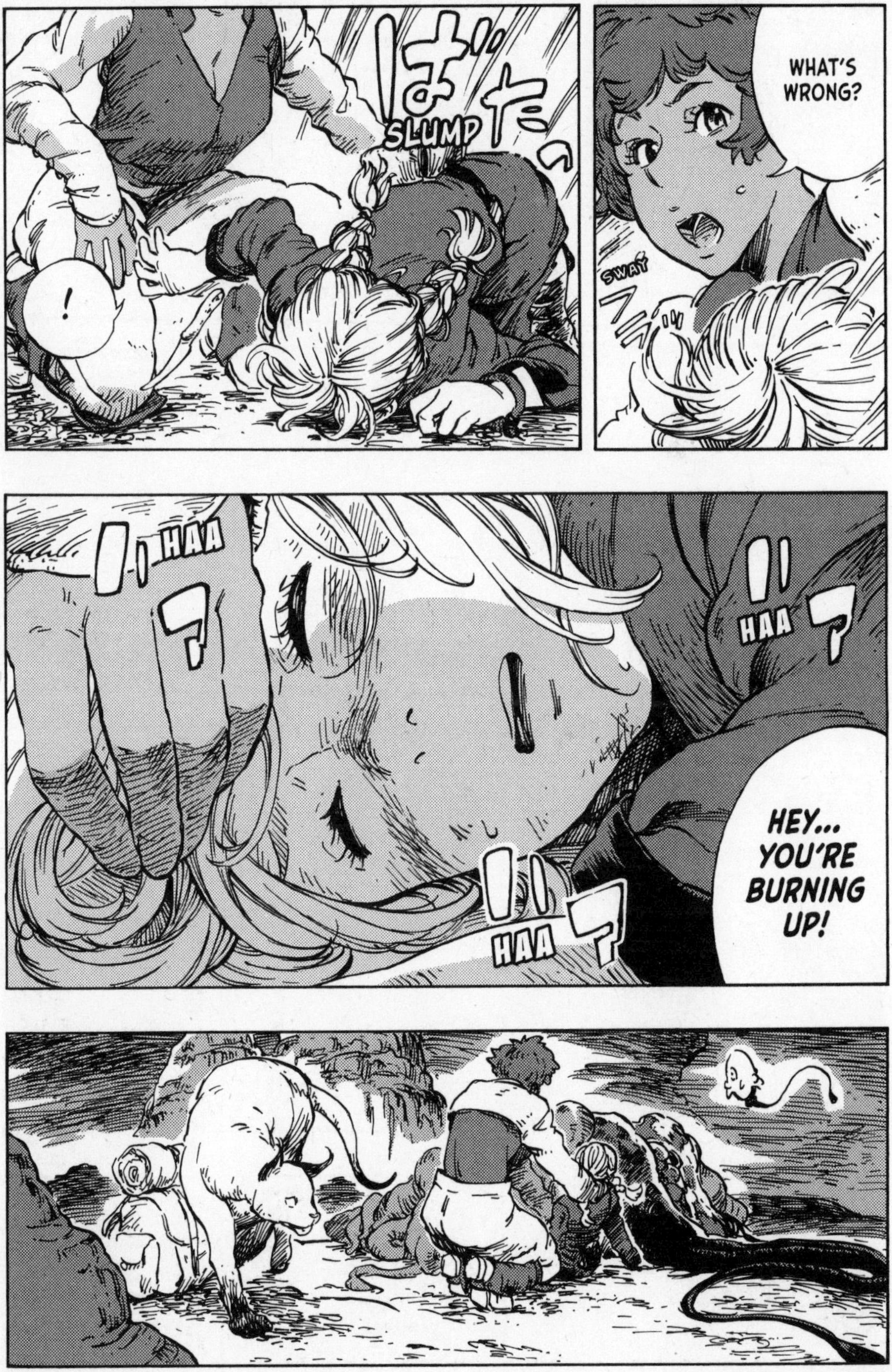
WHAT'S WRONG?
SWAY
SLUMP
!
HEY... YOU'RE BURNING UP!
HAA
HAA
HAA

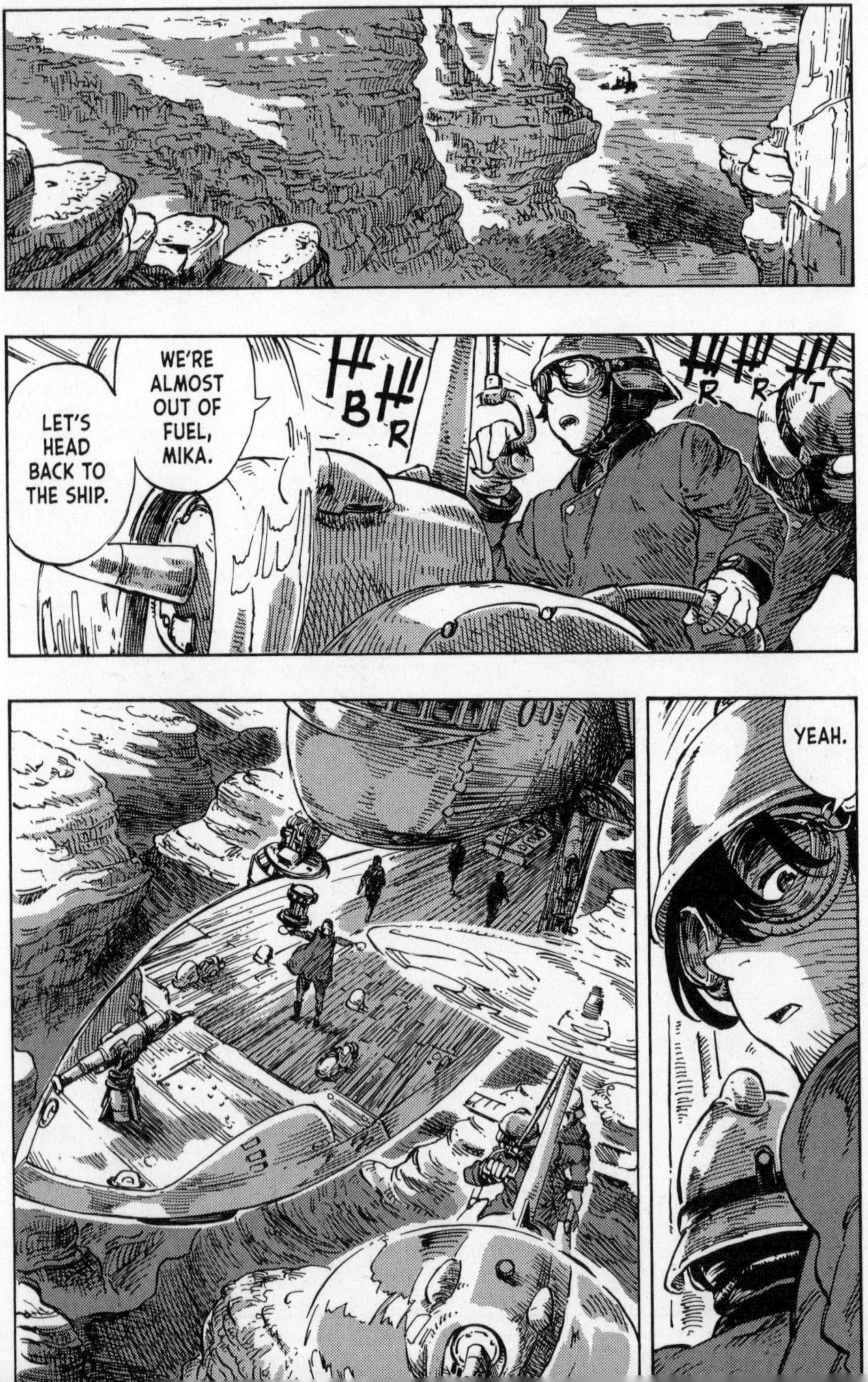
RRT
WE'RE ALMOST OUT OF FUEL, MIKA.
BR
LET'S HEAD BACK TO THE SHIP.
YEAH.

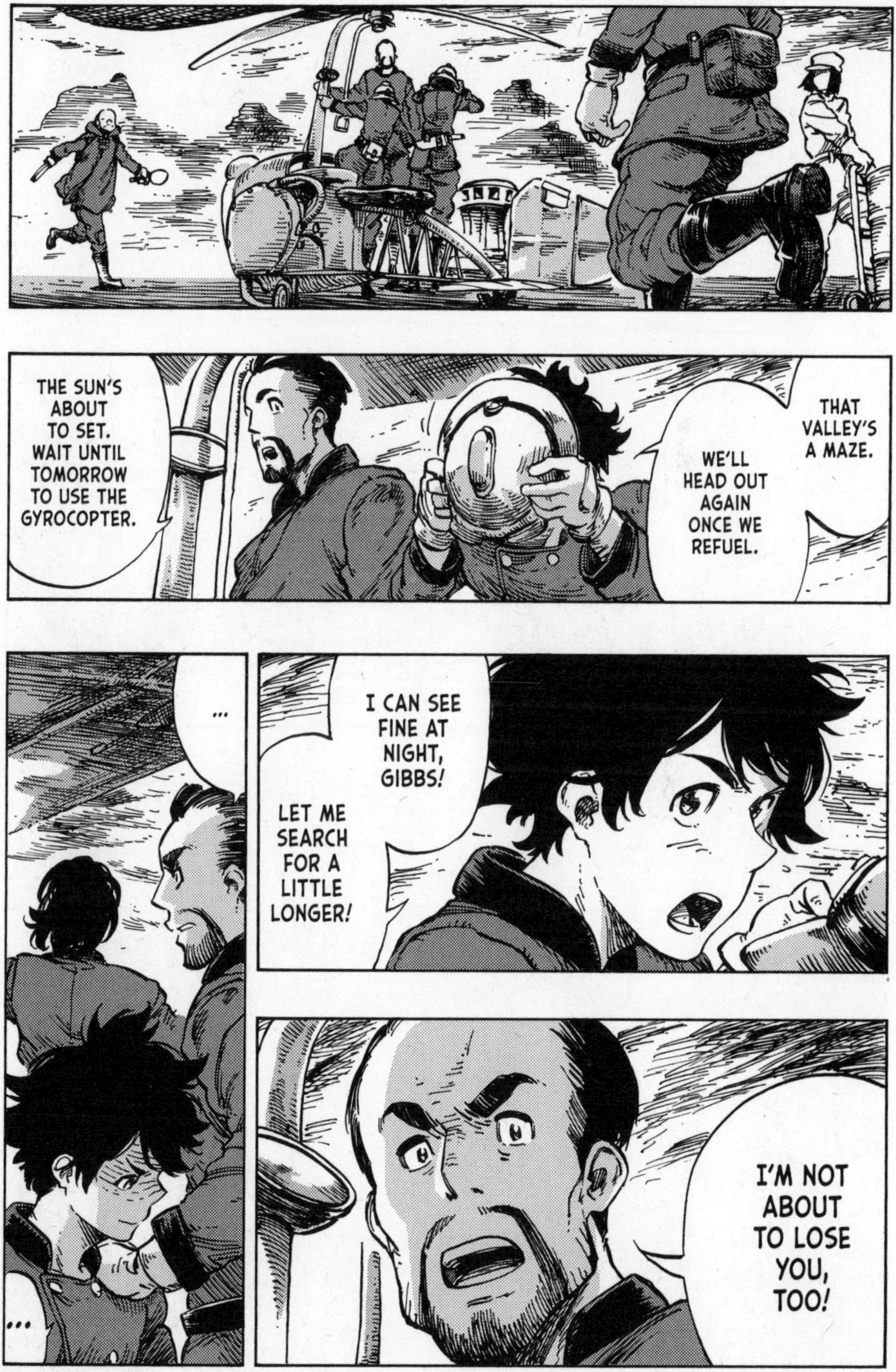
THAT VALLEY'S A MAZE.
WE'LL HEAD OUT AGAIN ONCE WE REFUEL.
THE SUN'S ABOUT TO SET. WAIT UNTIL TOMORROW TO USE THE GYROCOPTER.
I CAN SEE FINE AT NIGHT, GIBBS!
LET ME SEARCH FOR A LITTLE LONGER!
I'M NOT ABOUT TO LOSE YOU, TOO!
...
...

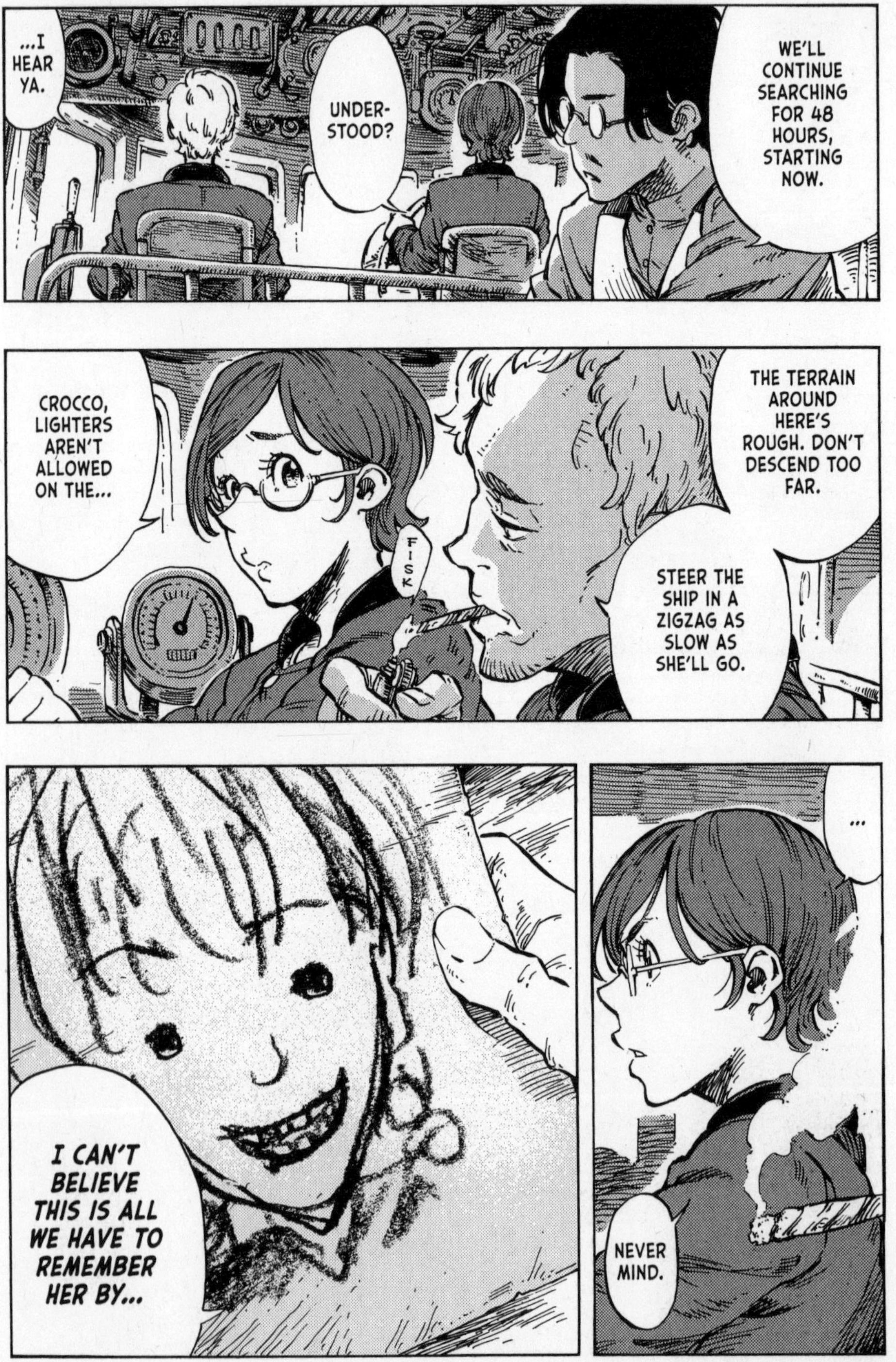
WE'LL CONTINUE SEARCHING FOR 48 HOURS, STARTING NOW.
UNDER-STOOD?
...I HEAR YA.
THE TERRAIN AROUND HERE'S ROUGH. DON'T DESCEND TOO FAR.
STEER THE SHIP IN A ZIGZAG AS SLOW AS SHE'LL GO.
FISK
CROCCO, LIGHTERS AREN'T ALLOWED ON THE...
...
NEVER MIND.
I CAN'T BELIEVE THIS IS ALL WE HAVE TO REMEMBER HER BY...

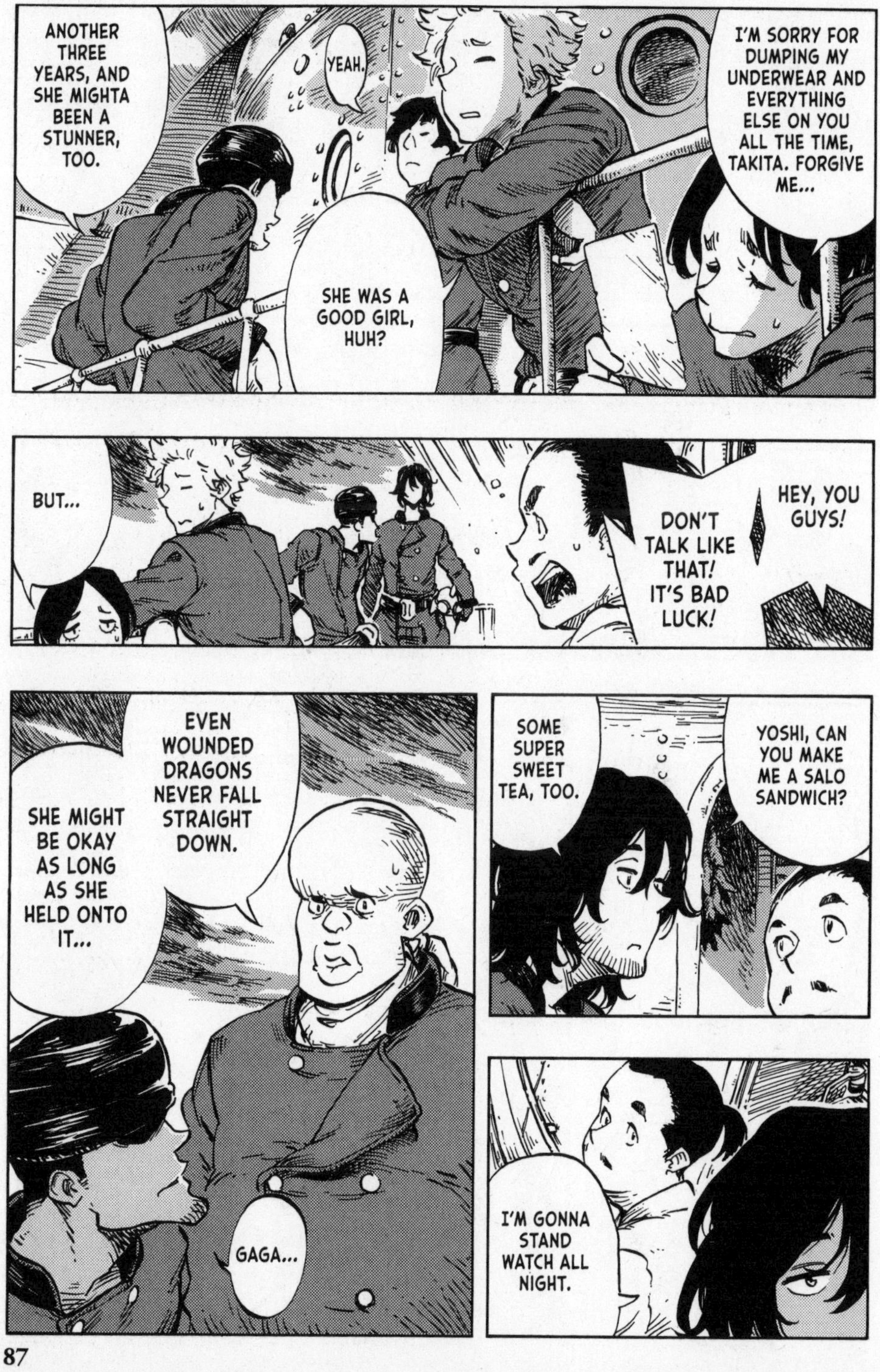
I'M SORRY FOR DUMPING MY UNDERWEAR AND EVERYTHING ELSE ON YOU ALL THE TIME, TAKITA. FORGIVE ME...
YEAH.
ANOTHER THREE YEARS, AND SHE MIGHTA BEEN A STUNNER, TOO.
SHE WAS A GOOD GIRL, HUH?
HEY, YOU GUYS!
DON'T TALK LIKE THAT! IT'S BAD LUCK!
BUT...
YOSHI, CAN YOU MAKE ME A SALO SANDWICH?
SOME SUPER SWEET TEA, TOO.
I'M GONNA STAND WATCH ALL NIGHT.
EVEN WOUNDED DRAGONS NEVER FALL STRAIGHT DOWN.
SHE MIGHT BE OKAY AS LONG AS SHE HELD ONTO IT...
GAGA...

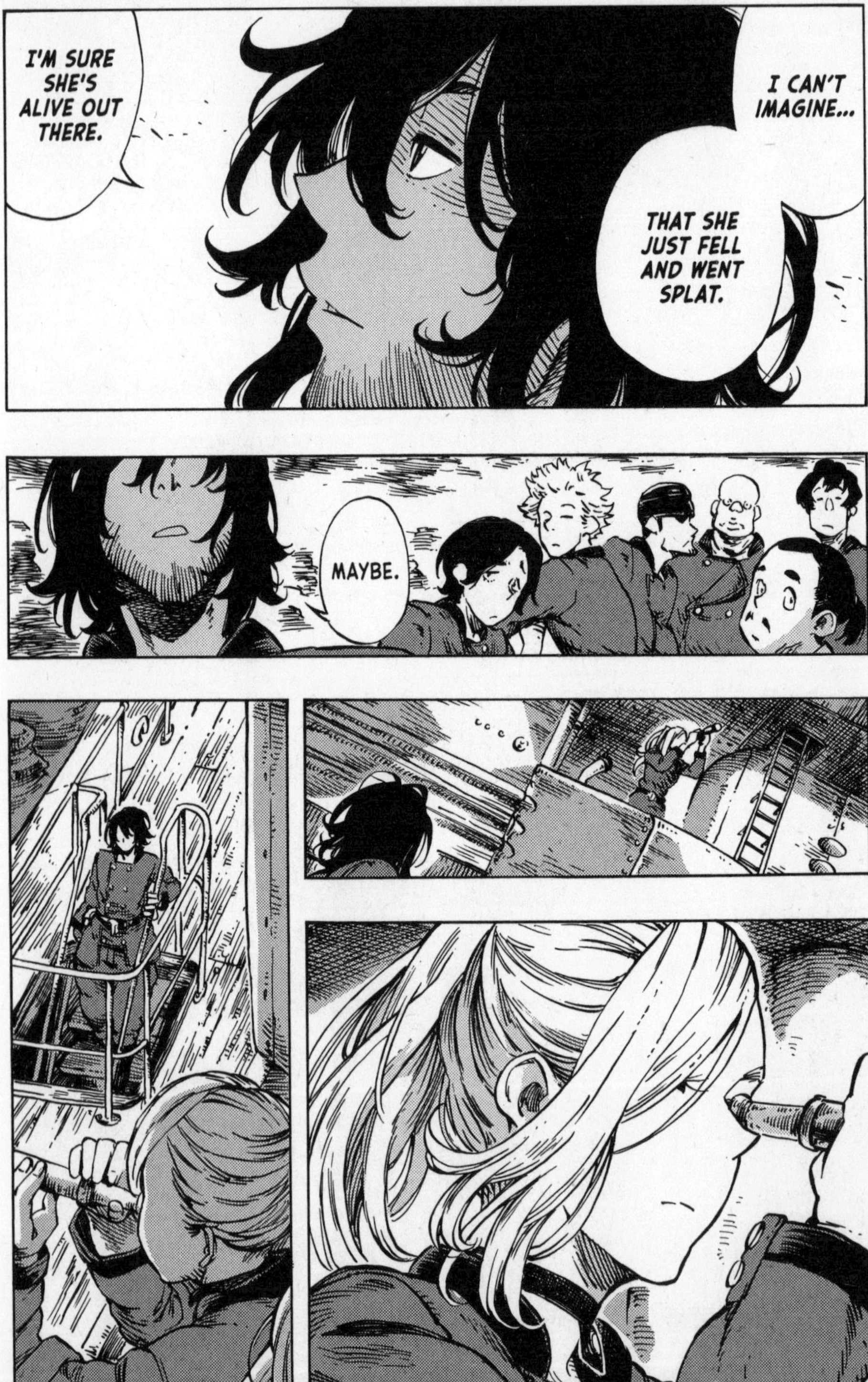
I CAN'T IMAGINE...
THAT SHE JUST FELL AND WENT SPLAT.
I'M SURE SHE'S ALIVE OUT THERE.
MAYBE.

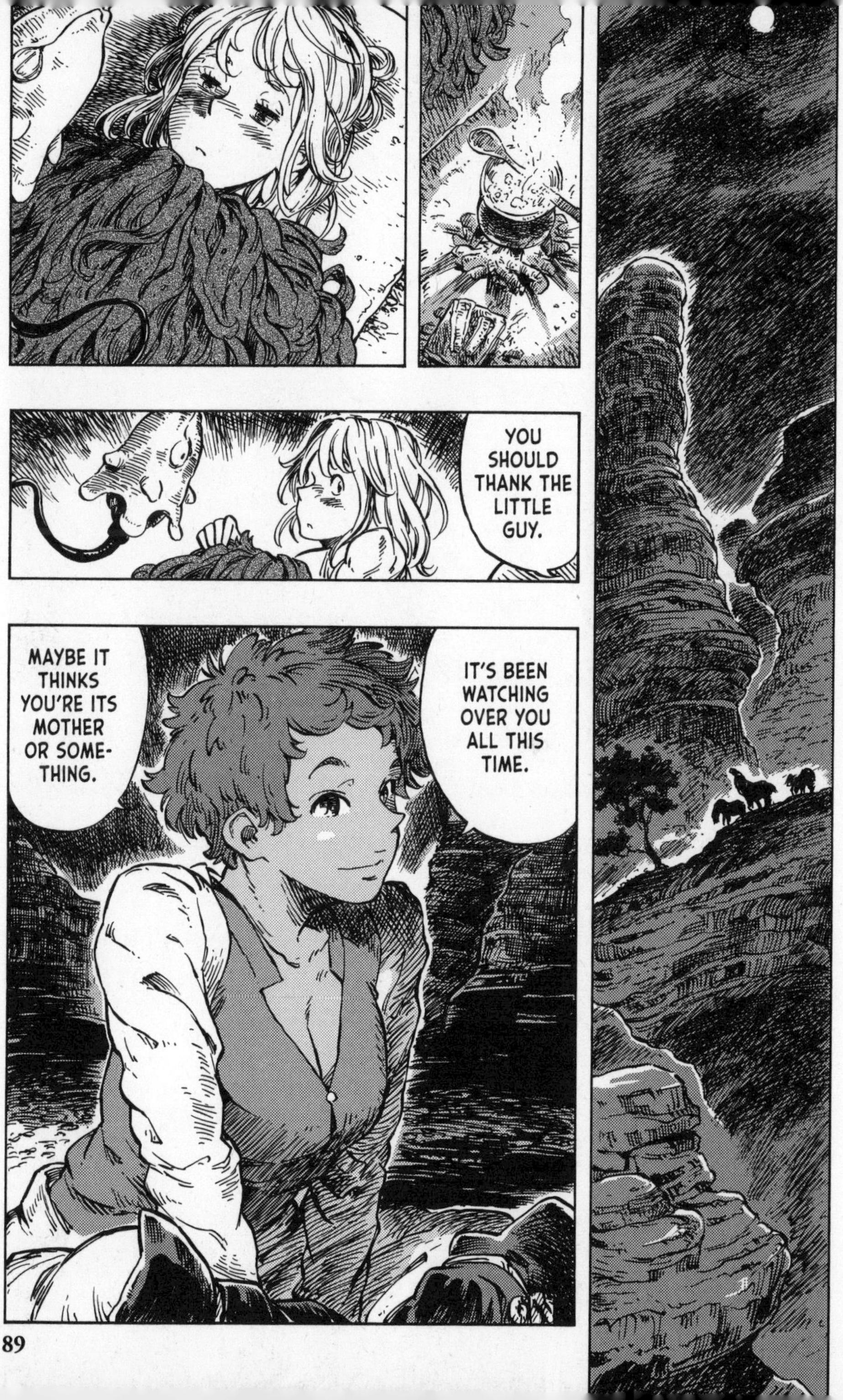
YOU SHOULD THANK THE LITTLE GUY.
IT'S BEEN WATCHING OVER YOU ALL THIS TIME.
MAYBE IT THINKS YOU'RE ITS MOTHER OR SOME-THING.

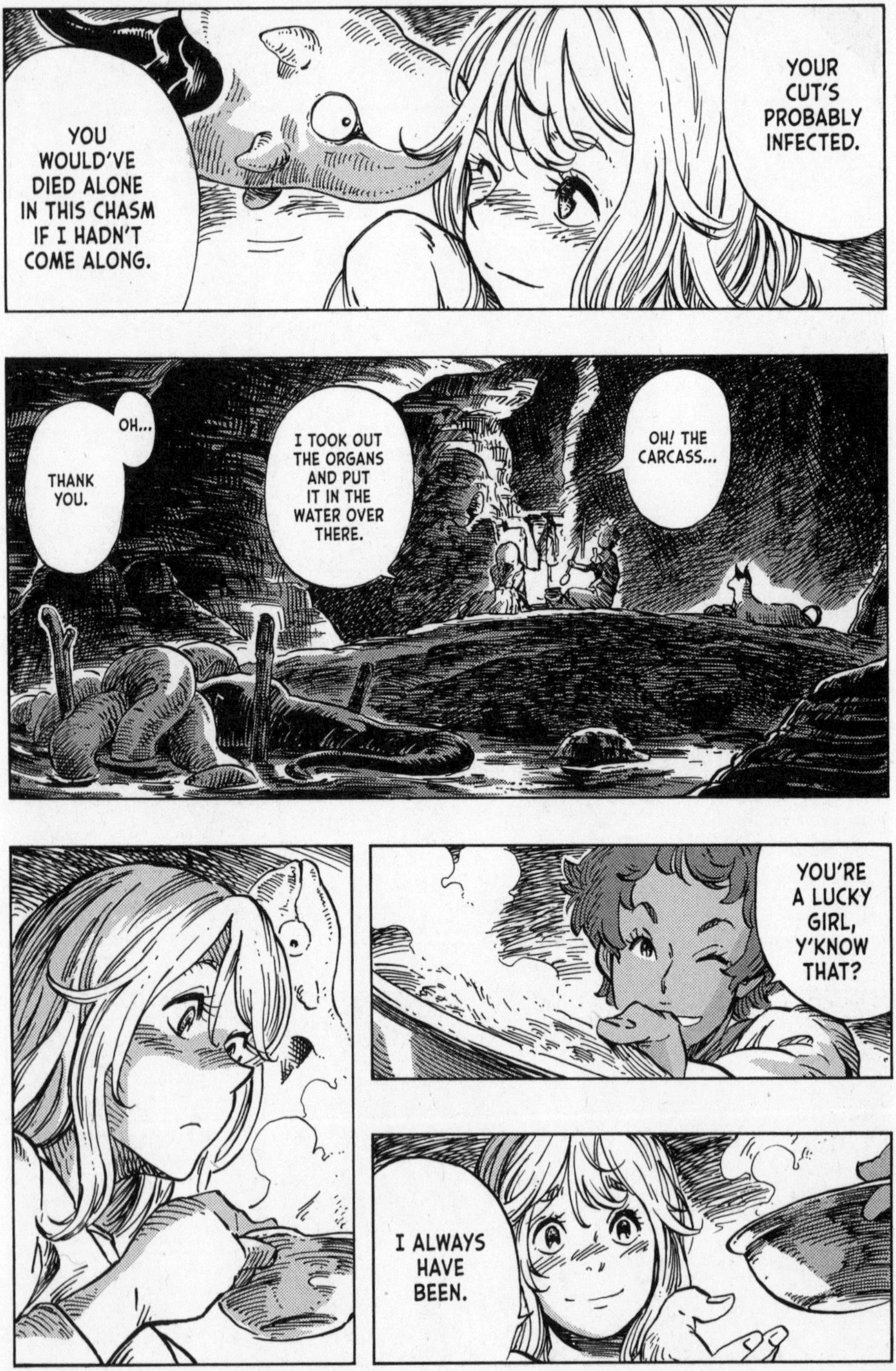
YOUR CUT'S PROBABLY INFECTED.
YOU WOULD'VE DIED ALONE IN THIS CHASM IF I HADN'T COME ALONG.
OH! THE CARCASS...
I TOOK OUT THE ORGANS AND PUT IT IN THE WATER OVER THERE.
OH...
THANK YOU.
YOU'RE A LUCKY GIRL, Y'KNOW THAT?
I ALWAYS HAVE BEEN.

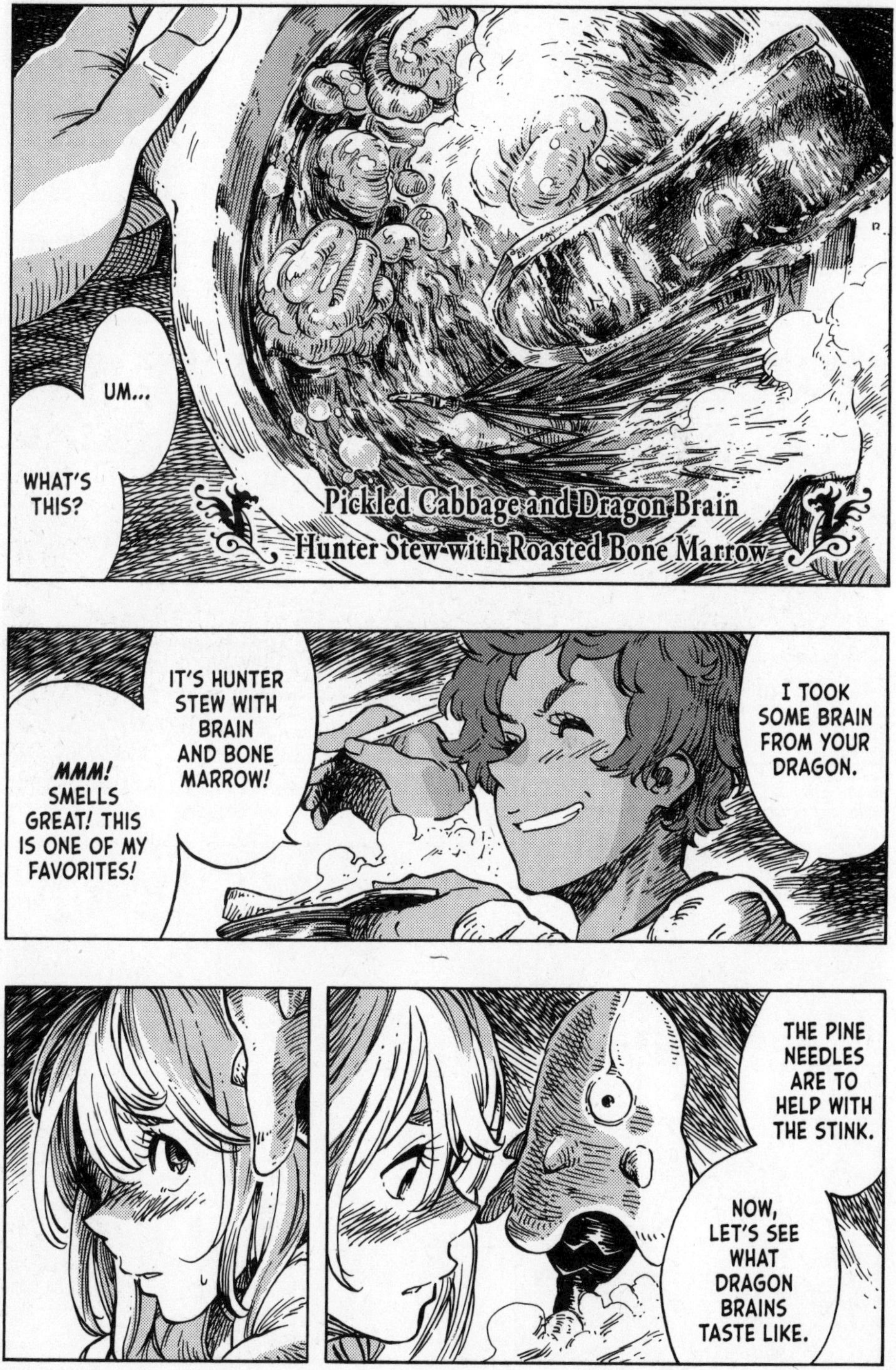
UM...
WHAT'S THIS?
Pickled Cabbage and Dragon Brain Hunter Stew with Roasted Bone Marrow
IT'S HUNTER STEW WITH BRAIN AND BONE MARROW!
I TOOK SOME BRAIN FROM YOUR DRAGON.
MMM! SMELLS GREAT! THIS IS ONE OF MY FAVORITES!
THE PINE NEEDLES ARE TO HELP WITH THE STINK.
NOW, LET'S SEE WHAT DRAGON BRAINS TASTE LIKE.

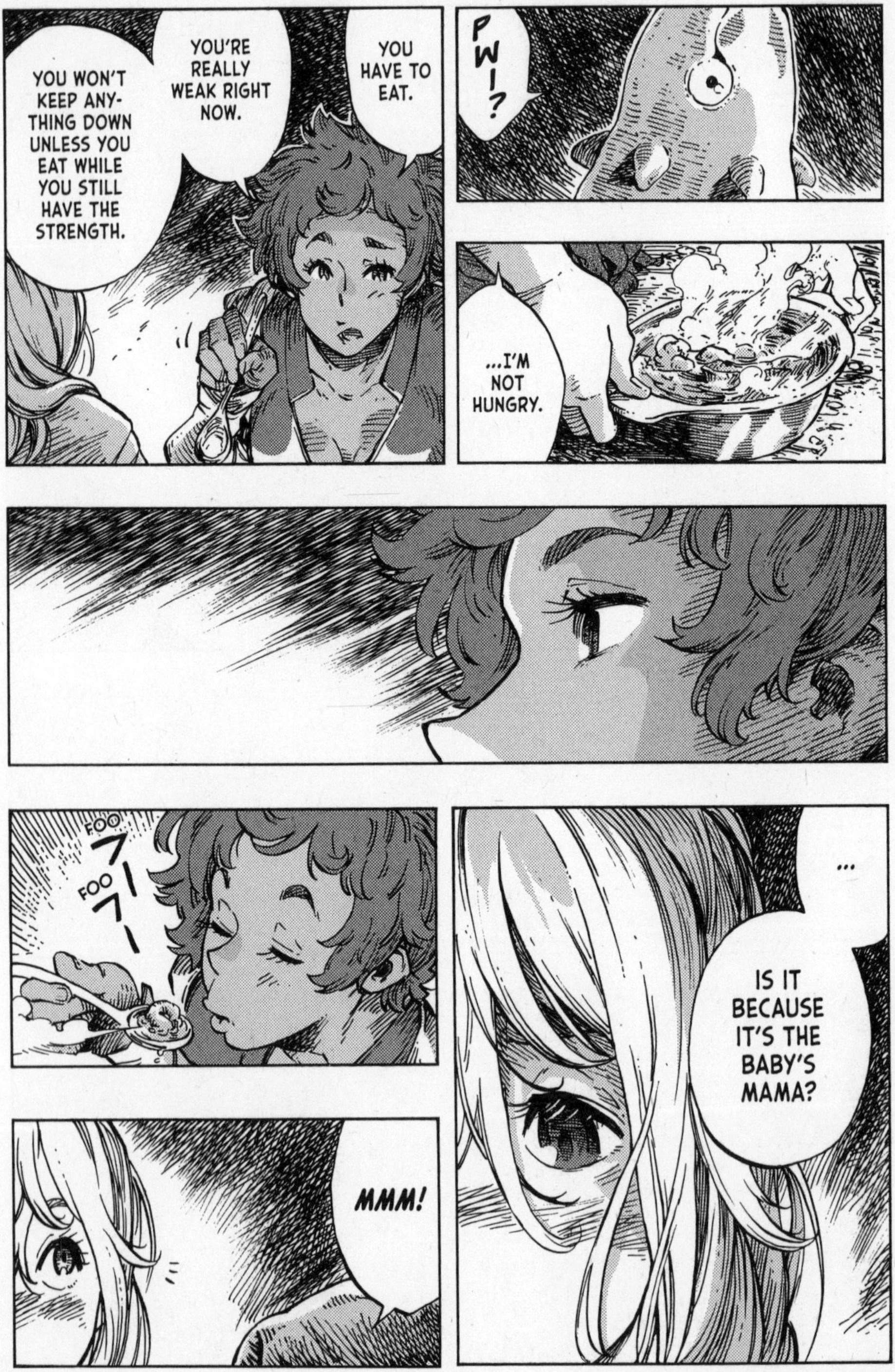
PWI?
...I'M NOT HUNGRY.
YOU HAVE TO EAT.
YOU'RE REALLY WEAK RIGHT NOW.
YOU WON'T KEEP ANYTHING DOWN UNLESS YOU EAT WHILE YOU STILL HAVE THE STRENGTH.
...
IS IT BECAUSE IT'S THE BABY'S MAMA?
FOO
FOO
MMM!

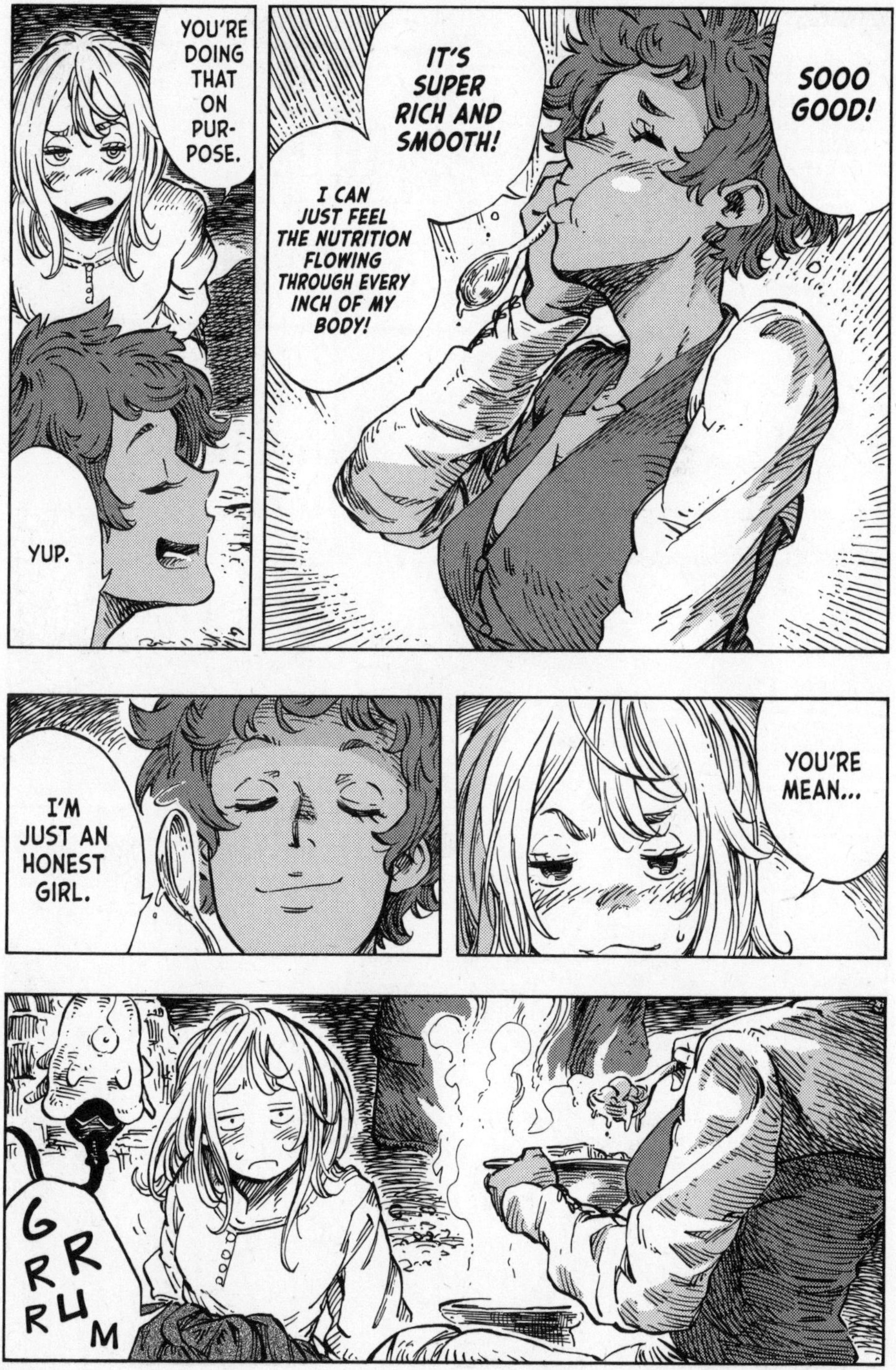
SOOO GOOD!
IT'S SUPER RICH AND SMOOTH!
I CAN JUST FEEL THE NUTRITION FLOWING THROUGH EVERY INCH OF MY BODY!
YOU'RE DOING THAT ON PURPOSE.
YUP.
YOU'RE MEAN...
I'M JUST AN HONEST GIRL.
GRRRUM

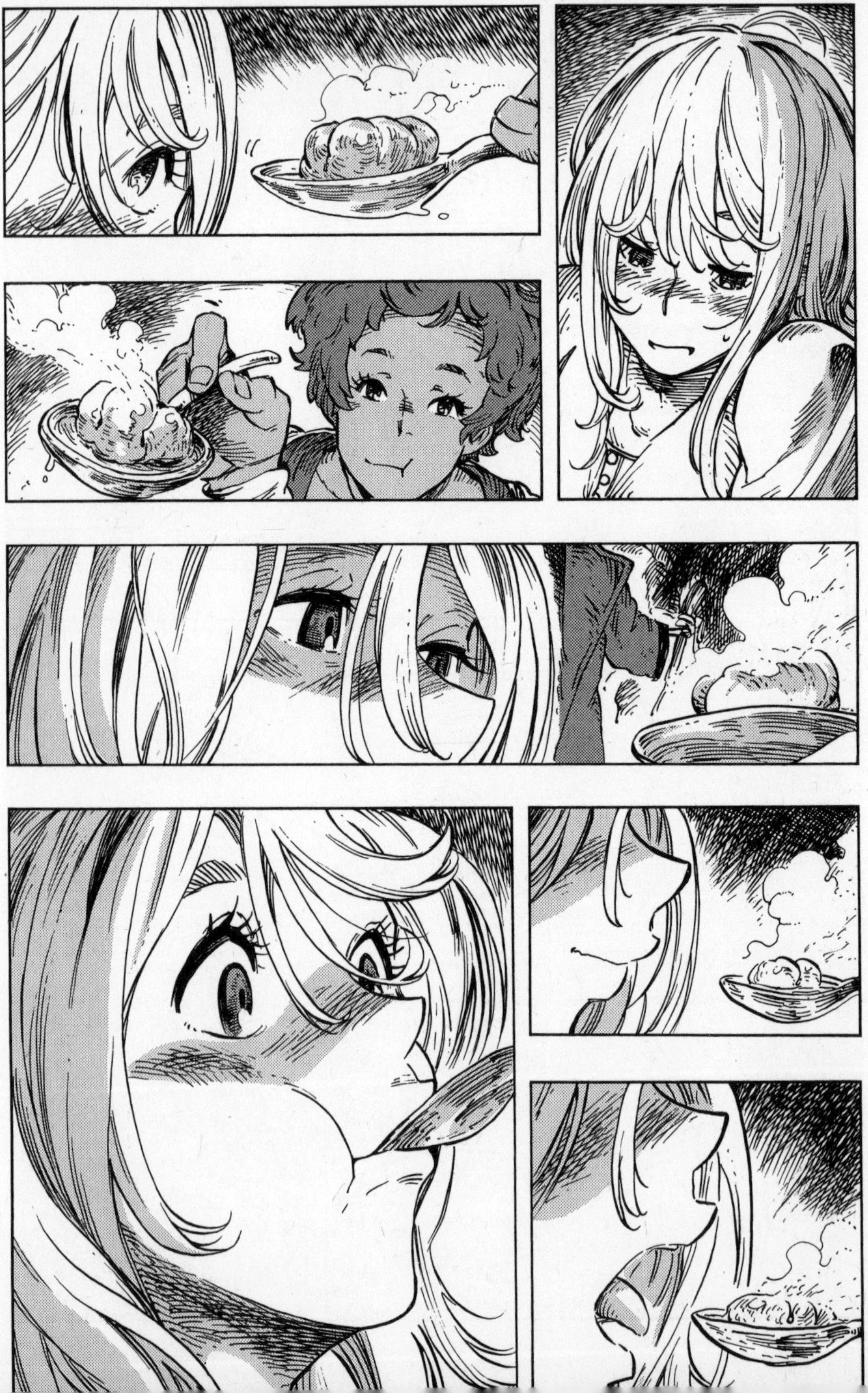

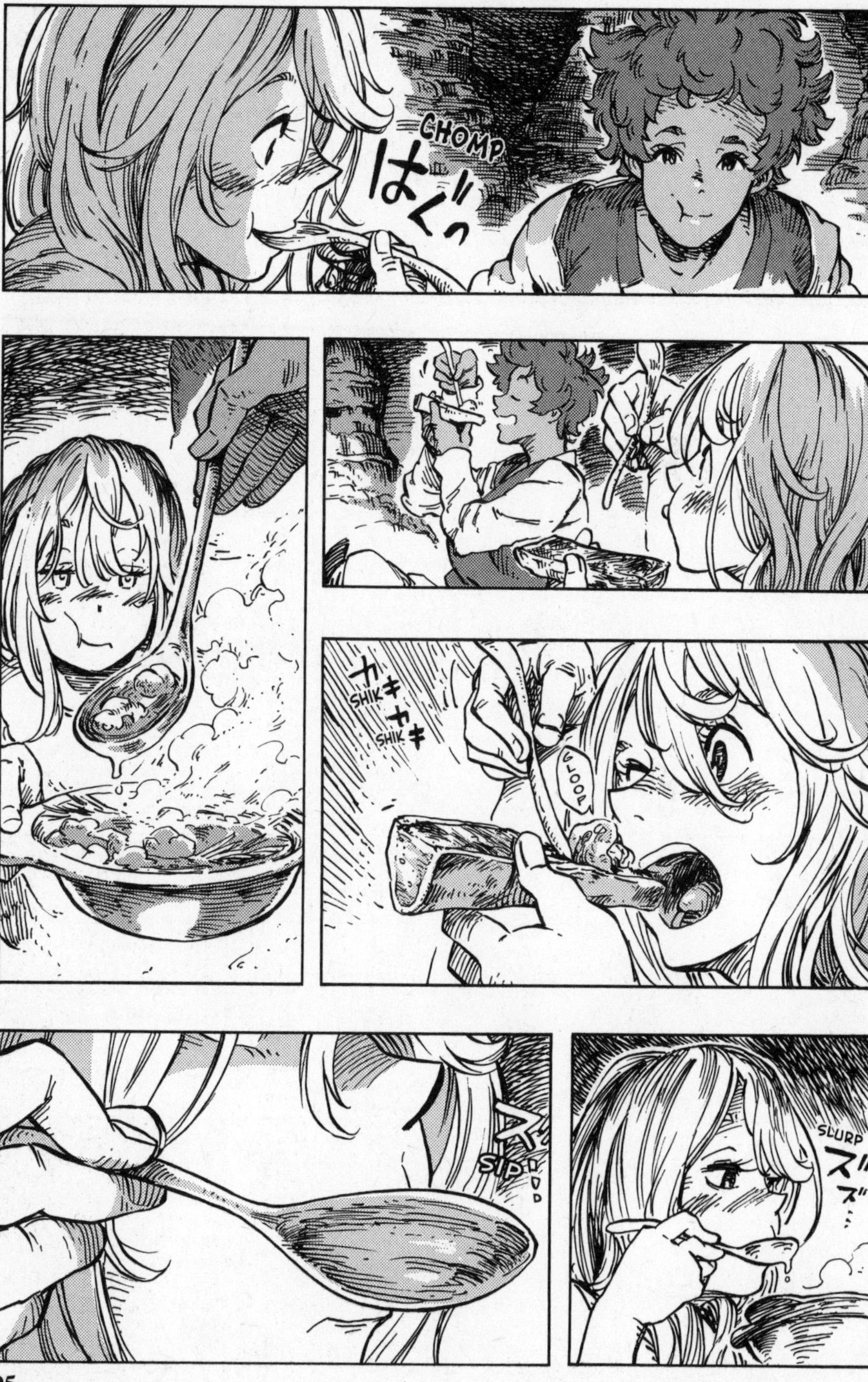
CHOMP
はぐっ
カキ
SHIK
カキ
SHIK
SLOOP
SLURP
ズズ…
ズ…
SIP

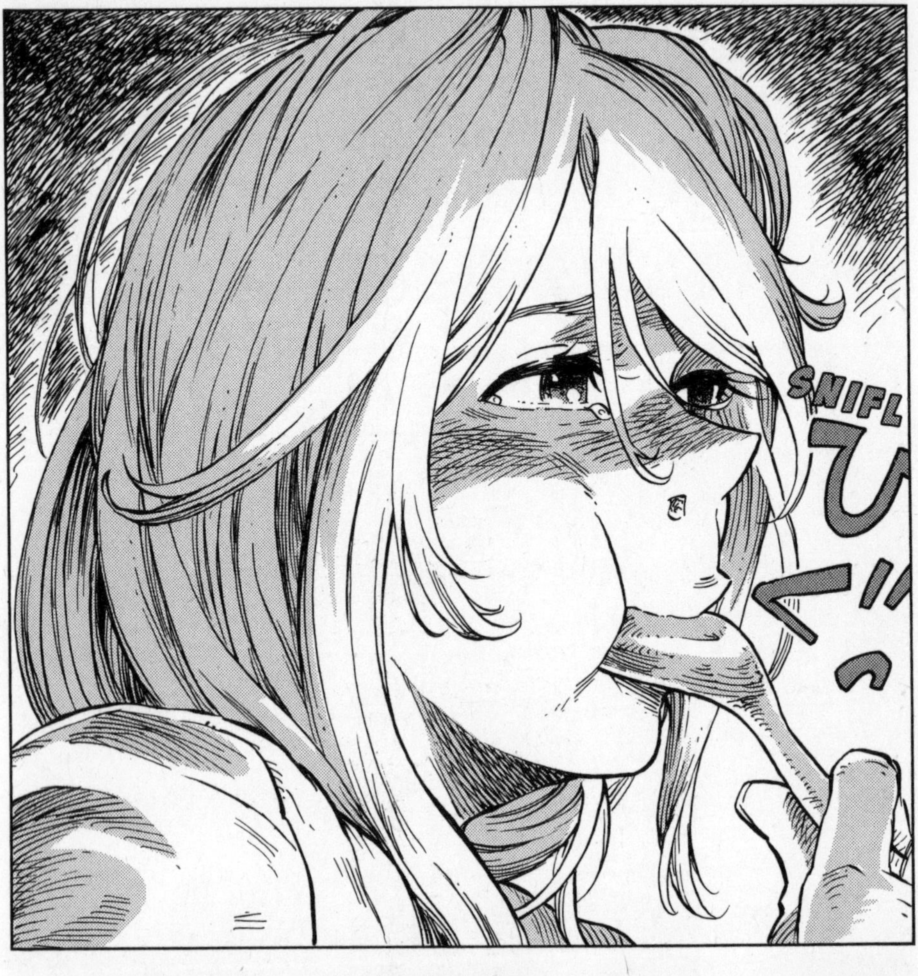
SNIFL
ひぐっ

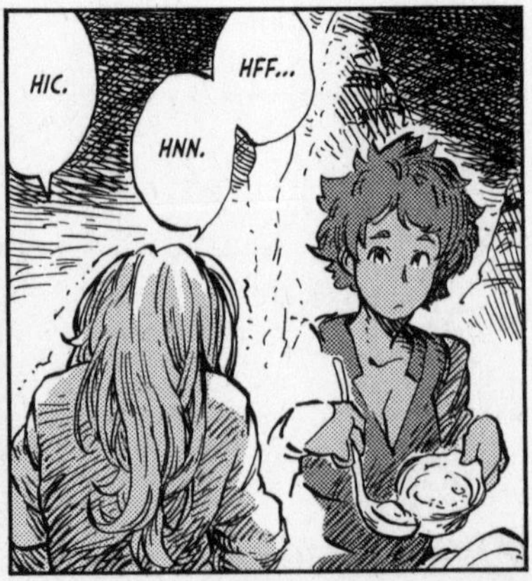
HFF...
HNN.
HIC.

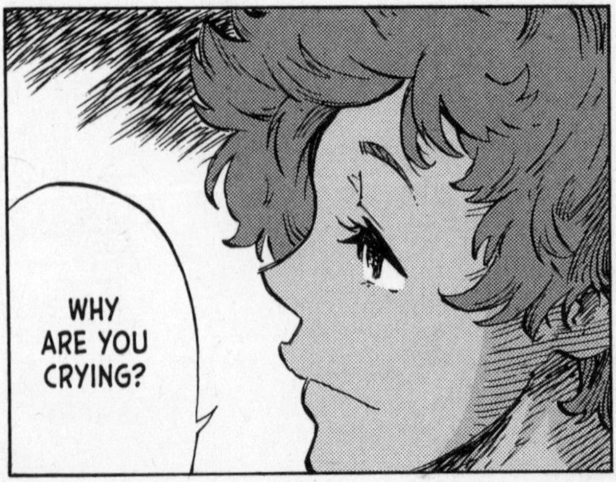
WHY ARE YOU CRYING?

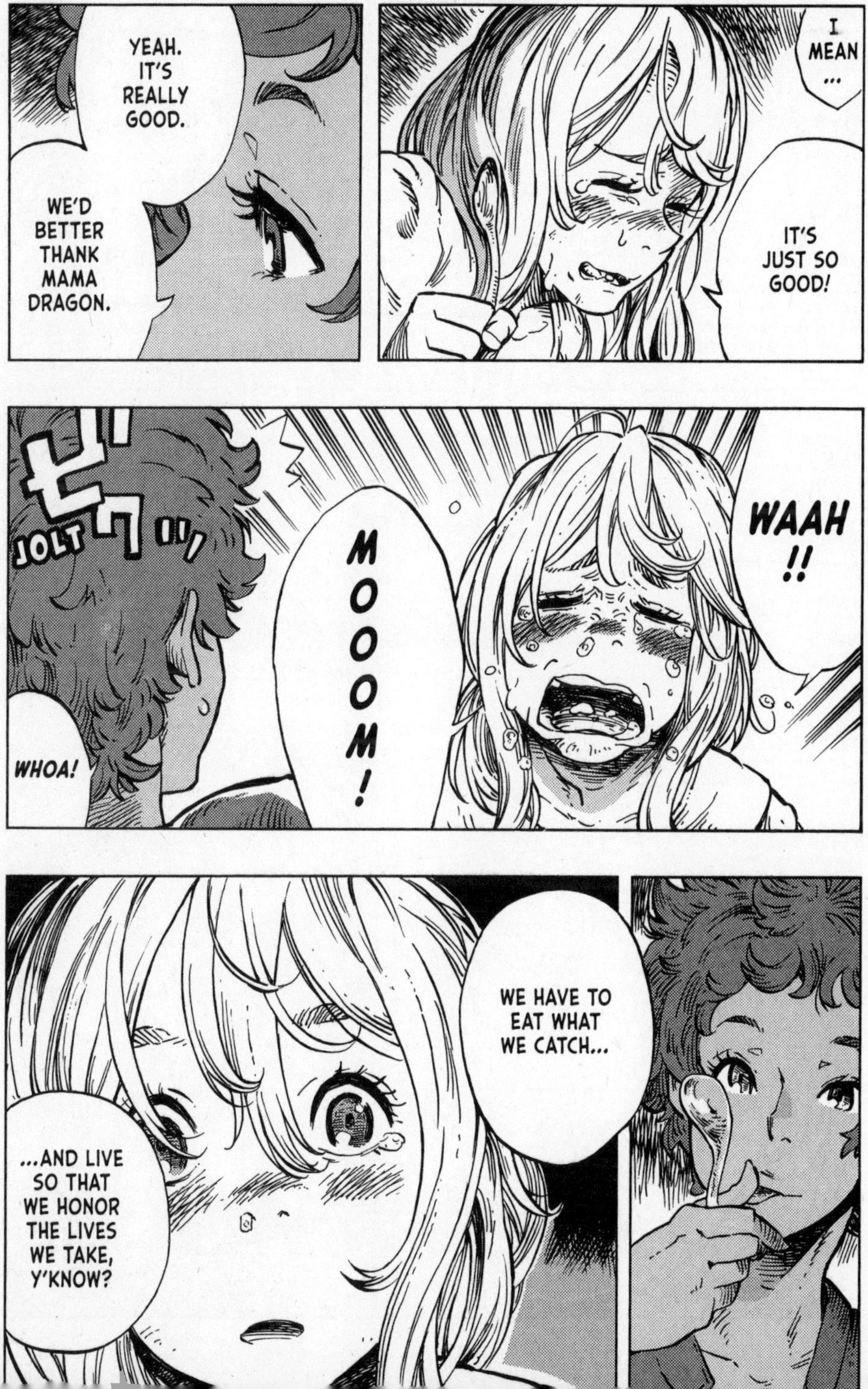
I MEAN ...
IT'S JUST SO GOOD!
YEAH. IT'S REALLY GOOD.
WE'D BETTER THANK MAMA DRAGON.
WAAH!!
MOOOOM!
JOLT
WHOA!
WE HAVE TO EAT WHAT WE CATCH...
...AND LIVE SO THAT WE HONOR THE LIVES WE TAKE, Y'KNOW?

YOU REMIND ME OF SOMEONE ON THE SHIP, ASCELLA. HE'S A GUY, THOUGH...

SNIFF

HM?

RUB RUB

THE OINTMENT?

WHAT DO YOU WANT?

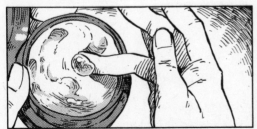

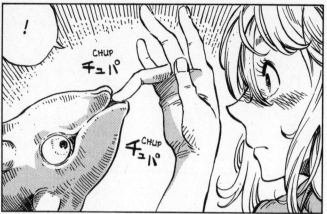

！

CHUP
チュパ

CHUP
チュパ

ALL
RIGHT.

...

I
SWEAR
...

...I'LL
GET YOU
BACK TO
YOUR
HERD!

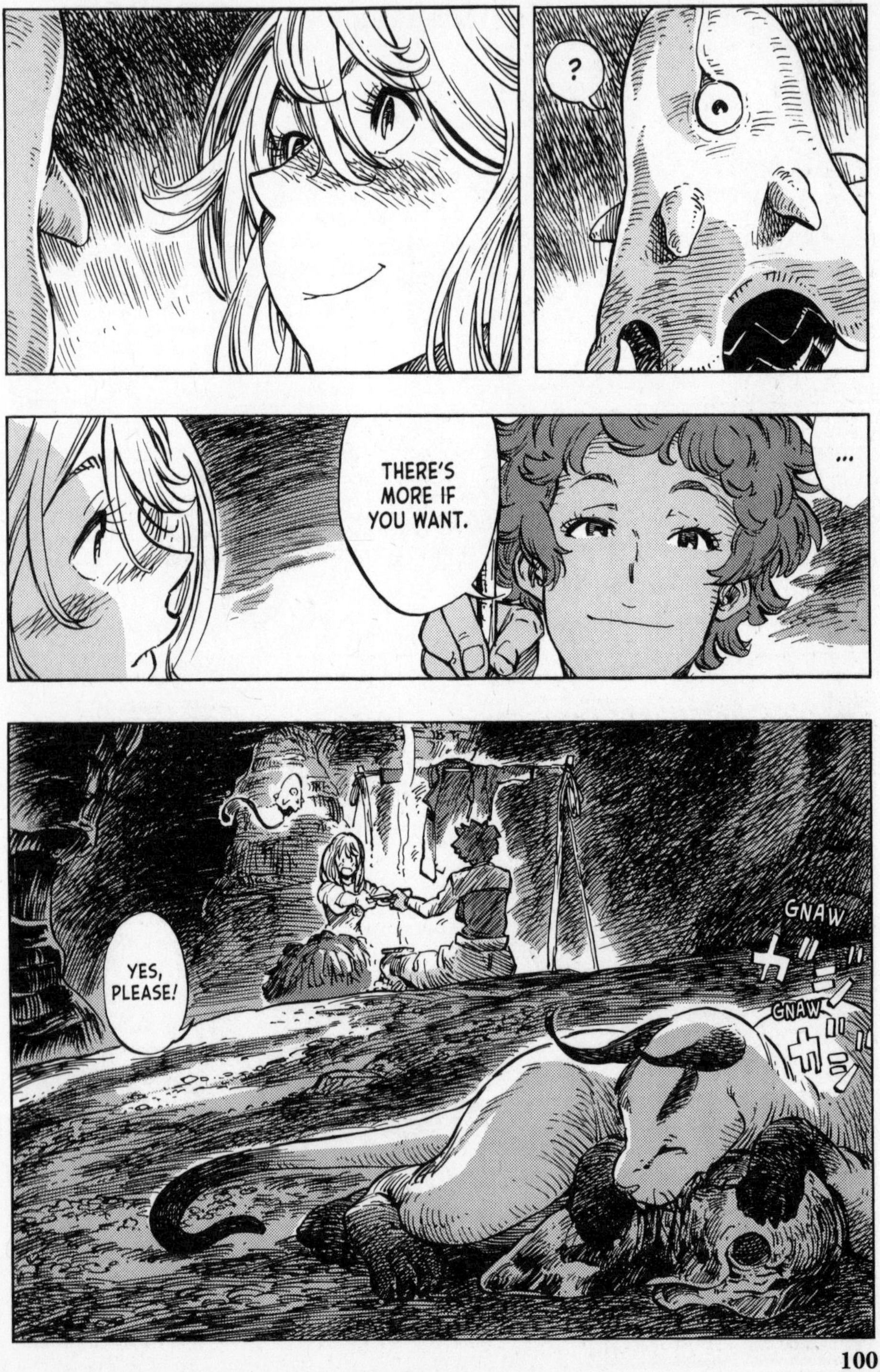
?
...
THERE'S MORE IF YOU WANT.
GNAW
GNAW
YES, PLEASE!

Hunter's Stew with Pickled Cabbage and Dragon Brains

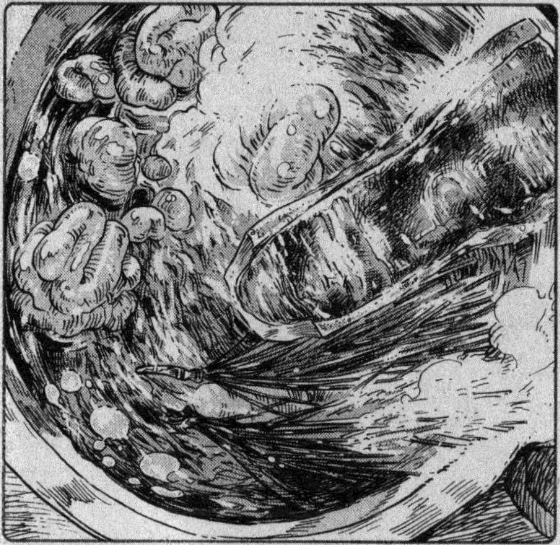

Ingredients (Serves 2-3)

- ✦ 400 g dragon brains
- ✦ 1 clove garlic
- ✦ 2 dried mushrooms (shiitake, porcini, morel, etc.)
- ✦ 300 g salted sour cabbage (sauerkraut)
- ✦ 3 sprigs pine needles
- ✦ 2 tbsp red wine or wine vodka
- ✦ Olive oil as needed
- ✦ Salt as needed
- ✦ Pepper as needed
- ✦ 1 tomato (if available)

01
Reconstitute the dried mushrooms in a half liter of water and chop finely. Reserve the liquid.

02
Cut open the dragon's skull with an axe or knife and cut away the thick membrane (called the dura mater) that surrounds the brain. Peel back the bone and take out the brain. Rinse under flowing water.

03
Heat olive oil in a pot and cook chopped garlic until fragrant.

04
Add mushrooms and pickled cabbage to the pot and cook until brown and tender.

05
Add bite-sized dragon brain pieces, mushroom liquid, red wine, pine needles, and chopped tomato if available. Bring mixture to a boil on high heat.

06
Once boiling, reduce the heat to low and simmer for 1 hour. Skim the scum from the surface throughout cooking.

07
Season to taste with salt and pepper, and it's ready.

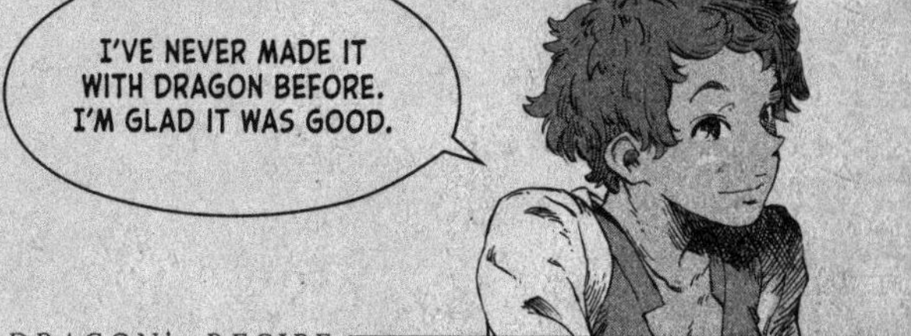
I'VE NEVER MADE IT WITH DRAGON BEFORE. I'M GLAD IT WAS GOOD.

Roasted Dragon Bone Marrow

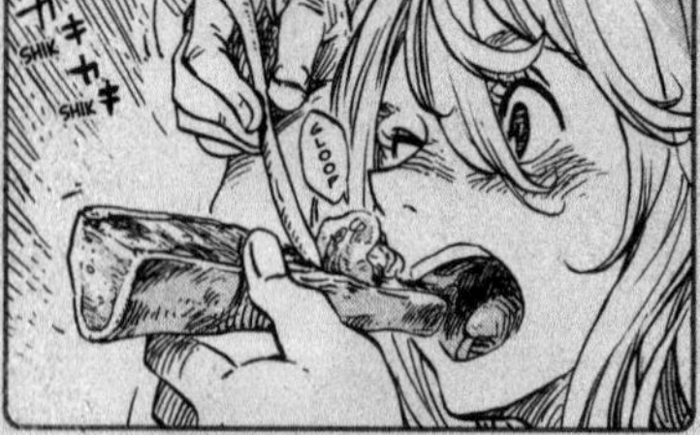
カキカキ
SHIK
SHIK
SLOOP

01
Chop dragon mandible in half with an axe.

02
Sprinkle with salt and pepper.

01
Roast slowly on indirect heat for about 20 minutes.

Ingredients (Serves 2-3)

- ✦ About 300 g dragon mandible
- ✦ Salt as needed
- ✦ Pepper as needed

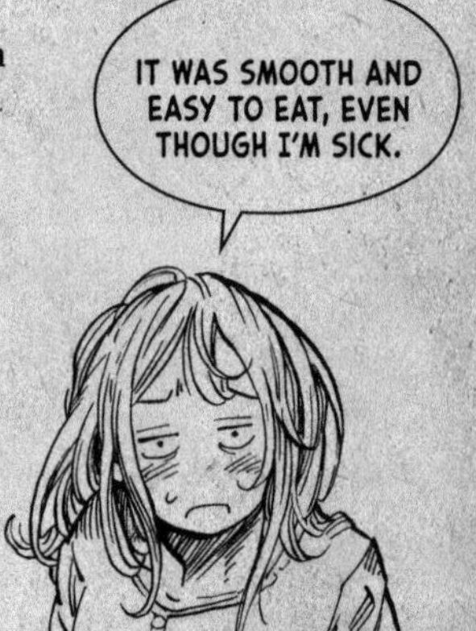
IT WAS SMOOTH AND EASY TO EAT, EVEN THOUGH I'M SICK.

Flight 15 Dragon Oil Mayonnaise & Mount Kin

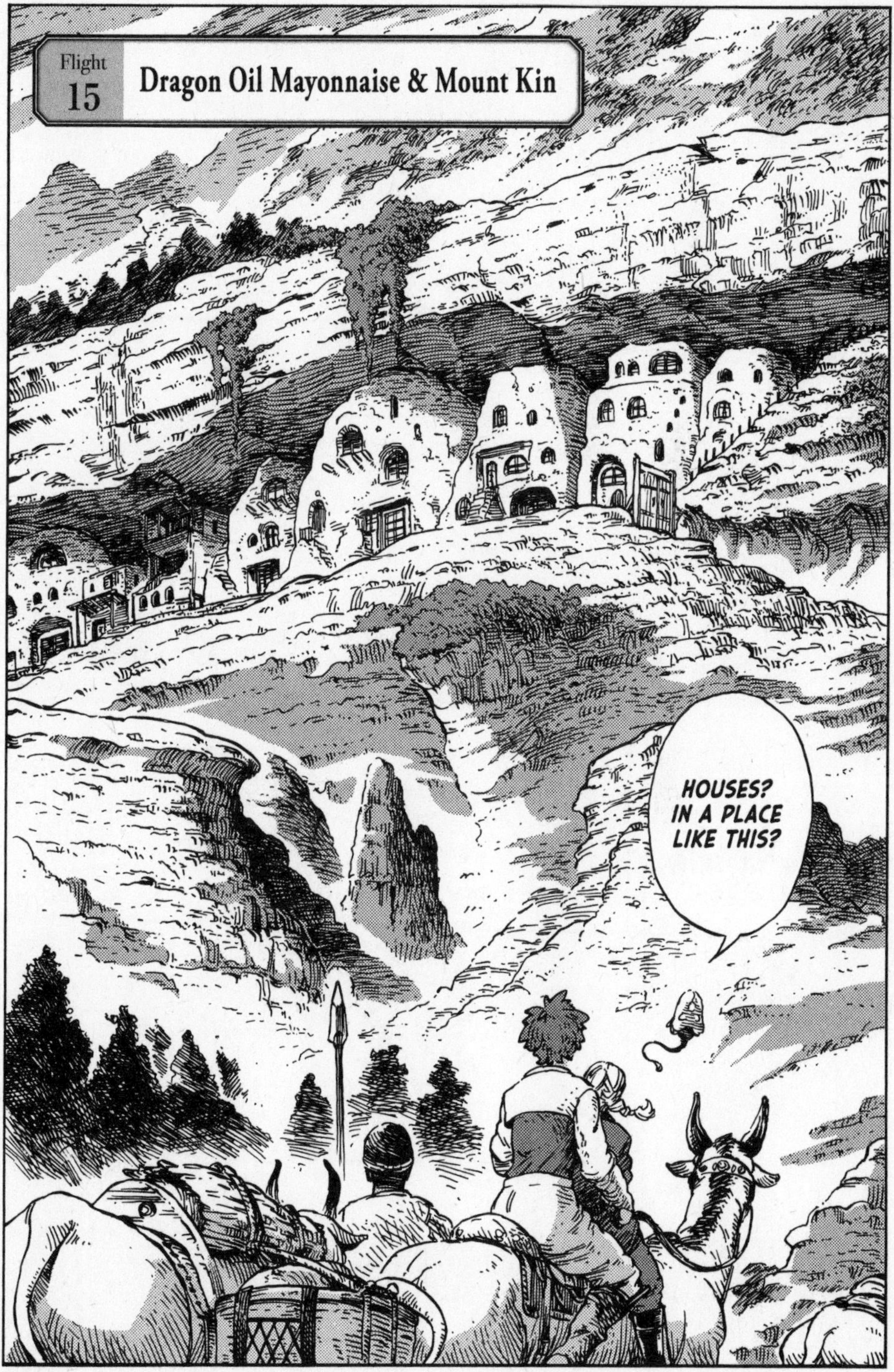
HOUSES? IN A PLACE LIKE THIS?

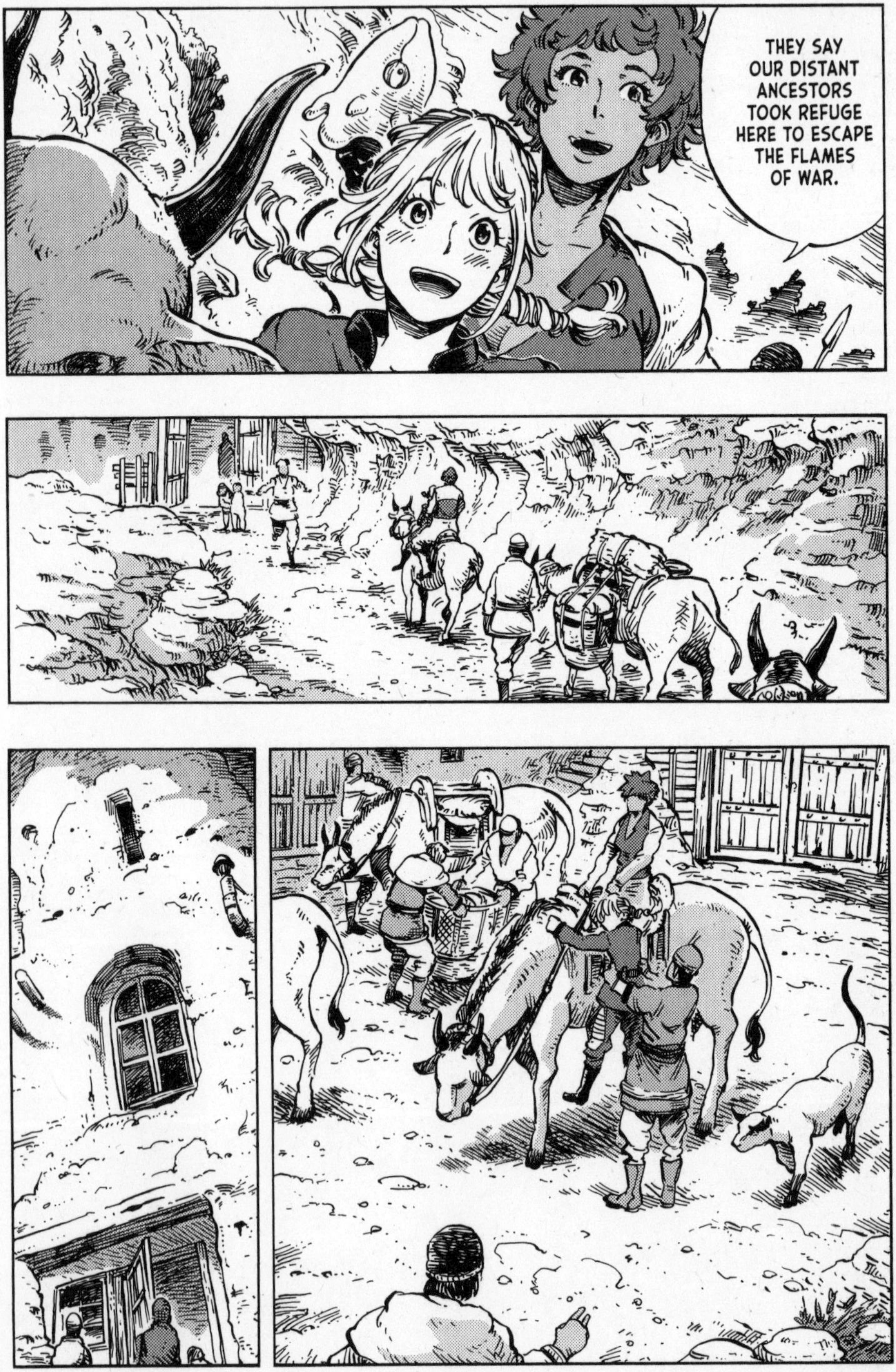
THEY SAY OUR DISTANT ANCESTORS TOOK REFUGE HERE TO ESCAPE THE FLAMES OF WAR.

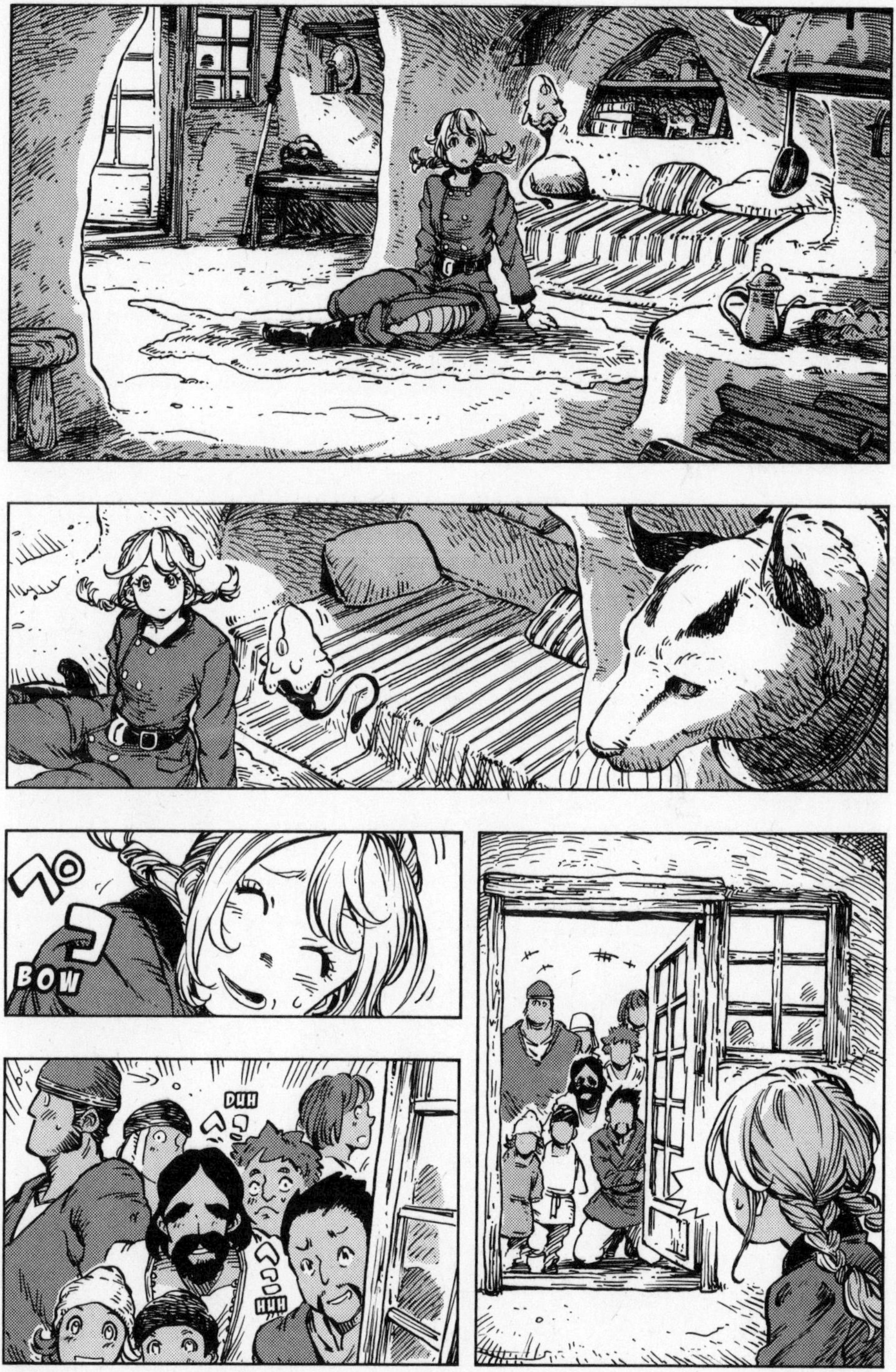
ペコ
BOW
へこ
DUH
へこっ
HUH

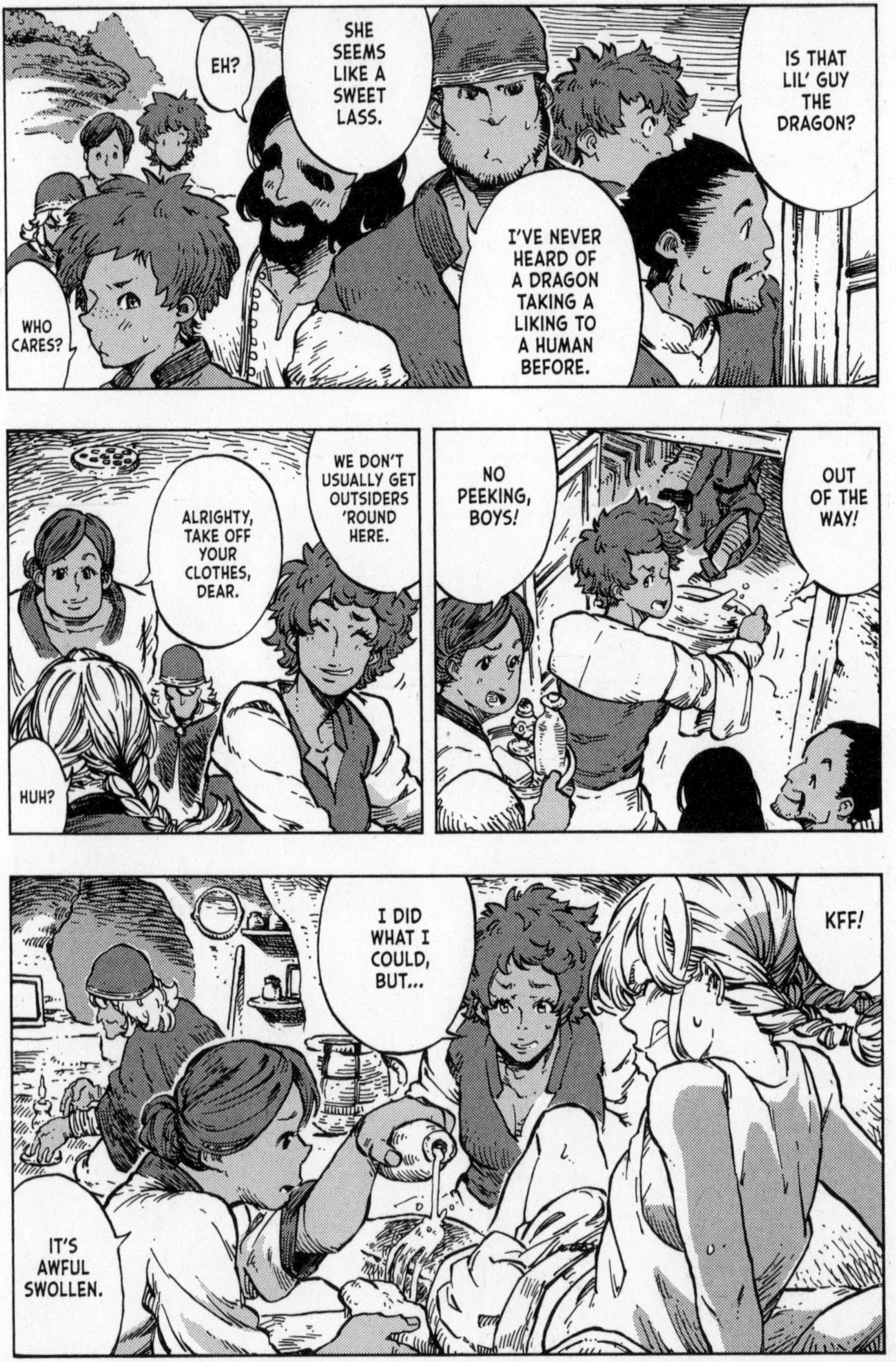
IS THAT LIL' GUY THE DRAGON?
I'VE NEVER HEARD OF A DRAGON TAKING A LIKING TO A HUMAN BEFORE.
SHE SEEMS LIKE A SWEET LASS.
EH?
WHO CARES?
OUT OF THE WAY!
NO PEEKING, BOYS!
WE DON'T USUALLY GET OUTSIDERS 'ROUND HERE.
ALRIGHTY, TAKE OFF YOUR CLOTHES, DEAR.
HUH?
KFF!
I DID WHAT I COULD, BUT...
IT'S AWFUL SWOLLEN.

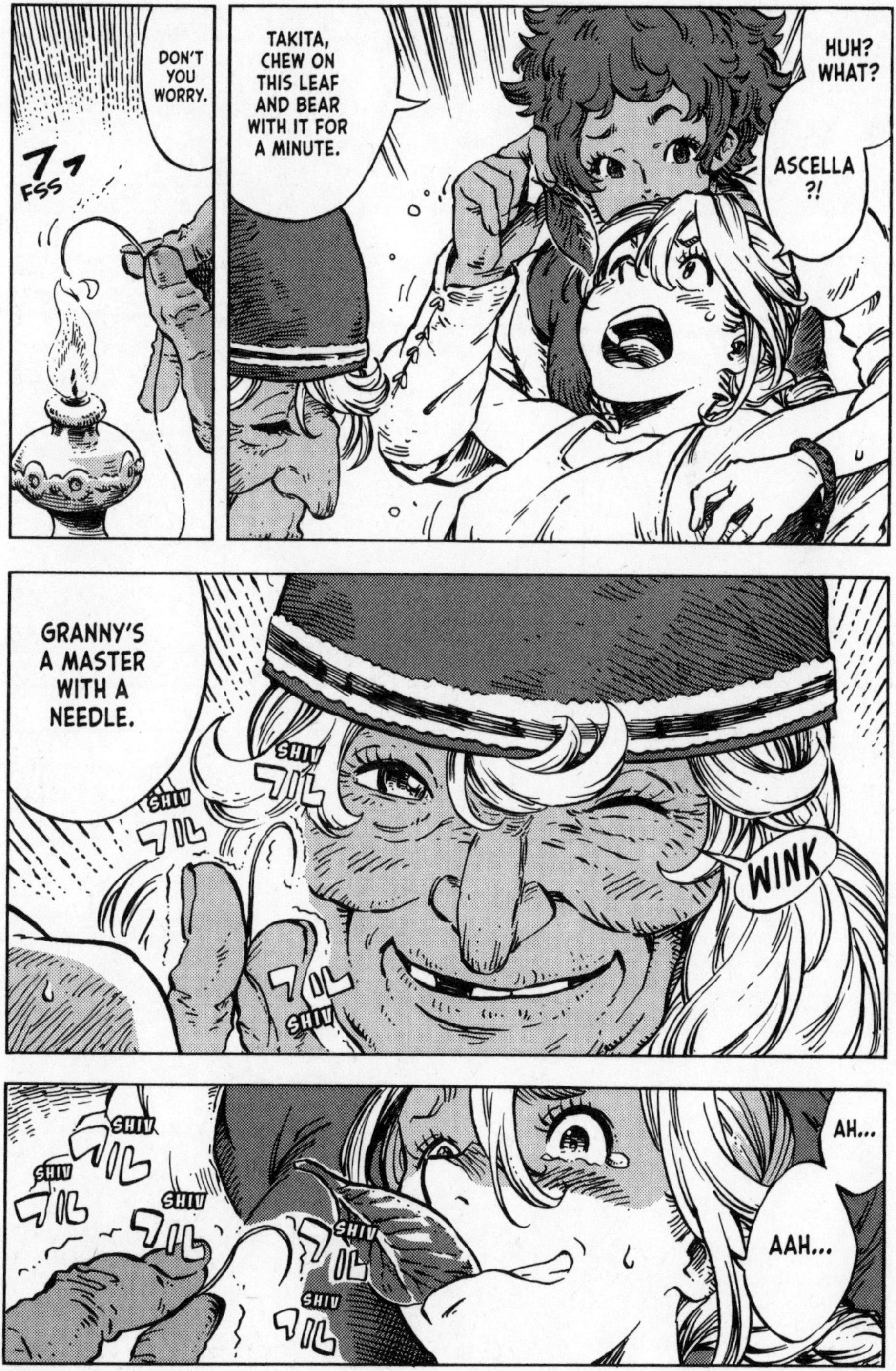
HUH? WHAT?
ASCELLA ?!
TAKITA, CHEW ON THIS LEAF AND BEAR WITH IT FOR A MINUTE.
DON'T YOU WORRY.
FSS
GRANNY'S A MASTER WITH A NEEDLE.
SHIV
SHIV
WINK
SHIV
AH...
AAH...
SHIV
SHIV
SHIV
SHIV
SHIV

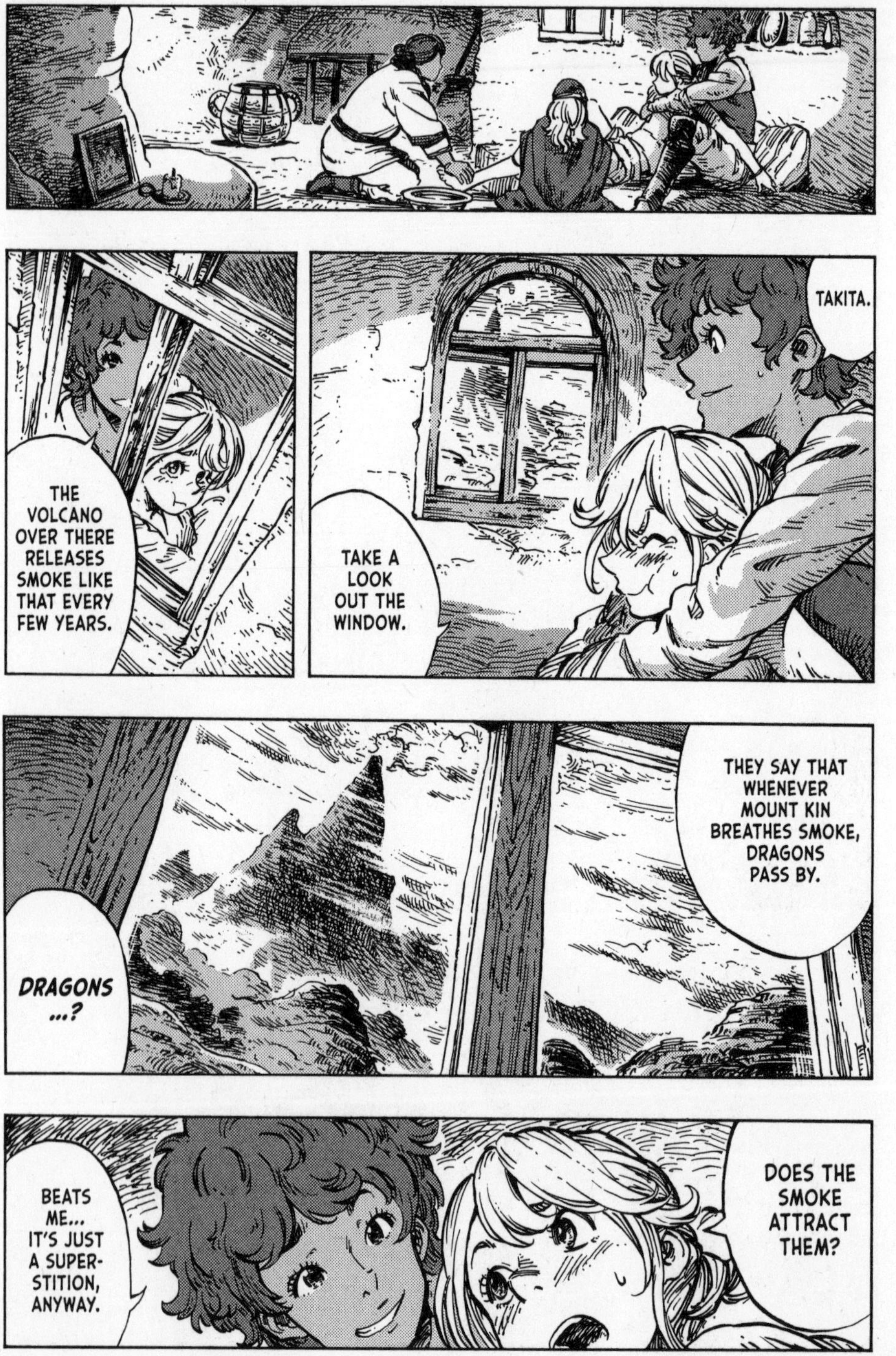
TAKITA.
TAKE A LOOK OUT THE WINDOW.
THE VOLCANO OVER THERE RELEASES SMOKE LIKE THAT EVERY FEW YEARS.
THEY SAY THAT WHENEVER MOUNT KIN BREATHES SMOKE, DRAGONS PASS BY.
DRAGONS ...?
DOES THE SMOKE ATTRACT THEM?
BEATS ME... IT'S JUST A SUPERSTITION, ANYWAY.

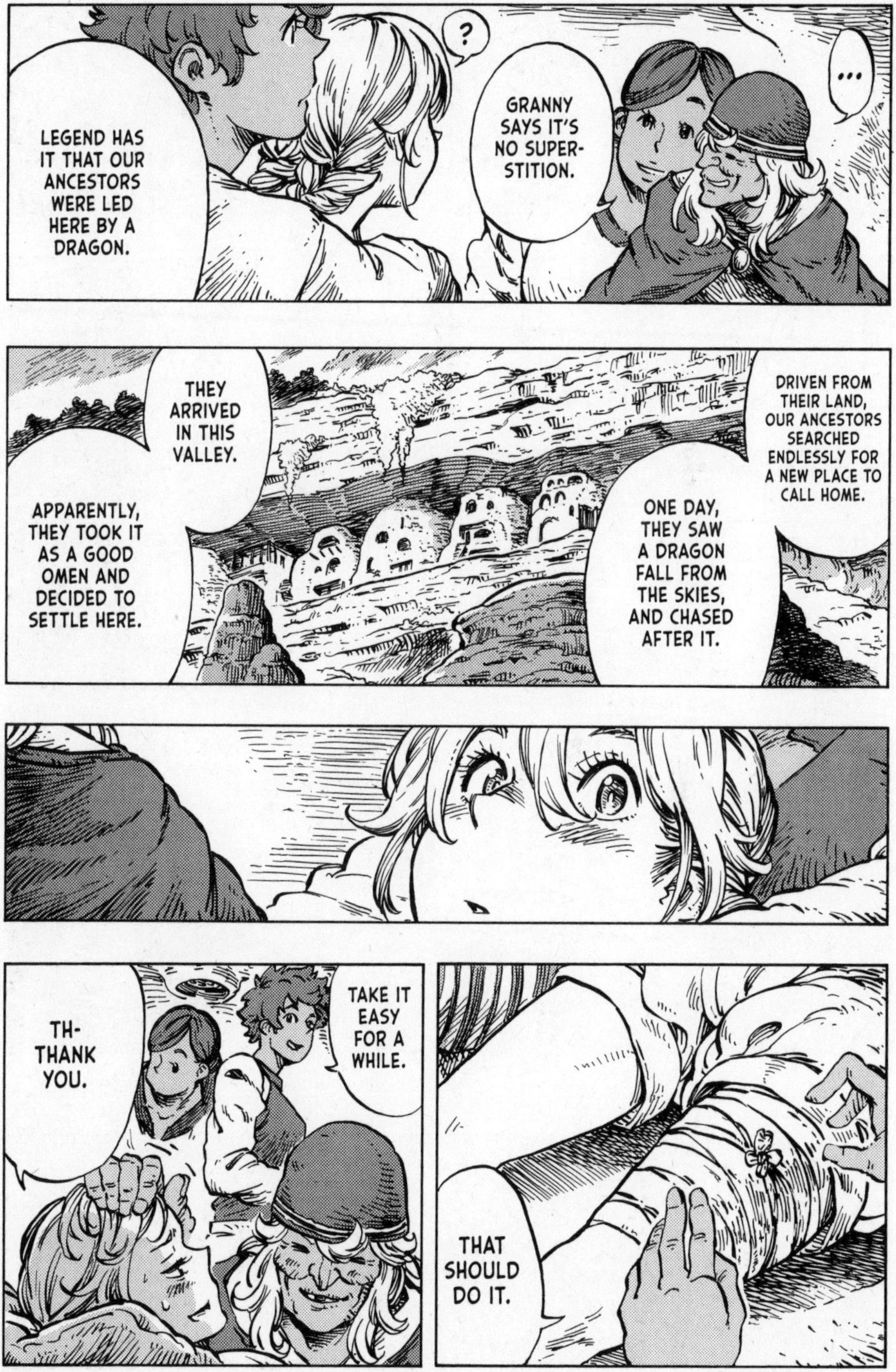
...
GRANNY SAYS IT'S NO SUPER-STITION.
?
LEGEND HAS IT THAT OUR ANCESTORS WERE LED HERE BY A DRAGON.
DRIVEN FROM THEIR LAND, OUR ANCESTORS SEARCHED ENDLESSLY FOR A NEW PLACE TO CALL HOME.
ONE DAY, THEY SAW A DRAGON FALL FROM THE SKIES, AND CHASED AFTER IT.
THEY ARRIVED IN THIS VALLEY.
APPARENTLY, THEY TOOK IT AS A GOOD OMEN AND DECIDED TO SETTLE HERE.
THAT SHOULD DO IT.
TAKE IT EASY FOR A WHILE.
TH-THANK YOU.

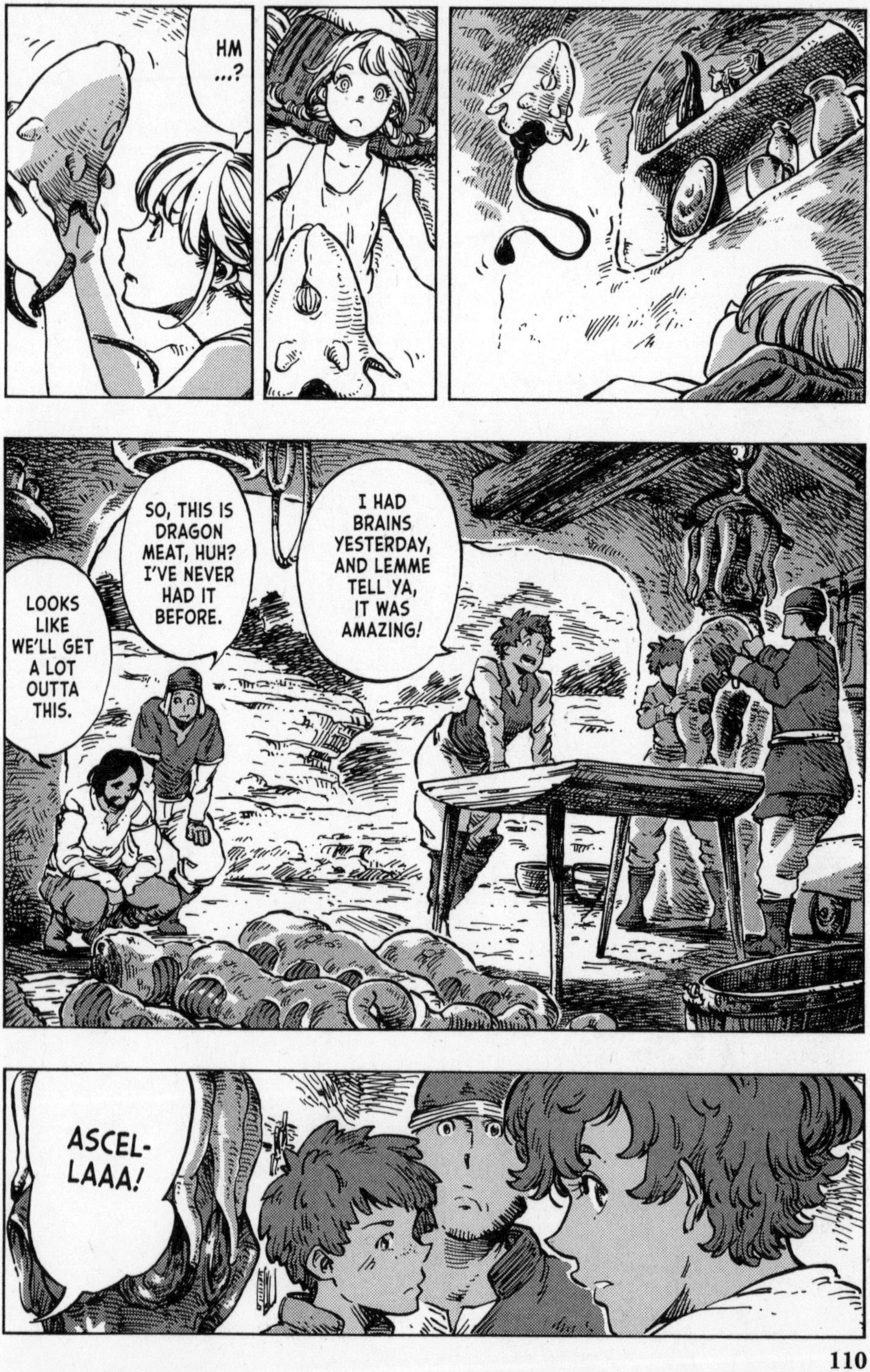
HM ...?
I HAD BRAINS YESTERDAY, AND LEMME TELL YA, IT WAS AMAZING!
SO, THIS IS DRAGON MEAT, HUH? I'VE NEVER HAD IT BEFORE.
LOOKS LIKE WE'LL GET A LOT OUTTA THIS.
ASCEL-LAAA!

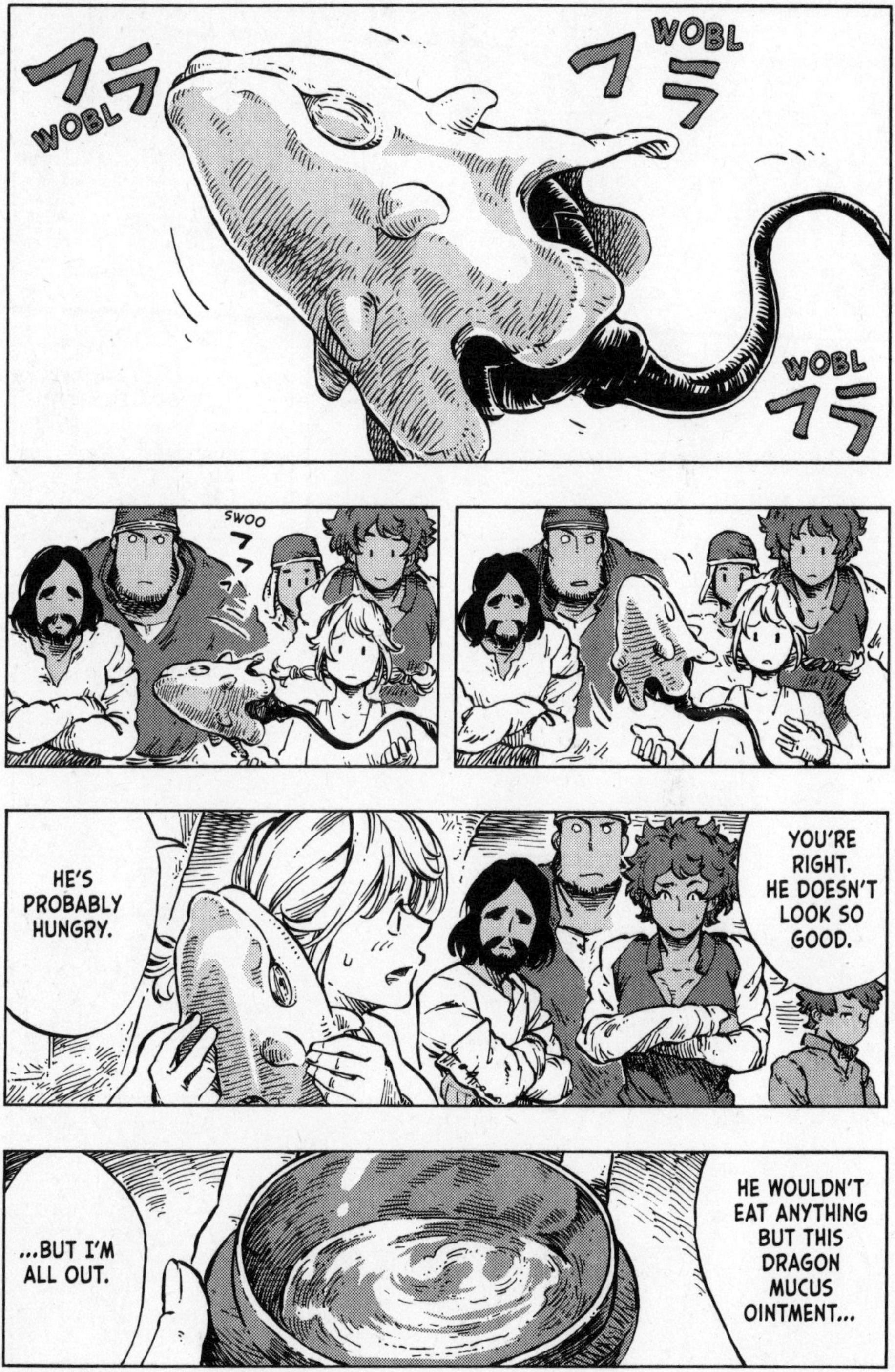
WOBL
フラ
フラ
WOBL
WOBL
フラ
SWOO
YOU'RE RIGHT. HE DOESN'T LOOK SO GOOD.
HE'S PROBABLY HUNGRY.
HE WOULDN'T EAT ANYTHING BUT THIS DRAGON MUCUS OINTMENT...
...BUT I'M ALL OUT.

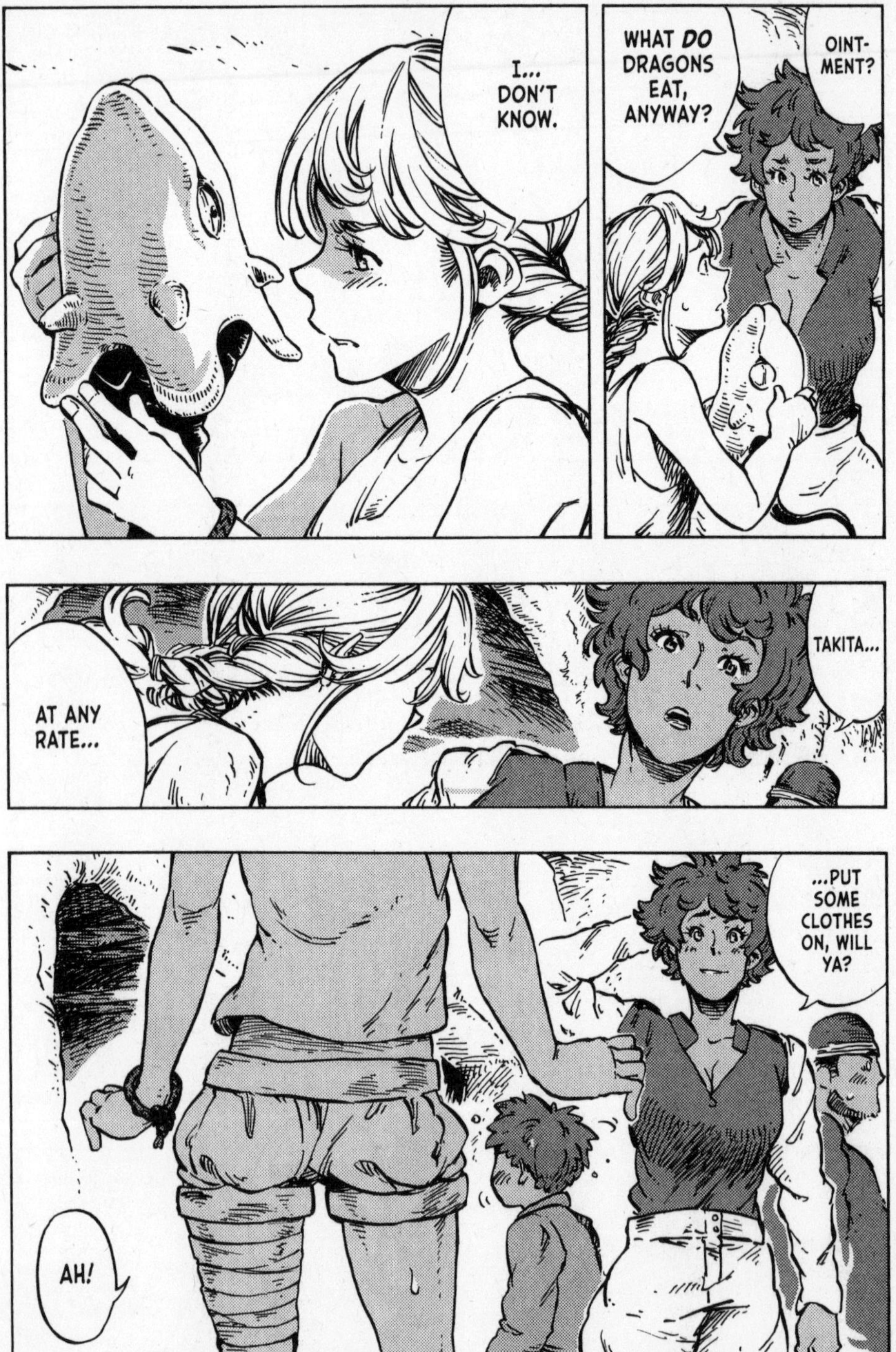
OINT-MENT?
WHAT *DO* DRAGONS EAT, ANYWAY?
I... DON'T KNOW.
TAKITA...
AT ANY RATE...
...PUT SOME CLOTHES ON, WILL YA?
AH!

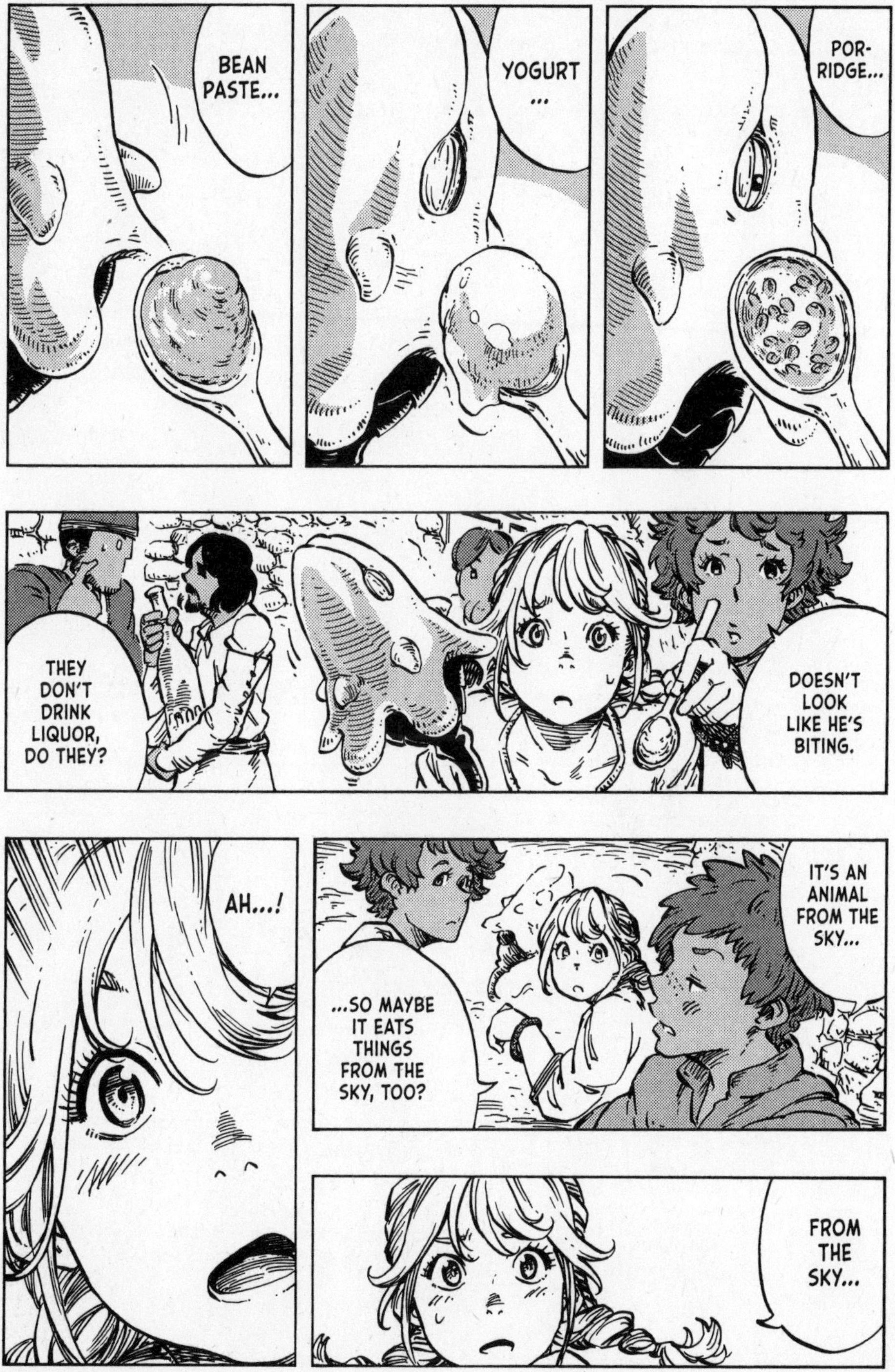
POR-
RIDGE...
YOGURT
...
BEAN
PASTE...
DOESN'T LOOK LIKE HE'S BITING.
THEY DON'T DRINK LIQUOR, DO THEY?
IT'S AN ANIMAL FROM THE SKY...
...SO MAYBE IT EATS THINGS FROM THE SKY, TOO?
FROM THE SKY...
AH...!

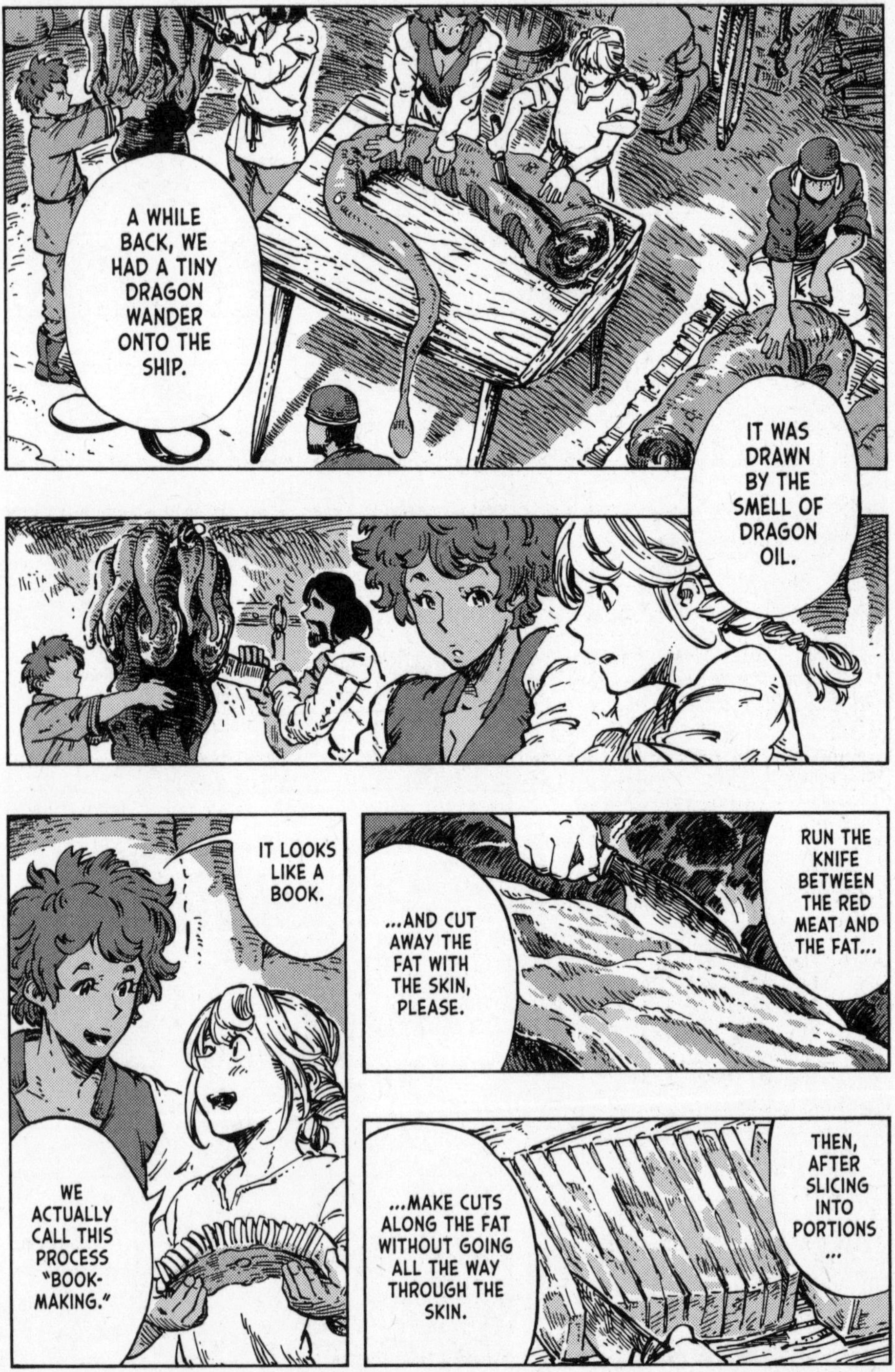
A WHILE BACK, WE HAD A TINY DRAGON WANDER ONTO THE SHIP.
IT WAS DRAWN BY THE SMELL OF DRAGON OIL.
RUN THE KNIFE BETWEEN THE RED MEAT AND THE FAT...
...AND CUT AWAY THE FAT WITH THE SKIN, PLEASE.
THEN, AFTER SLICING INTO PORTIONS...
...MAKE CUTS ALONG THE FAT WITHOUT GOING ALL THE WAY THROUGH THE SKIN.
IT LOOKS LIKE A BOOK.
WE ACTUALLY CALL THIS PROCESS "BOOK-MAKING."

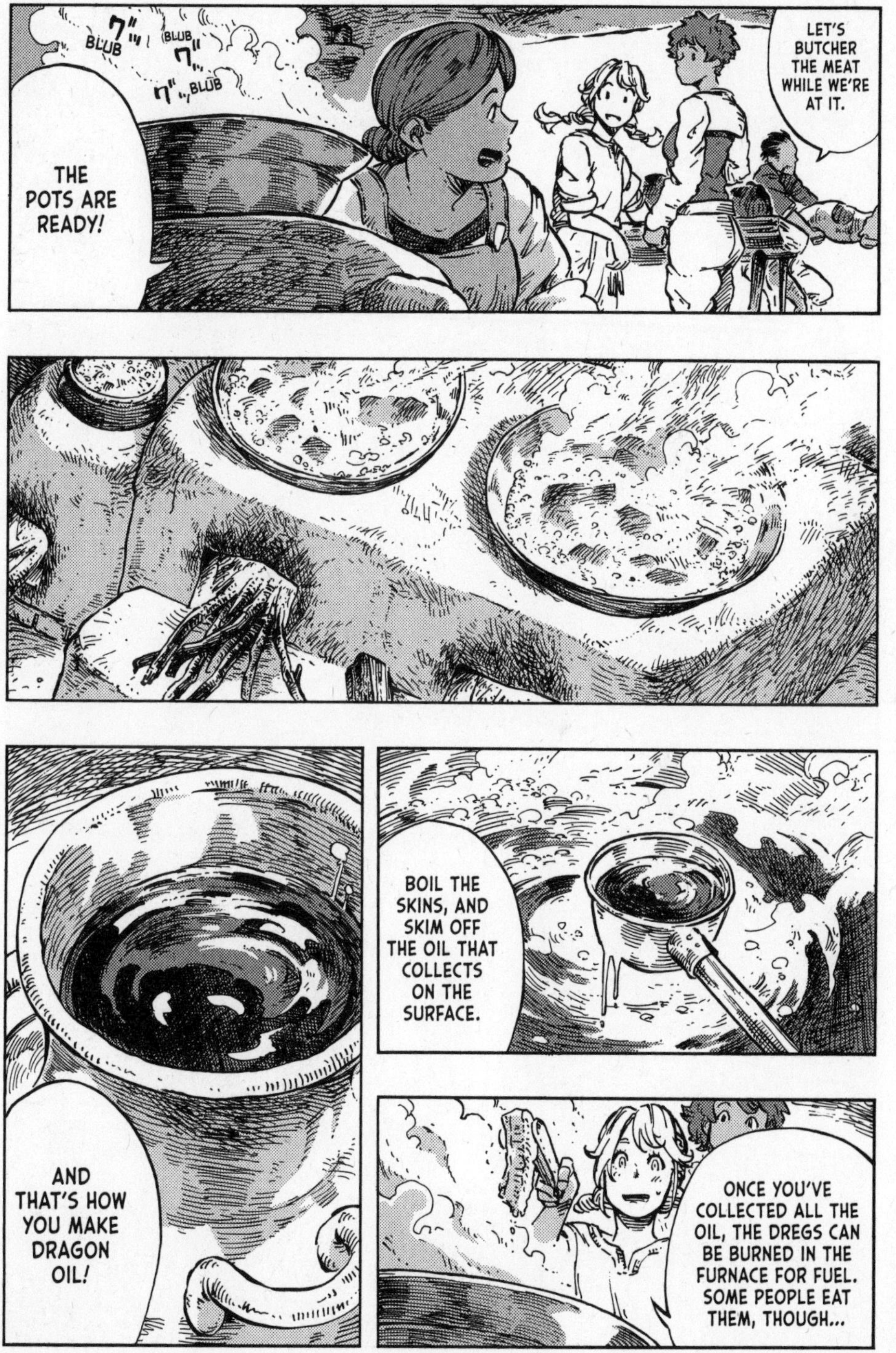
LET'S BUTCHER THE MEAT WHILE WE'RE AT IT.
BLUB
BLUB
BLUB
THE POTS ARE READY!
BOIL THE SKINS, AND SKIM OFF THE OIL THAT COLLECTS ON THE SURFACE.
ONCE YOU'VE COLLECTED ALL THE OIL, THE DREGS CAN BE BURNED IN THE FURNACE FOR FUEL. SOME PEOPLE EAT THEM, THOUGH...
AND THAT'S HOW YOU MAKE DRAGON OIL!

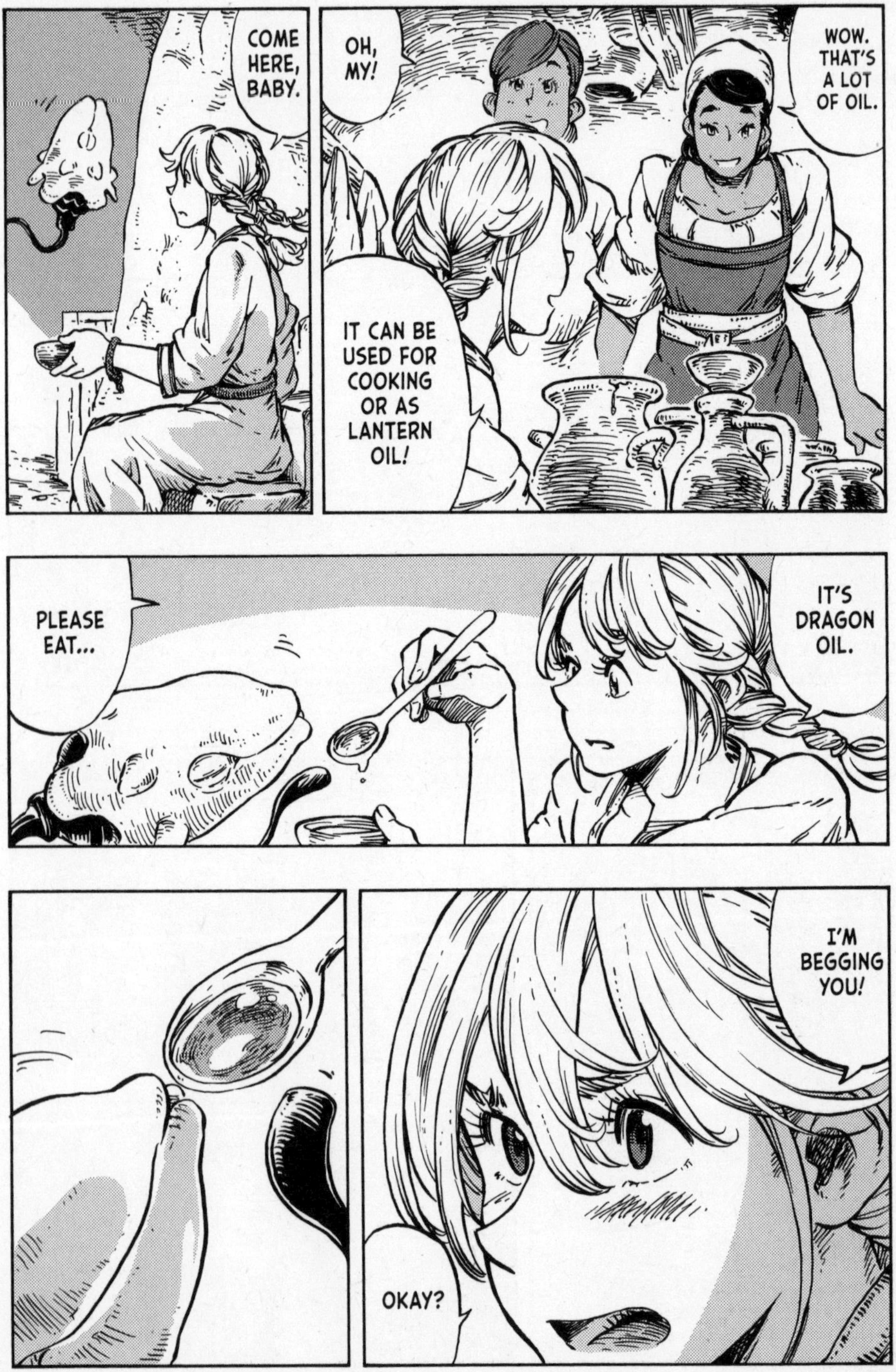
WOW. THAT'S A LOT OF OIL.
OH, MY!
IT CAN BE USED FOR COOKING OR AS LANTERN OIL!
COME HERE, BABY.
IT'S DRAGON OIL.
PLEASE EAT...
I'M BEGGING YOU!
OKAY?

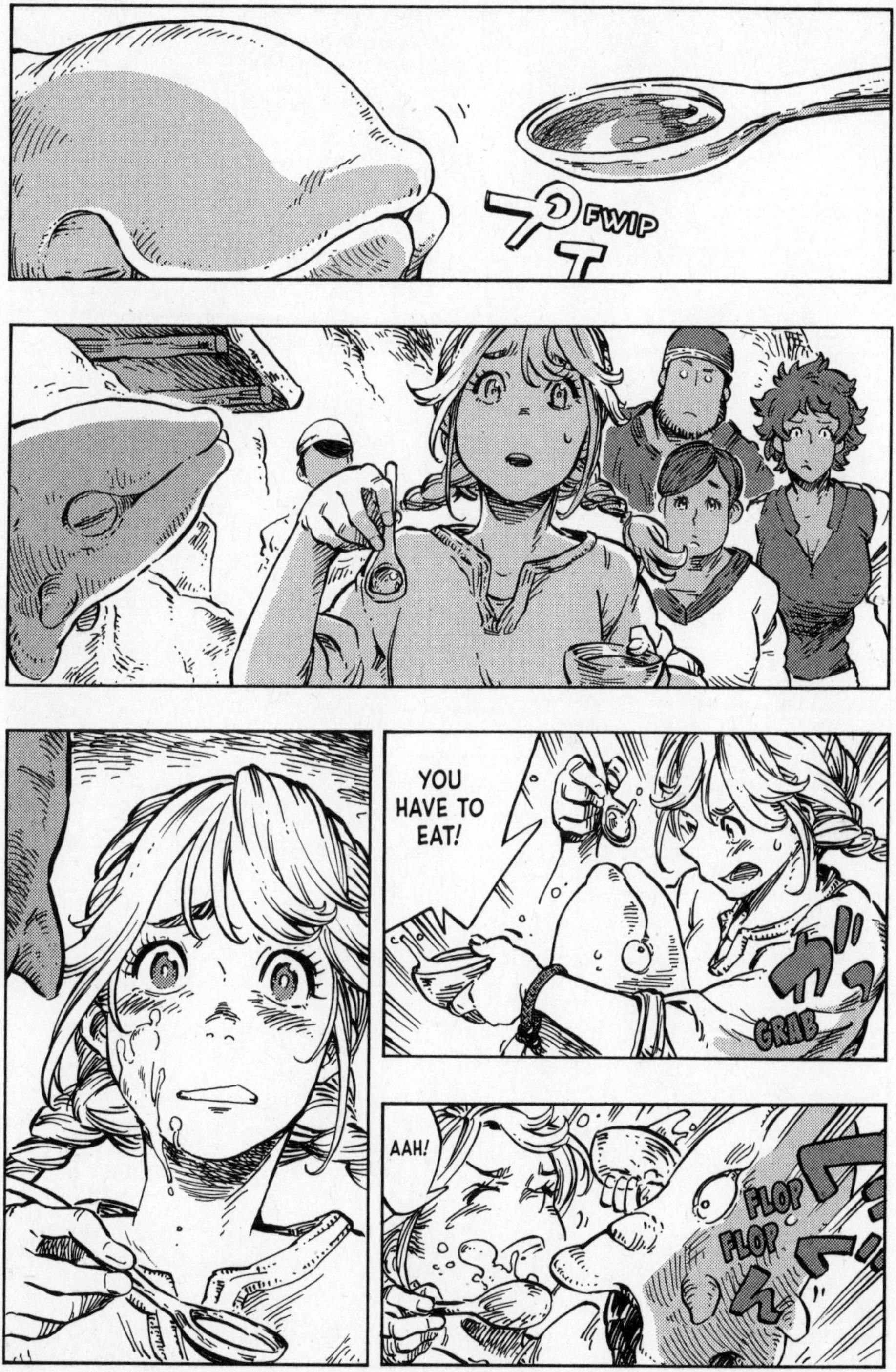
FWIP
YOU HAVE TO EAT!
GRAB
AAH!
FLOP
FLOP

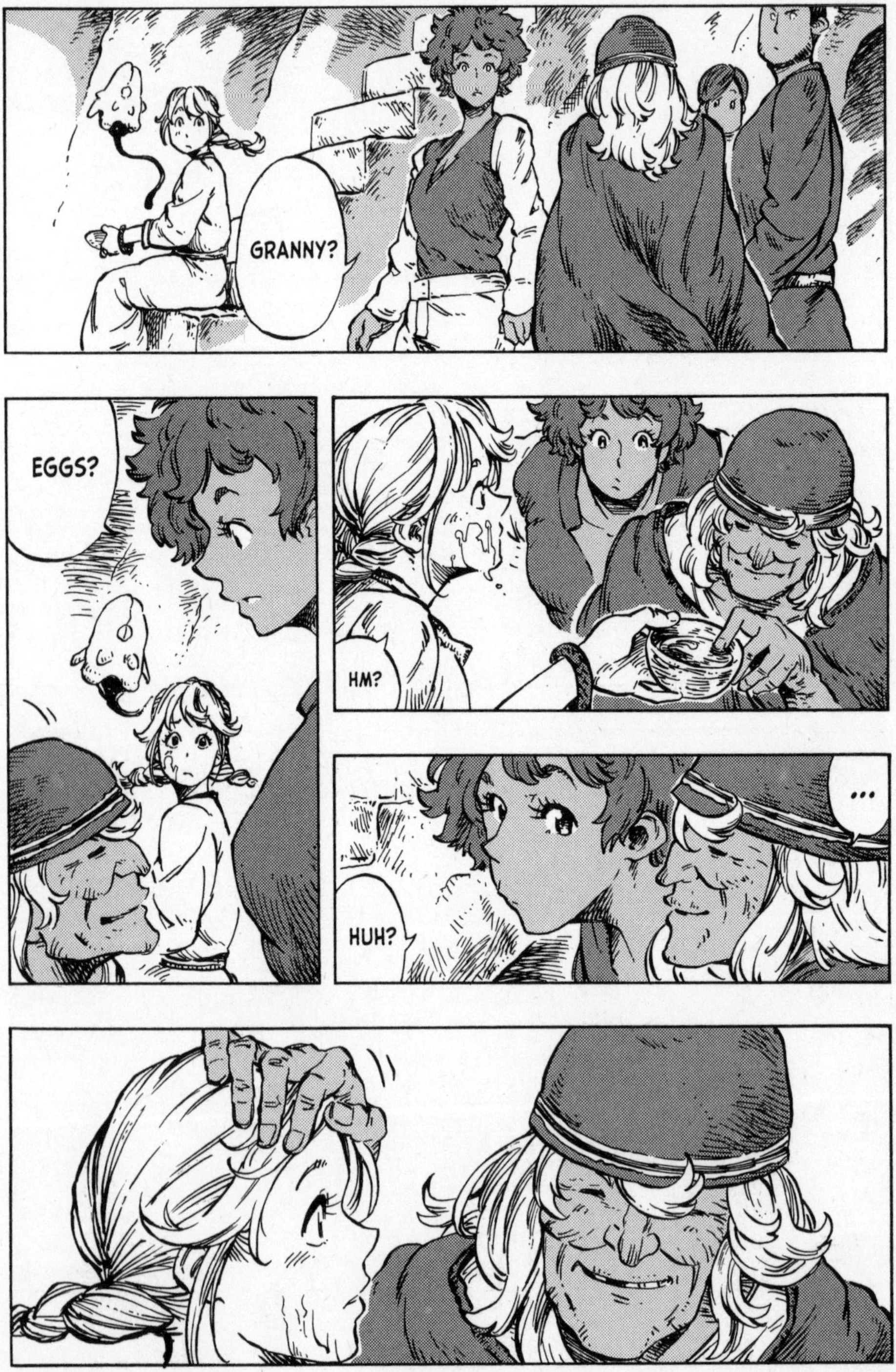
GRANNY?
HM?
...
HUH?
EGGS?

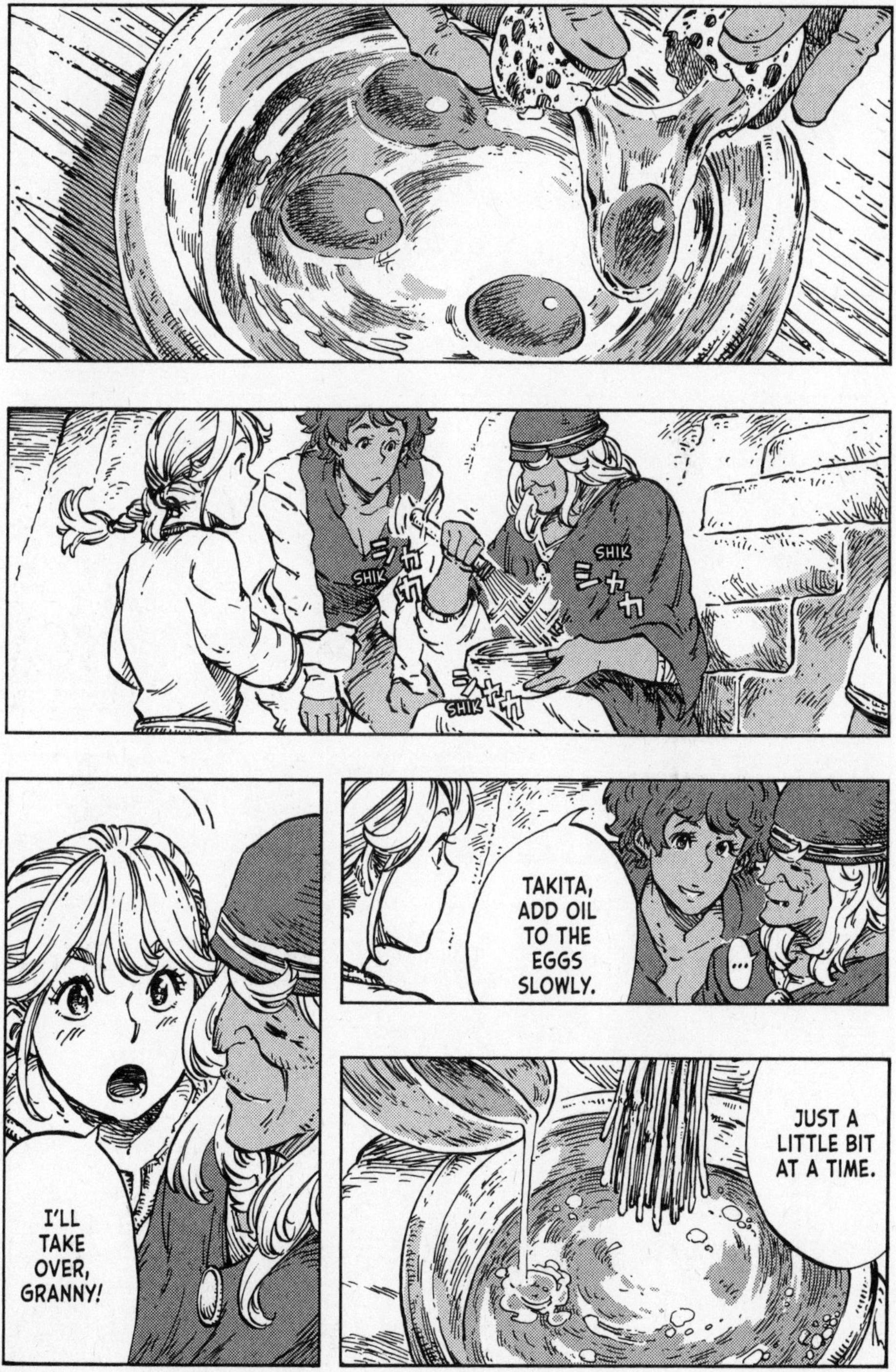
SHIK
SHIK
SHIK
TAKITA, ADD OIL TO THE EGGS SLOWLY.
...
JUST A LITTLE BIT AT A TIME.
I'LL TAKE OVER, GRANNY!

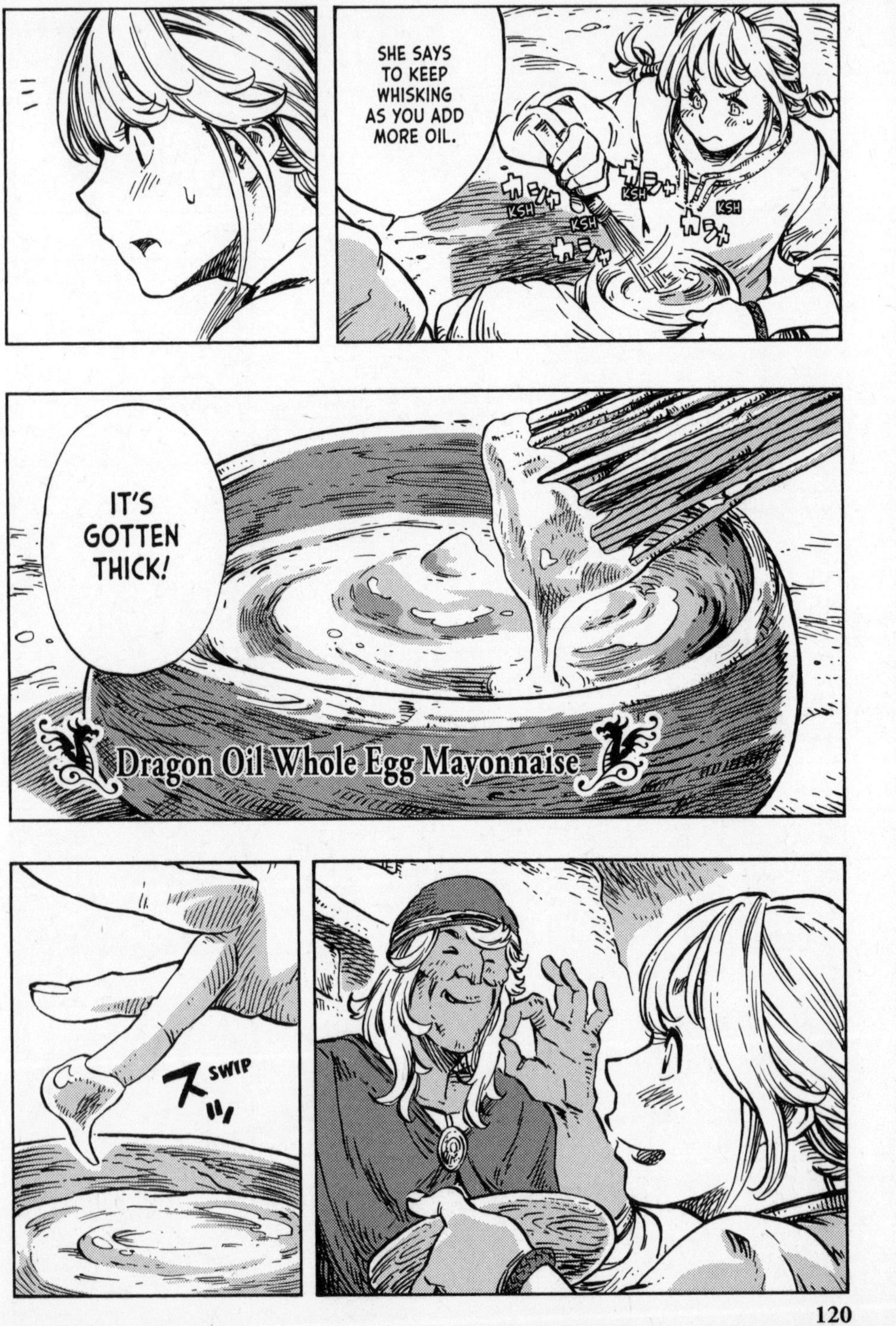
SHE SAYS TO KEEP WHISKING AS YOU ADD MORE OIL.
カシャ KSH
カシャ KSH
カシャ KSH
カシャ KSH
IT'S GOTTEN THICK!
Dragon Oil Whole Egg Mayonnaise
スッ SWIP

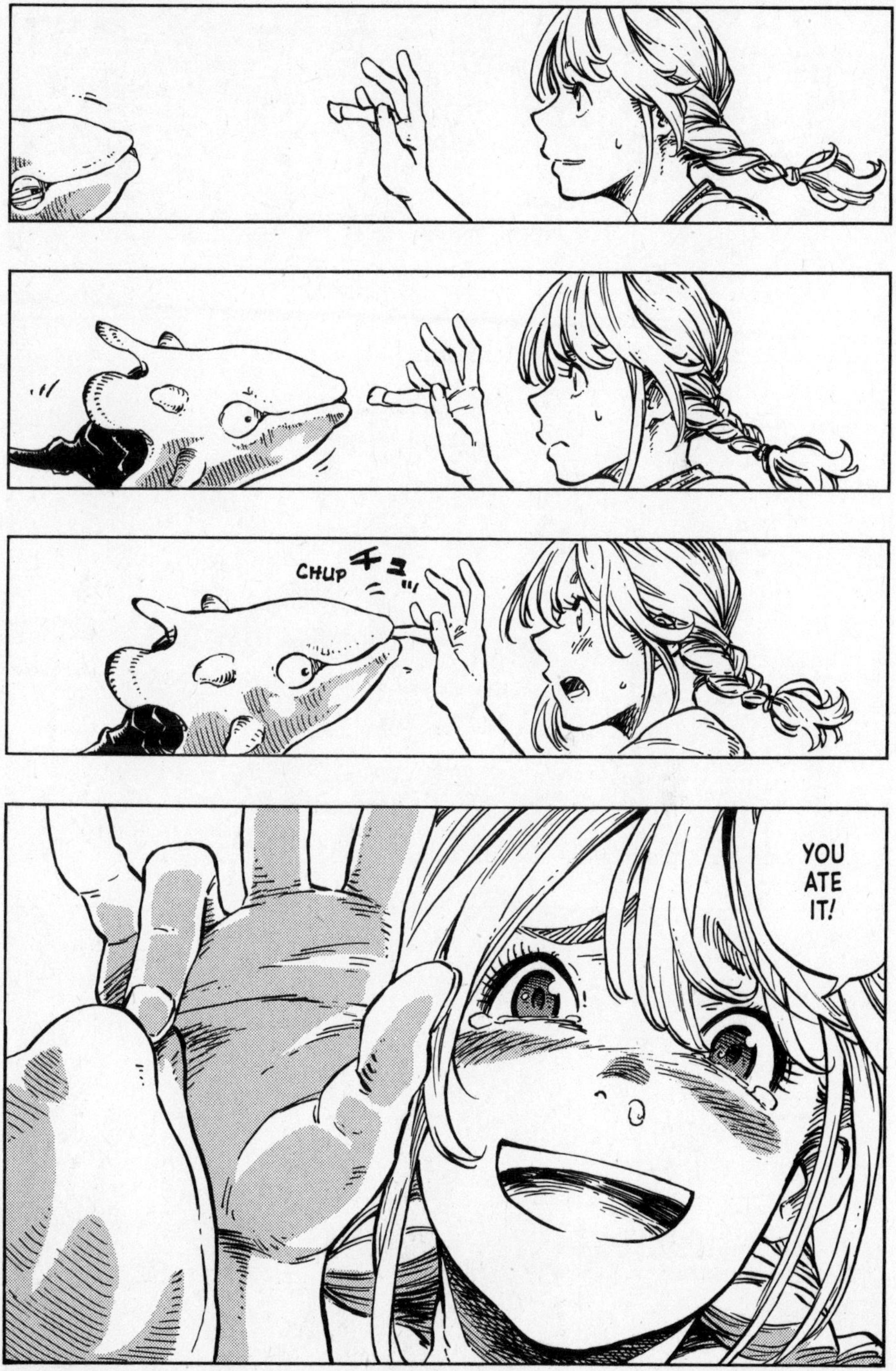
CHUP チュ
YOU ATE IT!

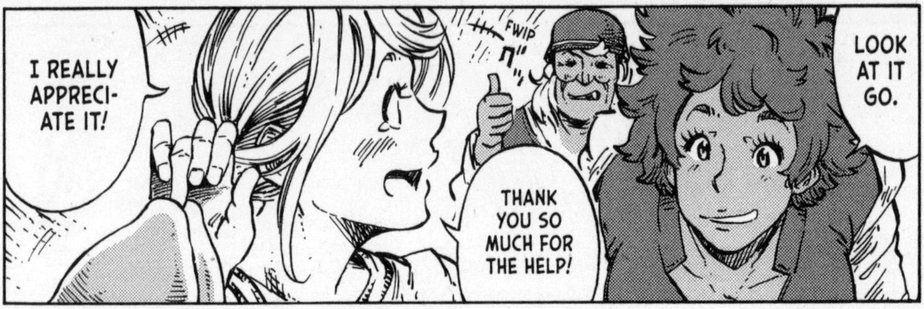
LOOK AT IT GO.
FWIP
THANK YOU SO MUCH FOR THE HELP!
I REALLY APPRECIATE IT!
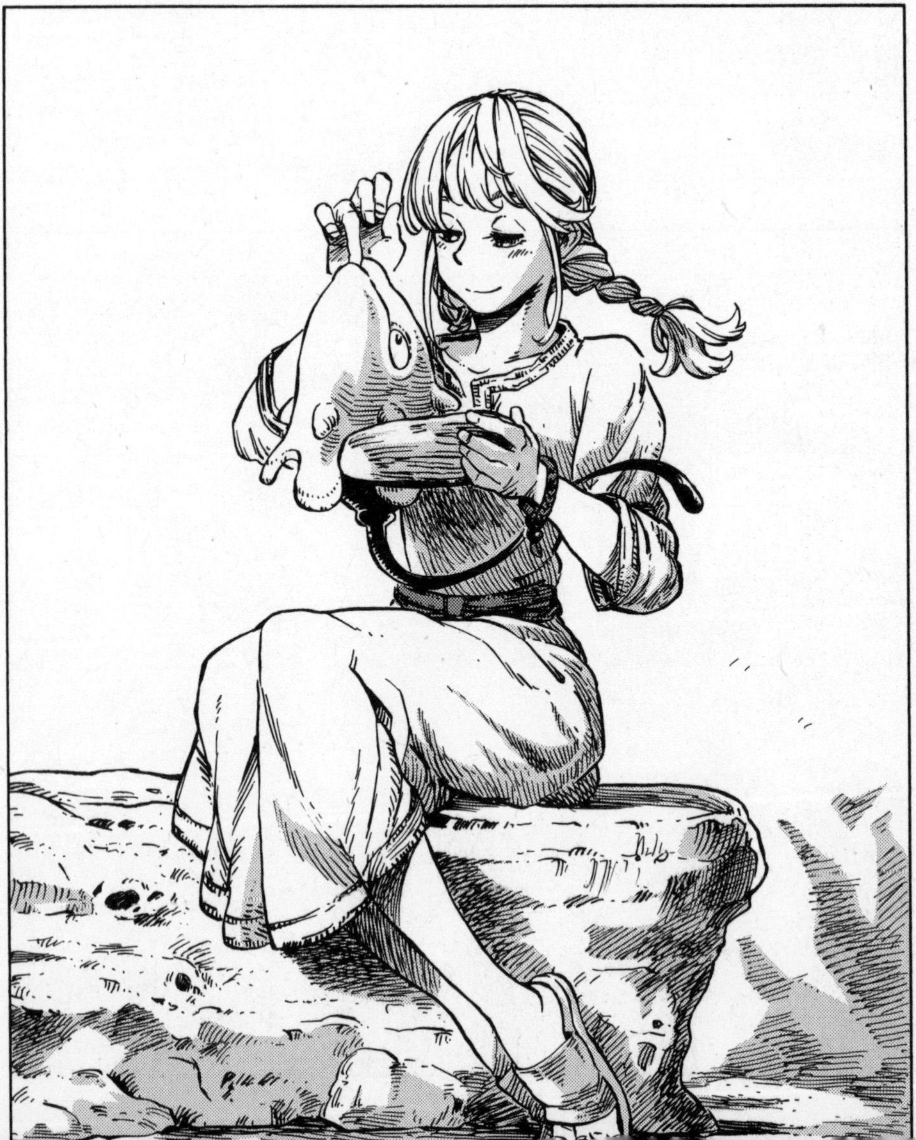

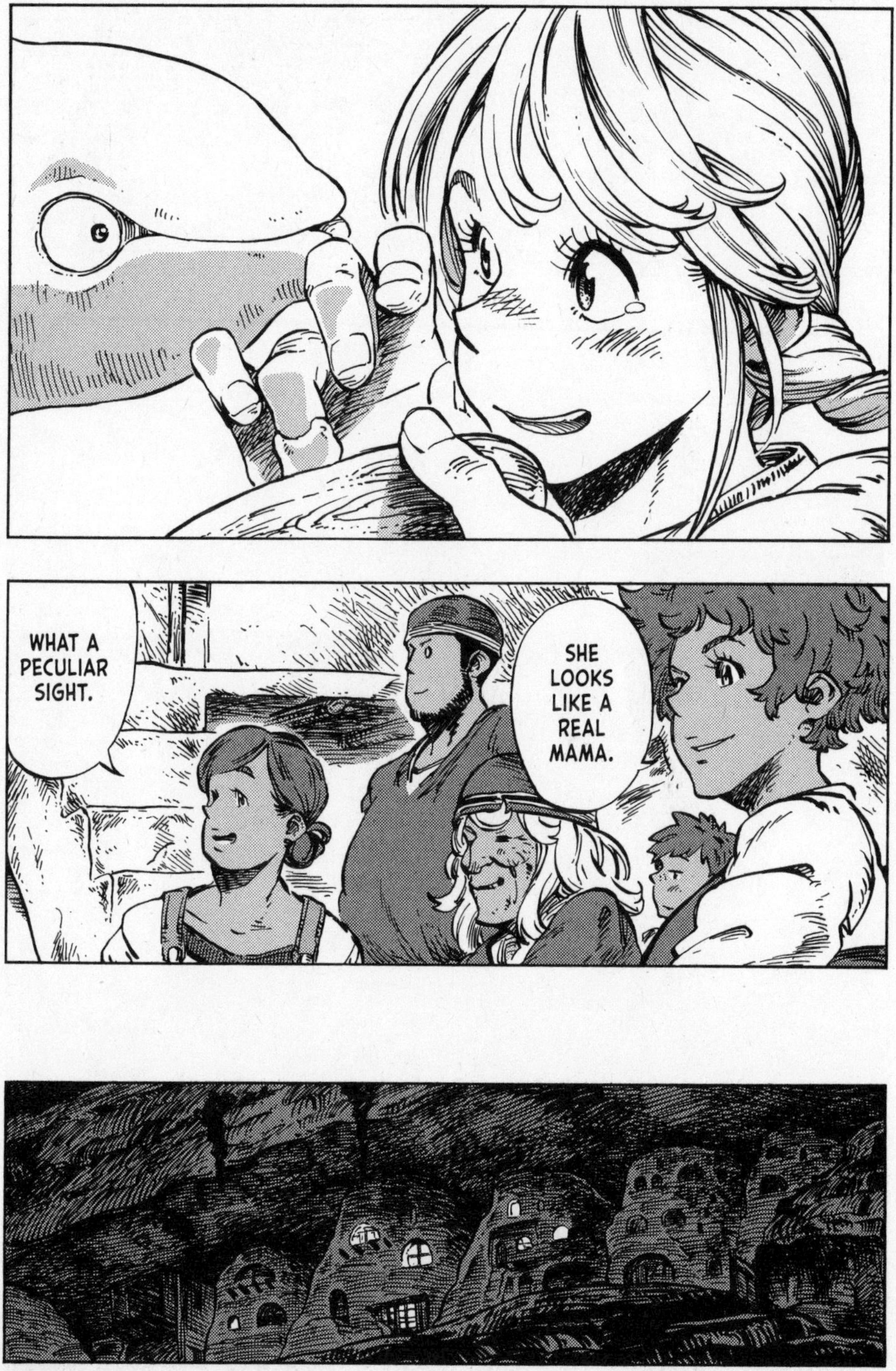
SHE LOOKS LIKE A REAL MAMA.
WHAT A PECULIAR SIGHT.

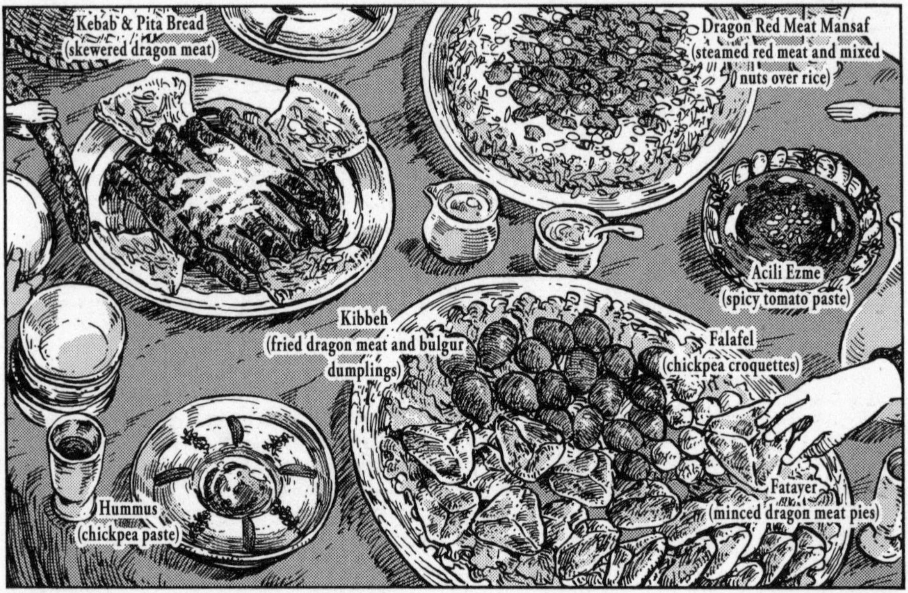
Dragon Red Meat Mansaf
(steamed red meat and mixed nuts over rice)
Kebab & Pita Bread
(skewered dragon meat)
Acili Ezme
(spicy tomato paste)
Falafel
(chickpea croquettes)
Kibbeh
(fried dragon meat and bulgur dumplings)
Fatayer
(minced dragon meat pies)
Hummus
(chickpea paste)

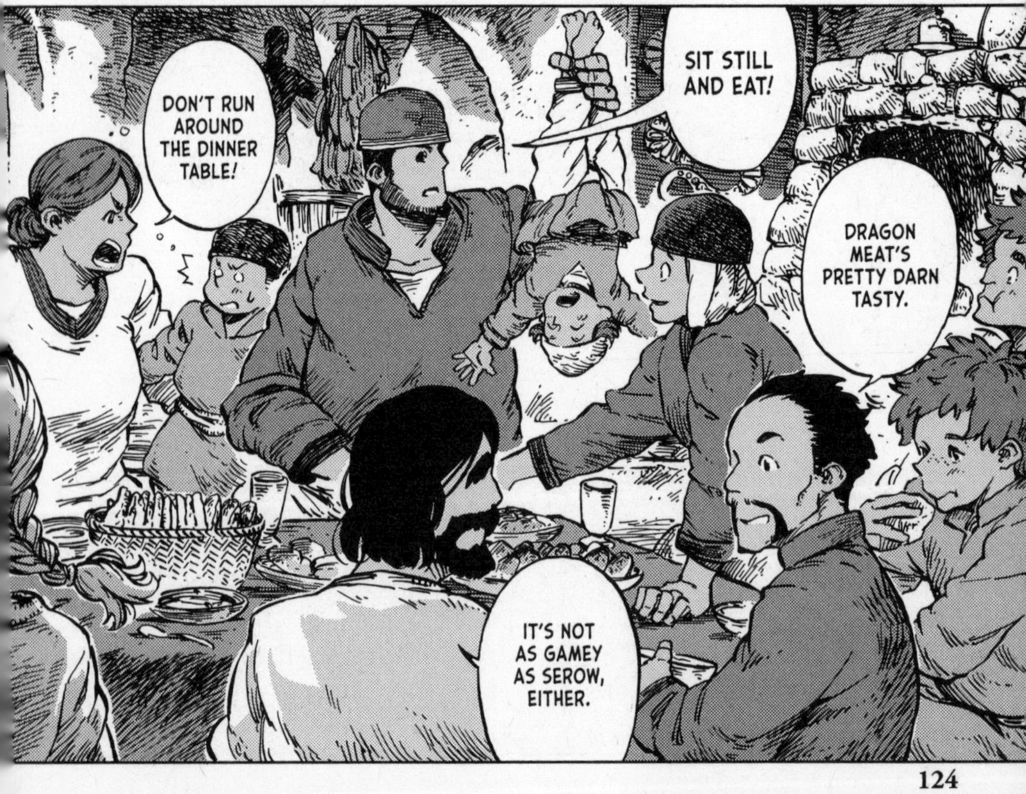
SIT STILL AND EAT!
DON'T RUN AROUND THE DINNER TABLE!
DRAGON MEAT'S PRETTY DARN TASTY.
IT'S NOT AS GAMEY AS SEROW, EITHER.

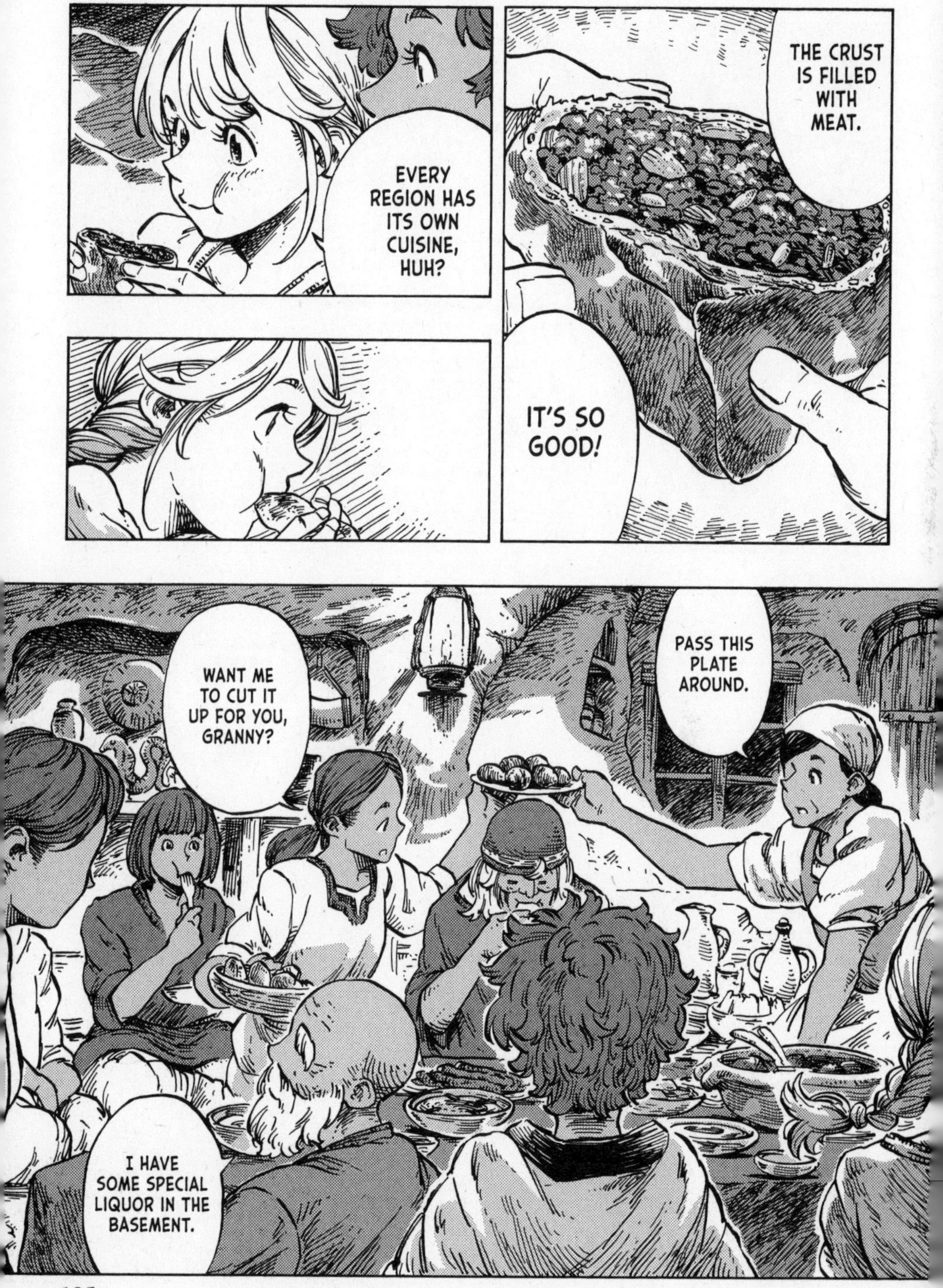
THE CRUST IS FILLED WITH MEAT.
IT'S SO GOOD!
EVERY REGION HAS ITS OWN CUISINE, HUH?
PASS THIS PLATE AROUND.
WANT ME TO CUT IT UP FOR YOU, GRANNY?
I HAVE SOME SPECIAL LIQUOR IN THE BASEMENT.

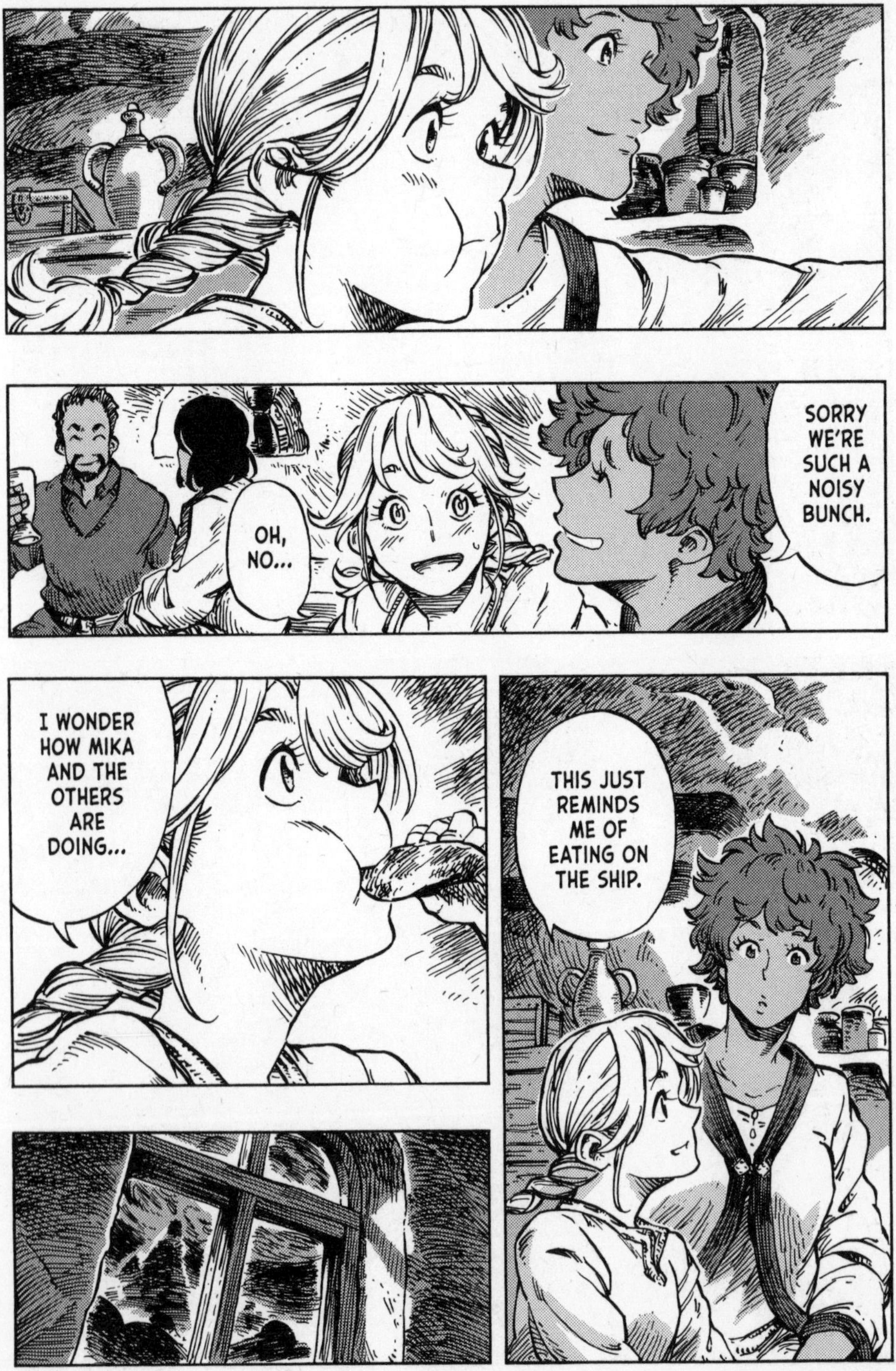
SORRY WE'RE SUCH A NOISY BUNCH.
OH, NO...
THIS JUST REMINDS ME OF EATING ON THE SHIP.
I WONDER HOW MIKA AND THE OTHERS ARE DOING...

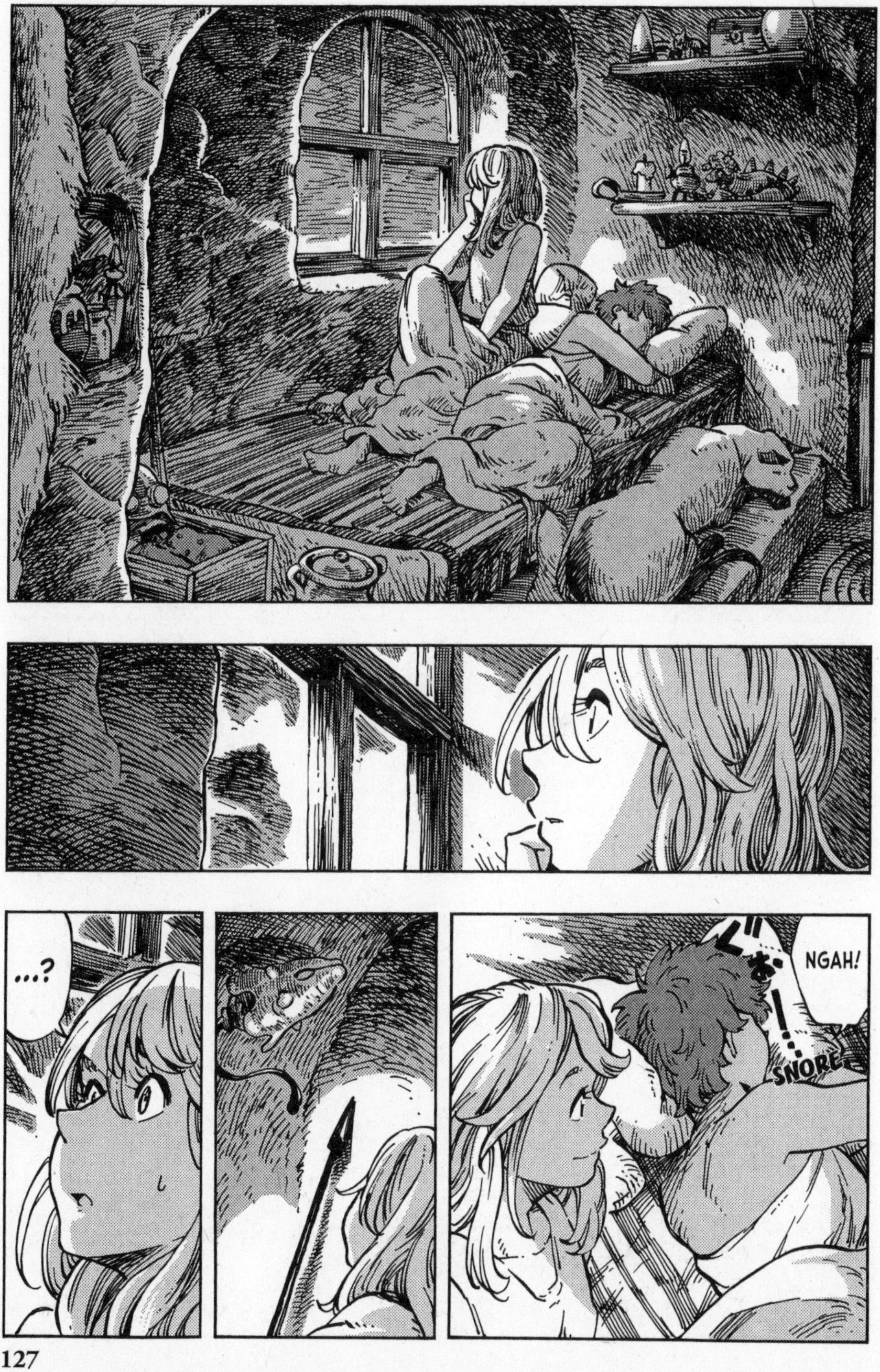
NGAH!
SNORE
...?

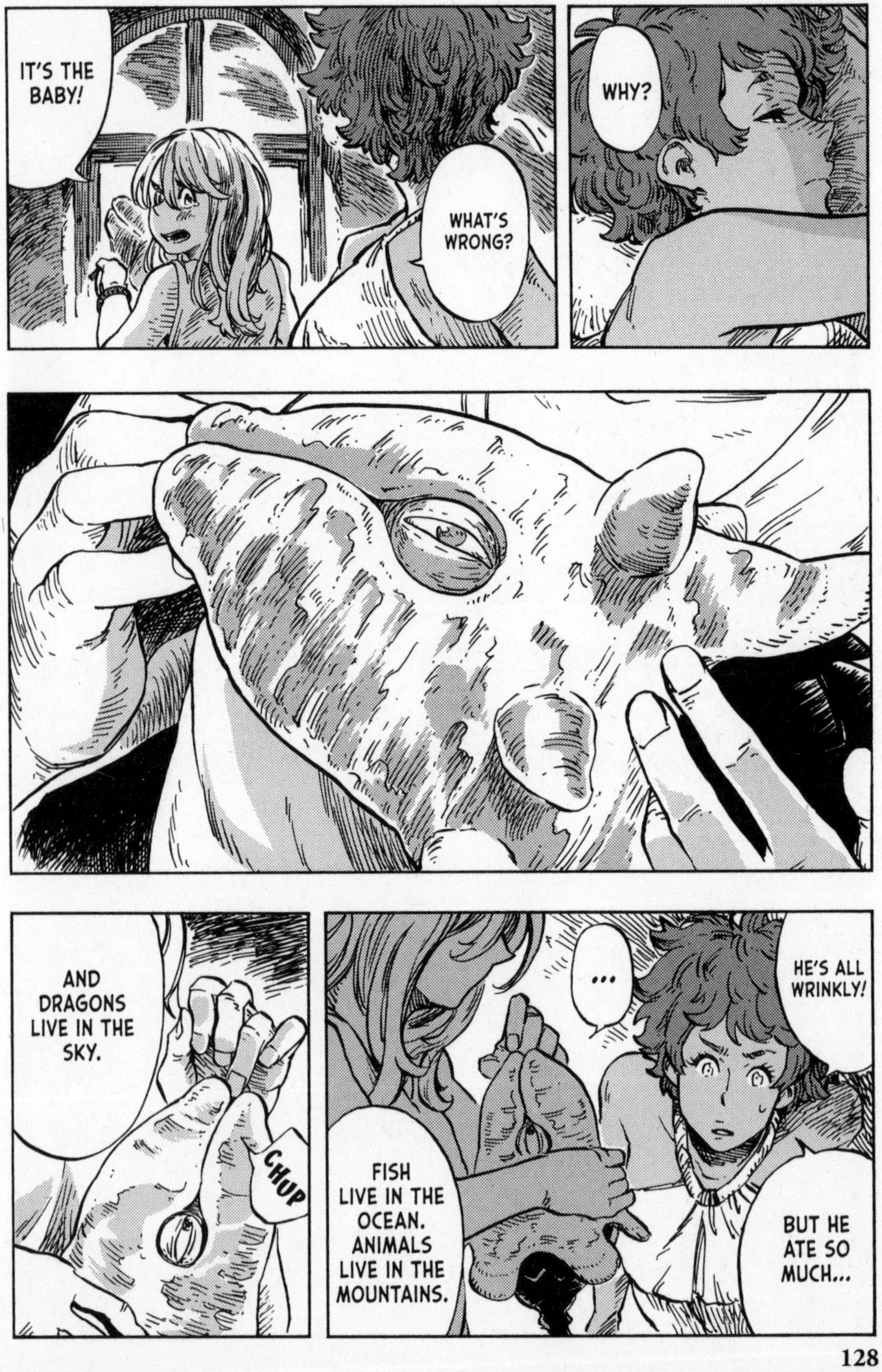
WHY?
WHAT'S WRONG?
IT'S THE BABY!
HE'S ALL WRINKLY!
...
BUT HE ATE SO MUCH...
FISH LIVE IN THE OCEAN. ANIMALS LIVE IN THE MOUNTAINS.
AND DRAGONS LIVE IN THE SKY.
CHUP

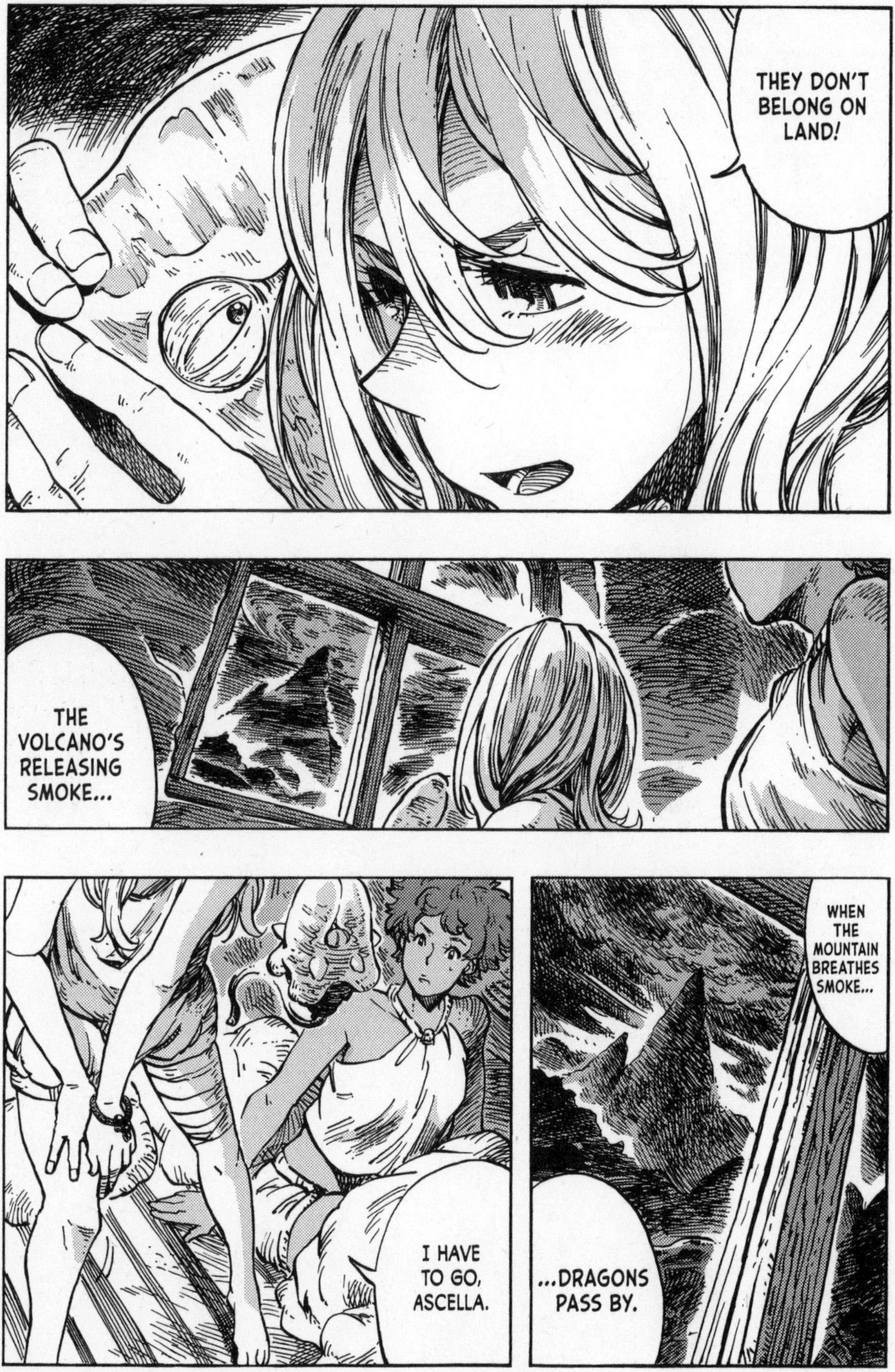
THEY DON'T BELONG ON LAND!
THE VOLCANO'S RELEASING SMOKE...
WHEN THE MOUNTAIN BREATHES SMOKE...
...DRAGONS PASS BY.
I HAVE TO GO, ASCELLA.

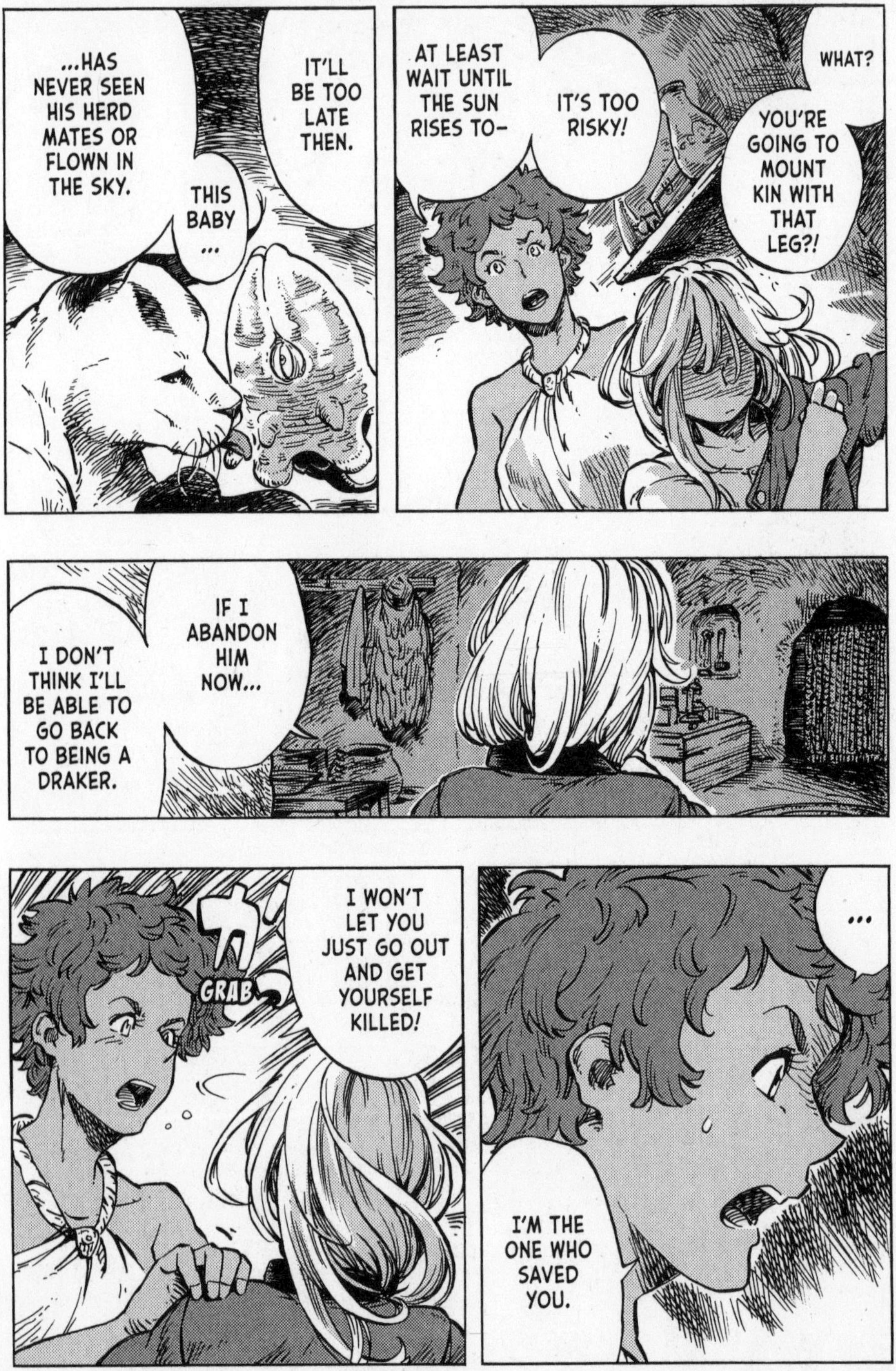
WHAT?
YOU'RE GOING TO MOUNT KIN WITH THAT LEG?!
IT'S TOO RISKY!
AT LEAST WAIT UNTIL THE SUN RISES TO–
IT'LL BE TOO LATE THEN.
THIS BABY ...
...HAS NEVER SEEN HIS HERD MATES OR FLOWN IN THE SKY.
IF I ABANDON HIM NOW...
I DON'T THINK I'LL BE ABLE TO GO BACK TO BEING A DRAKER.
...
I'M THE ONE WHO SAVED YOU.
I WON'T LET YOU JUST GO OUT AND GET YOURSELF KILLED!
GRAB

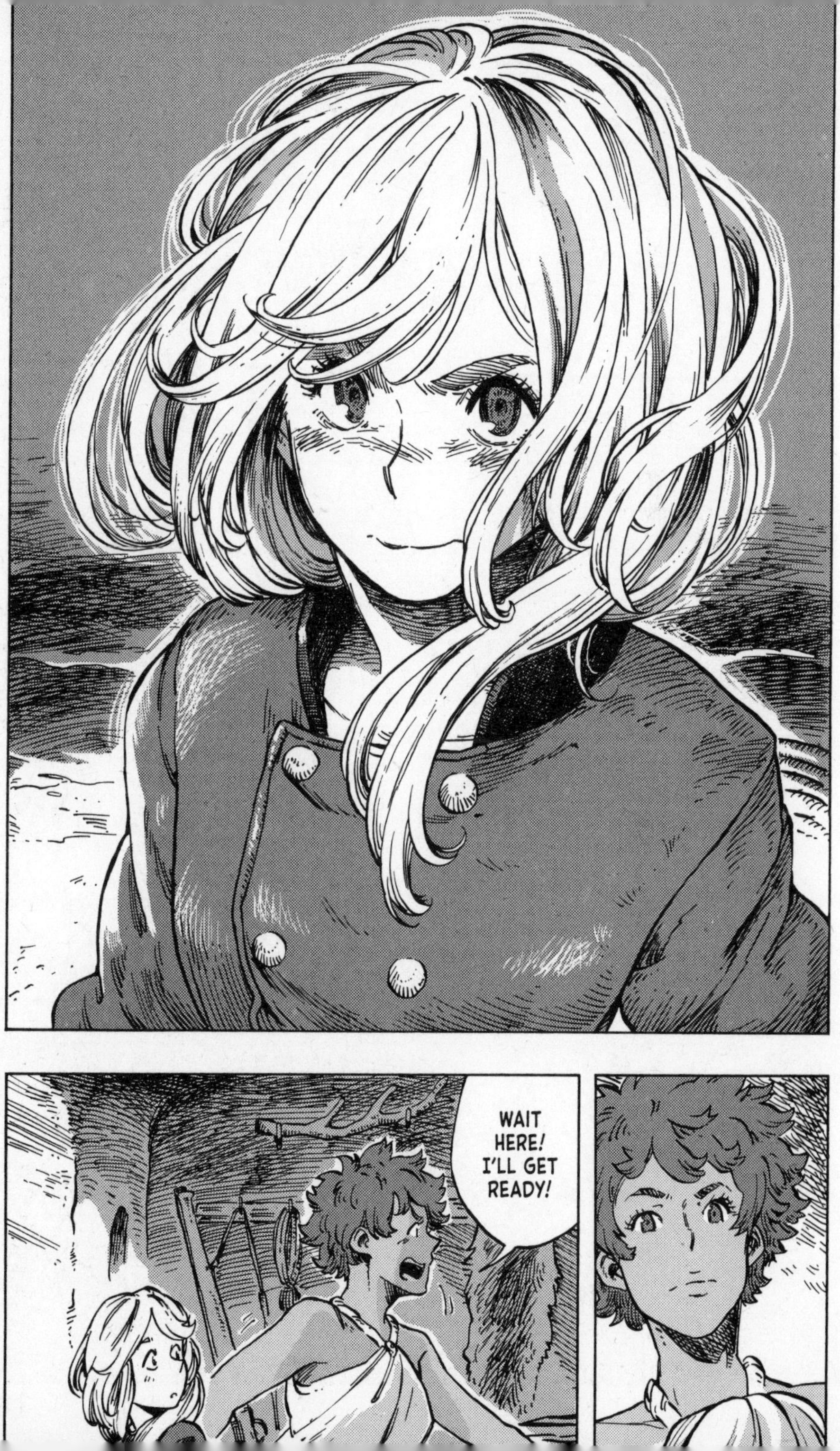
WAIT HERE! I'LL GET READY!

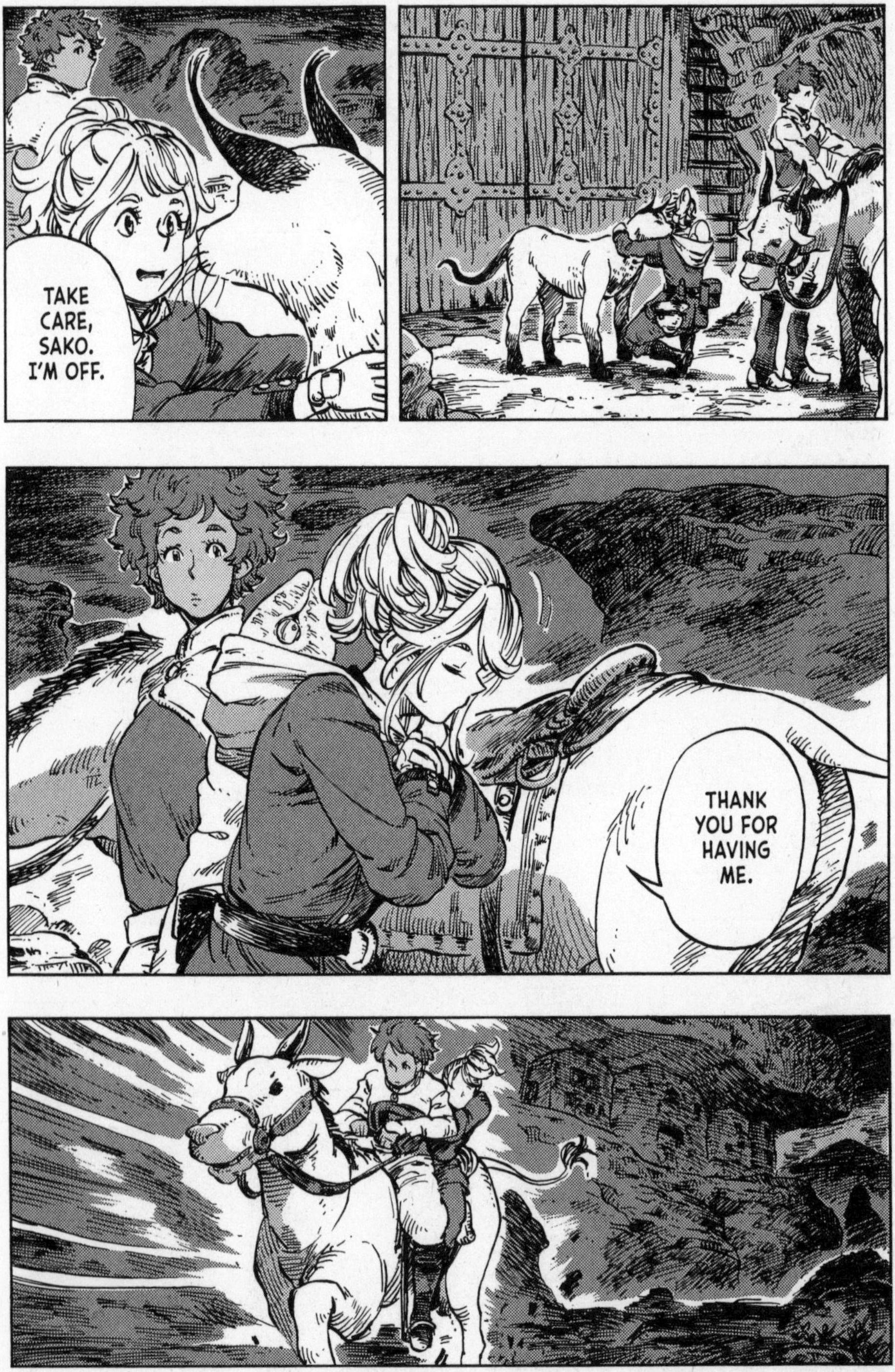
TAKE CARE, SAKO. I'M OFF.
THANK YOU FOR HAVING ME.

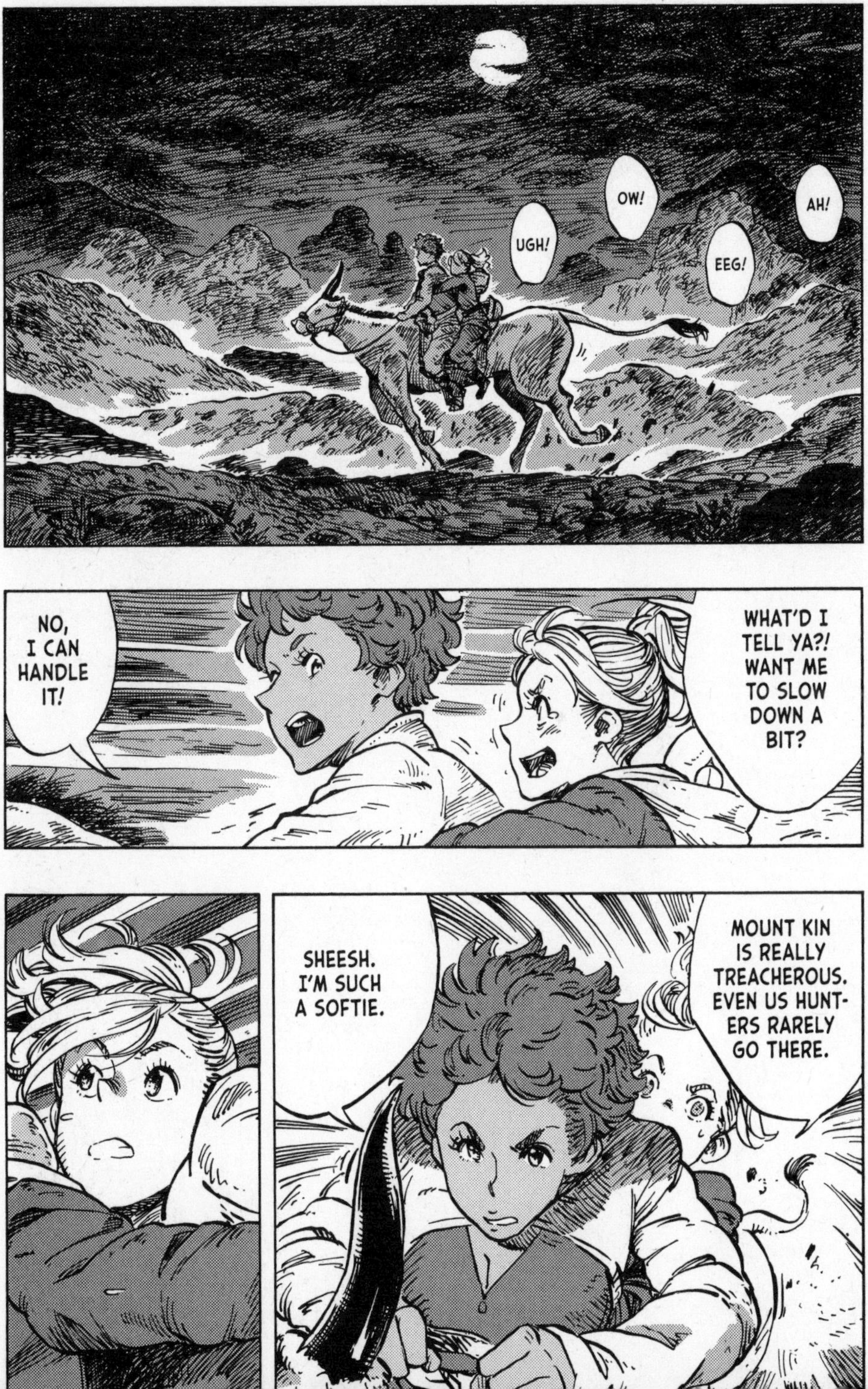
AH!
EEG!
OW!
UGH!
WHAT'D I TELL YA?! WANT ME TO SLOW DOWN A BIT?
NO, I CAN HANDLE IT!
MOUNT KIN IS REALLY TREACHEROUS. EVEN US HUNTERS RARELY GO THERE.
SHEESH. I'M SUCH A SOFTIE.

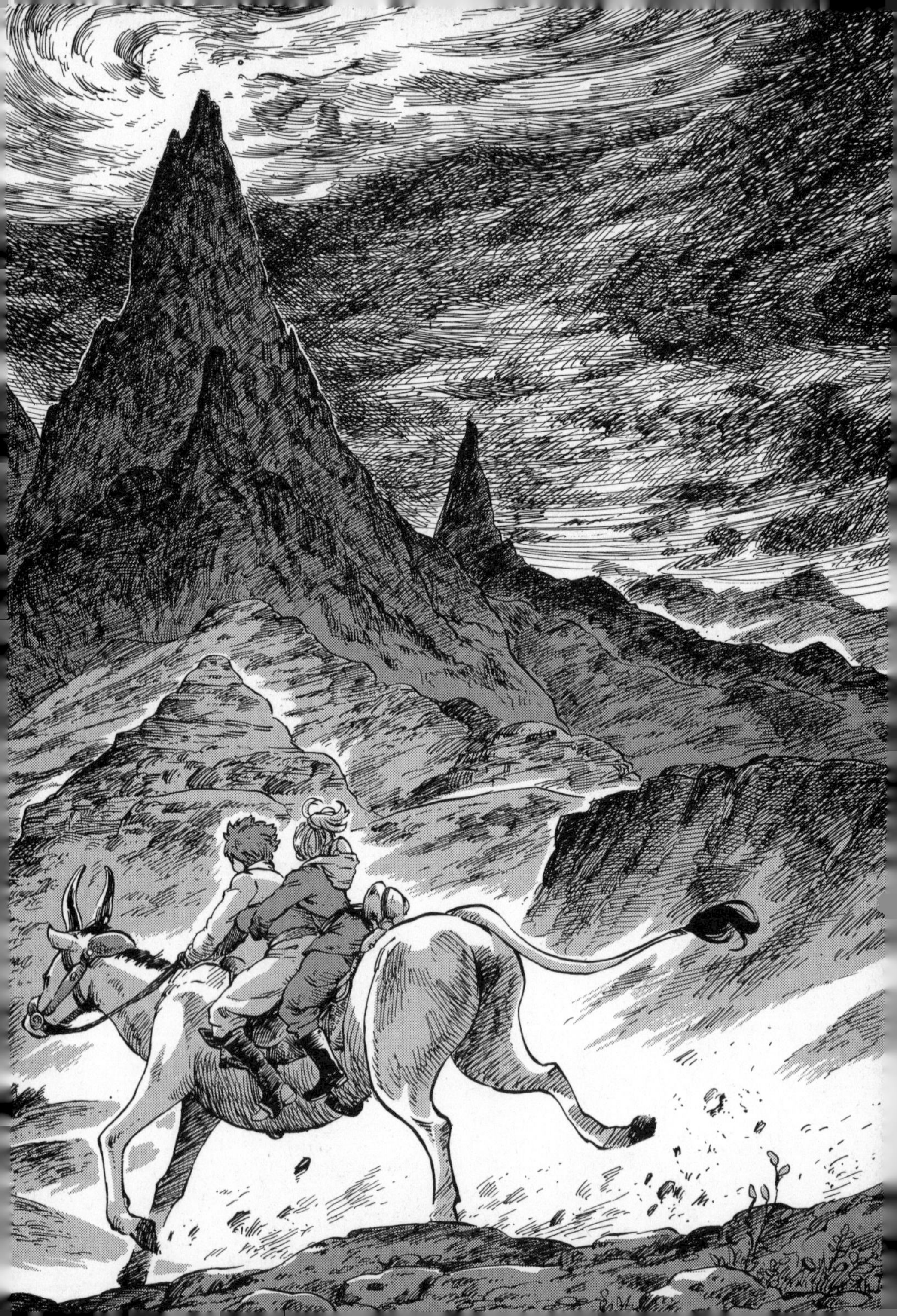

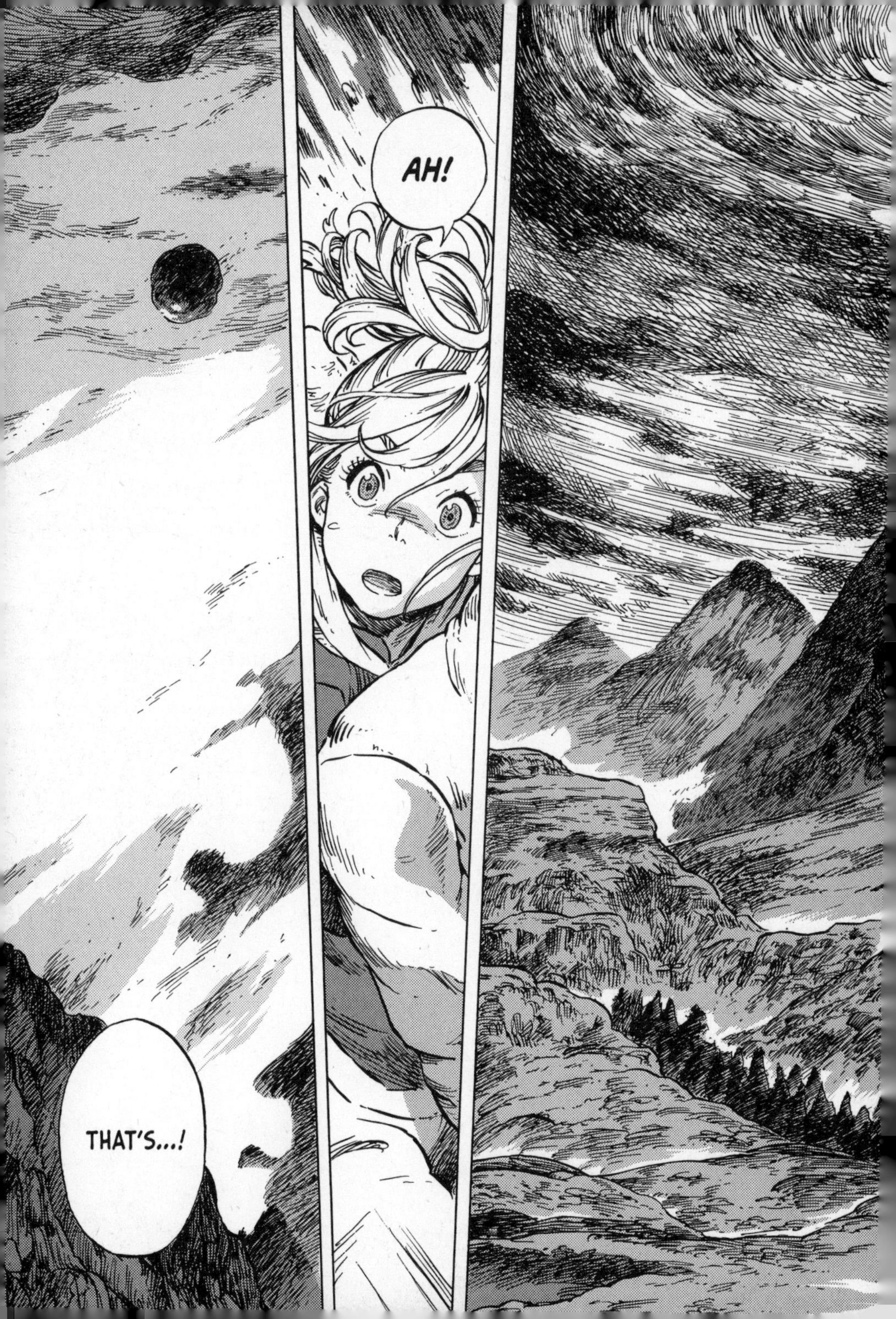
AH!
THAT'S...!

Dragon Oil Whole Egg Mayonnaise

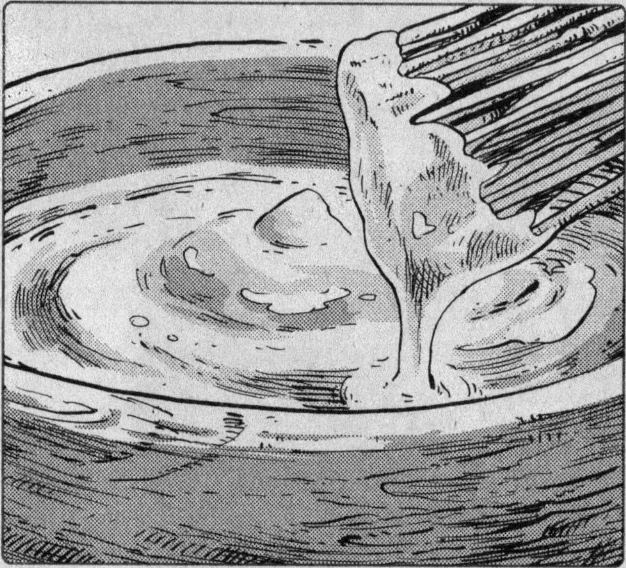

Ingredients

- ✦ 4 quail eggs
- ✦ 1 Tbsp Vinegar
- ✦ 1 tsp salt
- ✦ A pinch of pepper
- ✦ 120 ml dragon oil

01

Crack the eggs into a bowl with the vinegar and whisk until frothy.

02

Continue to whisk while slowly drizzling in dragon oil.

03

Once the mixture thickens, season with salt and pepper and it's done.

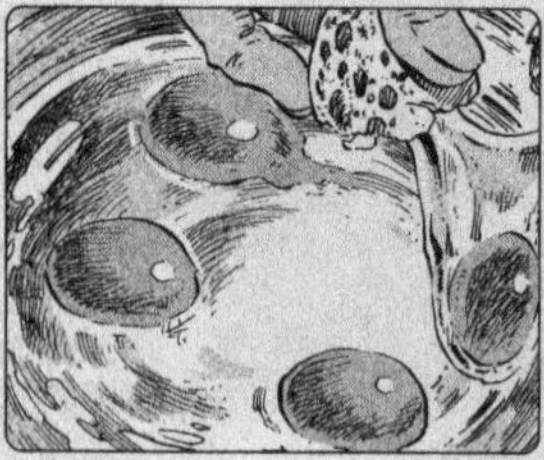

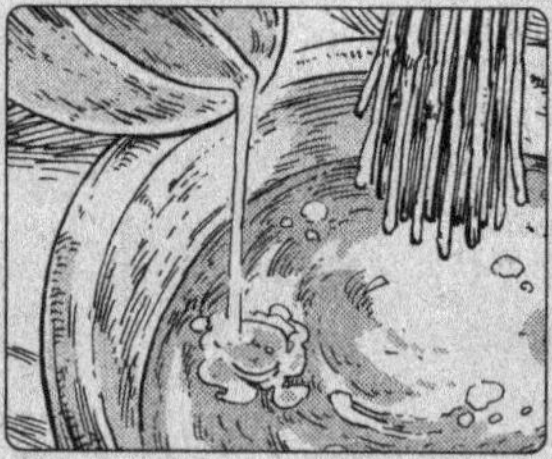

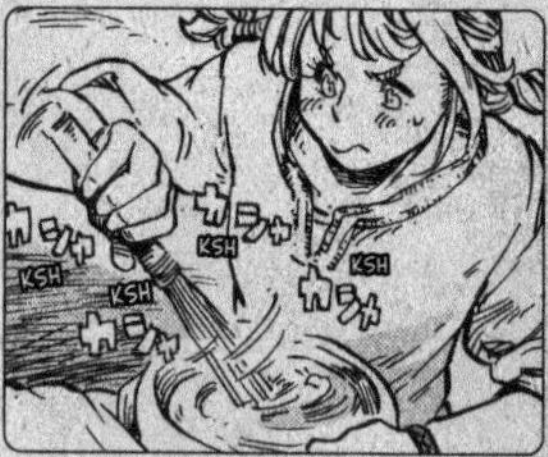
KSH
KSH
KSH
KSH

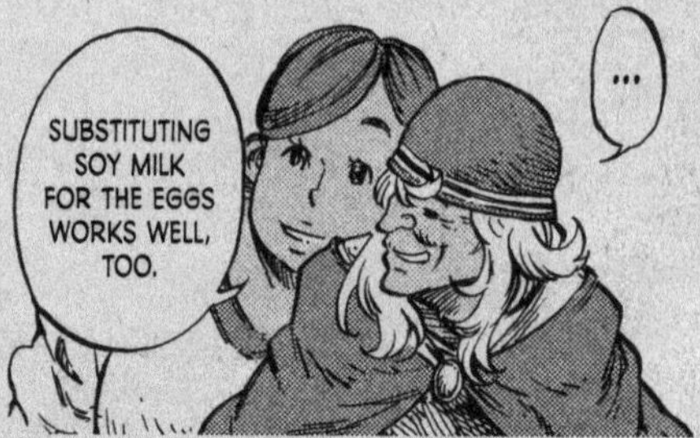
...
SUBSTITUTING SOY MILK FOR THE EGGS WORKS WELL, TOO.

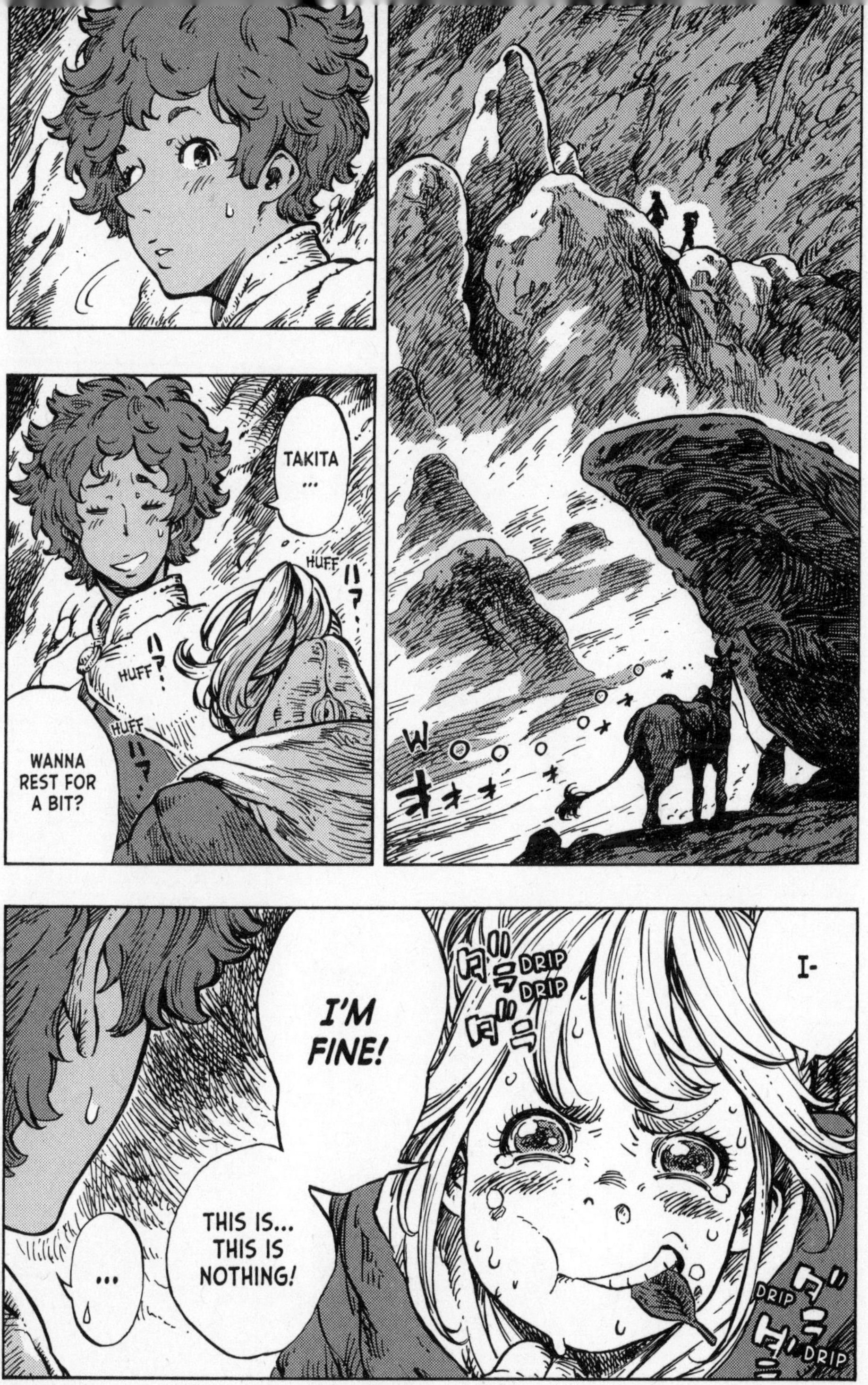
WOOOOO
TAKITA ...
HUFF
HUFF
HUFF
WANNA REST FOR A BIT?
I-
DRIP DRIP
I'M FINE!
DRIP DRIP
THIS IS... THIS IS NOTHING!
...

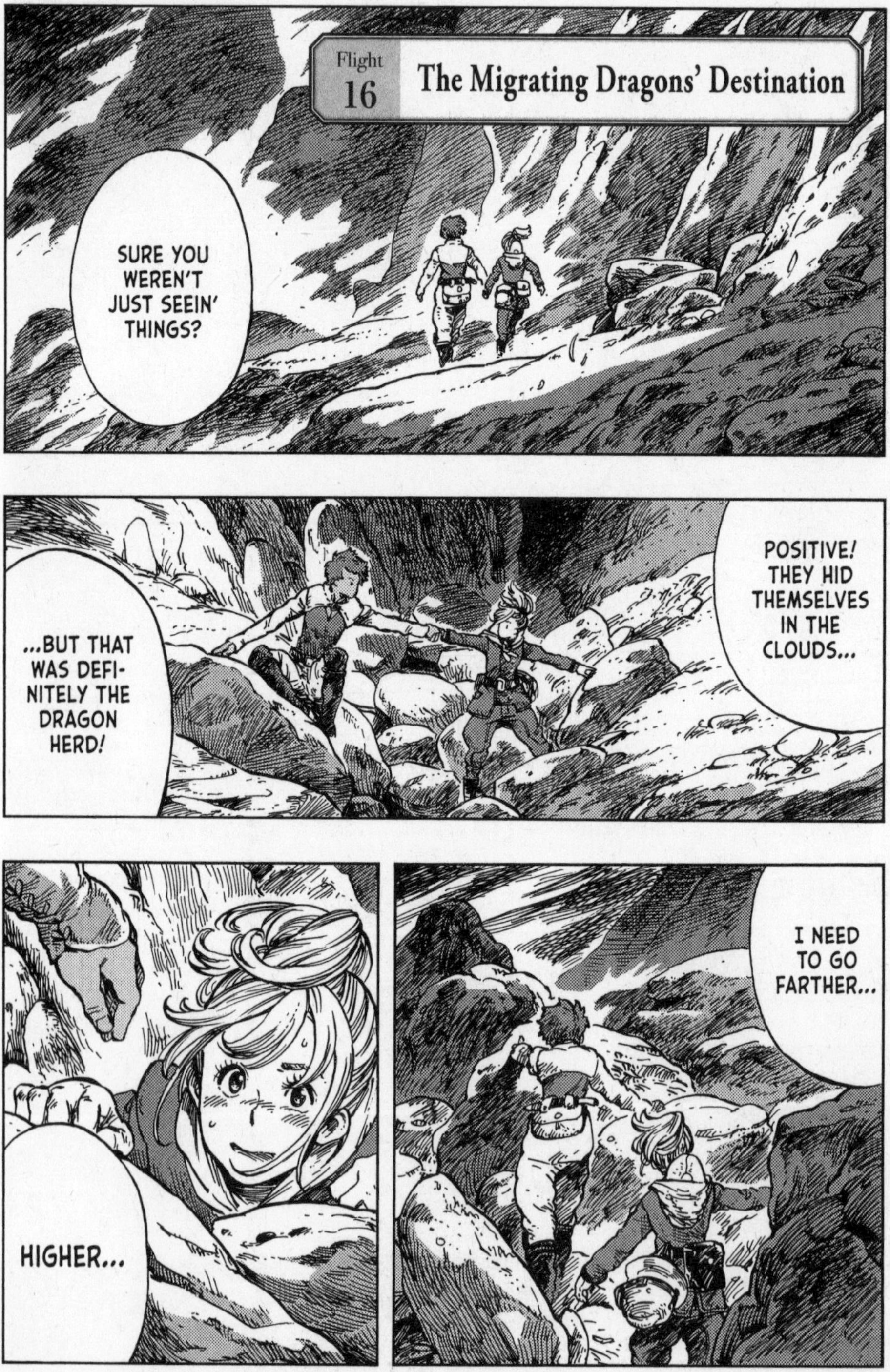
Flight 16
The Migrating Dragons' Destination
SURE YOU WEREN'T JUST SEEIN' THINGS?
POSITIVE! THEY HID THEMSELVES IN THE CLOUDS...
...BUT THAT WAS DEFI-NITELY THE DRAGON HERD!
I NEED TO GO FARTHER...
HIGHER...

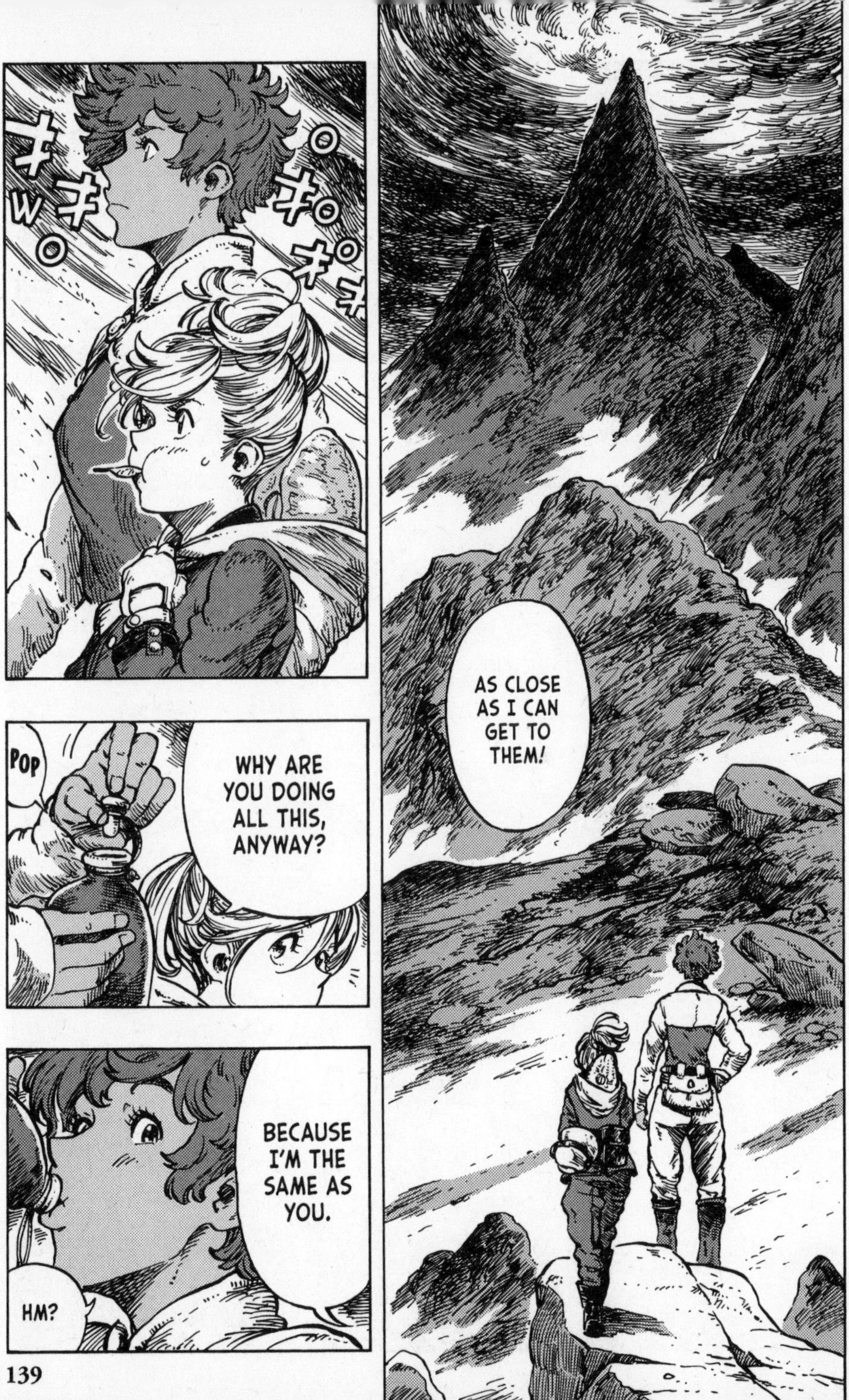
AS CLOSE AS I CAN GET TO THEM!
POP
WHY ARE YOU DOING ALL THIS, ANYWAY?
BECAUSE I'M THE SAME AS YOU.
HM?

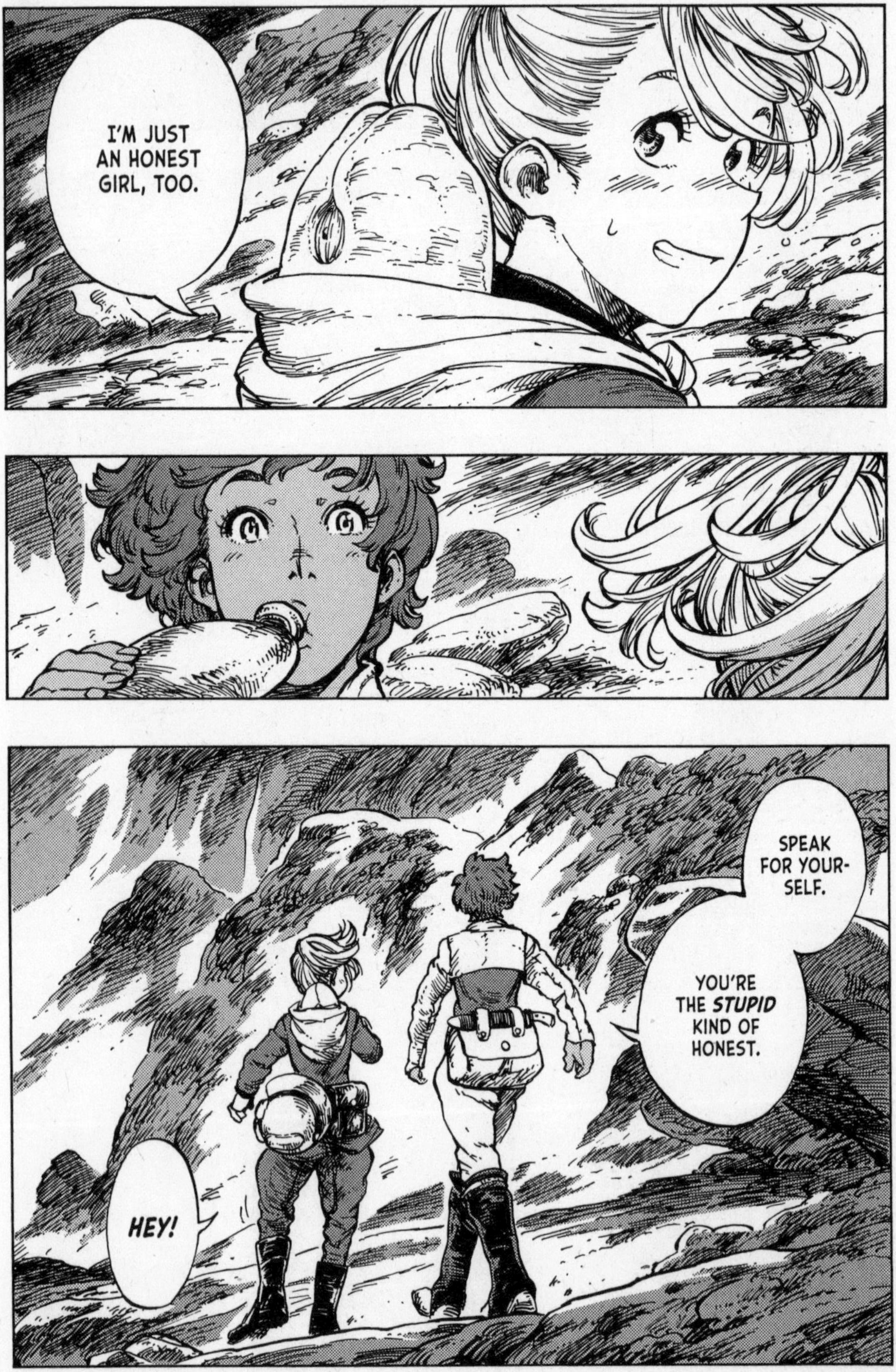
I'M JUST AN HONEST GIRL, TOO.
SPEAK FOR YOUR-SELF.
YOU'RE THE *STUPID* KIND OF HONEST.
HEY!

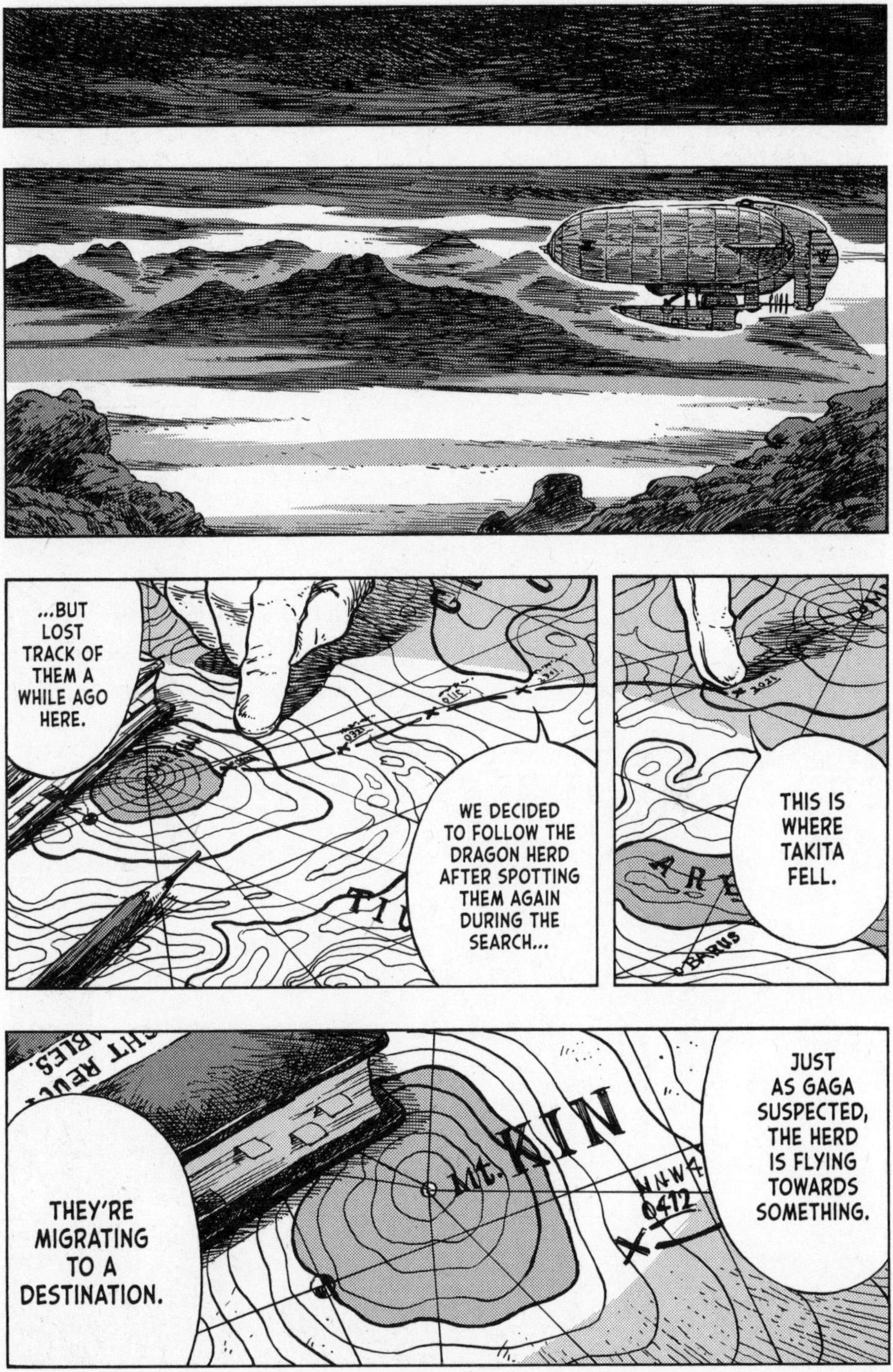
THIS IS WHERE TAKITA FELL.
BARUS
WE DECIDED TO FOLLOW THE DRAGON HERD AFTER SPOTTING THEM AGAIN DURING THE SEARCH...
...BUT LOST TRACK OF THEM A WHILE AGO HERE.
JUST AS GAGA SUSPECTED, THE HERD IS FLYING TOWARDS SOMETHING.
Mt. KIN
THEY'RE MIGRATING TO A DESTINATION.

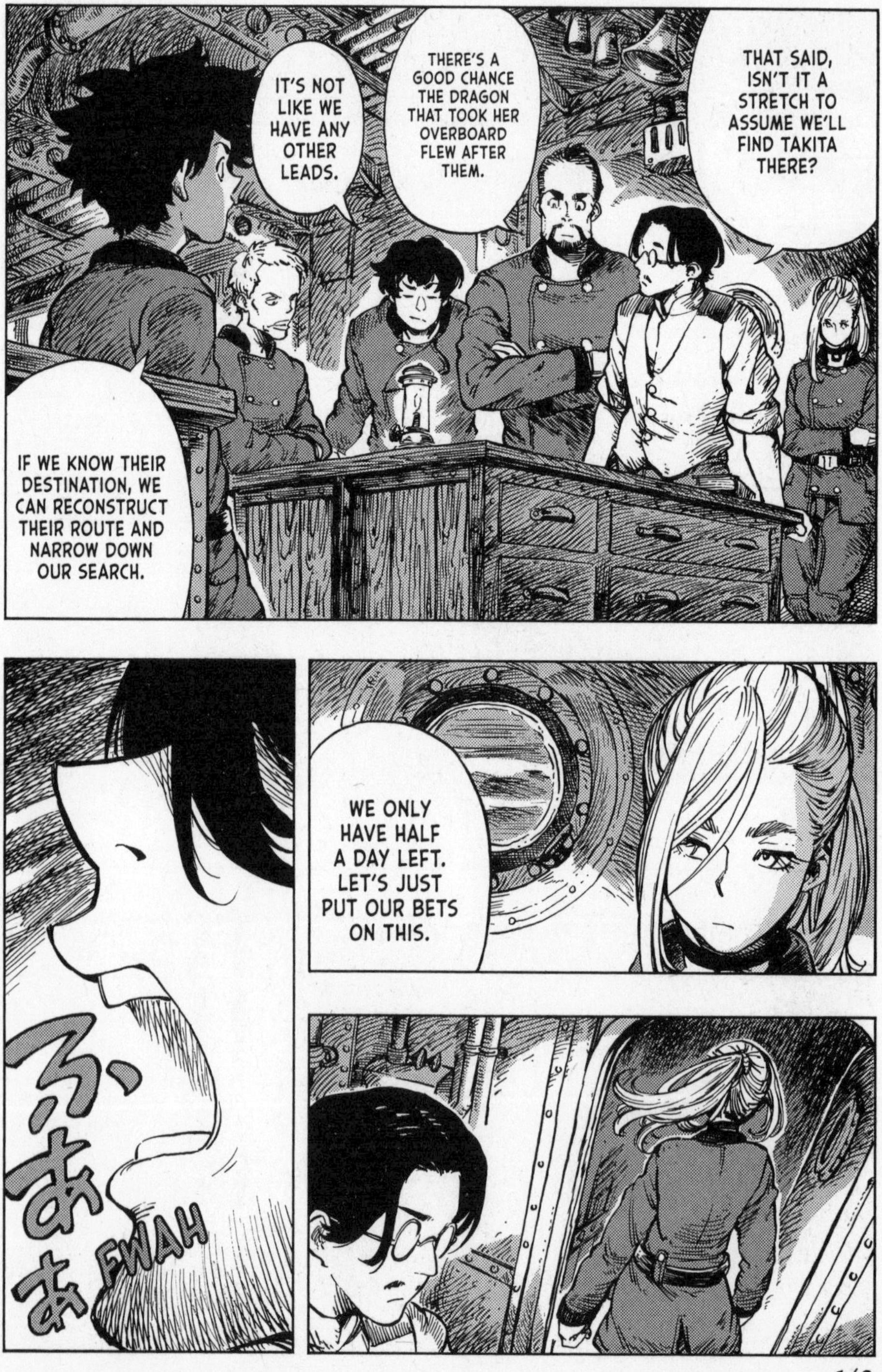
THAT SAID, ISN'T IT A STRETCH TO ASSUME WE'LL FIND TAKITA THERE?
THERE'S A GOOD CHANCE THE DRAGON THAT TOOK HER OVERBOARD FLEW AFTER THEM.
IT'S NOT LIKE WE HAVE ANY OTHER LEADS.
IF WE KNOW THEIR DESTINATION, WE CAN RECONSTRUCT THEIR ROUTE AND NARROW DOWN OUR SEARCH.
WE ONLY HAVE HALF A DAY LEFT. LET'S JUST PUT OUR BETS ON THIS.
ふぁぁ
FWAH

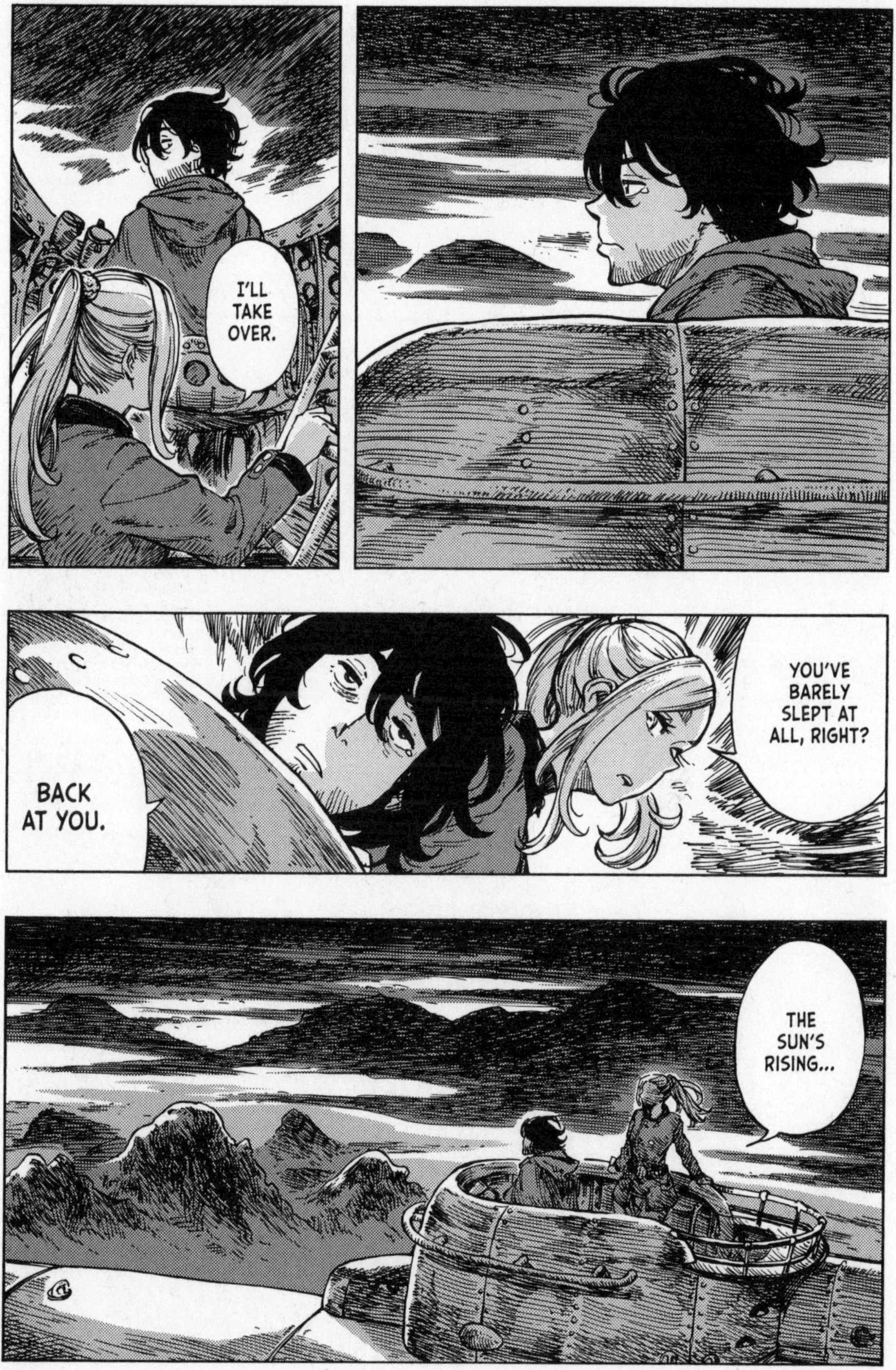
I'LL TAKE OVER.
YOU'VE BARELY SLEPT AT ALL, RIGHT?
BACK AT YOU.
THE SUN'S RISING...

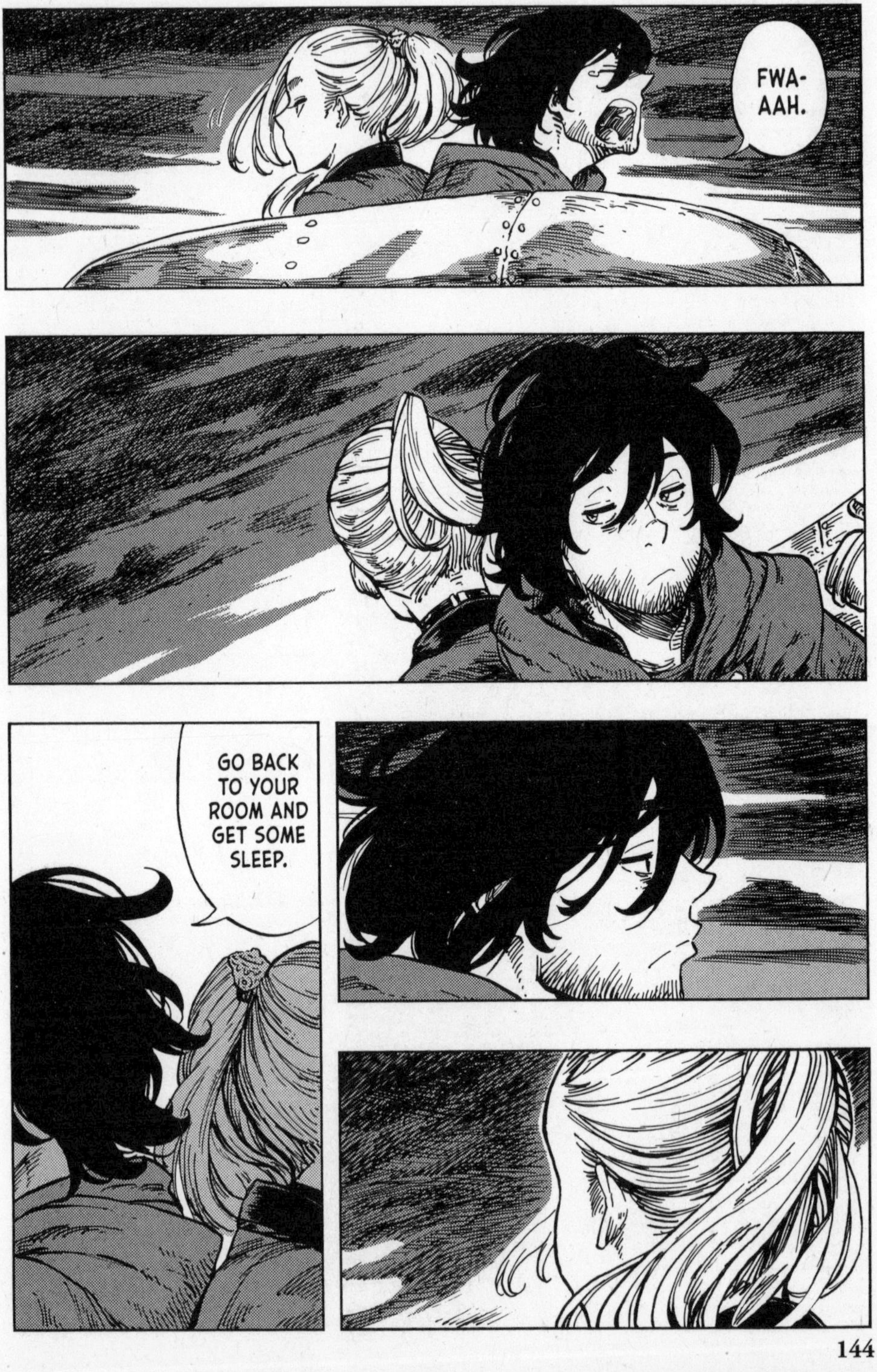
FWA- AAH.
GO BACK TO YOUR ROOM AND GET SOME SLEEP.

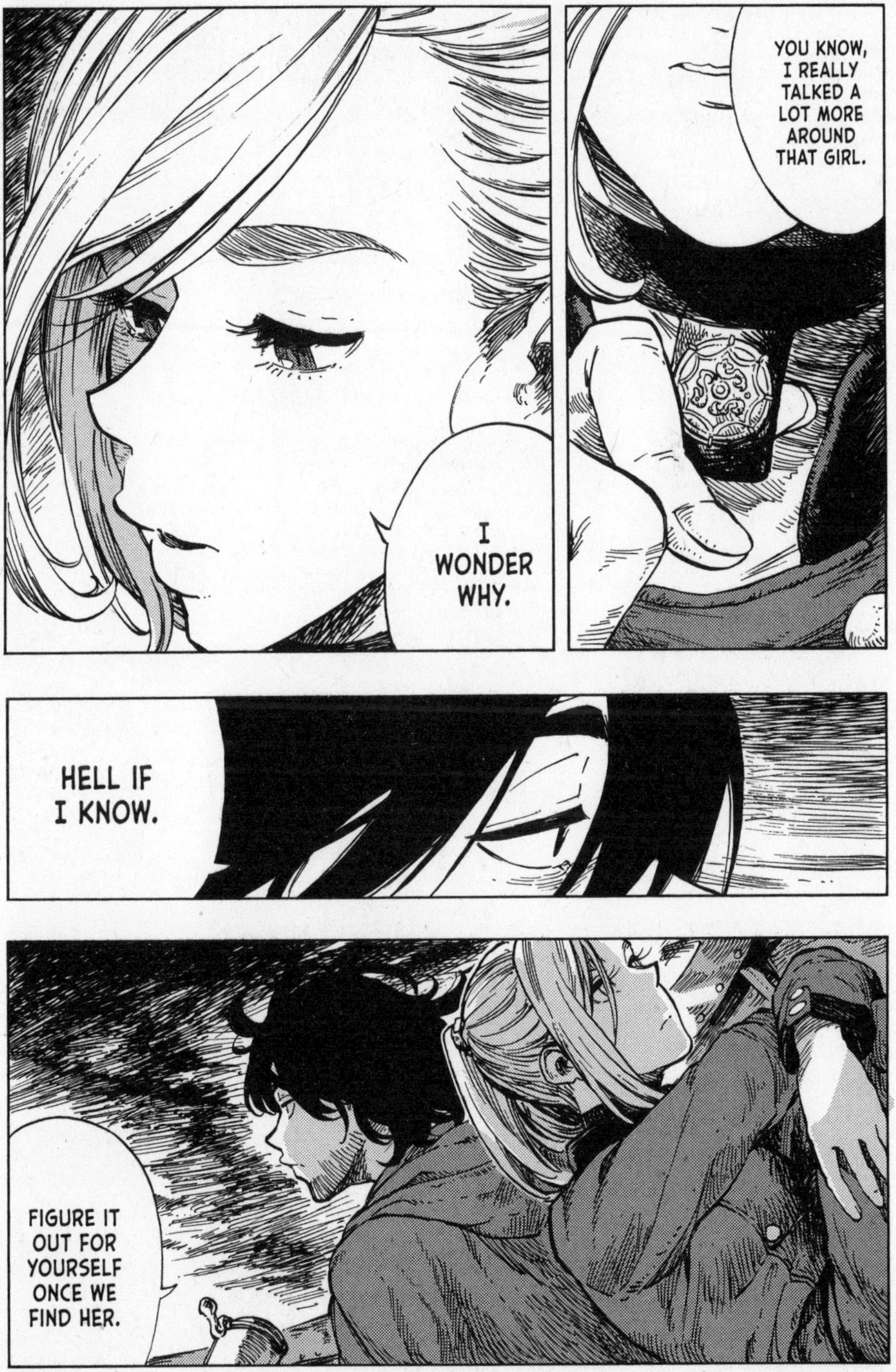
YOU KNOW, I REALLY TALKED A LOT MORE AROUND THAT GIRL.
I WONDER WHY.
HELL IF I KNOW.
FIGURE IT OUT FOR YOURSELF ONCE WE FIND HER.

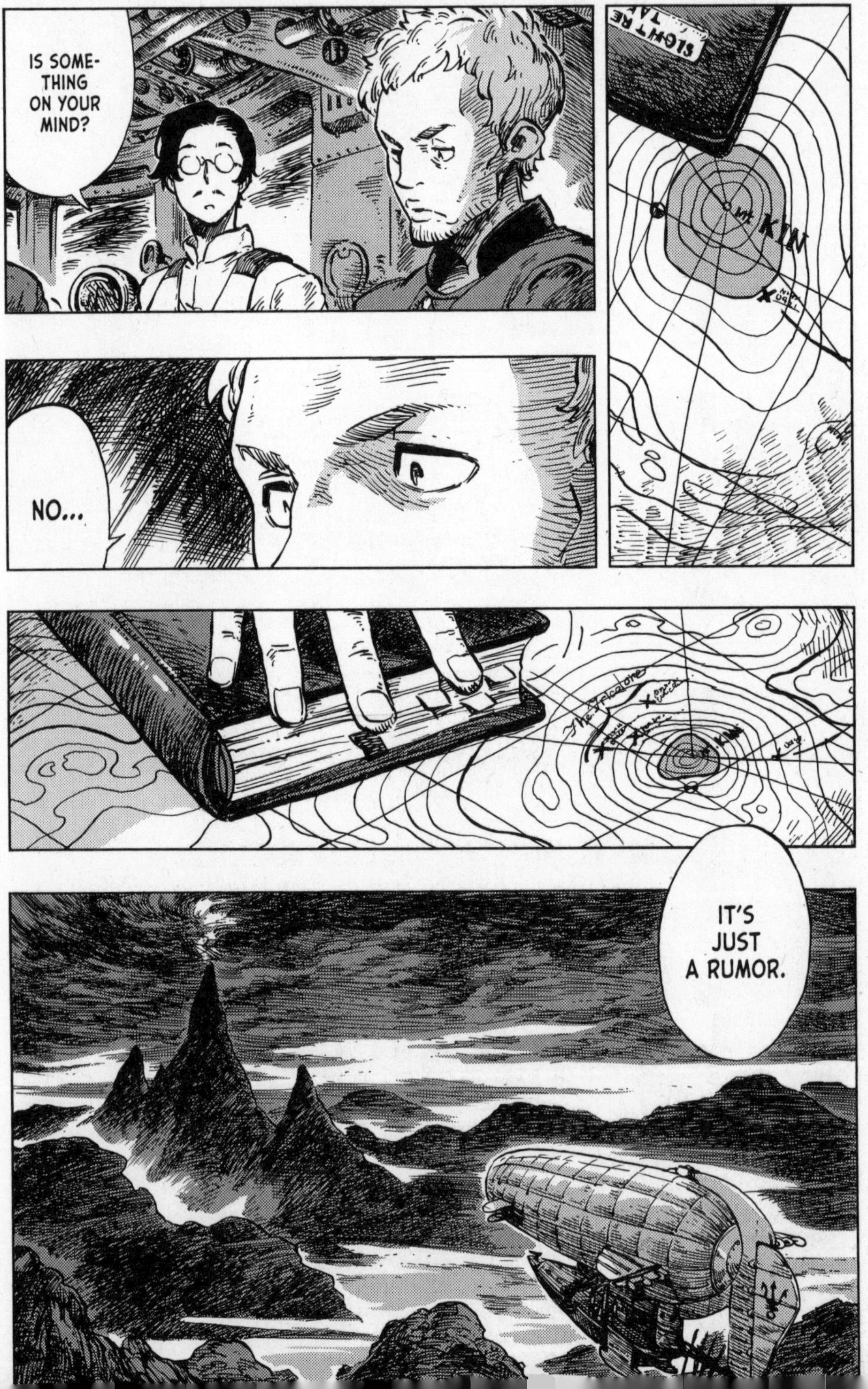
IS SOME-THING ON YOUR MIND?
NO...
IT'S JUST A RUMOR.

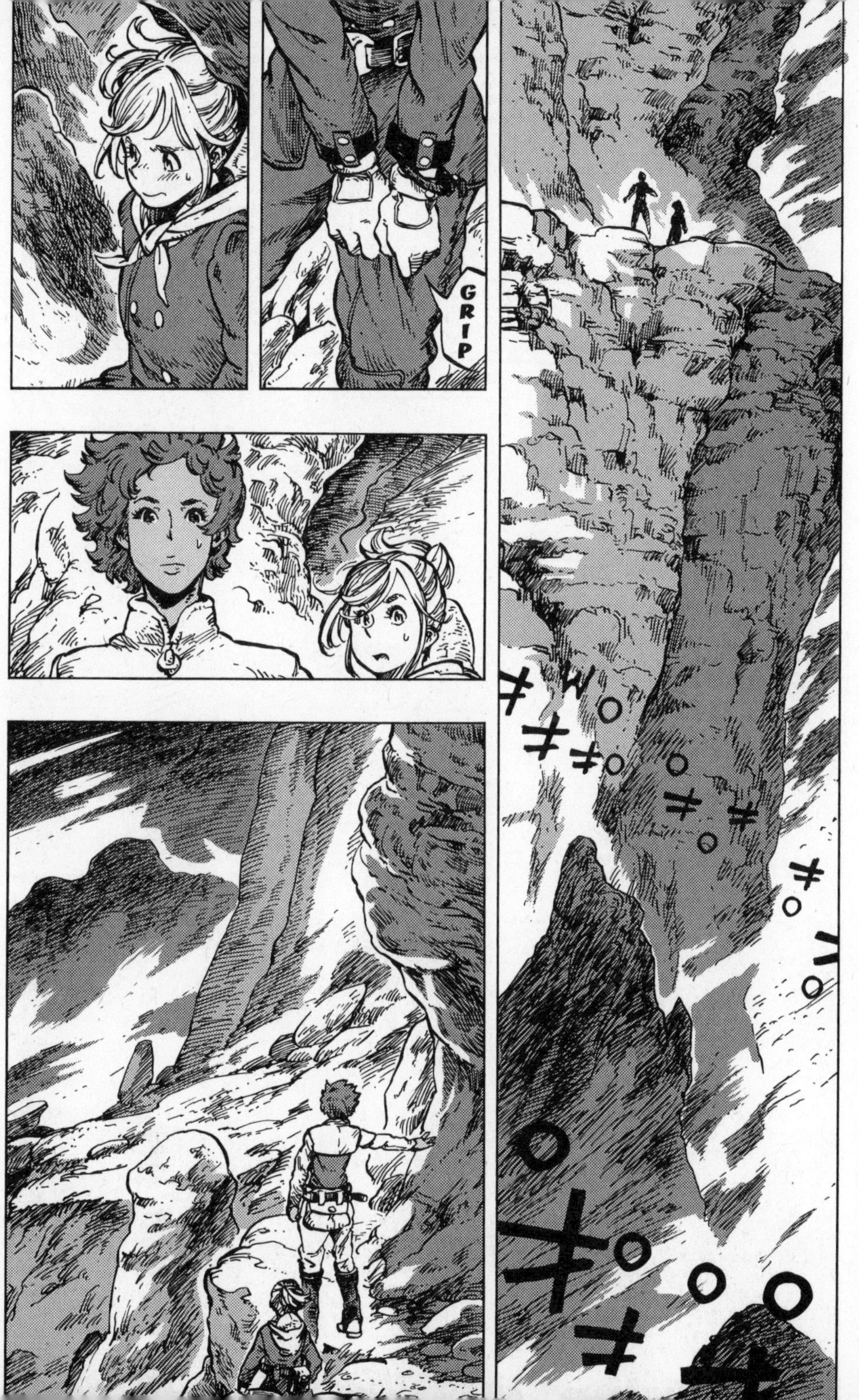
GRIP

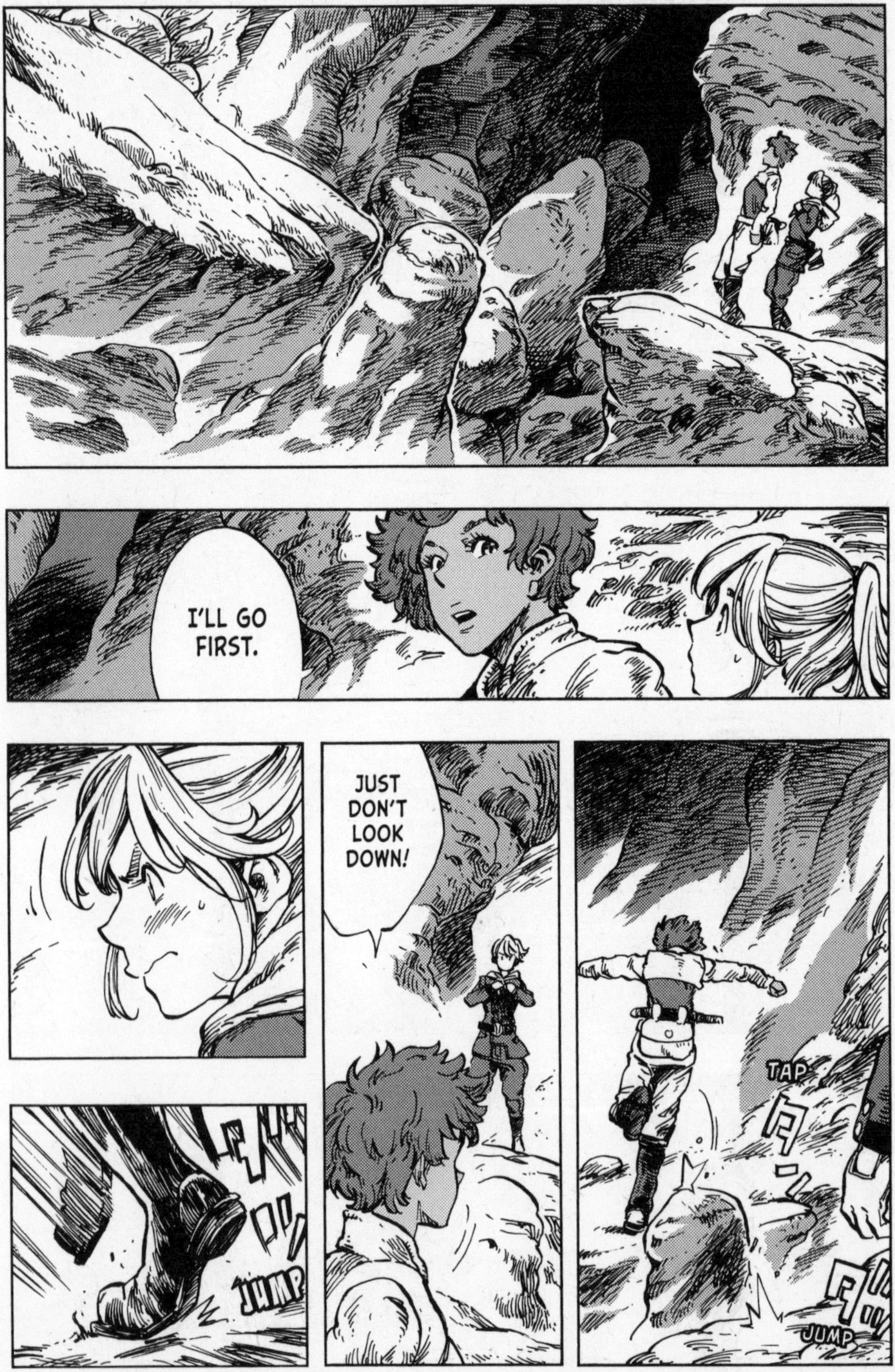
I'LL GO FIRST.
TAP
JUMP
JUST DON'T LOOK DOWN!
JUMP

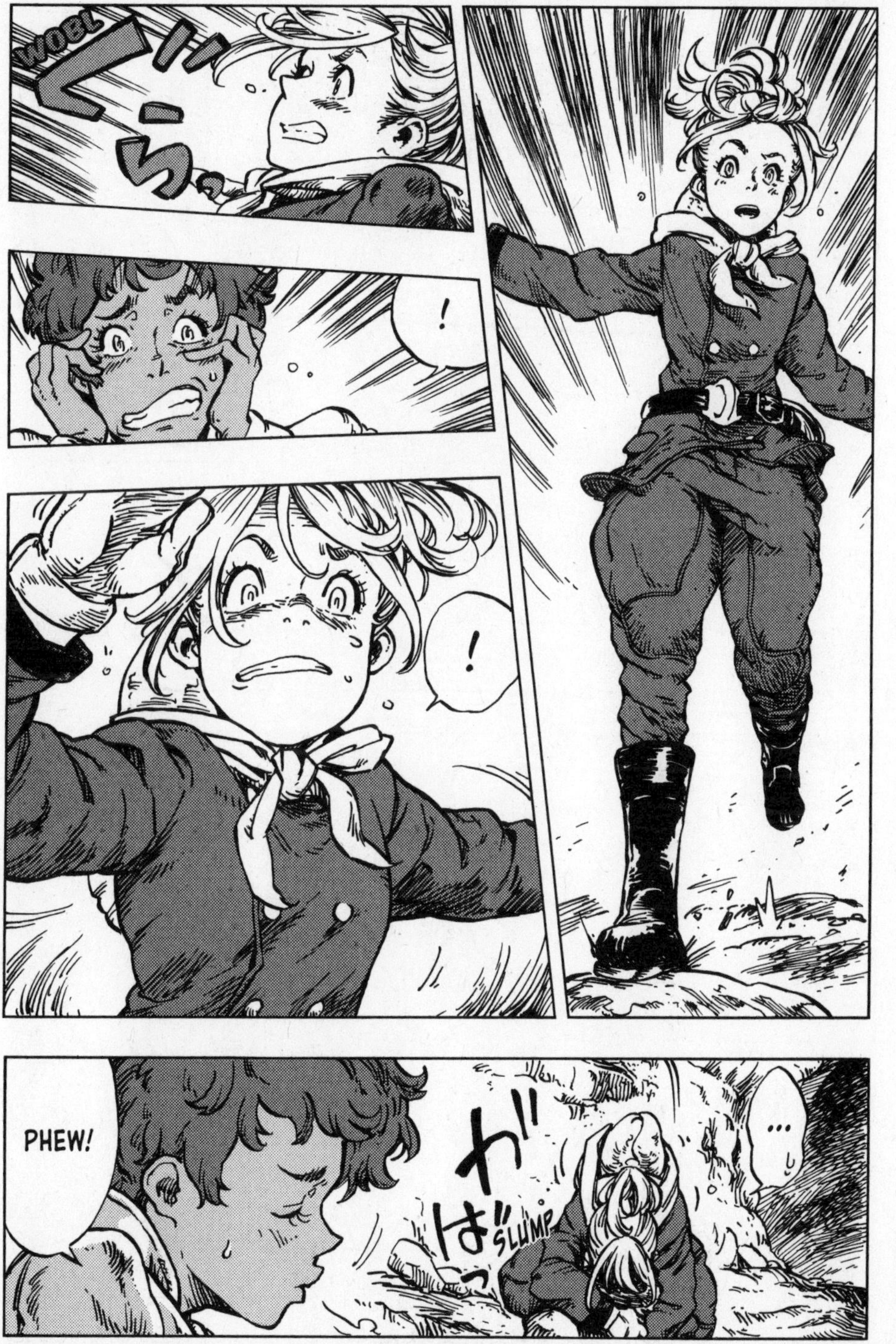

WOBL
ぐらっ
!
!
...
わ゛
ばっ
SLUMP
PHEW!

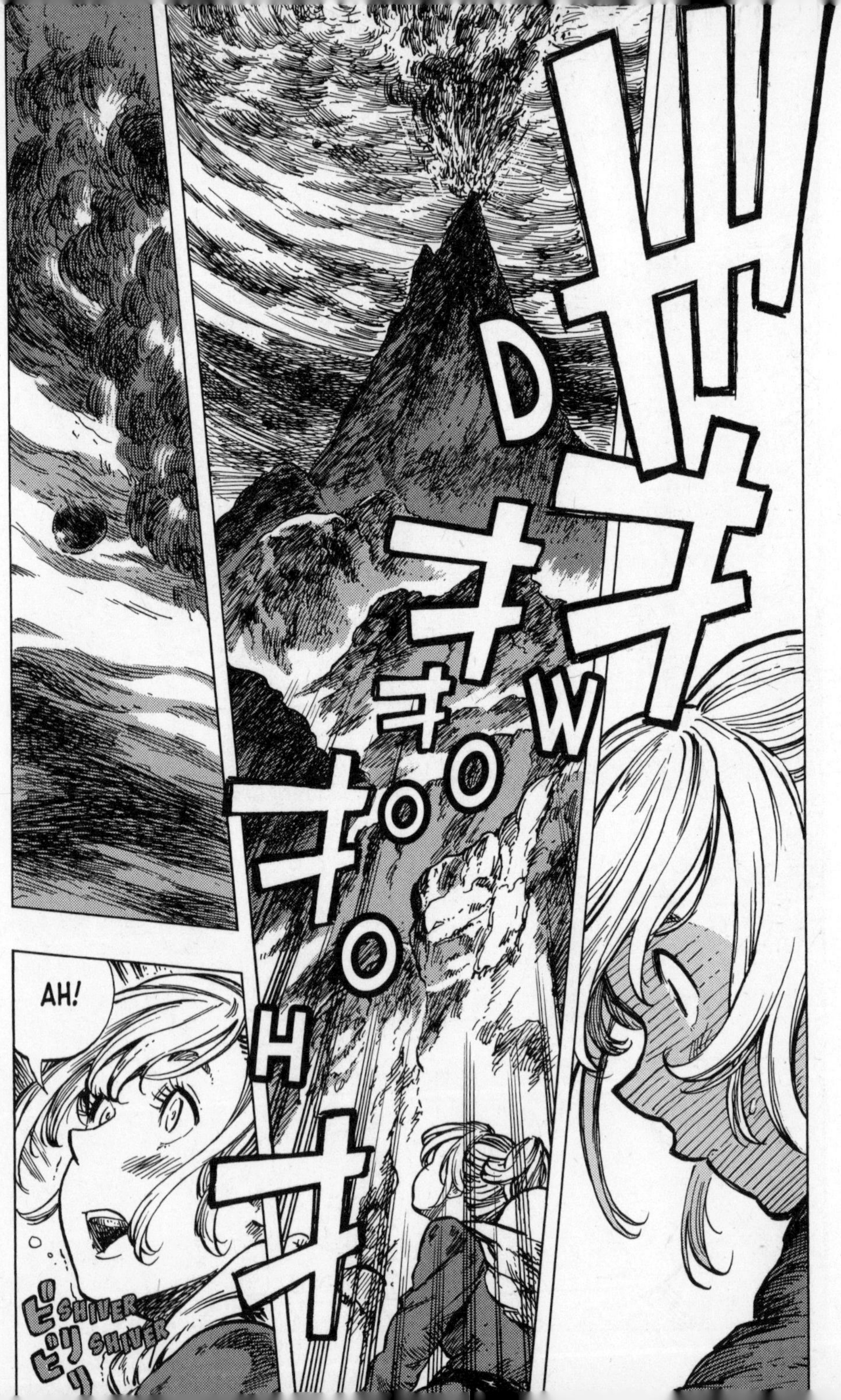
DWOOOH
AH!
SHIVER
SHIVER

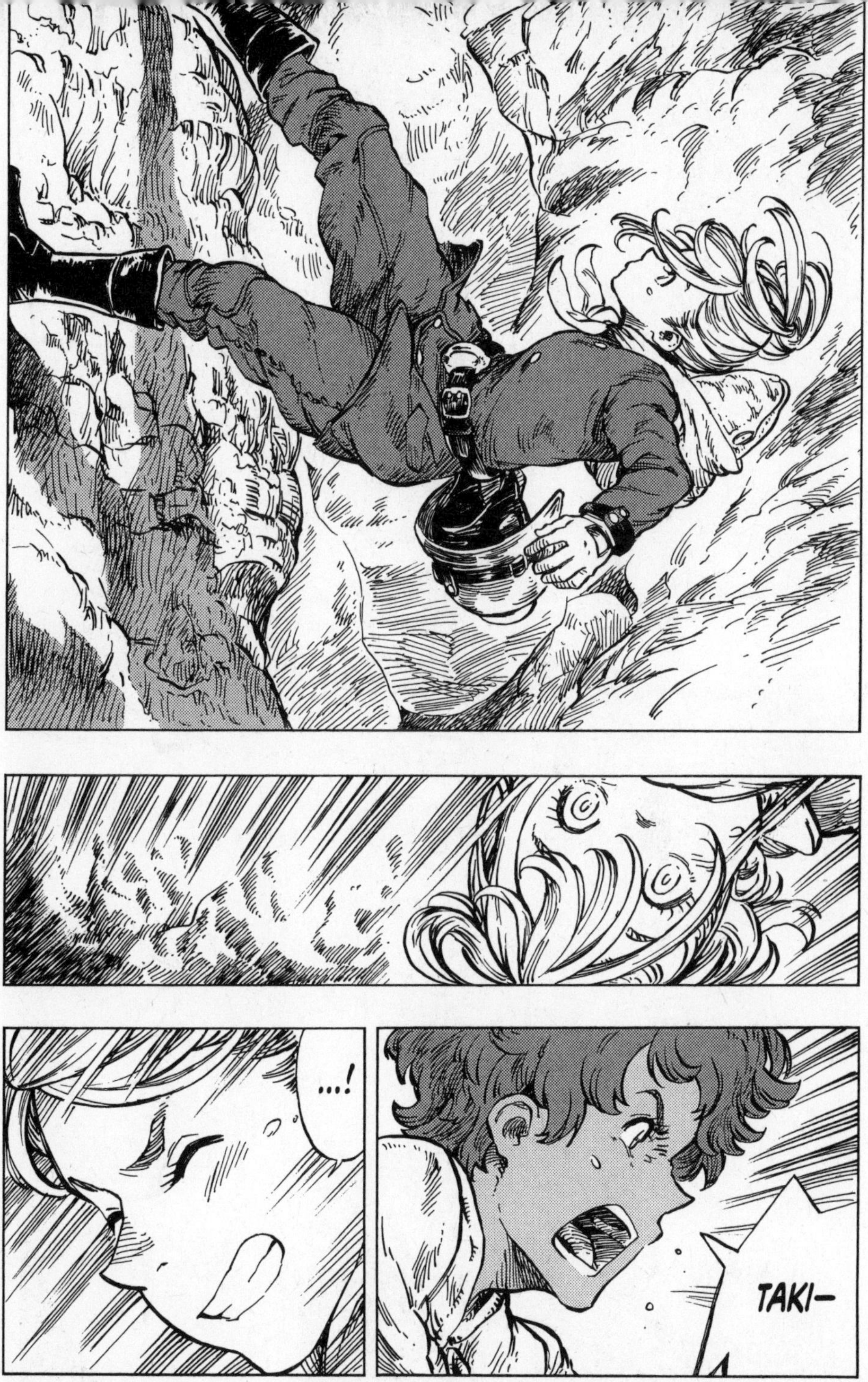
TAKI-
...!

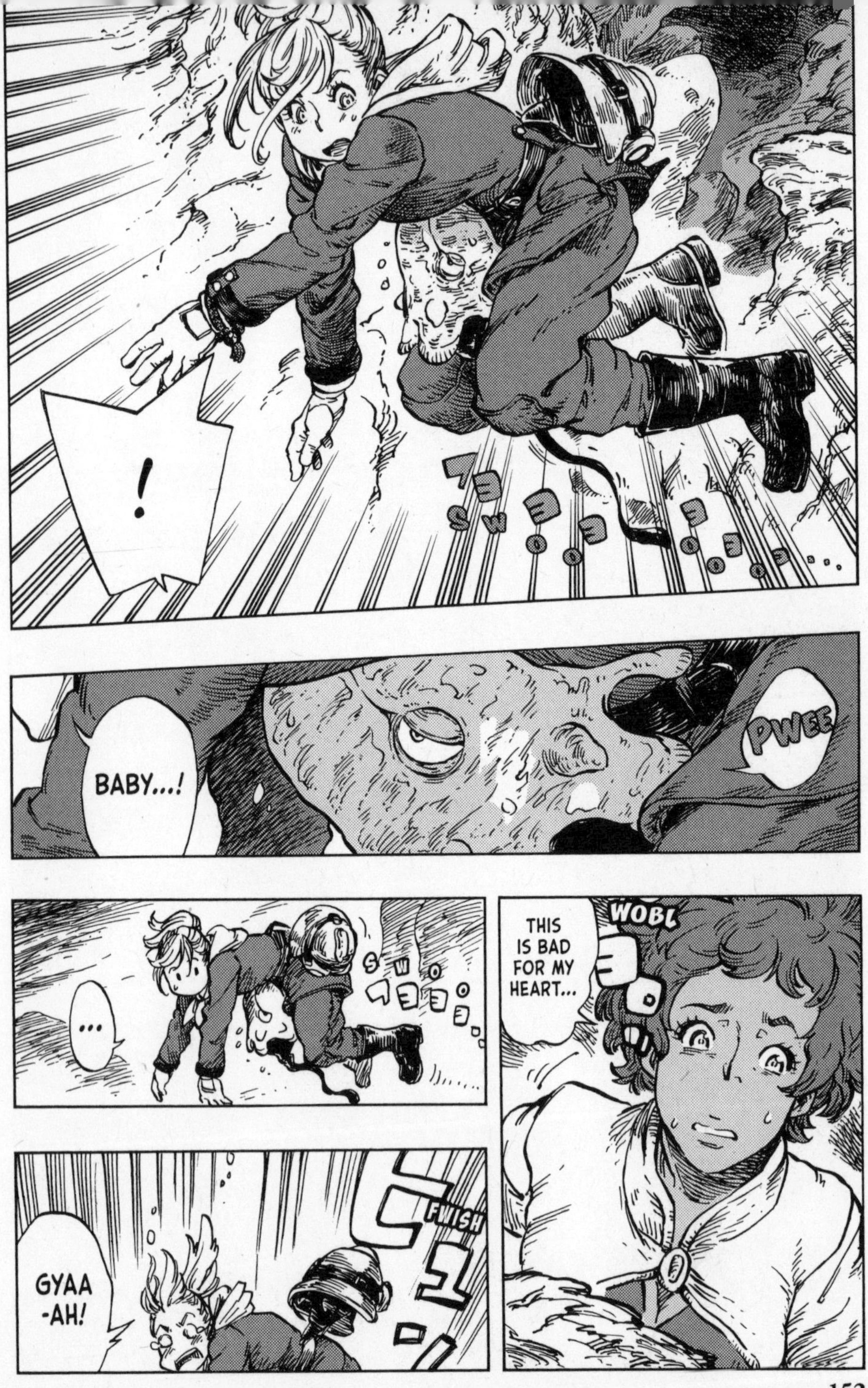
!
PWEE
BABY...!
WOBL
THIS IS BAD FOR MY HEART...
...
FWISH
GYAA-AH!

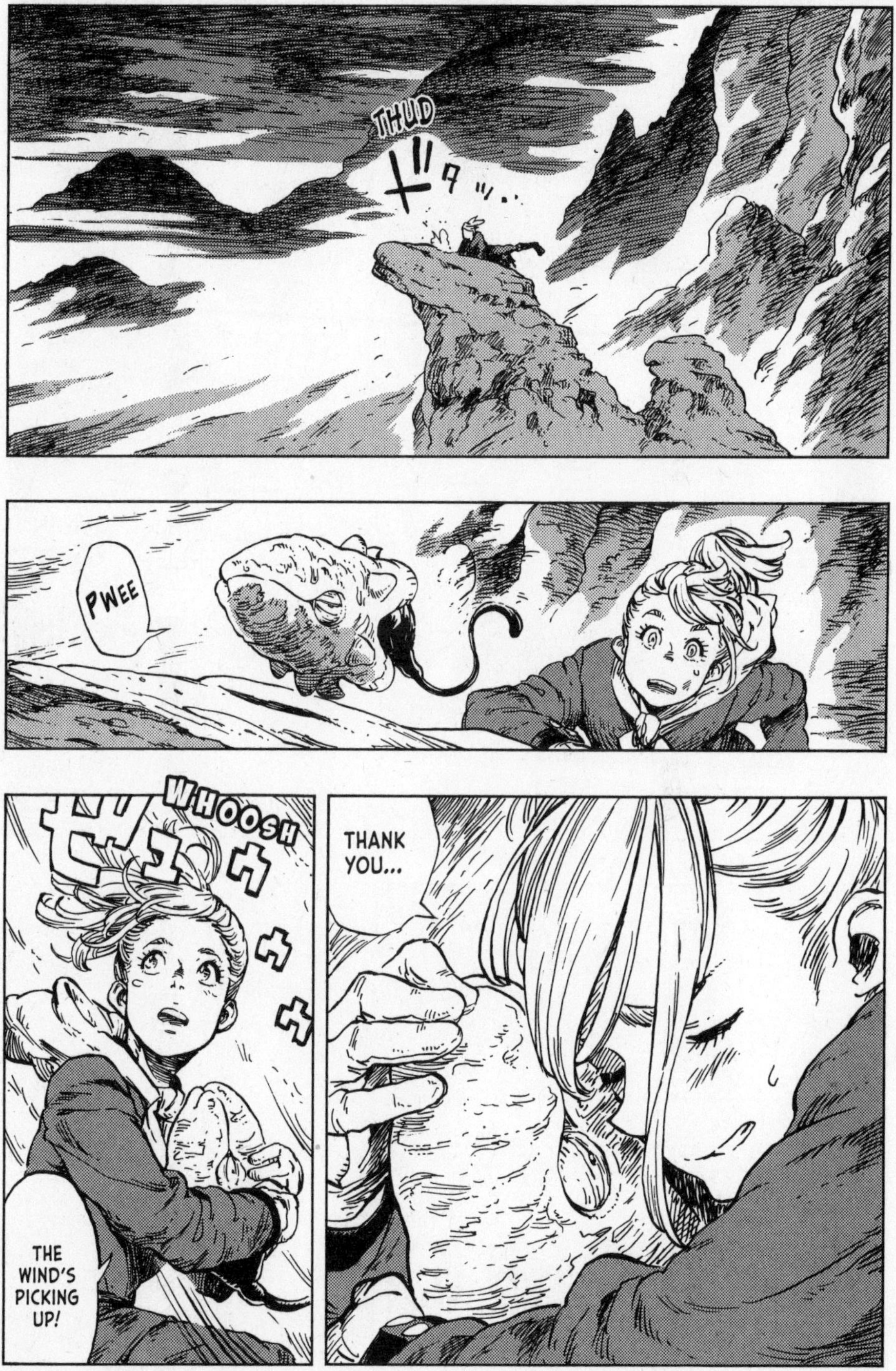
THUD
PWEE
THANK YOU...
WHOOSH
THE WIND'S PICKING UP!

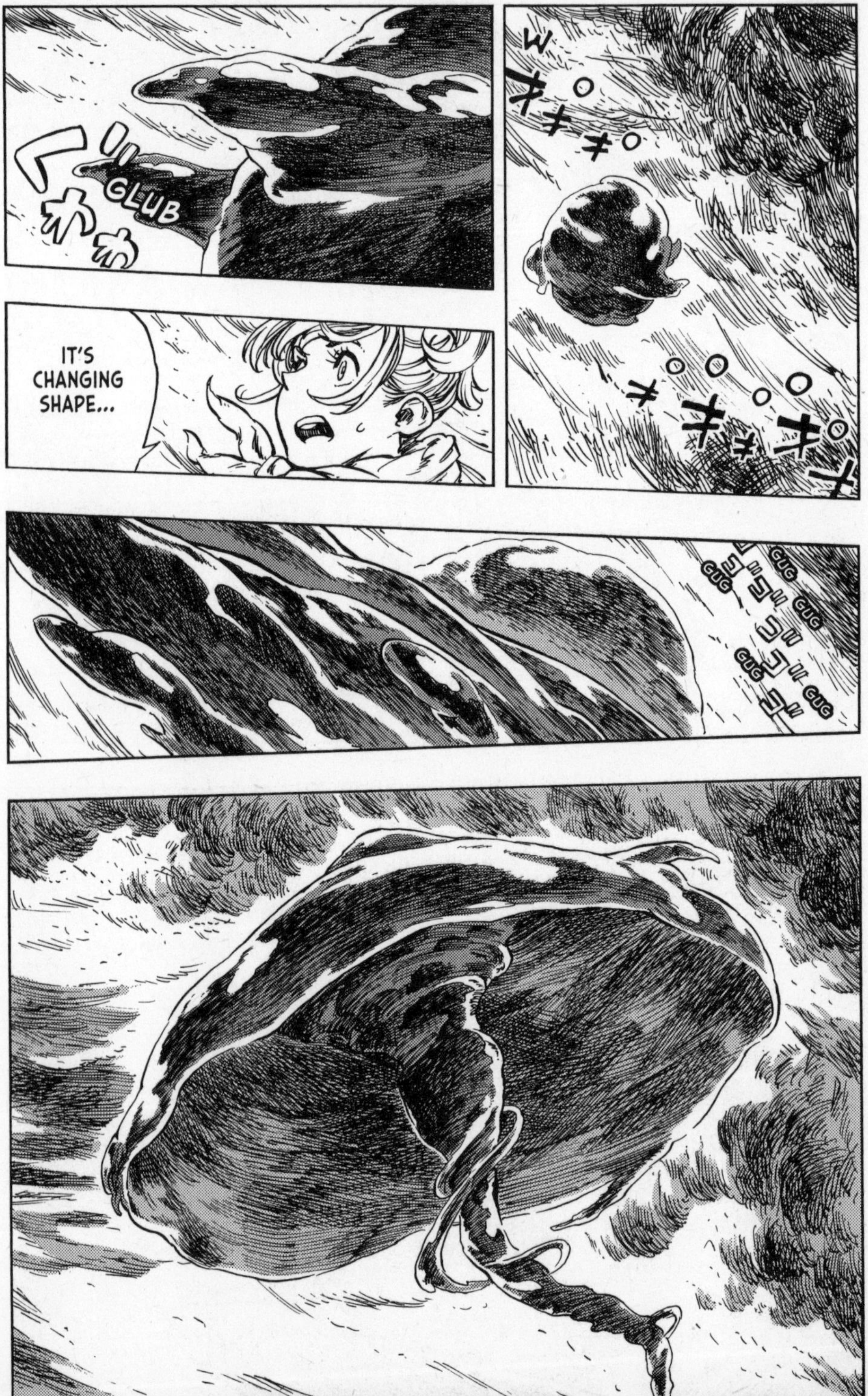
W
GLUB
IT'S CHANGING SHAPE...
GUG GUG GUG GUG GUG GUG

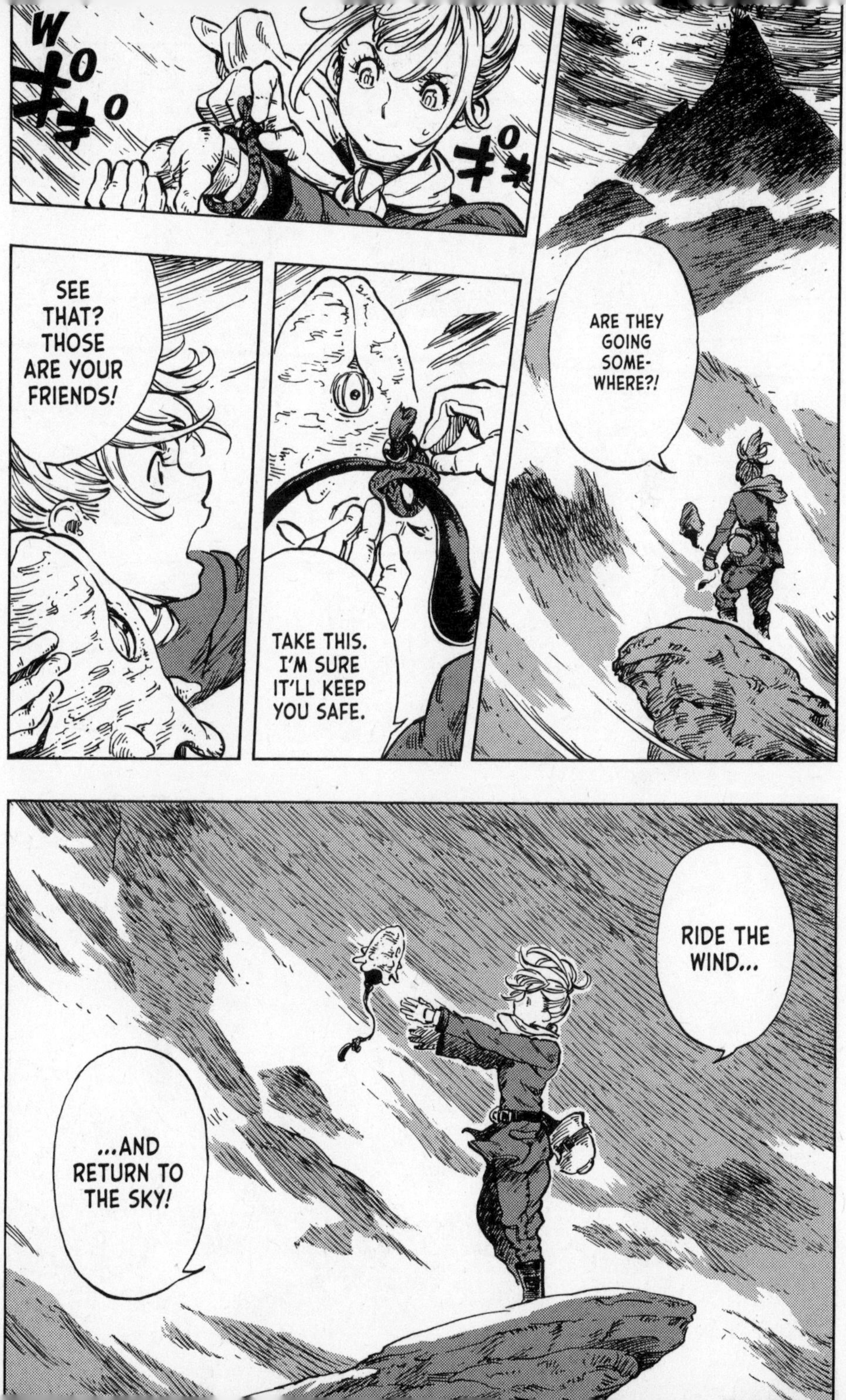
ARE THEY GOING SOME-WHERE?!
WOO
TAKE THIS. I'M SURE IT'LL KEEP YOU SAFE.
SEE THAT? THOSE ARE YOUR FRIENDS!
RIDE THE WIND...
...AND RETURN TO THE SKY!

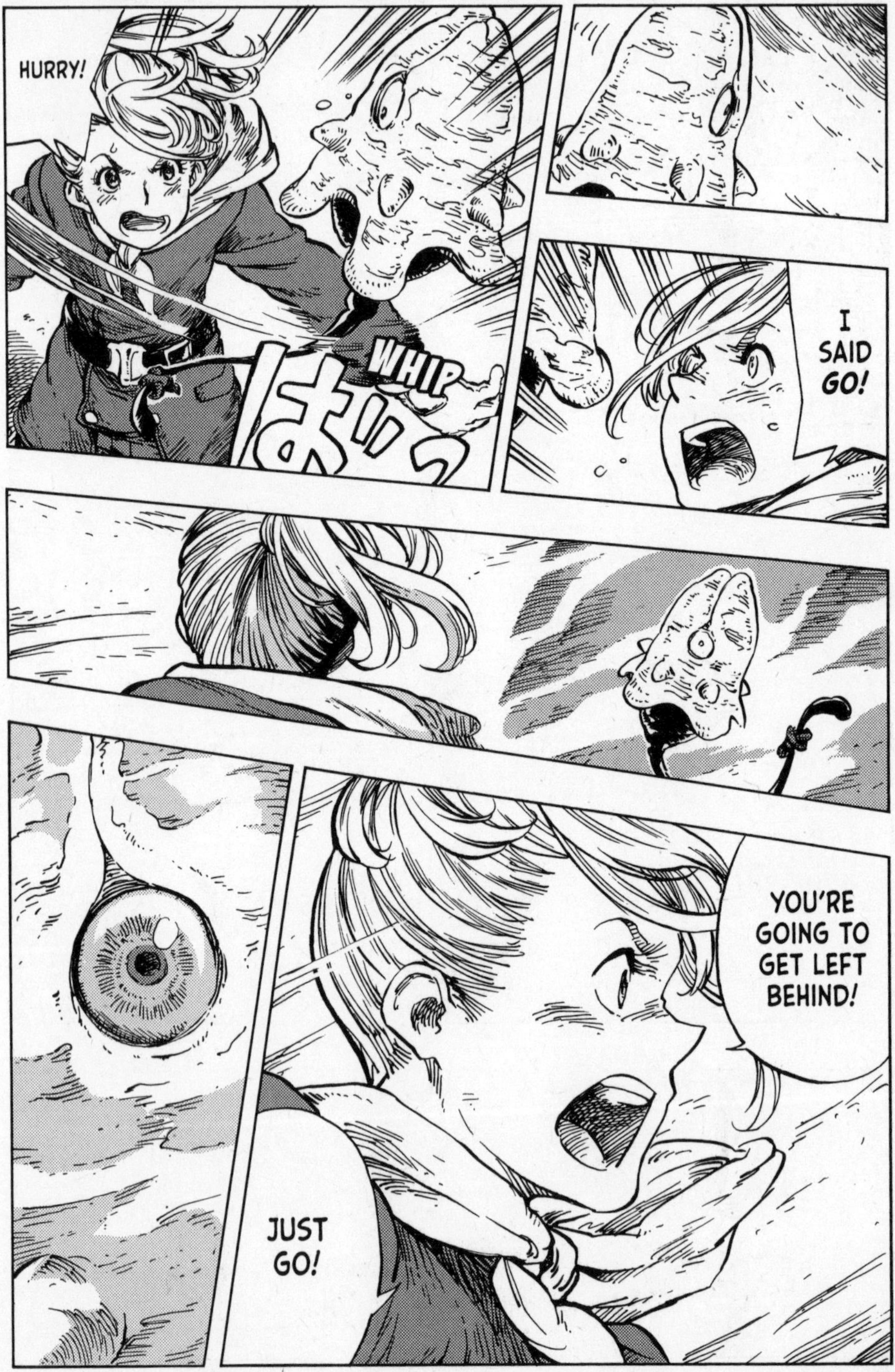
I SAID GO!
HURRY!
WHIP
YOU'RE GOING TO GET LEFT BEHIND!
JUST GO!

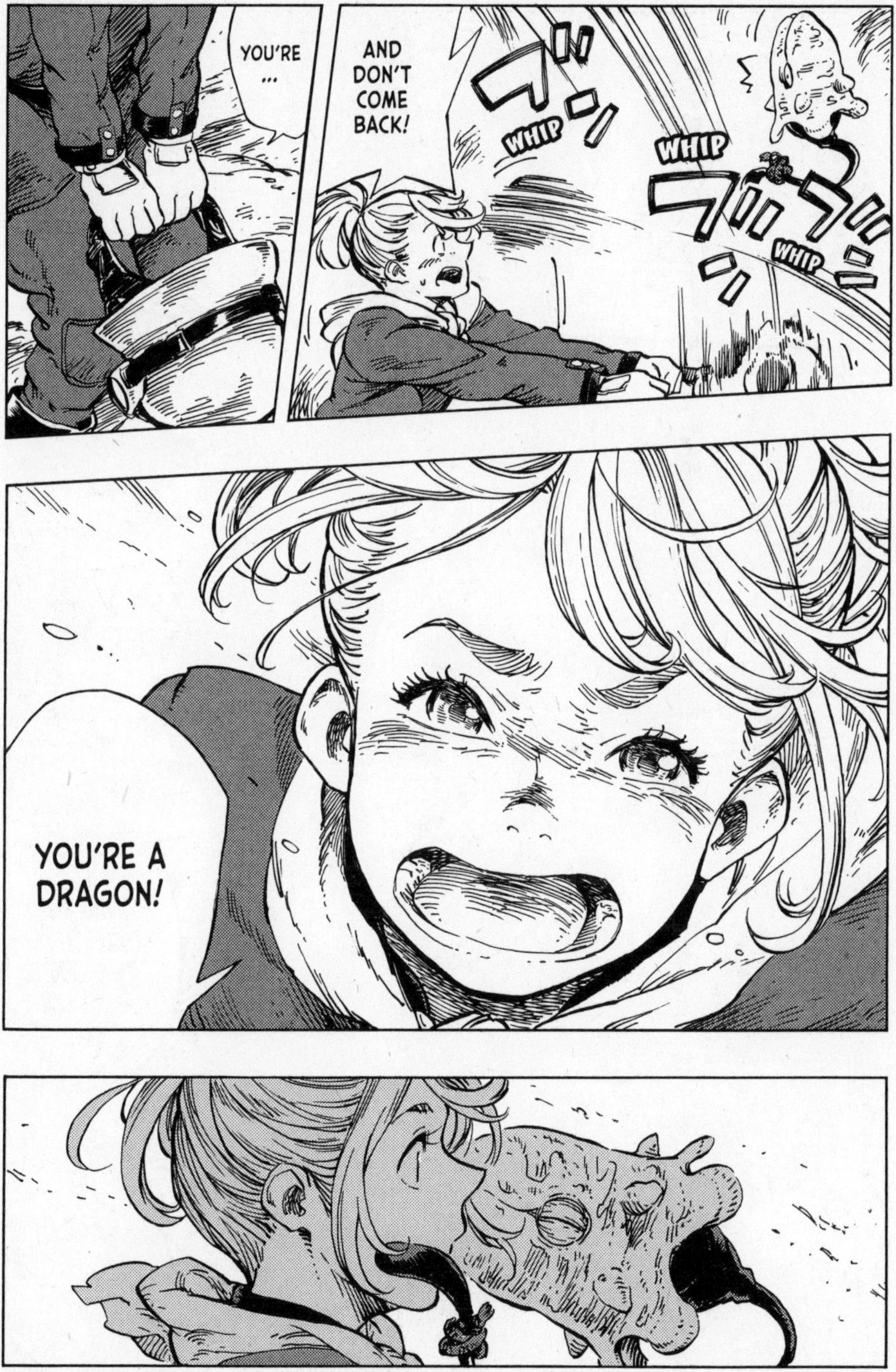
AND DON'T COME BACK!
WHIP
WHIP
WHIP
YOU'RE ...
YOU'RE A DRAGON!

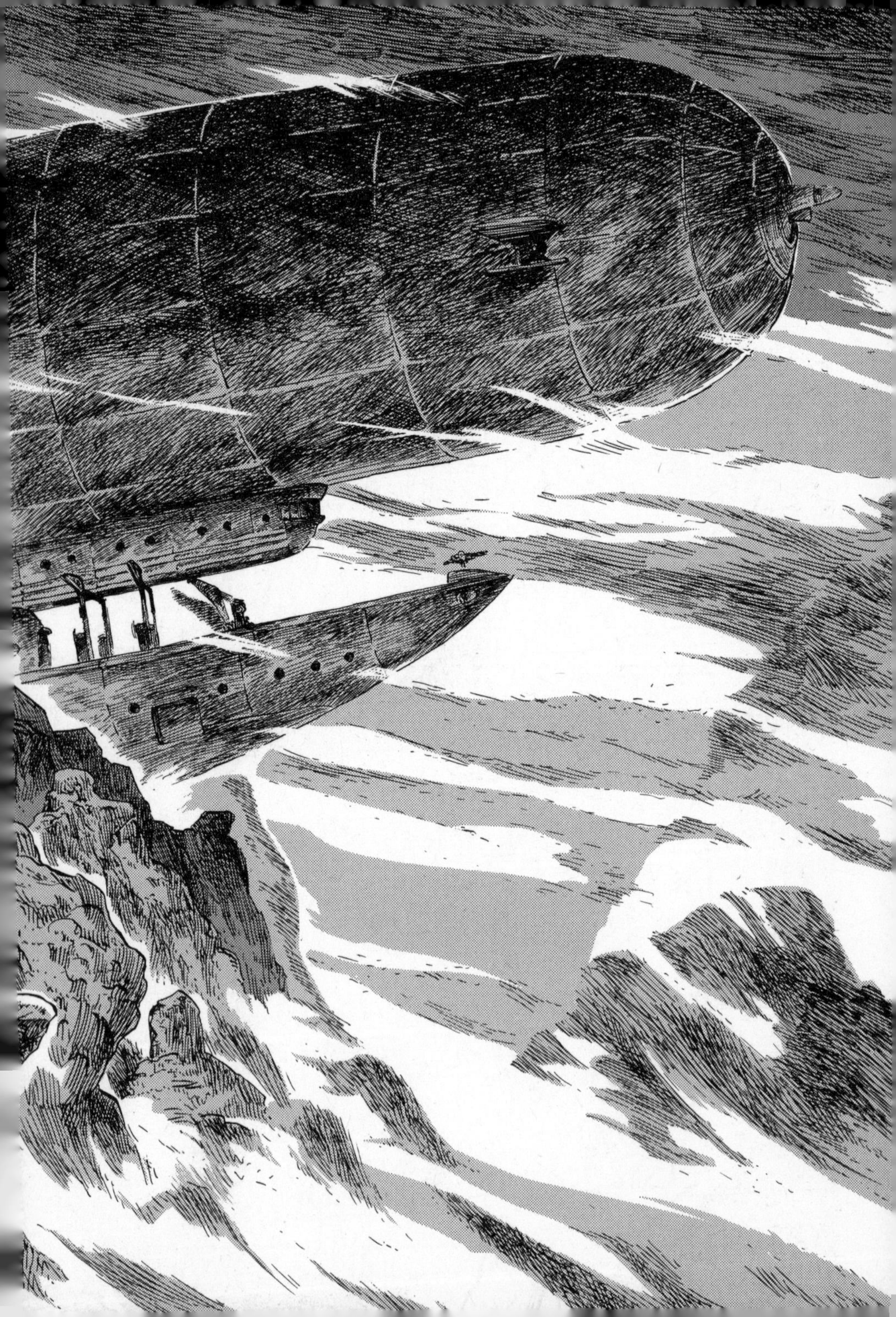

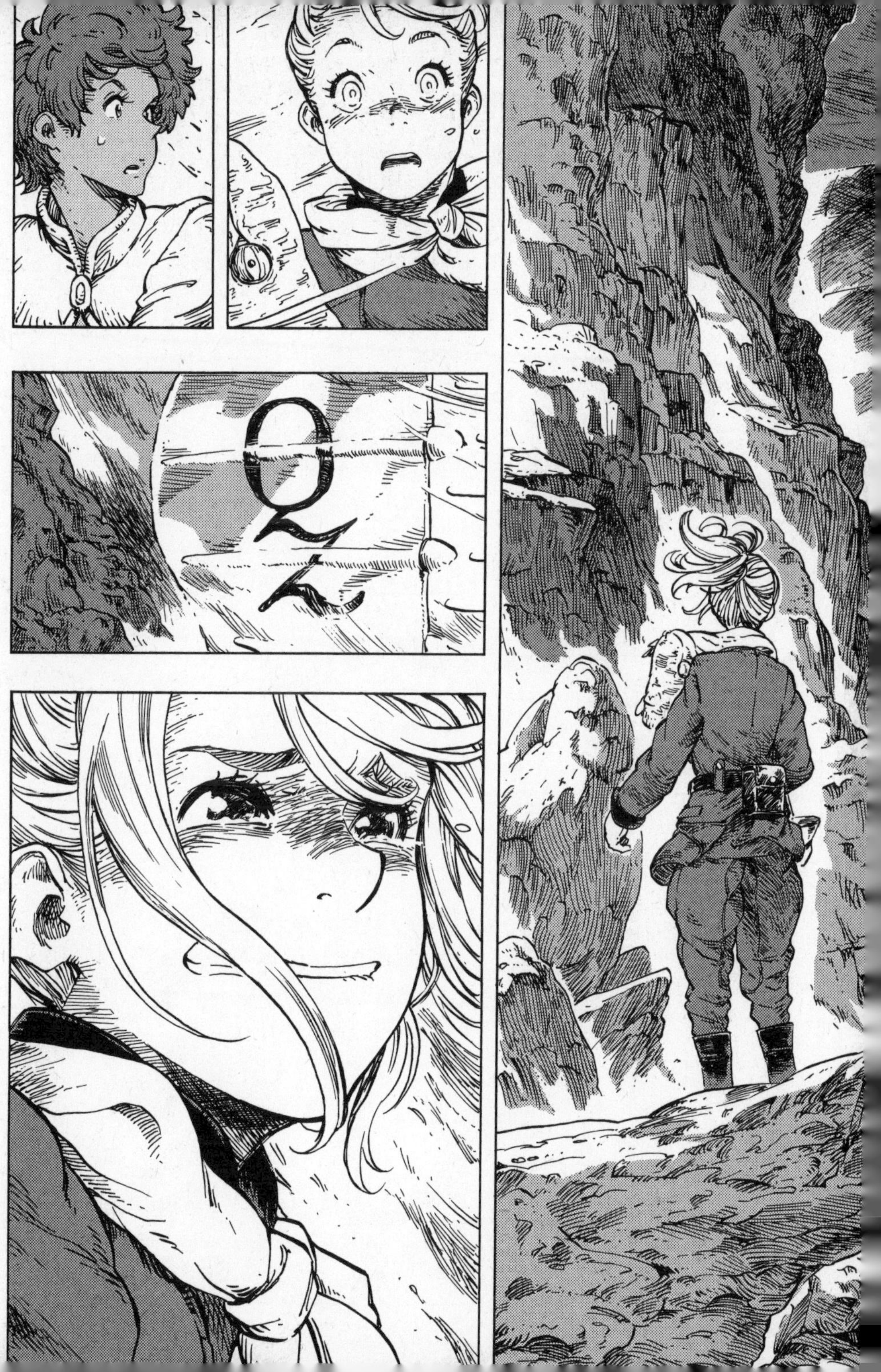

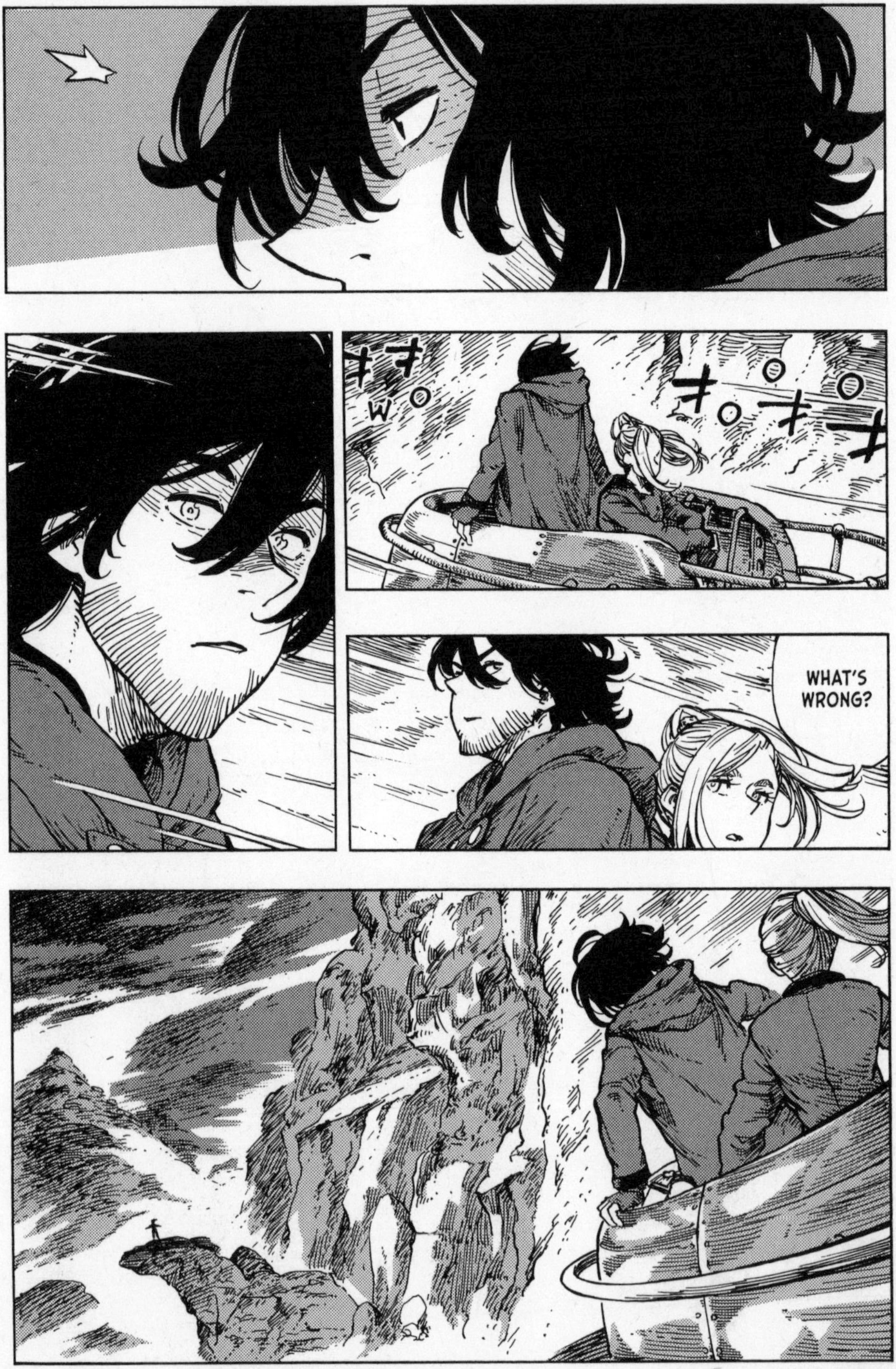
WHAT'S WRONG?

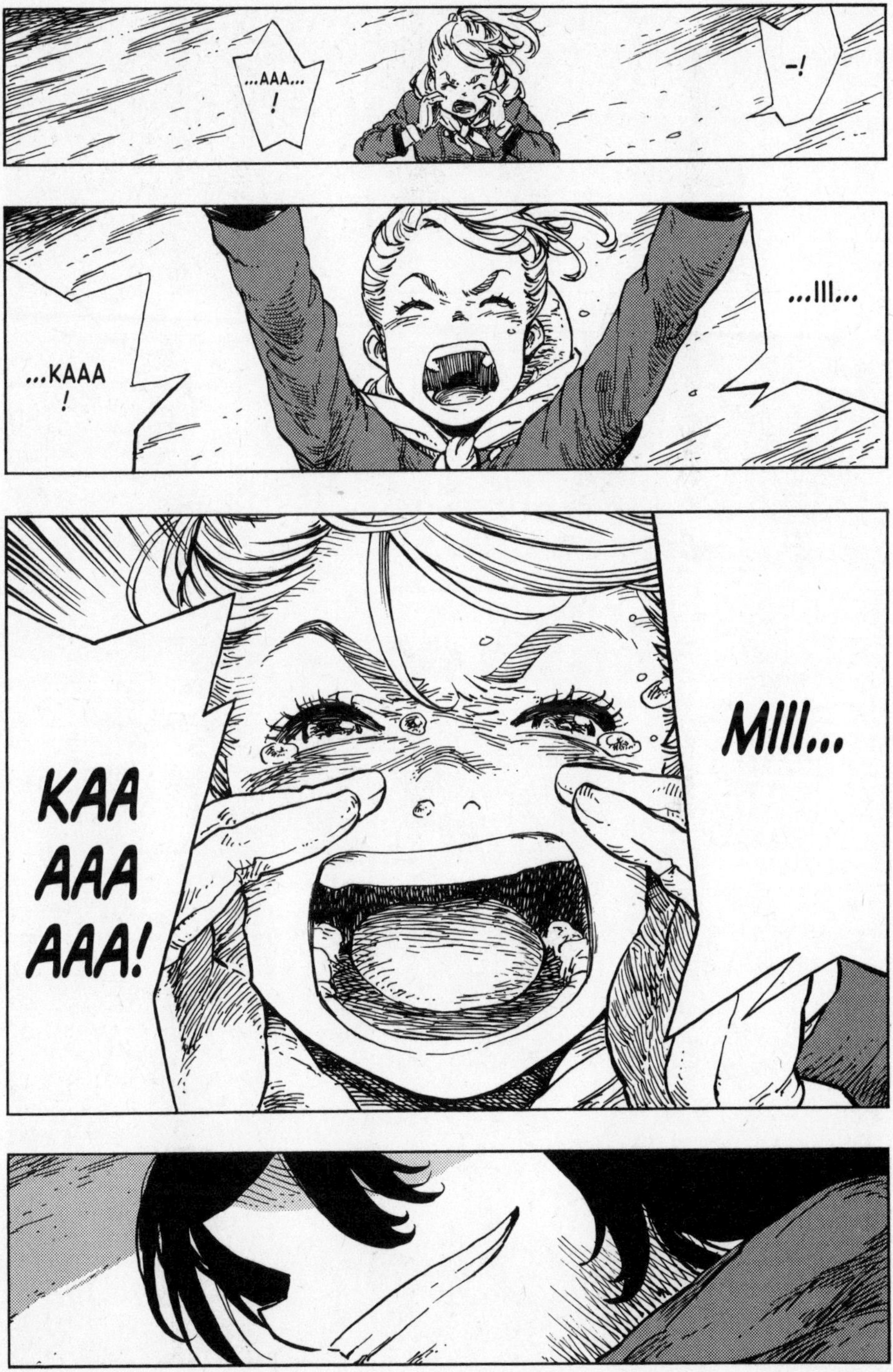
–!
...AAA... !
...III...
...KAAA !
MIII...
KAA AAA AAA!

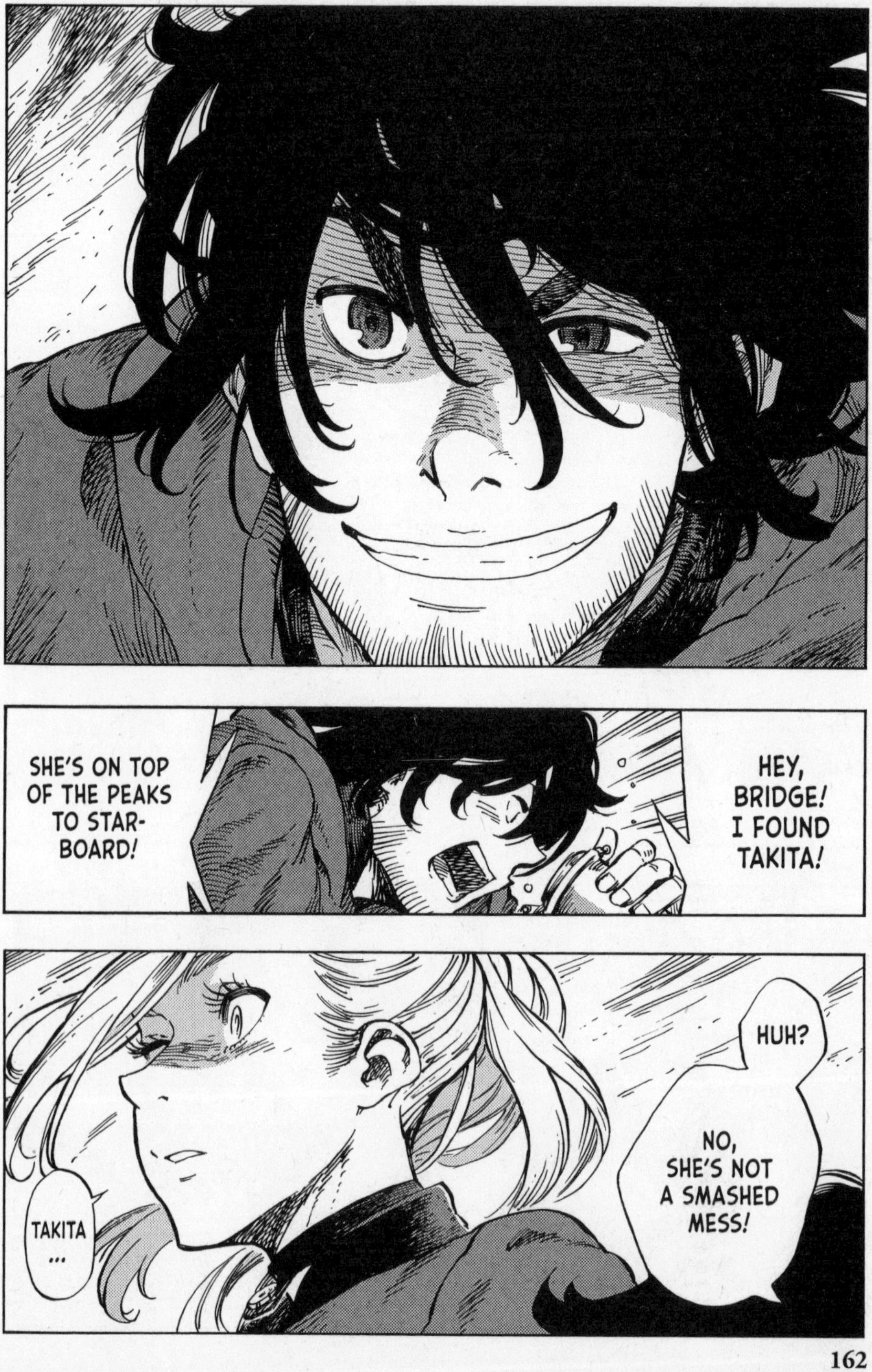
HEY, BRIDGE! I FOUND TAKITA!
SHE'S ON TOP OF THE PEAKS TO STAR-BOARD!
HUH?
NO, SHE'S NOT A SMASHED MESS!
TAKITA ...

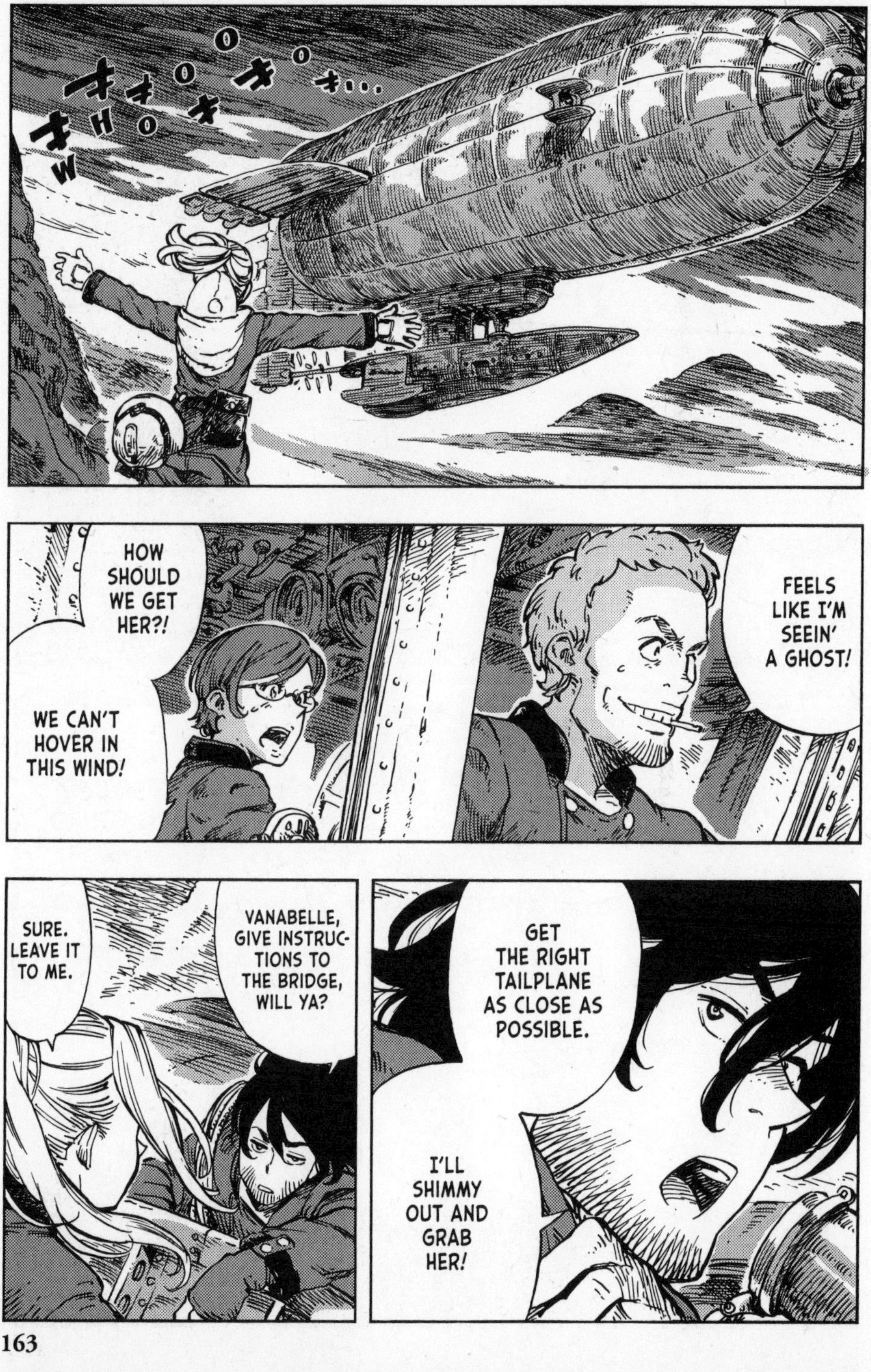
WHOOOO
FEELS LIKE I'M SEEIN' A GHOST!
HOW SHOULD WE GET HER?!
WE CAN'T HOVER IN THIS WIND!
GET THE RIGHT TAILPLANE AS CLOSE AS POSSIBLE.
I'LL SHIMMY OUT AND GRAB HER!
VANABELLE, GIVE INSTRUCTIONS TO THE BRIDGE, WILL YA?
SURE. LEAVE IT TO ME.

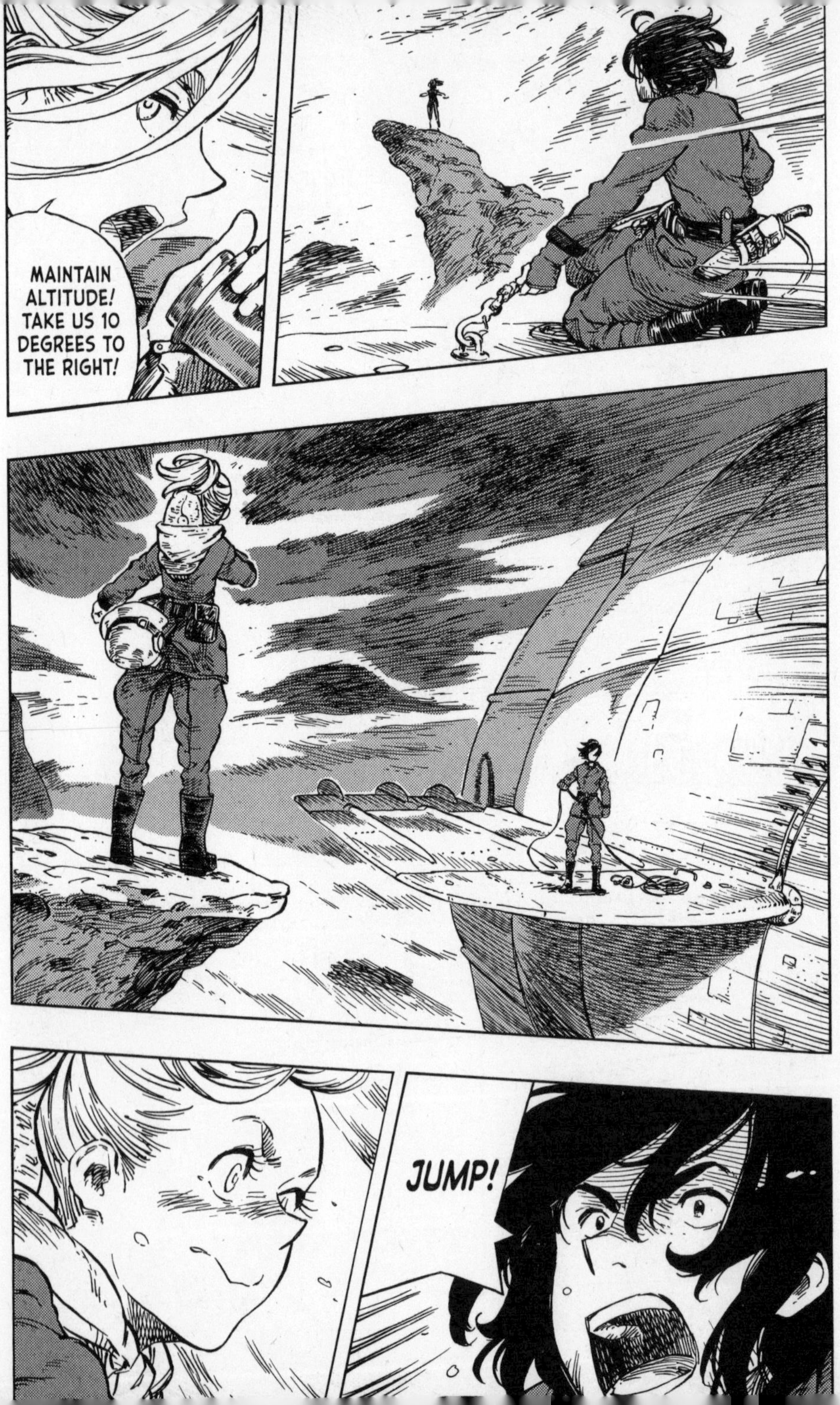
MAINTAIN ALTITUDE! TAKE US 10 DEGREES TO THE RIGHT!
JUMP!

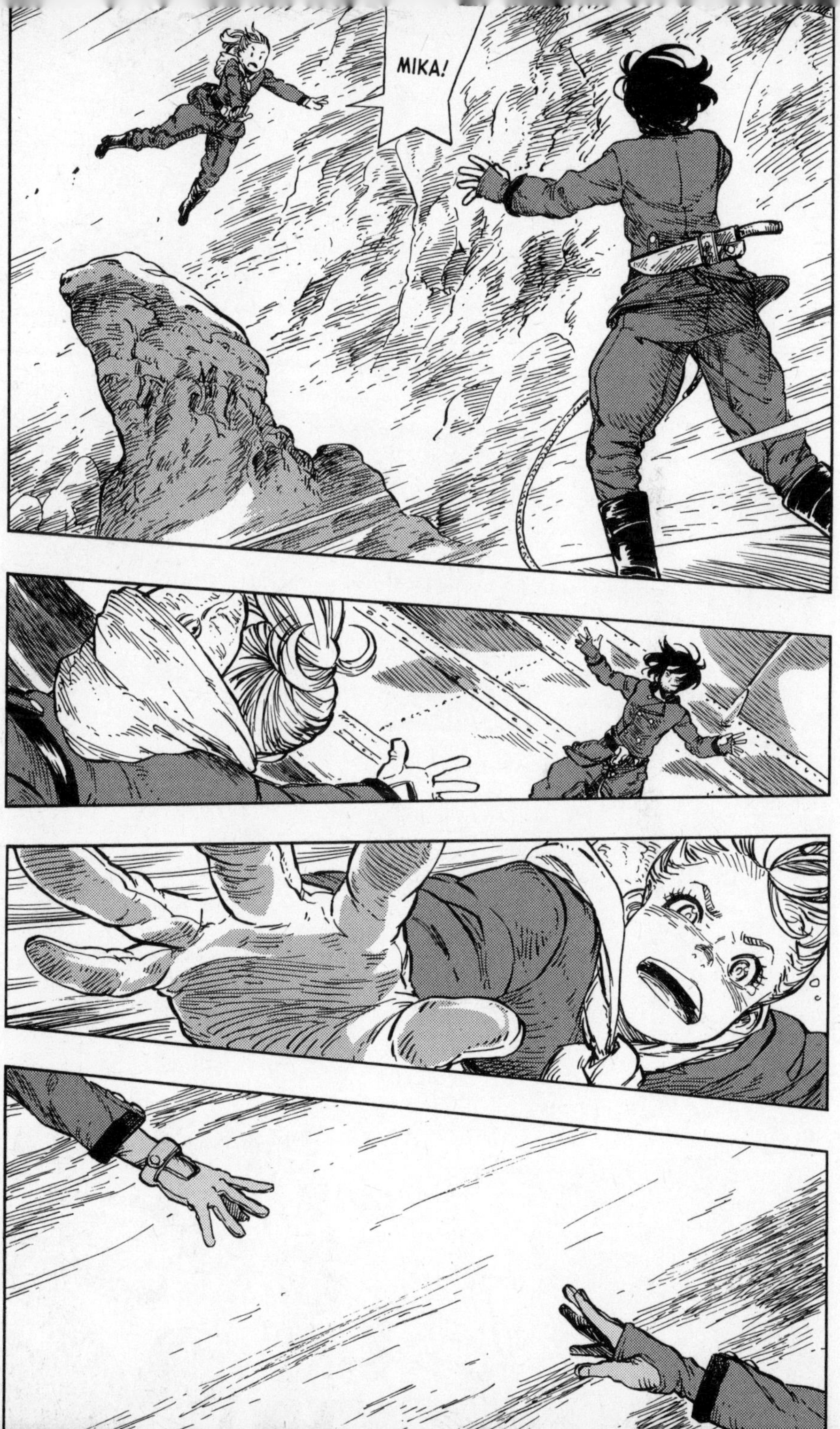
MIKA!

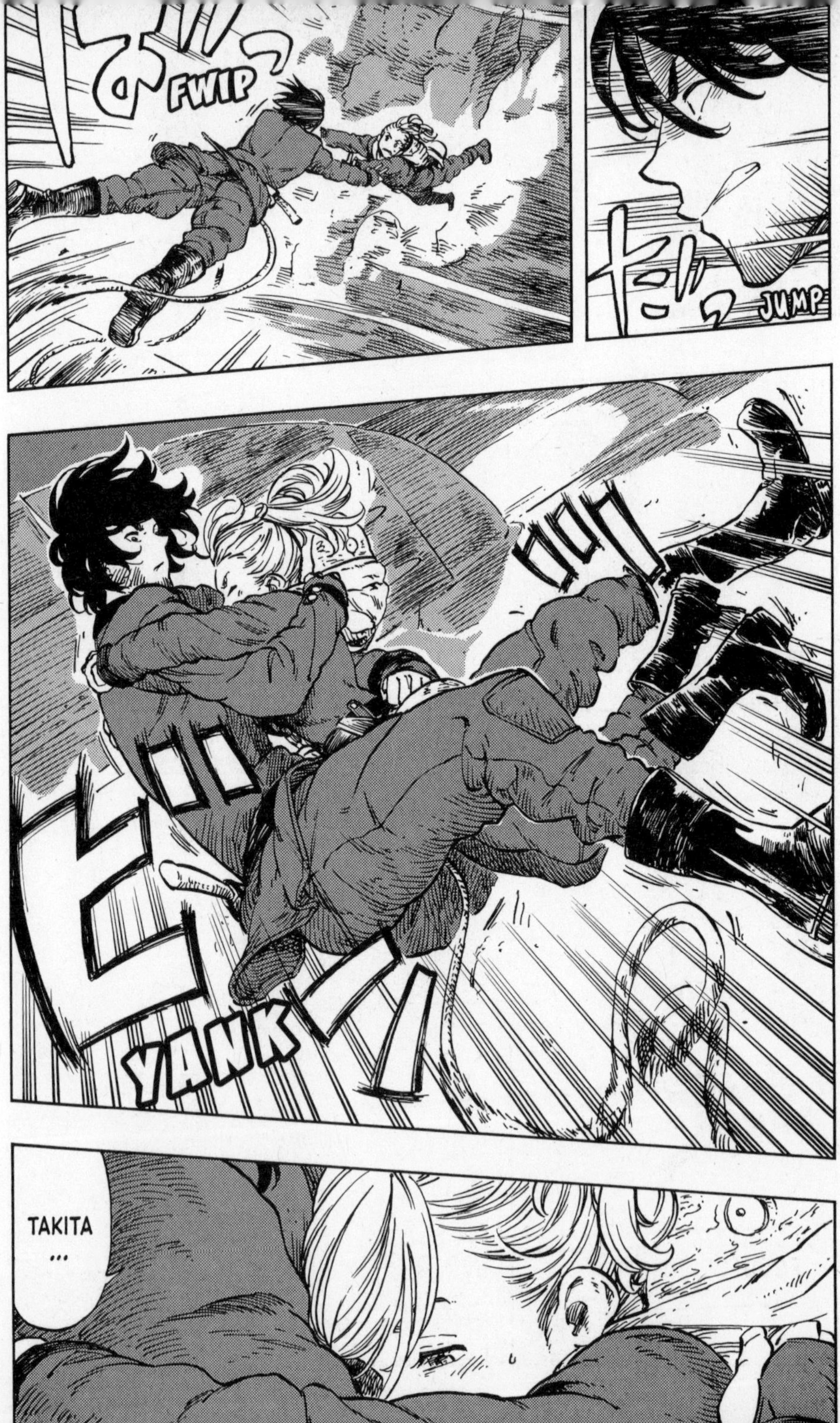
JUMP
FWIP
YANK
TAKITA ...

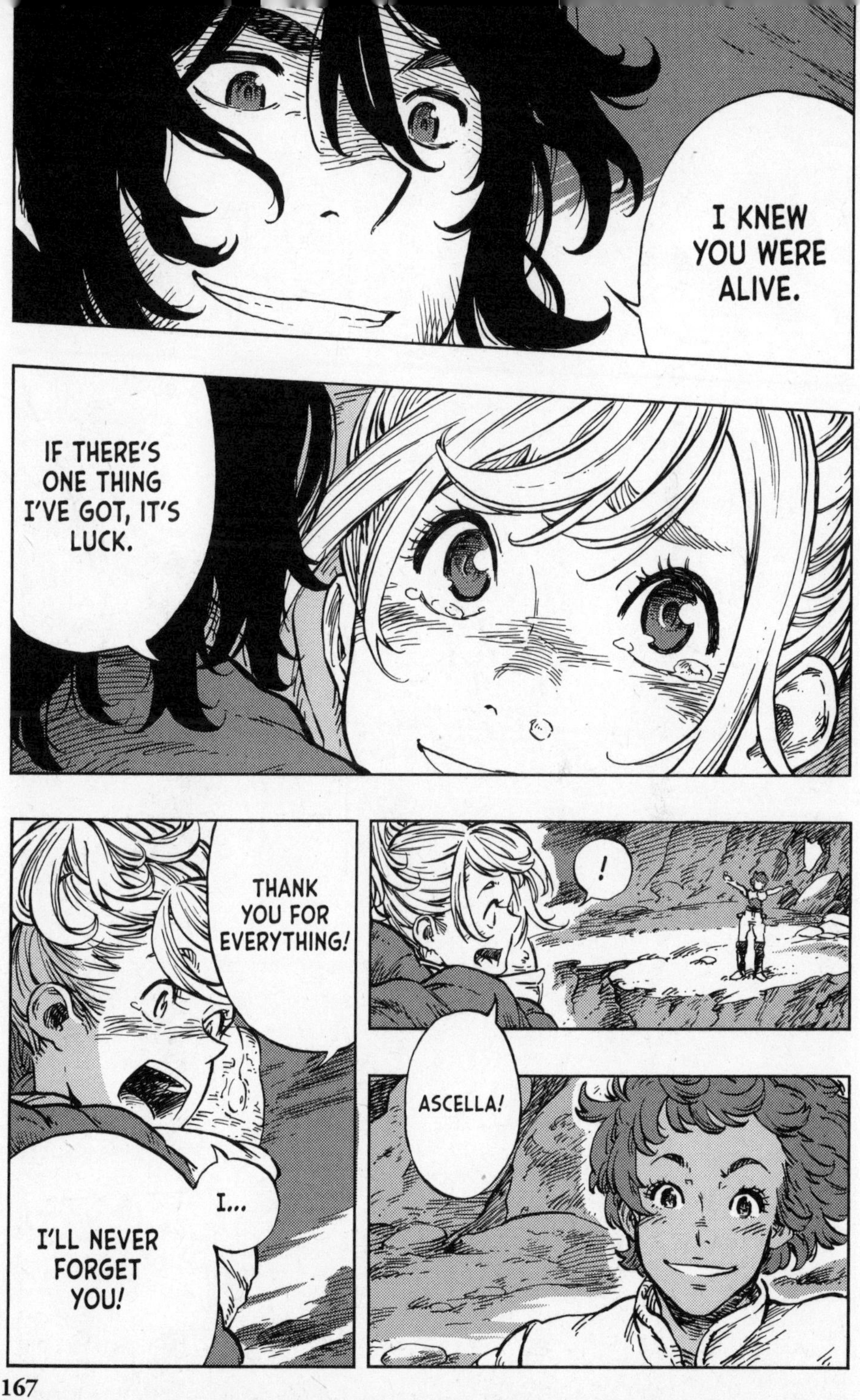
I KNEW YOU WERE ALIVE.
IF THERE'S ONE THING I'VE GOT, IT'S LUCK.
!
ASCELLA!
THANK YOU FOR EVERYTHING!
I...
I'LL NEVER FORGET YOU!

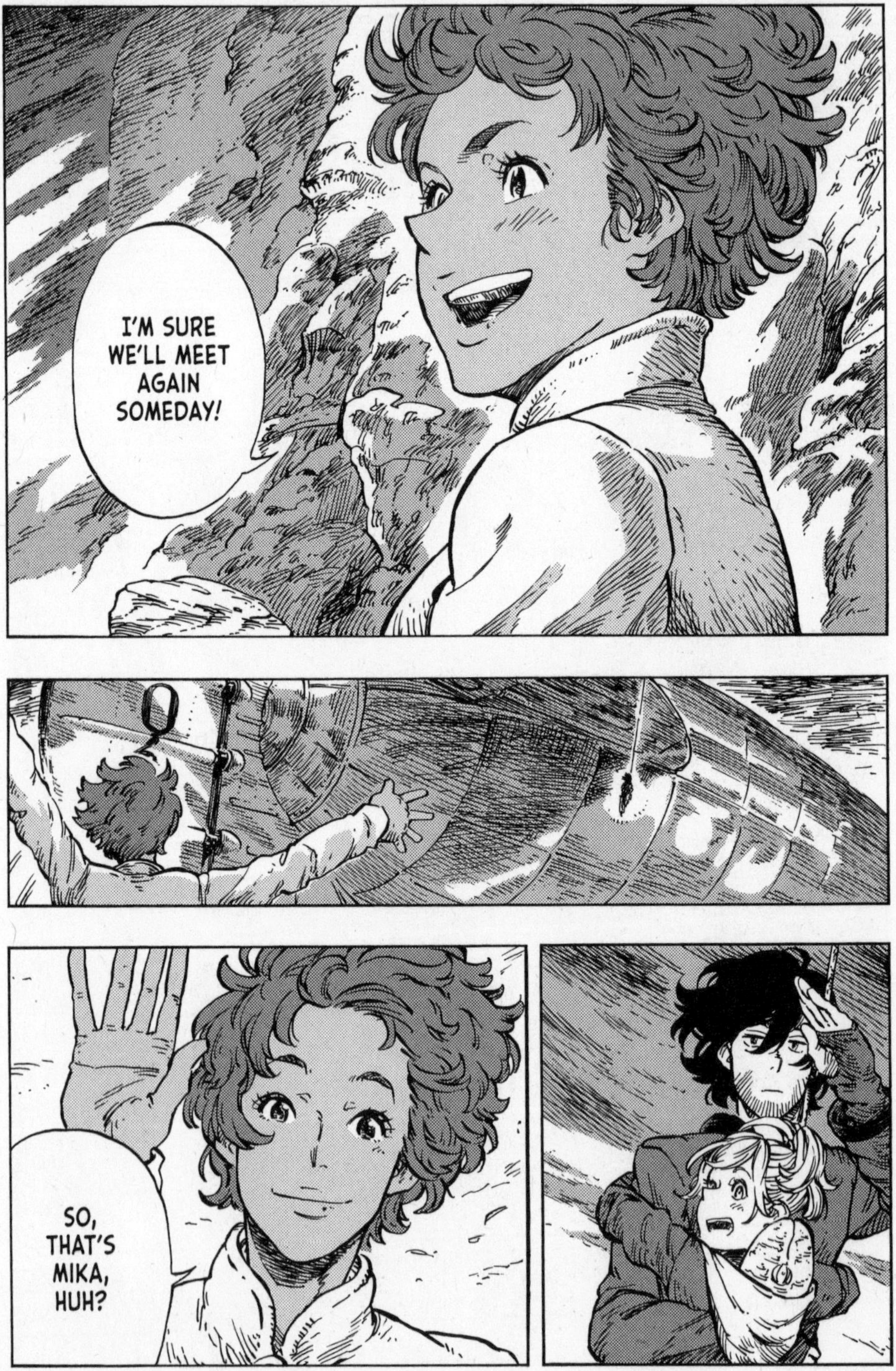
I'M SURE WE'LL MEET AGAIN SOMEDAY!
SO, THAT'S MIKA, HUH?

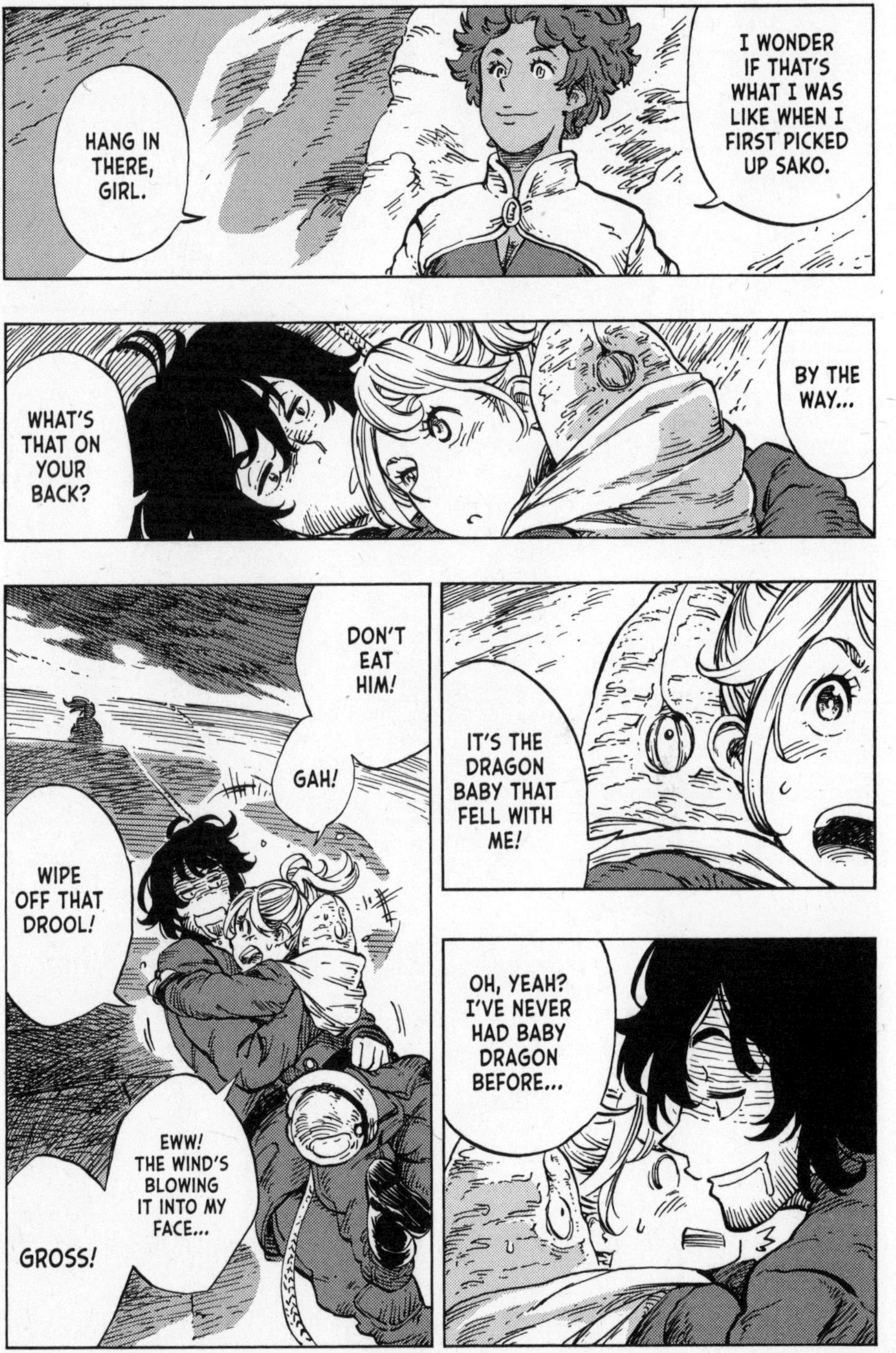
I WONDER IF THAT'S WHAT I WAS LIKE WHEN I FIRST PICKED UP SAKO.
HANG IN THERE, GIRL.
BY THE WAY...
WHAT'S THAT ON YOUR BACK?
IT'S THE DRAGON BABY THAT FELL WITH ME!
OH, YEAH? I'VE NEVER HAD BABY DRAGON BEFORE...
DON'T EAT HIM!
GAH!
WIPE OFF THAT DROOL!
EWW! THE WIND'S BLOWING IT INTO MY FACE...
GROSS!

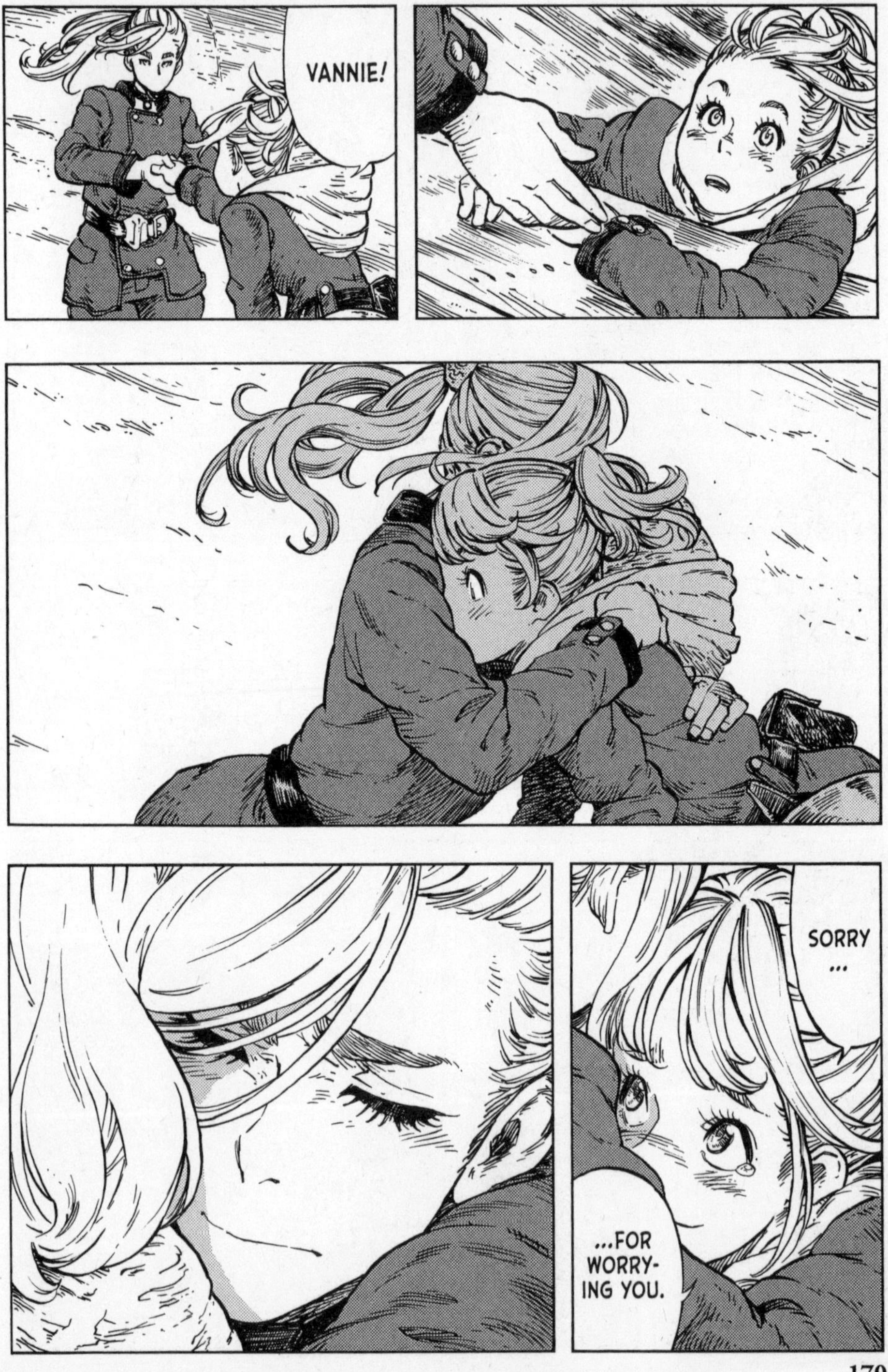
VANNIE!
SORRY ...
...FOR WORRYING YOU.

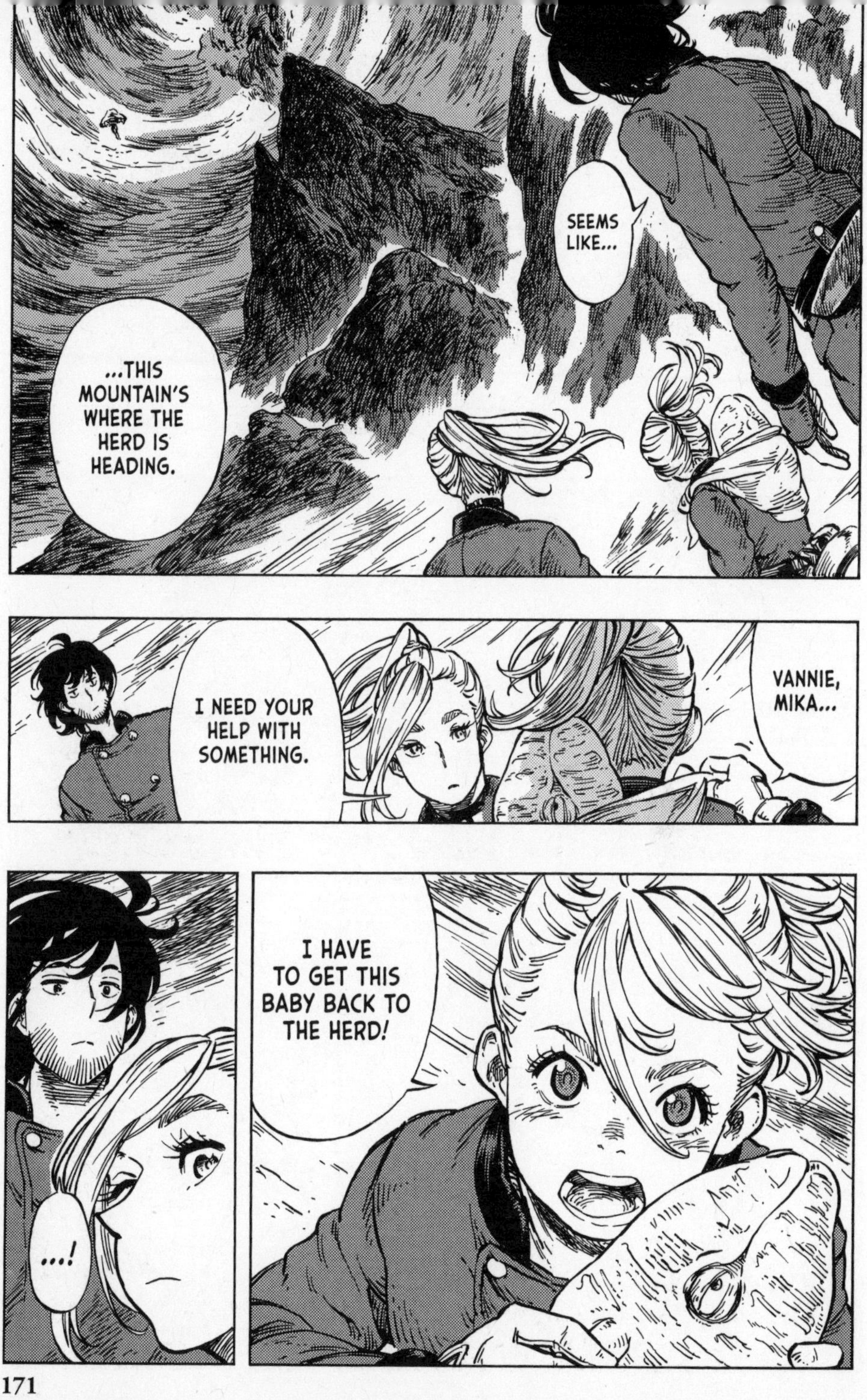
SEEMS LIKE...
...THIS MOUNTAIN'S WHERE THE HERD IS HEADING.
VANNIE, MIKA...
I NEED YOUR HELP WITH SOMETHING.
I HAVE TO GET THIS BABY BACK TO THE HERD!
...!

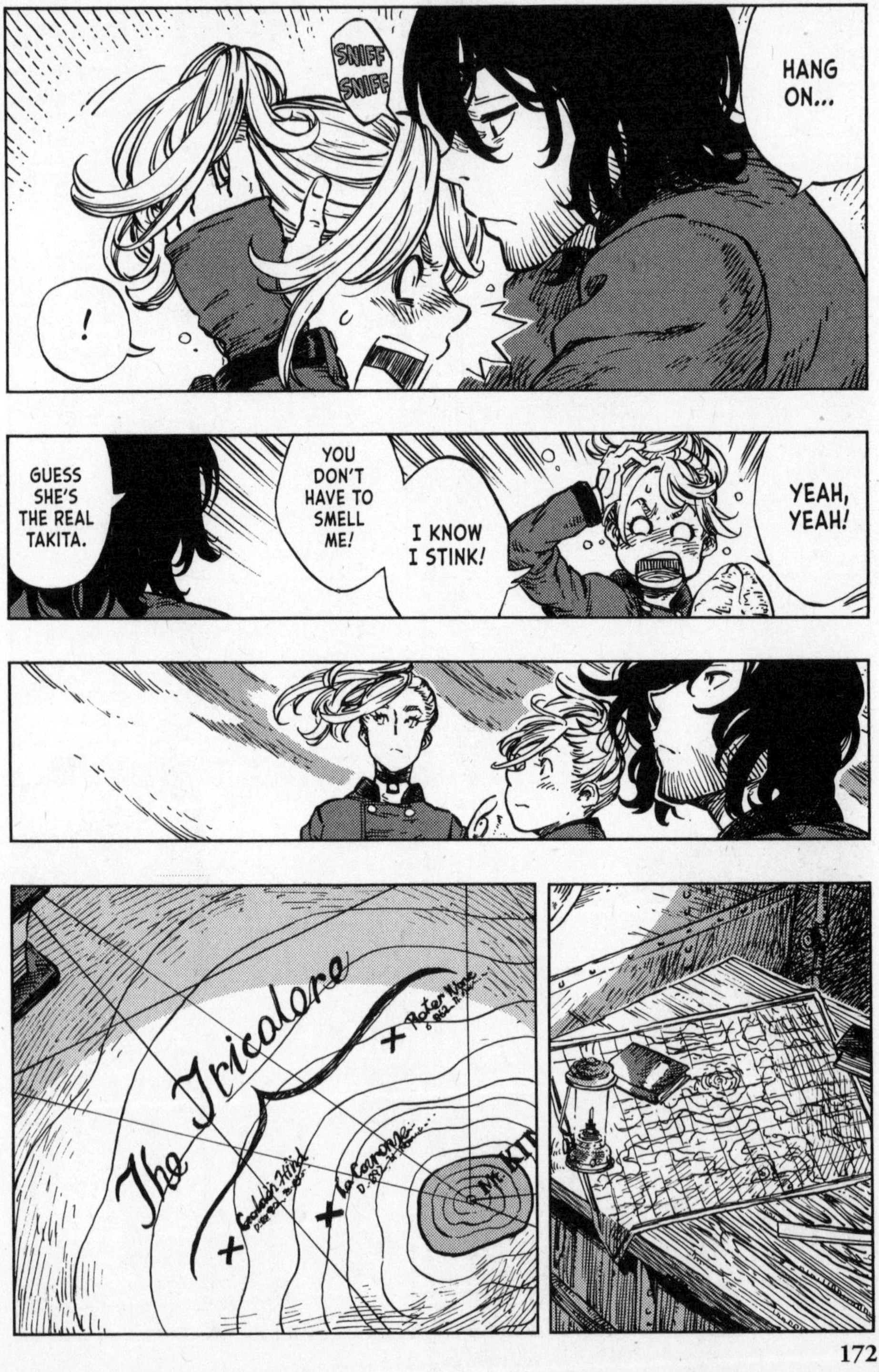
HANG ON...
SNIFF SNIFF
!
YEAH, YEAH!
I KNOW I STINK!
YOU DON'T HAVE TO SMELL ME!
GUESS SHE'S THE REAL TAKITA.
The Tricolore
Golden Hind
La Couronne

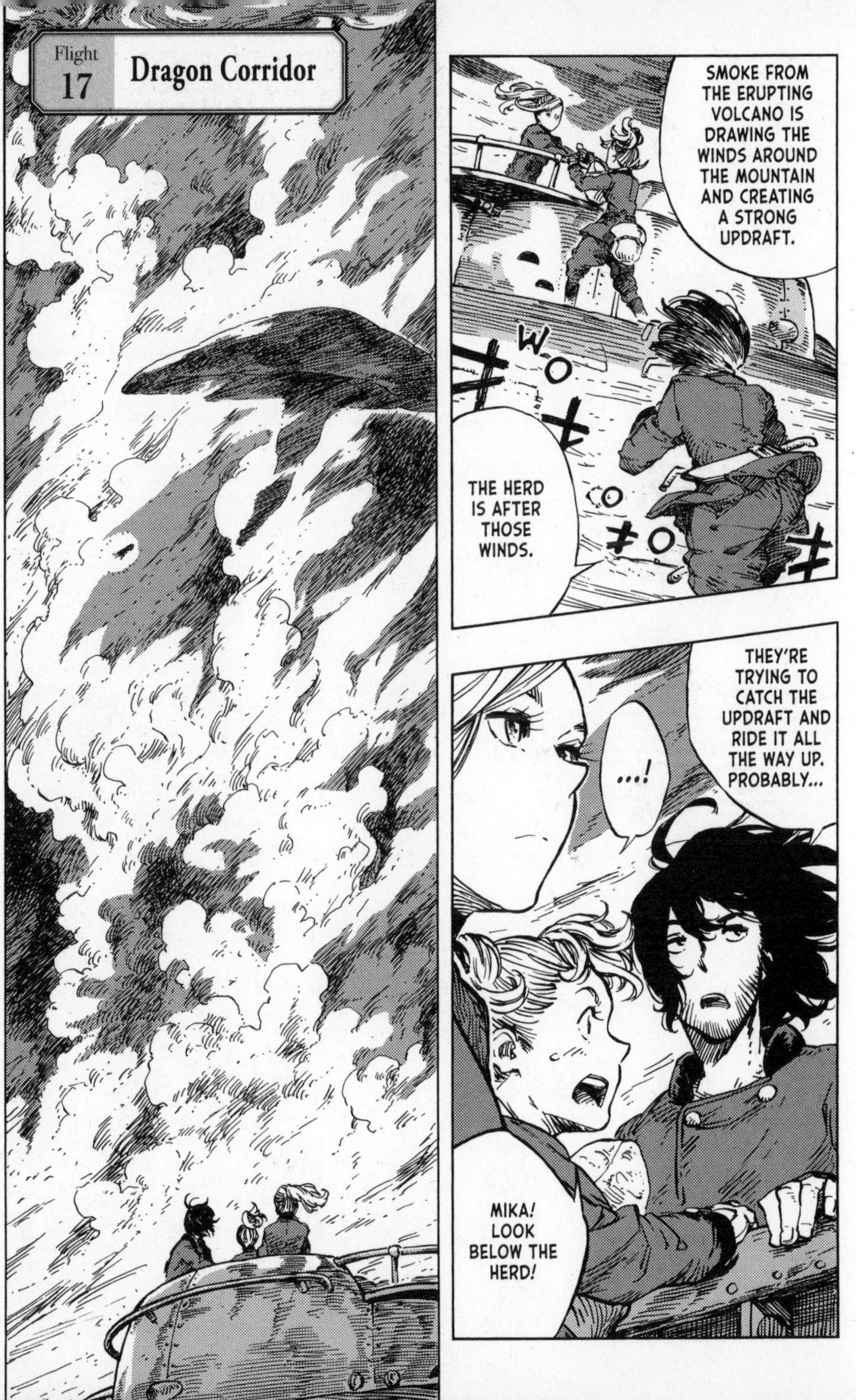
SMOKE FROM THE ERUPTING VOLCANO IS DRAWING THE WINDS AROUND THE MOUNTAIN AND CREATING A STRONG UPDRAFT.
THE HERD IS AFTER THOSE WINDS.
THEY'RE TRYING TO CATCH THE UPDRAFT AND RIDE IT ALL THE WAY UP. PROBABLY...
...!
MIKA! LOOK BELOW THE HERD!
Flight 17
Dragon Corridor

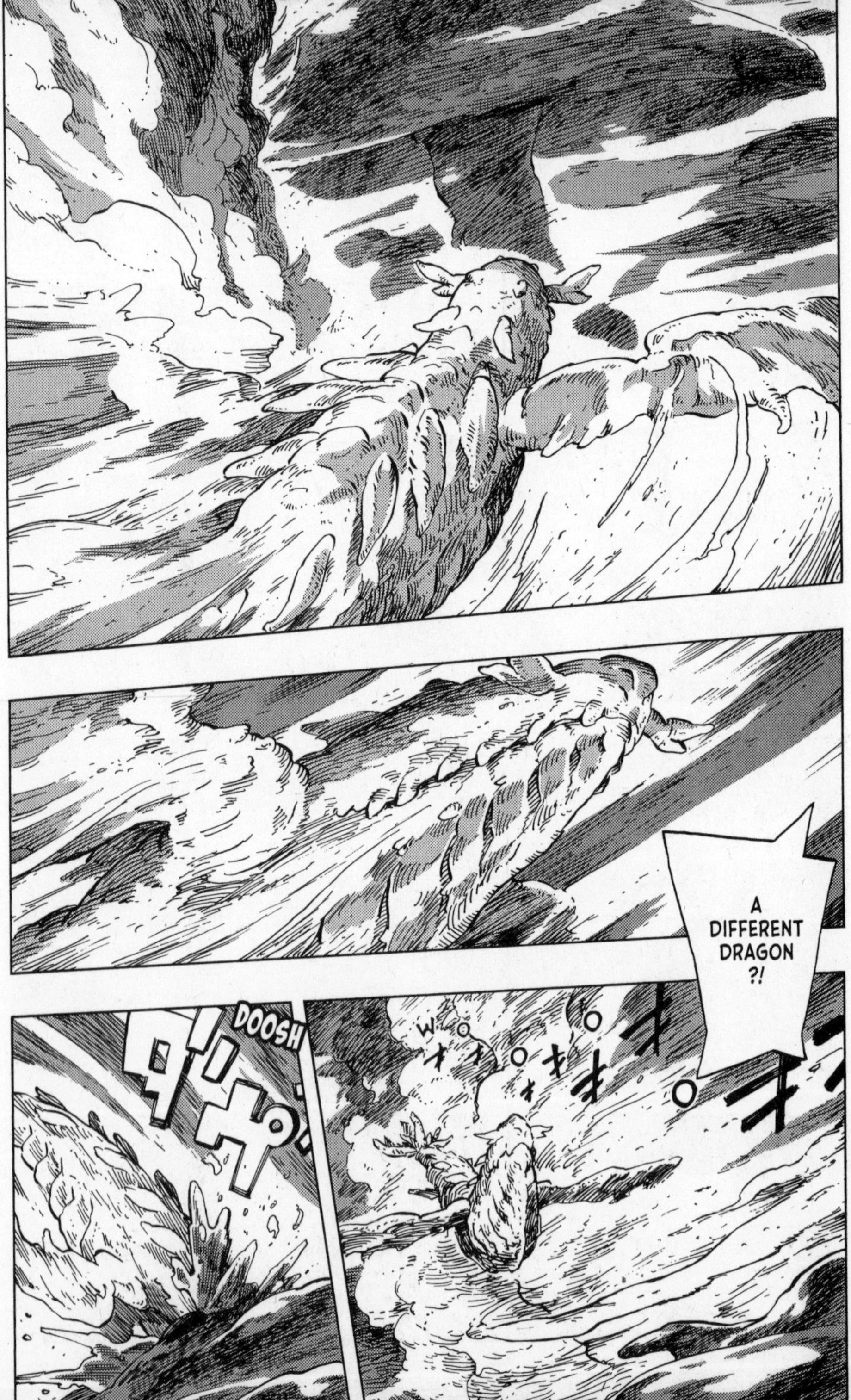
A DIFFERENT DRAGON ?!
DOOSH

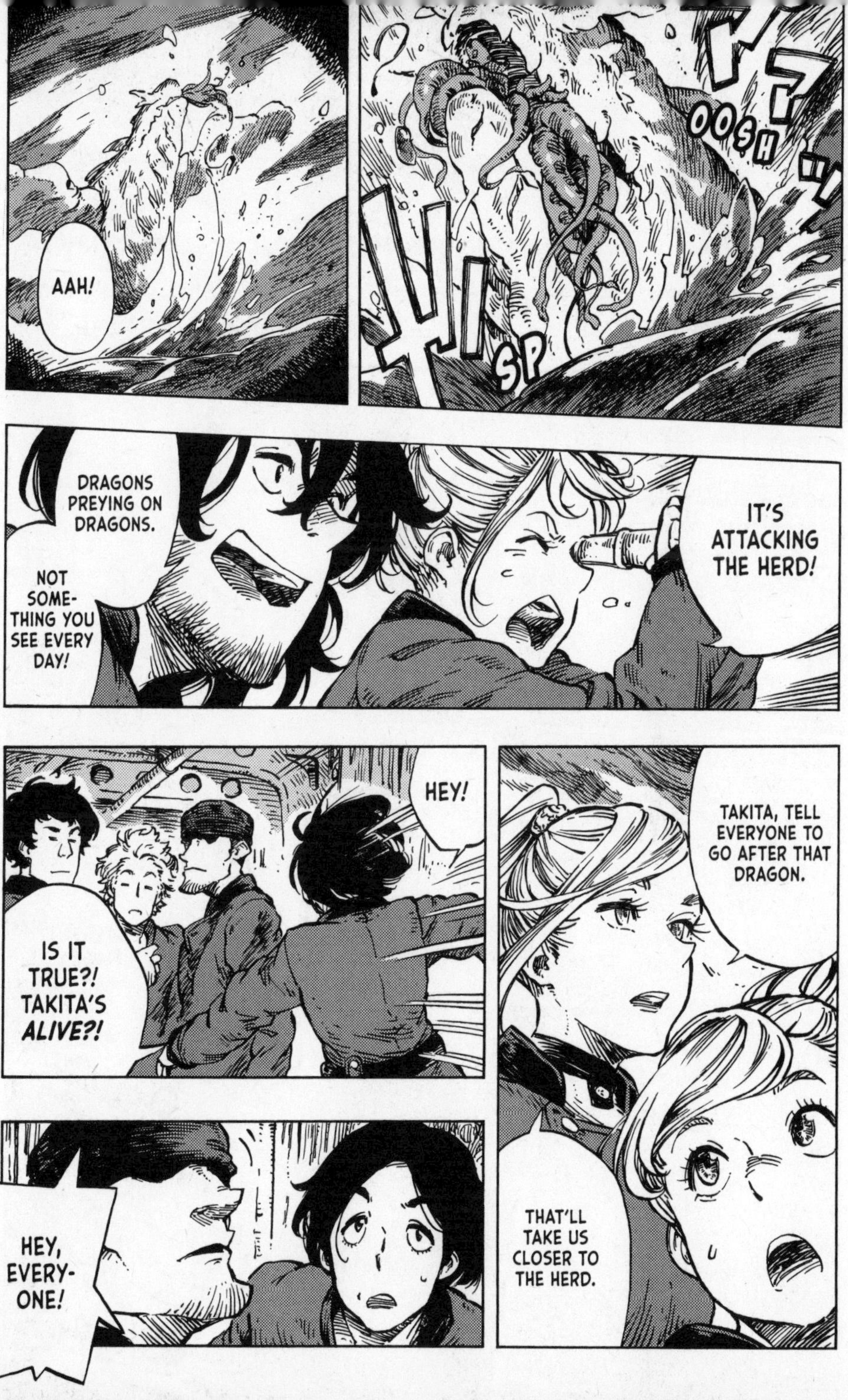
OOSH
SP
AAH!
IT'S ATTACKING THE HERD!
DRAGONS PREYING ON DRAGONS.
NOT SOMETHING YOU SEE EVERY DAY!
TAKITA, TELL EVERYONE TO GO AFTER THAT DRAGON.
THAT'LL TAKE US CLOSER TO THE HERD.
HEY!
IS IT TRUE?! TAKITA'S *ALIVE?!*
HEY, EVERYONE!

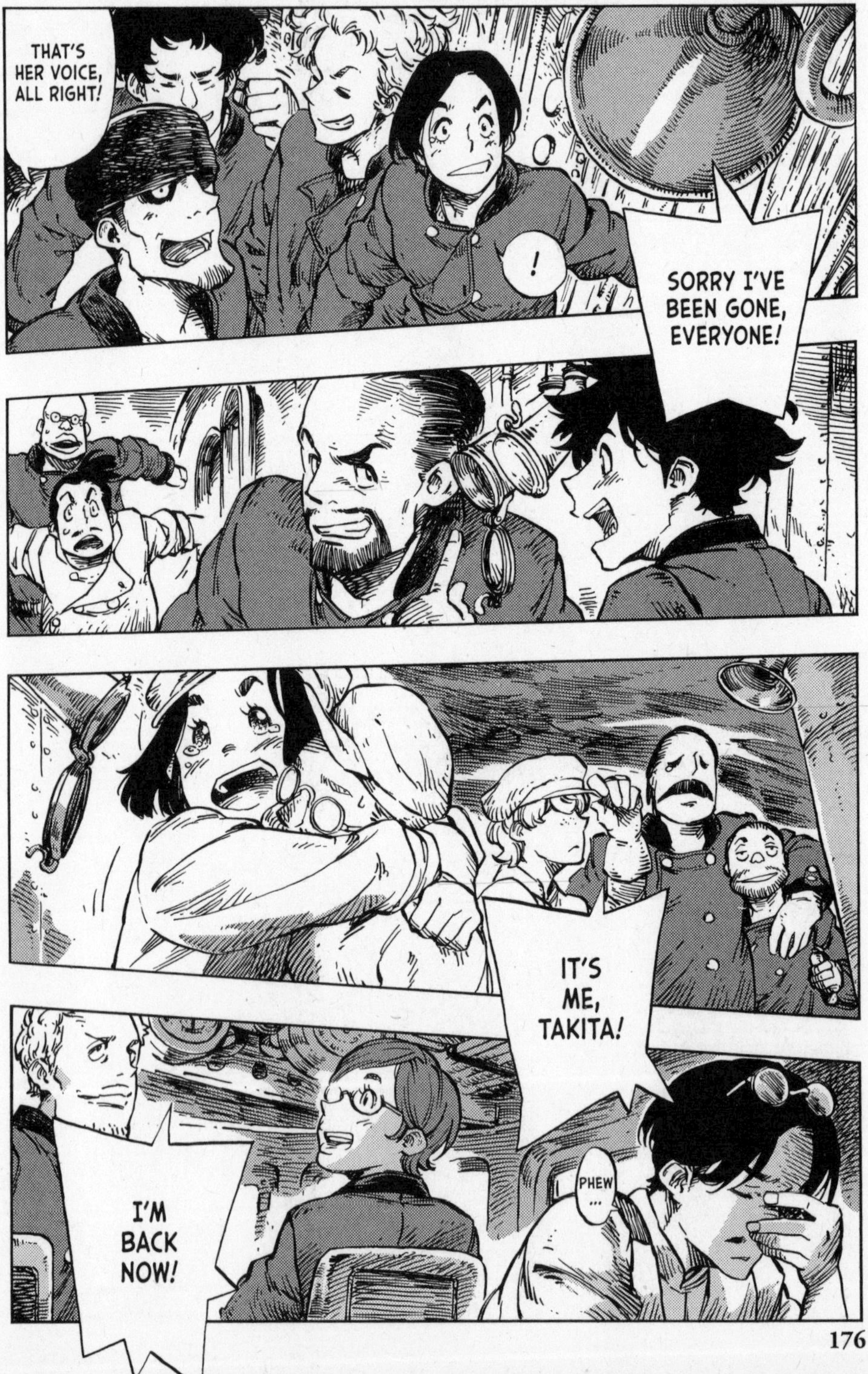
SORRY I'VE BEEN GONE, EVERYONE!
!
THAT'S HER VOICE, ALL RIGHT!
IT'S ME, TAKITA!
PHEW...
I'M BACK NOW!

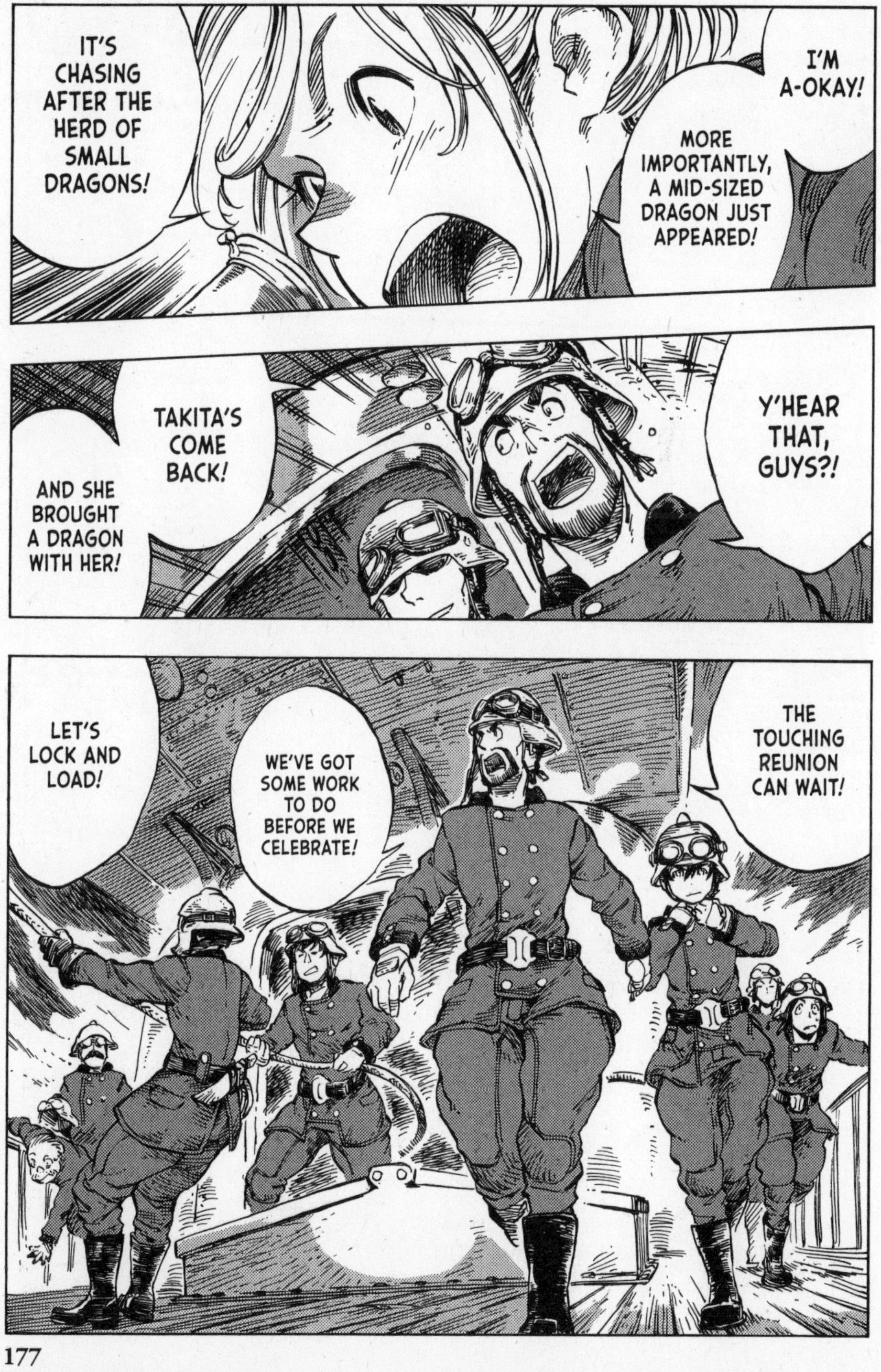
I'M A-OKAY!
MORE IMPORTANTLY, A MID-SIZED DRAGON JUST APPEARED!
IT'S CHASING AFTER THE HERD OF SMALL DRAGONS!
Y'HEAR THAT, GUYS?!
TAKITA'S COME BACK!
AND SHE BROUGHT A DRAGON WITH HER!
THE TOUCHING REUNION CAN WAIT!
WE'VE GOT SOME WORK TO DO BEFORE WE CELEBRATE!
LET'S LOCK AND LOAD!

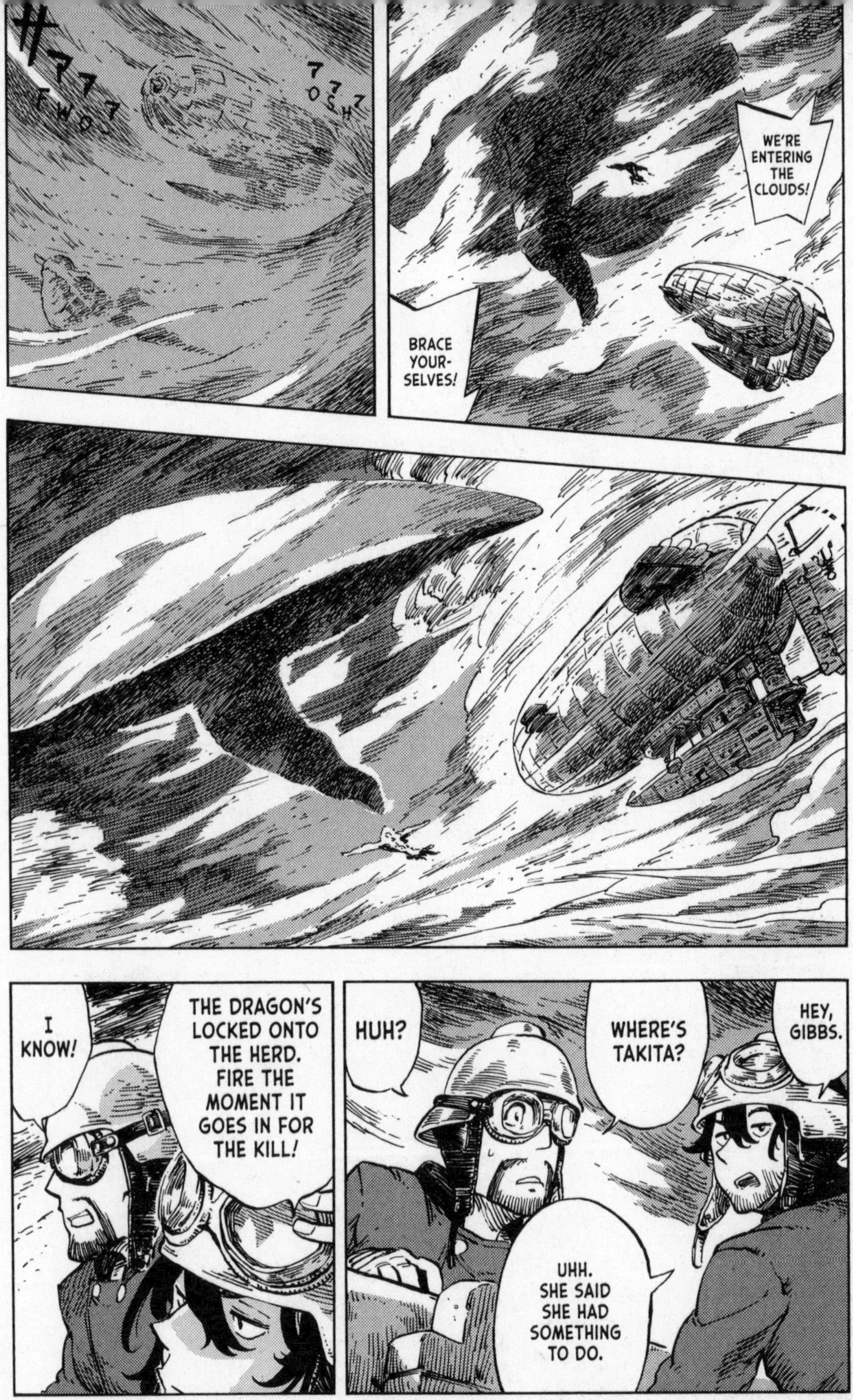
WE'RE ENTERING THE CLOUDS!
BRACE YOUR-SELVES!
HEY, GIBBS.
WHERE'S TAKITA?
HUH?
UHH. SHE SAID SHE HAD SOMETHING TO DO.
THE DRAGON'S LOCKED ONTO THE HERD. FIRE THE MOMENT IT GOES IN FOR THE KILL!
I KNOW!

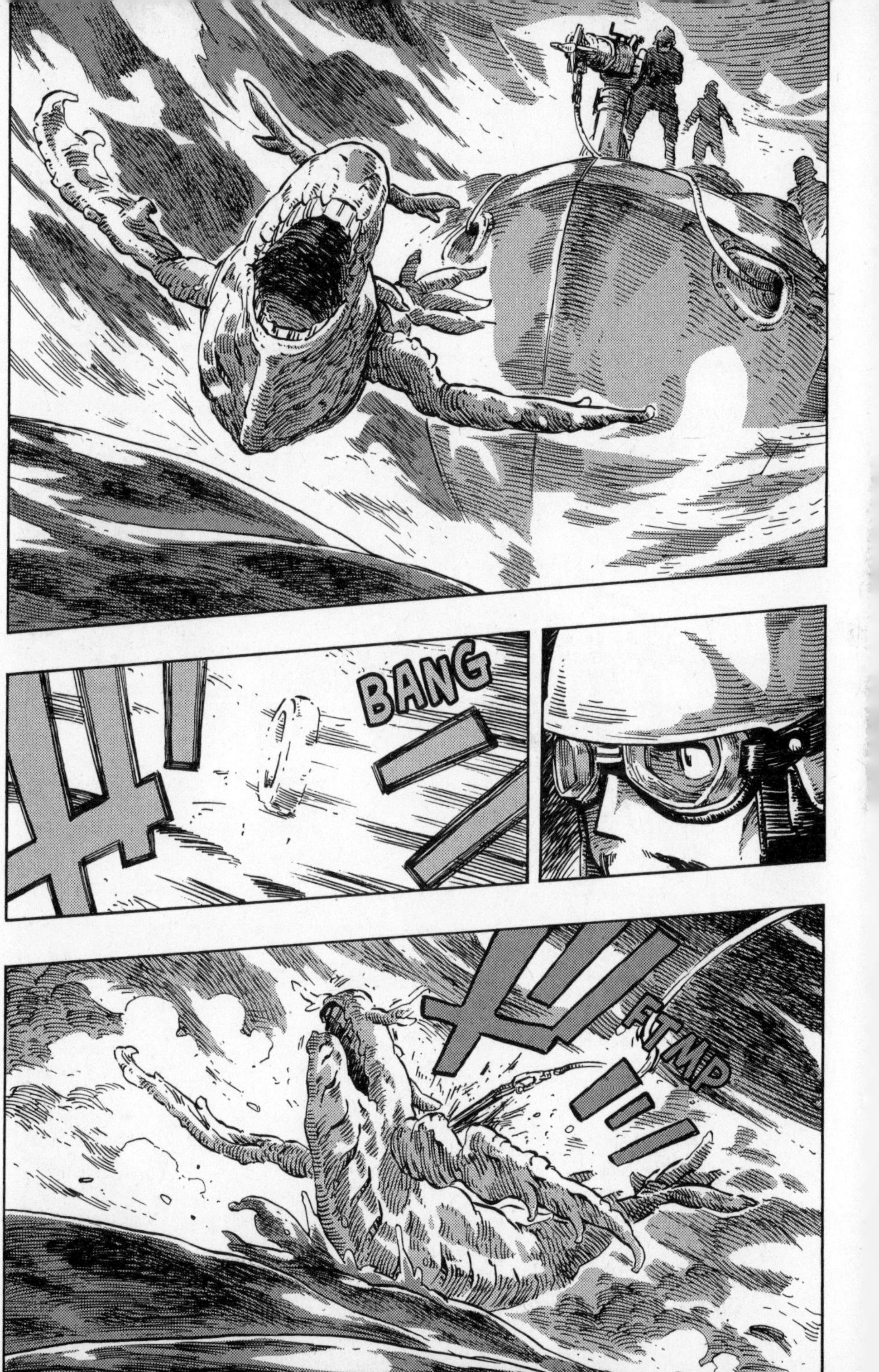
BANG
FTMP

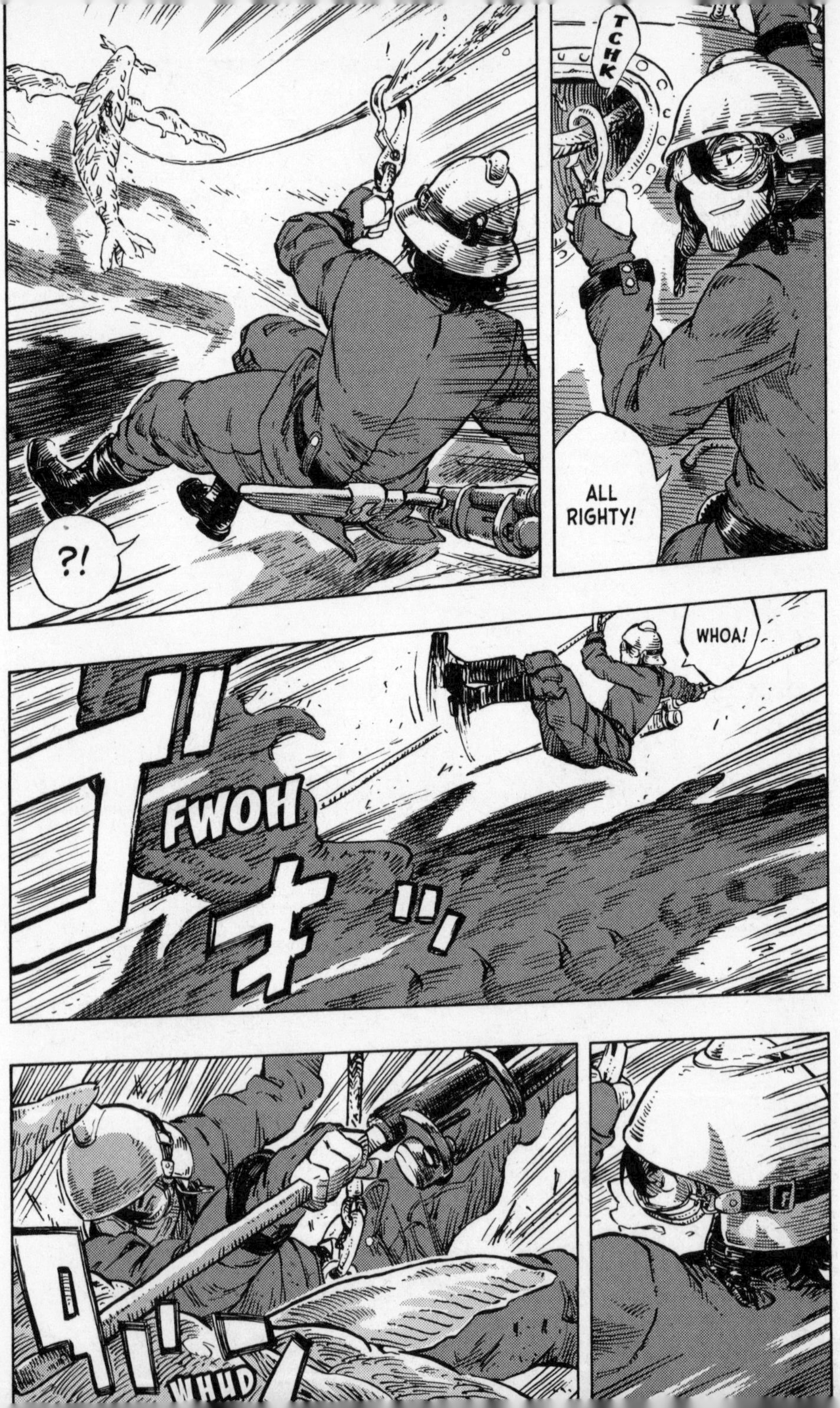
TCHK
ALL RIGHTY!
?!
WHOA!
FWOH
WHUD

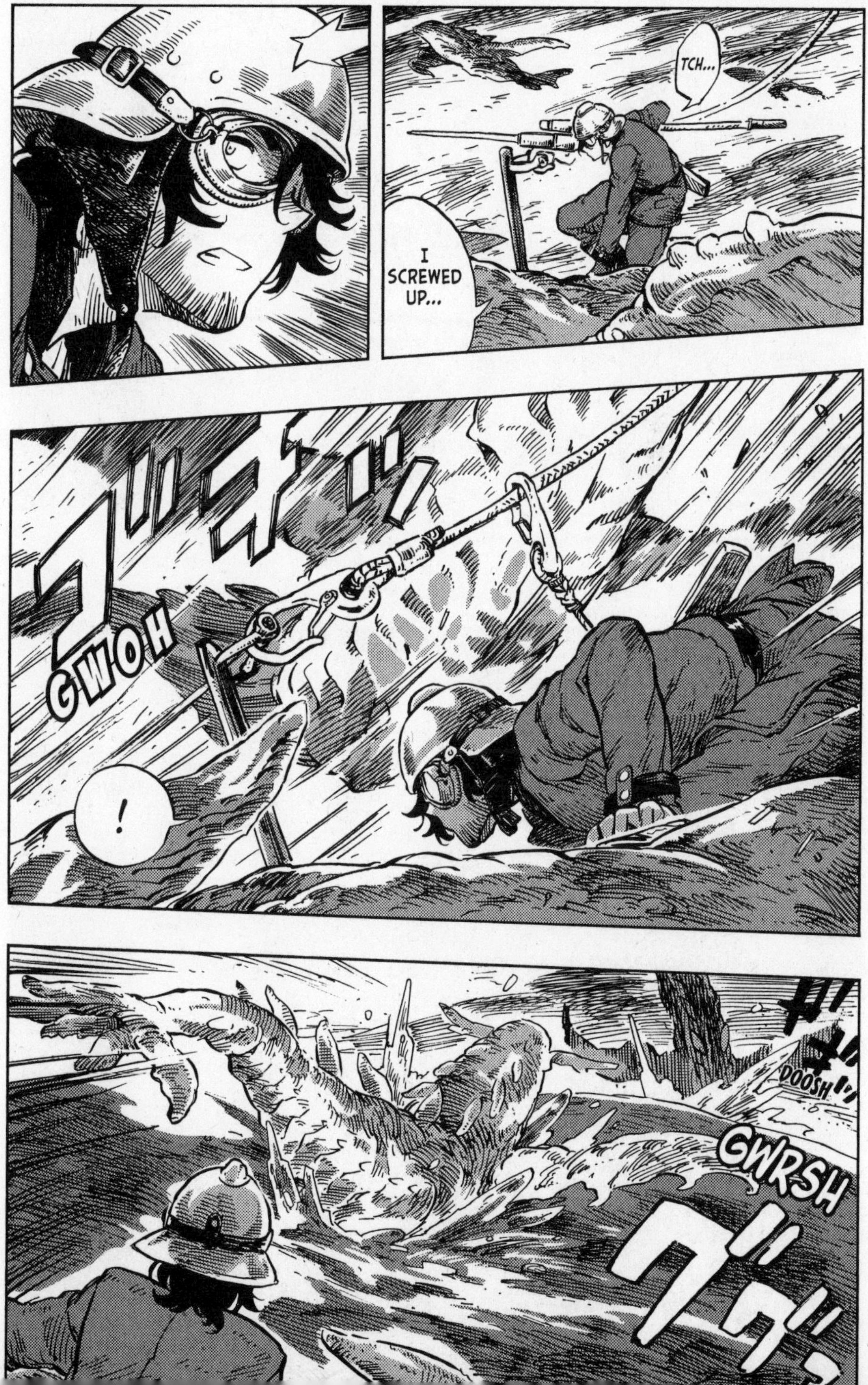
TCH...
I SCREWED UP...
GWOH
!
DOOSH
GWRSH

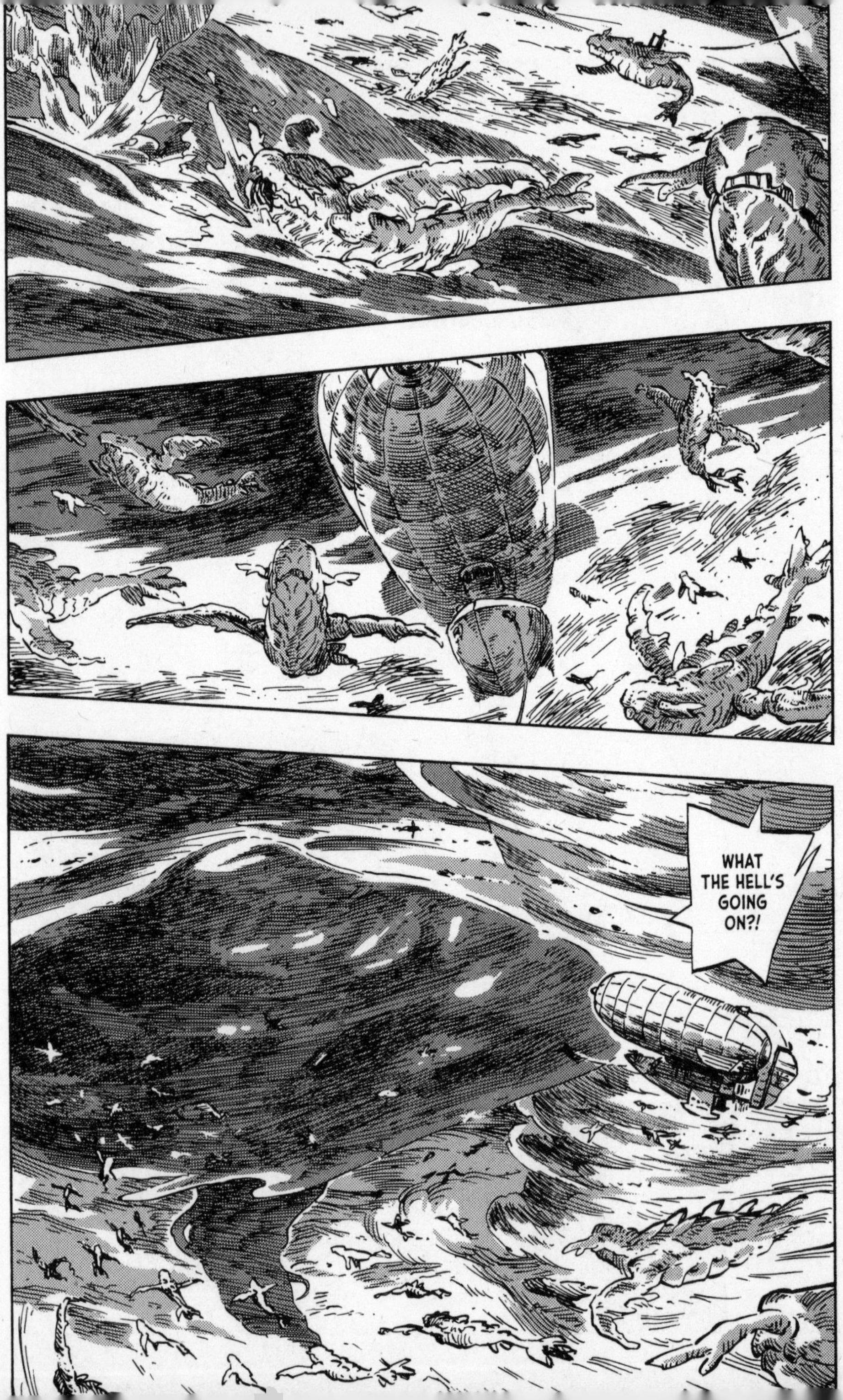
WHAT THE HELL'S GOING ON?!

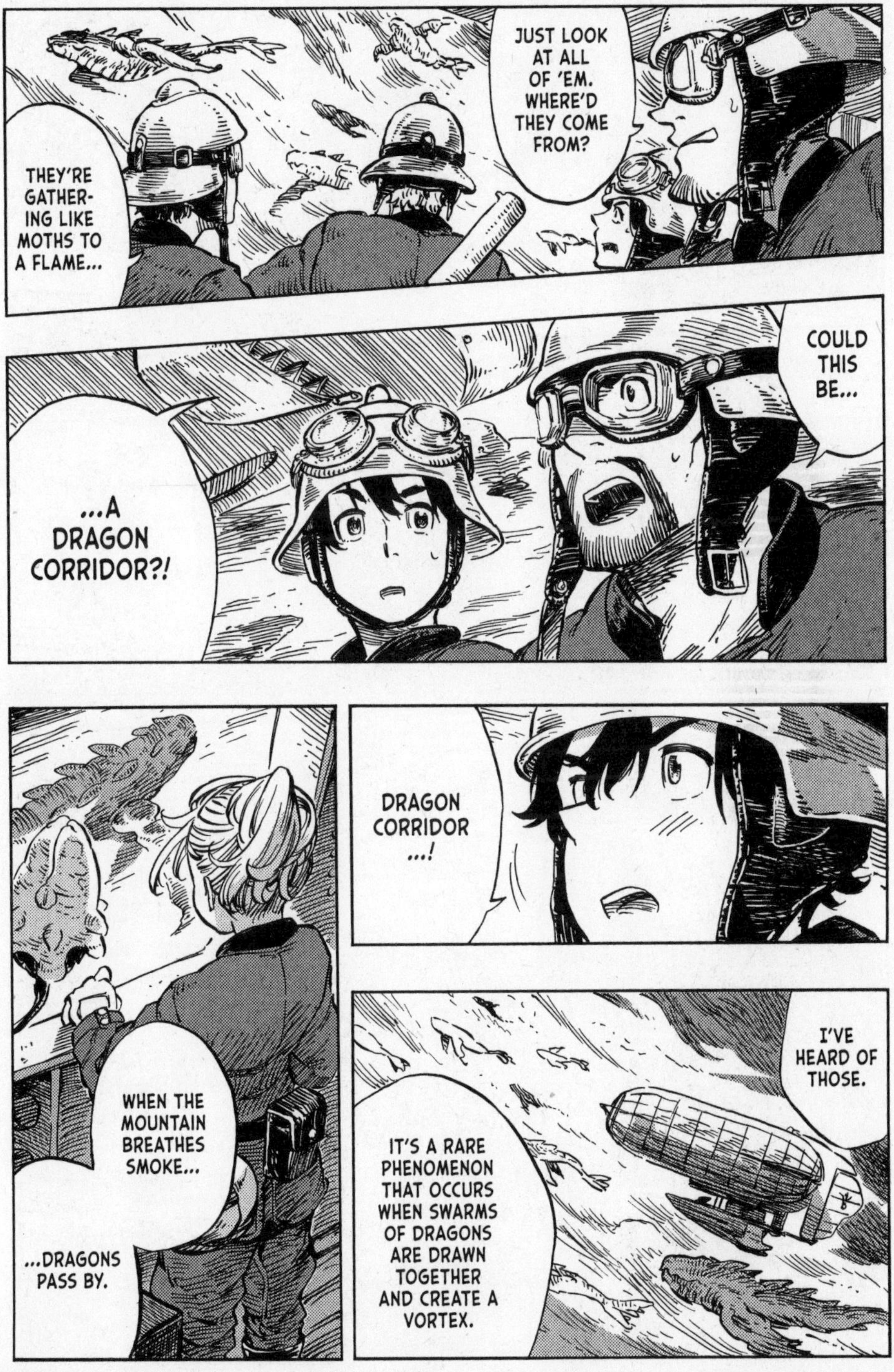
JUST LOOK AT ALL OF 'EM. WHERE'D THEY COME FROM?
THEY'RE GATHER-ING LIKE MOTHS TO A FLAME...
COULD THIS BE...
...A DRAGON CORRIDOR?!
DRAGON CORRIDOR ...!
I'VE HEARD OF THOSE.
IT'S A RARE PHENOMENON THAT OCCURS WHEN SWARMS OF DRAGONS ARE DRAWN TOGETHER AND CREATE A VORTEX.
WHEN THE MOUNTAIN BREATHES SMOKE...
...DRAGONS PASS BY.

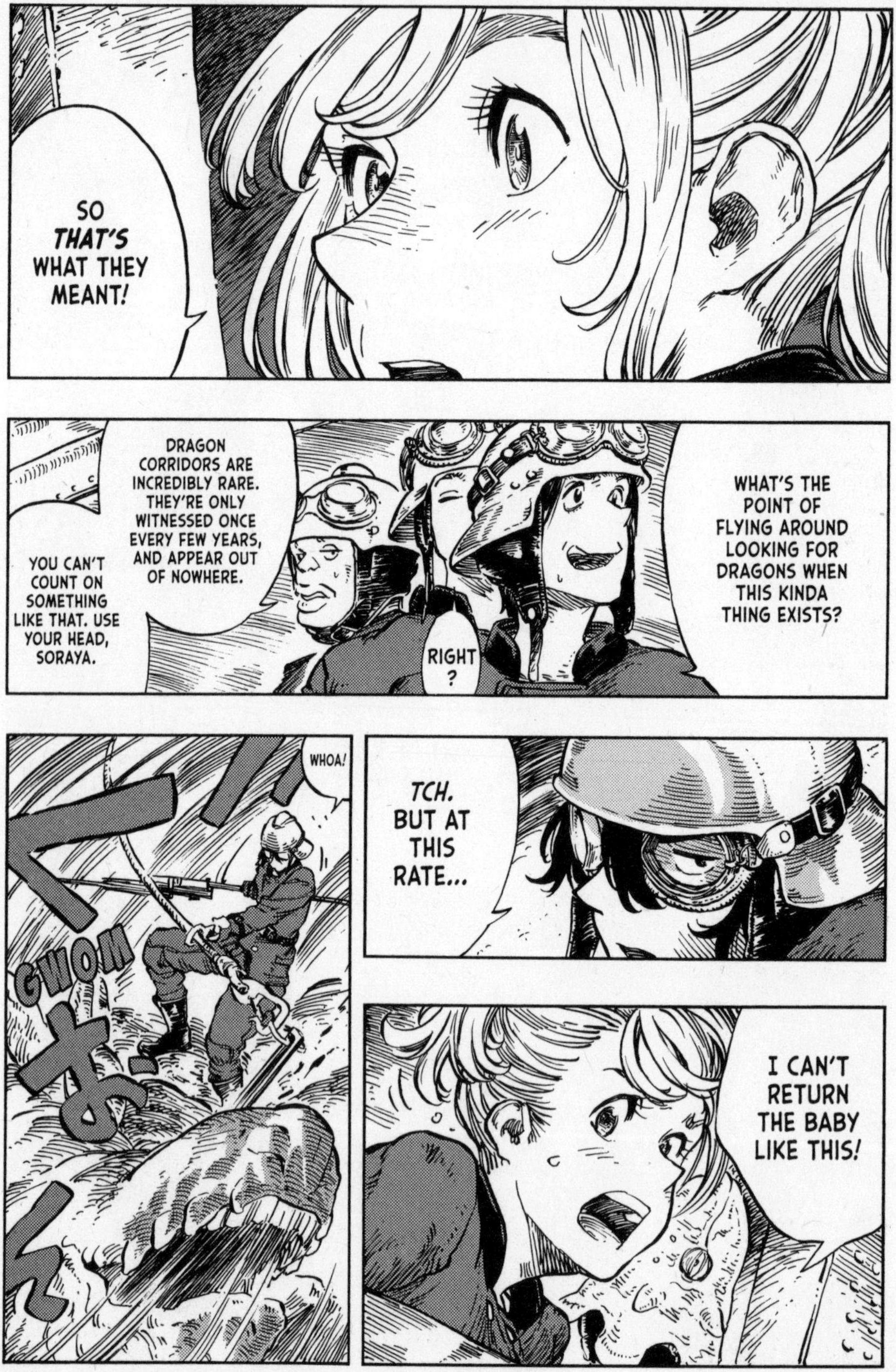
SO *THAT'S* WHAT THEY MEANT!
WHAT'S THE POINT OF FLYING AROUND LOOKING FOR DRAGONS WHEN THIS KINDA THING EXISTS?
RIGHT?
DRAGON CORRIDORS ARE INCREDIBLY RARE. THEY'RE ONLY WITNESSED ONCE EVERY FEW YEARS, AND APPEAR OUT OF NOWHERE.
YOU CAN'T COUNT ON SOMETHING LIKE THAT. USE YOUR HEAD, SORAYA.
TCH. BUT AT THIS RATE...
I CAN'T RETURN THE BABY LIKE THIS!
WHOA!
GWOM

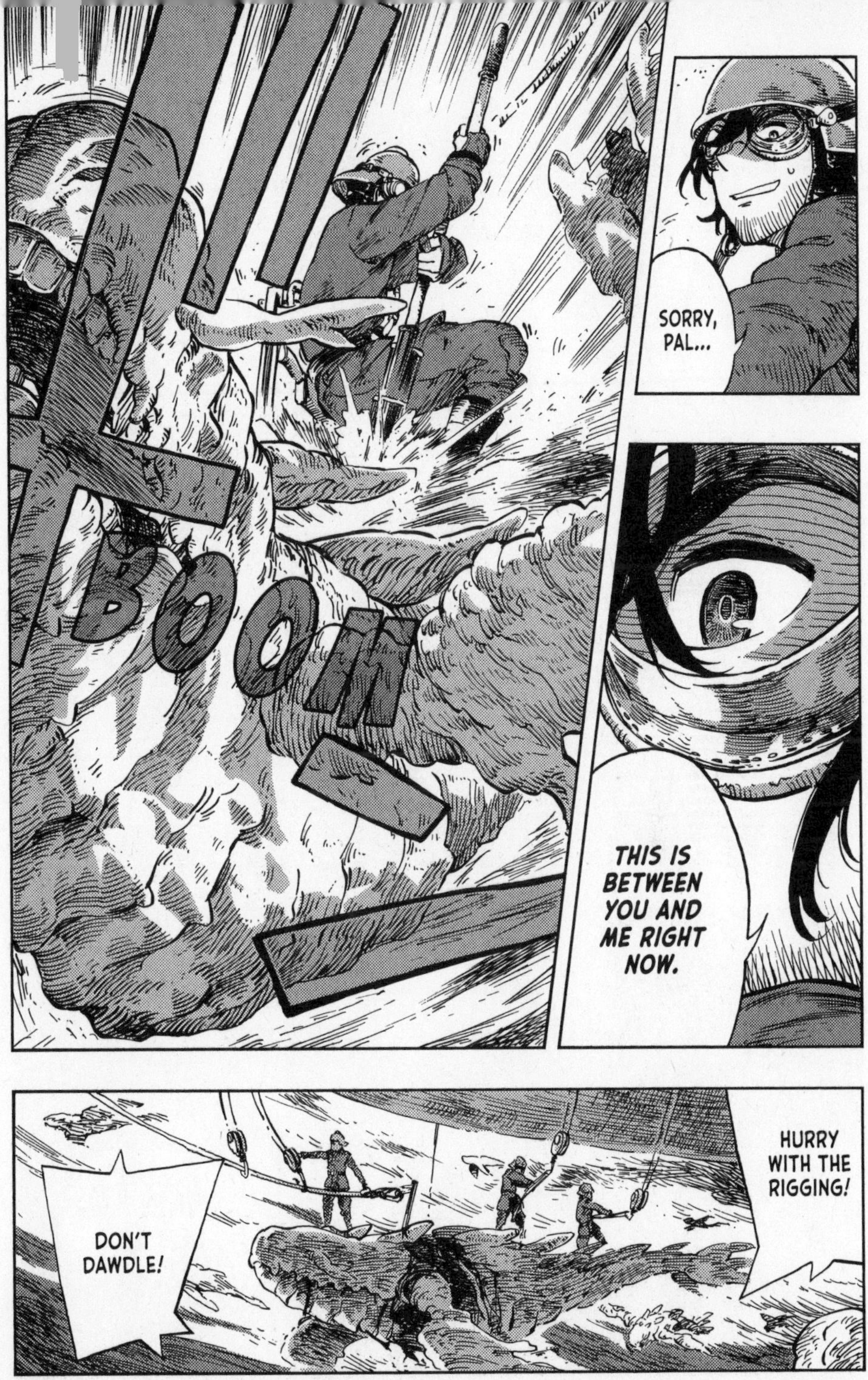
SORRY, PAL...
THIS IS BETWEEN YOU AND ME RIGHT NOW.
BOOM
HURRY WITH THE RIGGING!
DON'T DAWDLE!

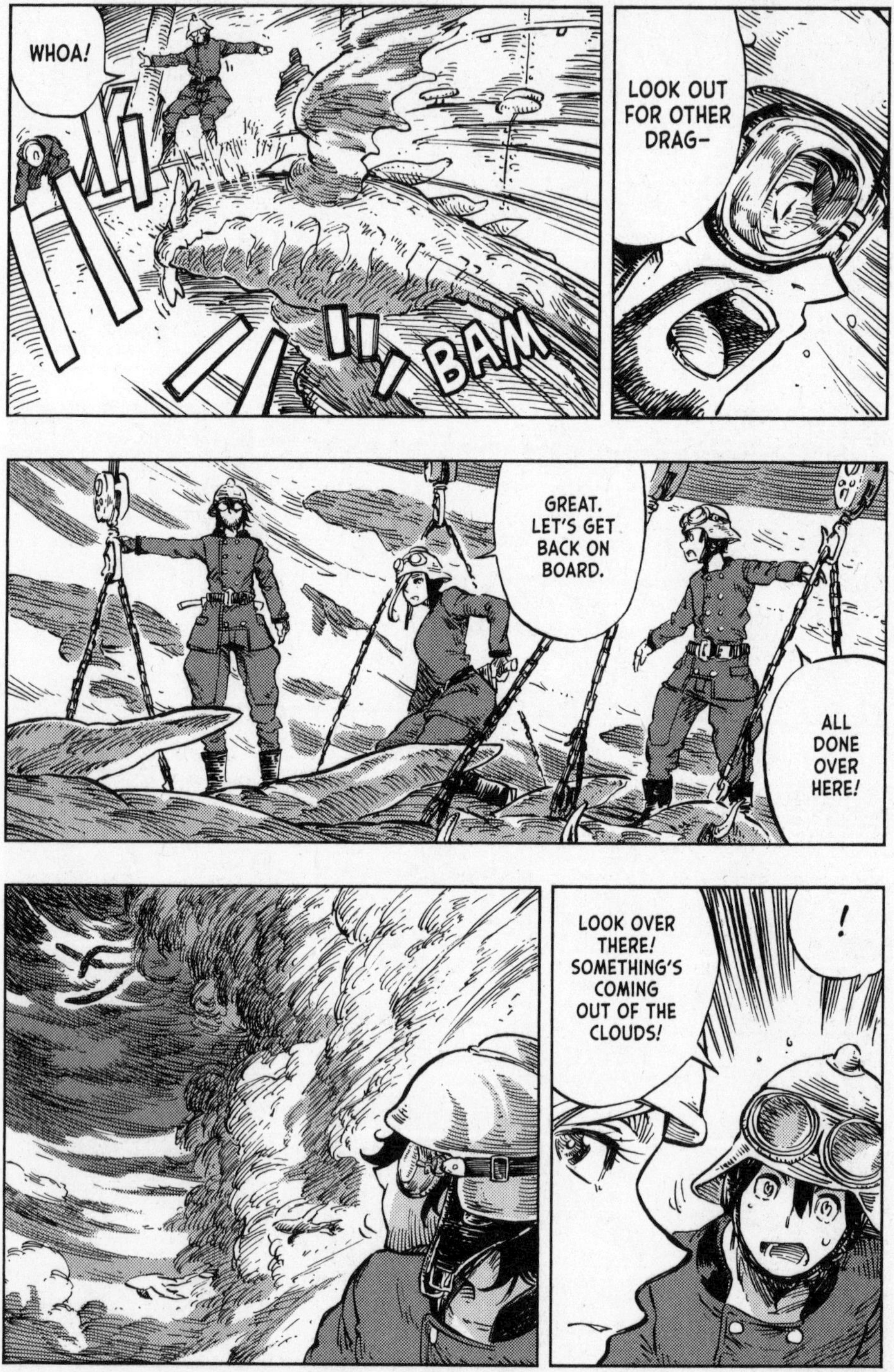
LOOK OUT FOR OTHER DRAG–
WHOA!
BAM
ALL DONE OVER HERE!
GREAT. LET'S GET BACK ON BOARD.
!
LOOK OVER THERE! SOMETHING'S COMING OUT OF THE CLOUDS!

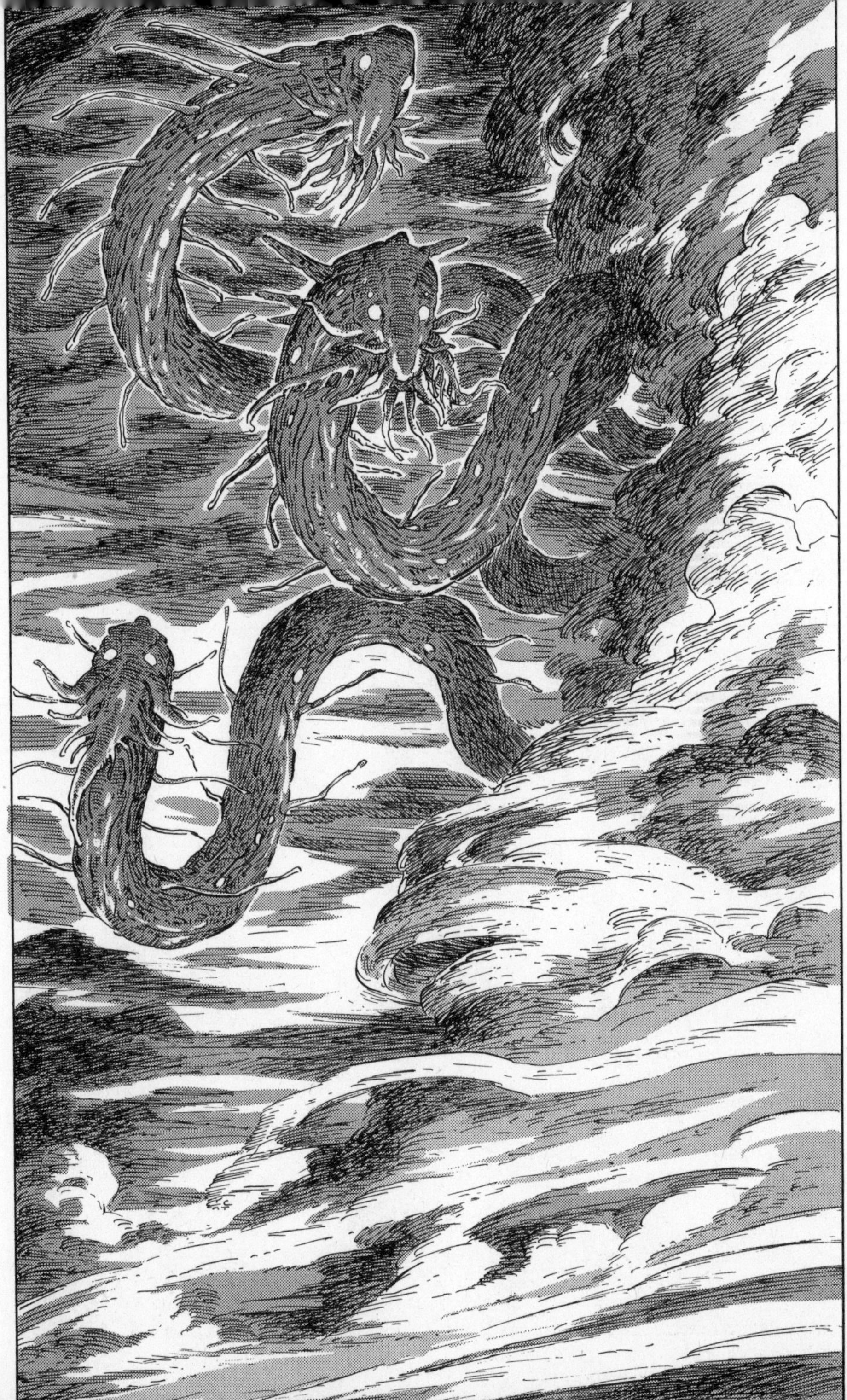

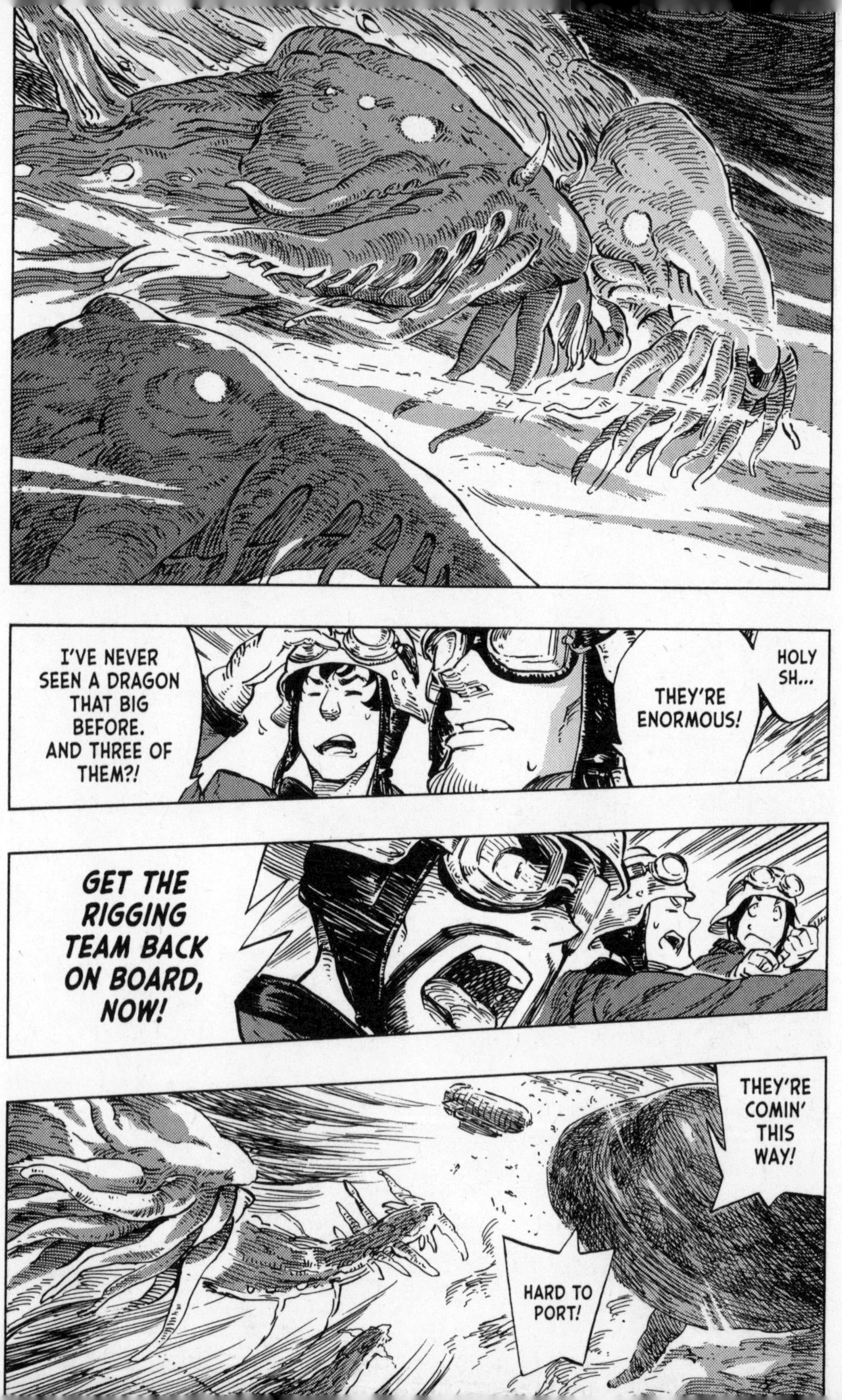
HOLY SH...
THEY'RE ENORMOUS!
I'VE NEVER SEEN A DRAGON THAT BIG BEFORE. AND THREE OF THEM?!
GET THE RIGGING TEAM BACK ON BOARD, NOW!
THEY'RE COMIN' THIS WAY!
HARD TO PORT!

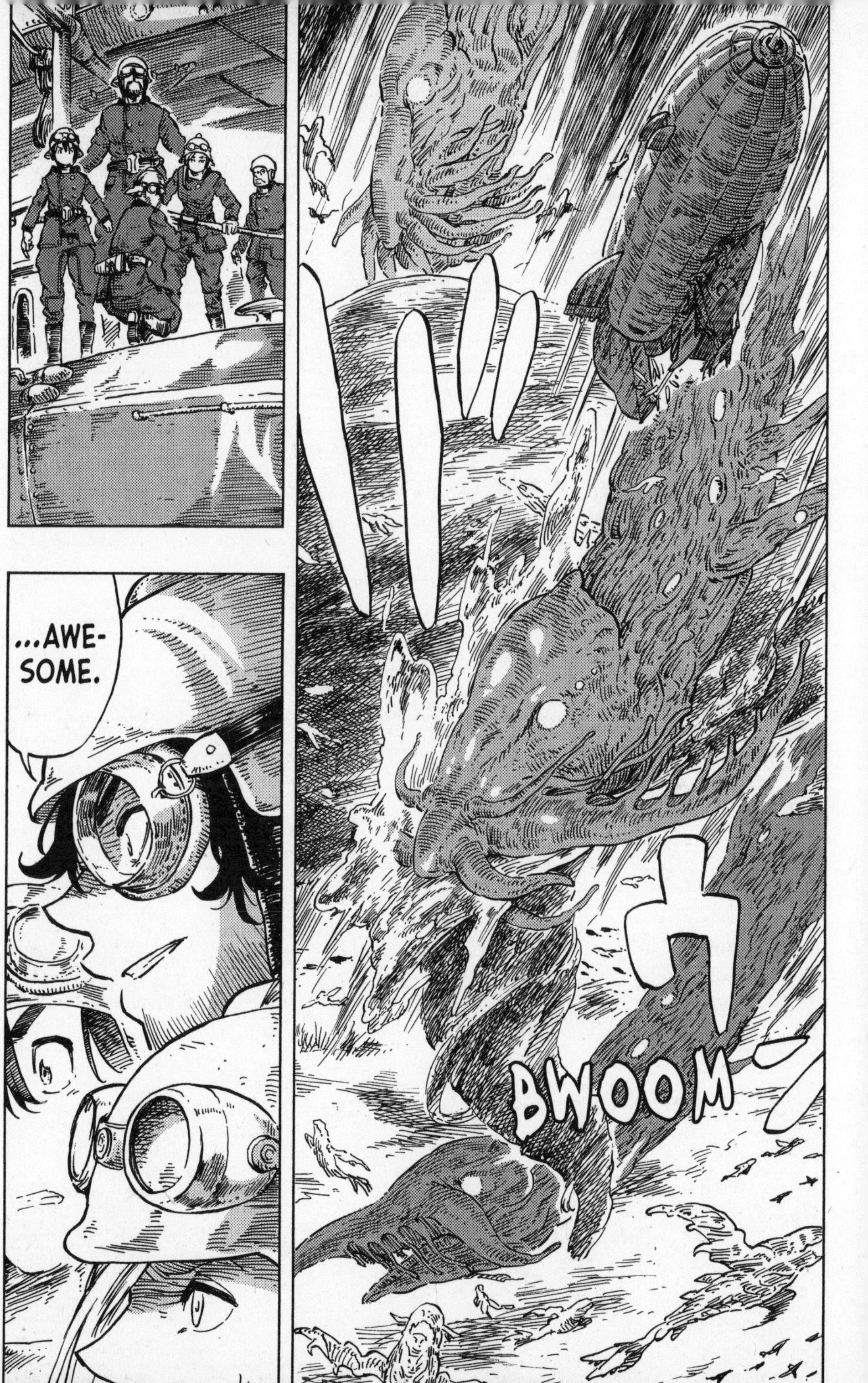
BWOOM
...AWE-
SOME.

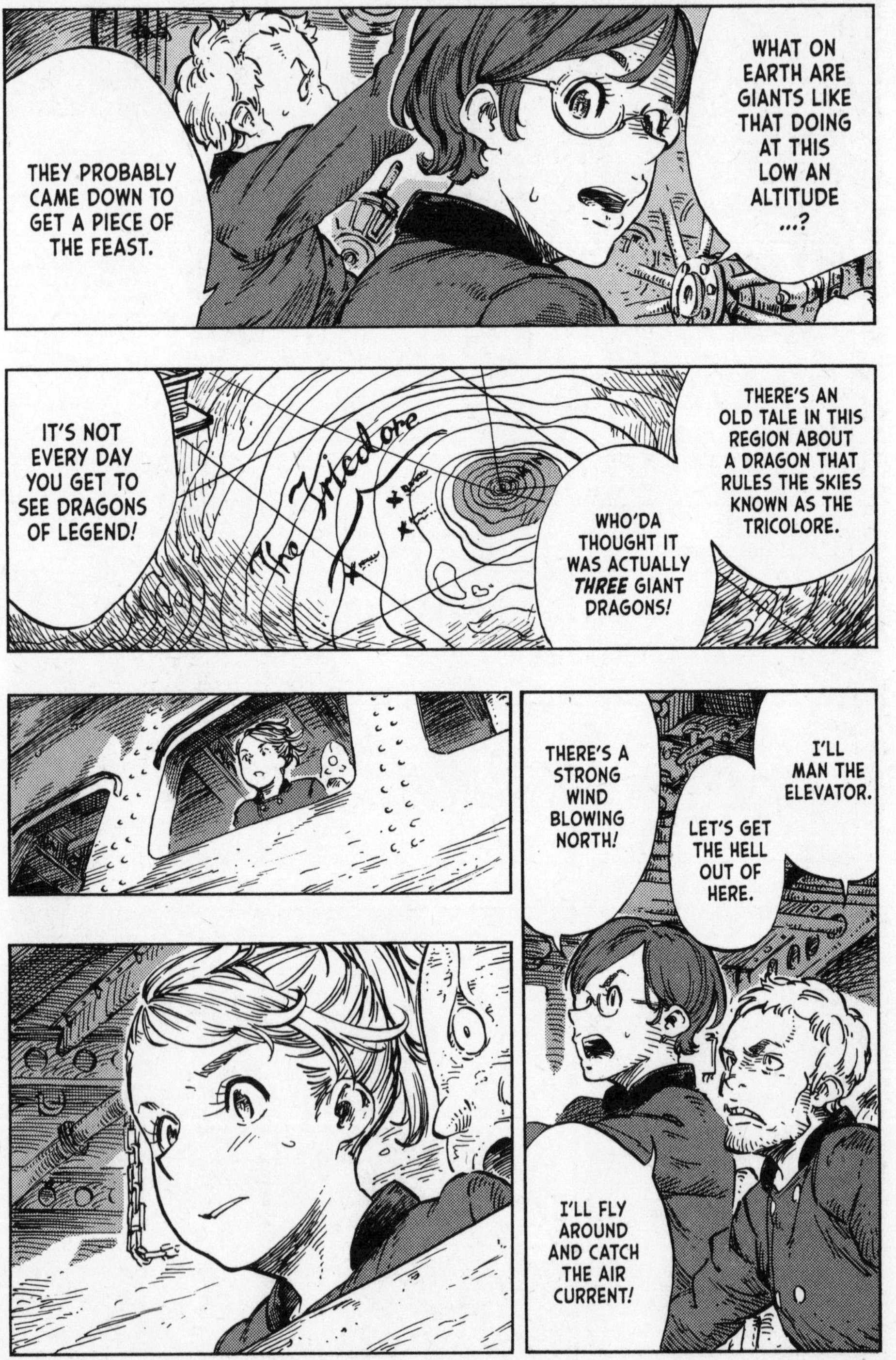
WHAT ON EARTH ARE GIANTS LIKE THAT DOING AT THIS LOW AN ALTITUDE ...?
THEY PROBABLY CAME DOWN TO GET A PIECE OF THE FEAST.
THERE'S AN OLD TALE IN THIS REGION ABOUT A DRAGON THAT RULES THE SKIES KNOWN AS THE TRICOLORE.
WHO'DA THOUGHT IT WAS ACTUALLY *THREE* GIANT DRAGONS!
IT'S NOT EVERY DAY YOU GET TO SEE DRAGONS OF LEGEND!
I'LL MAN THE ELEVATOR.
LET'S GET THE HELL OUT OF HERE.
THERE'S A STRONG WIND BLOWING NORTH!
I'LL FLY AROUND AND CATCH THE AIR CURRENT!

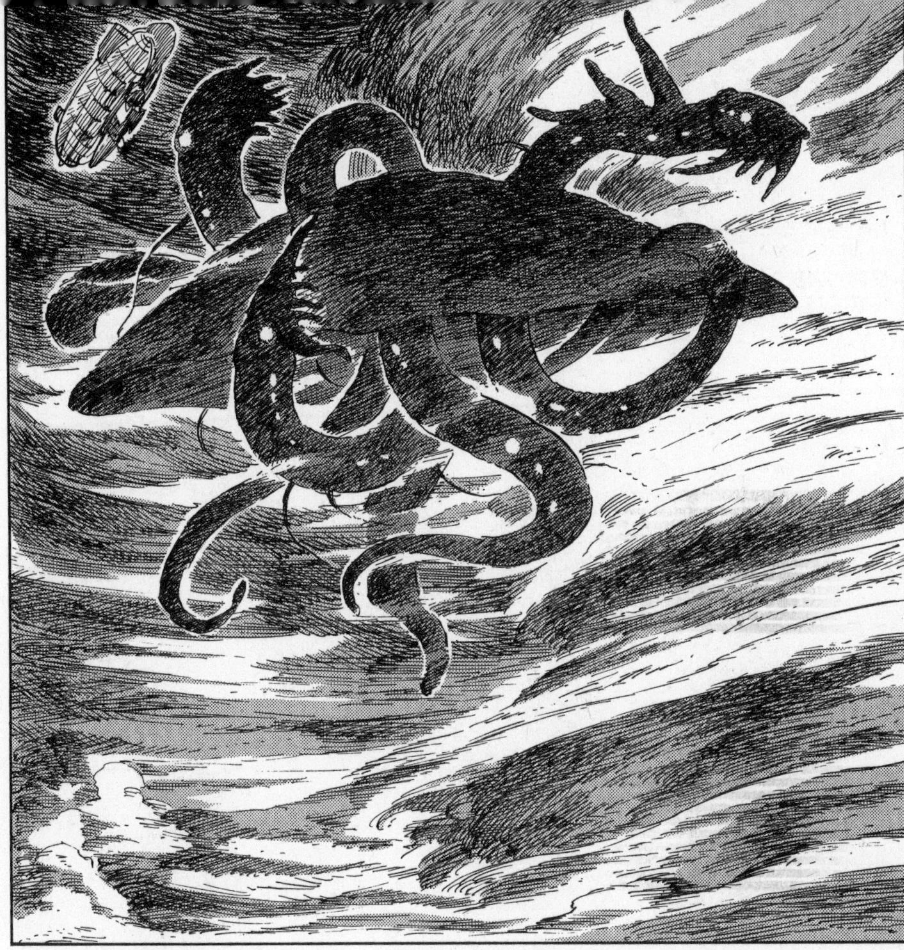

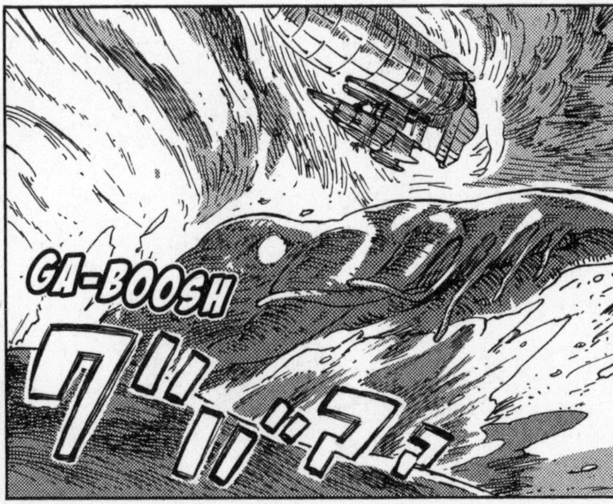
GA-BOOSH

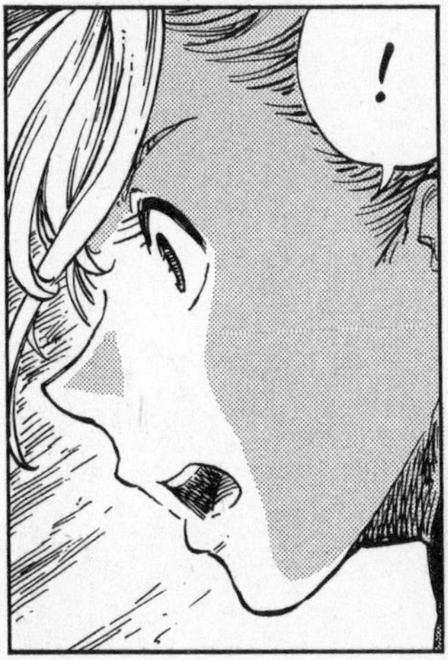
!

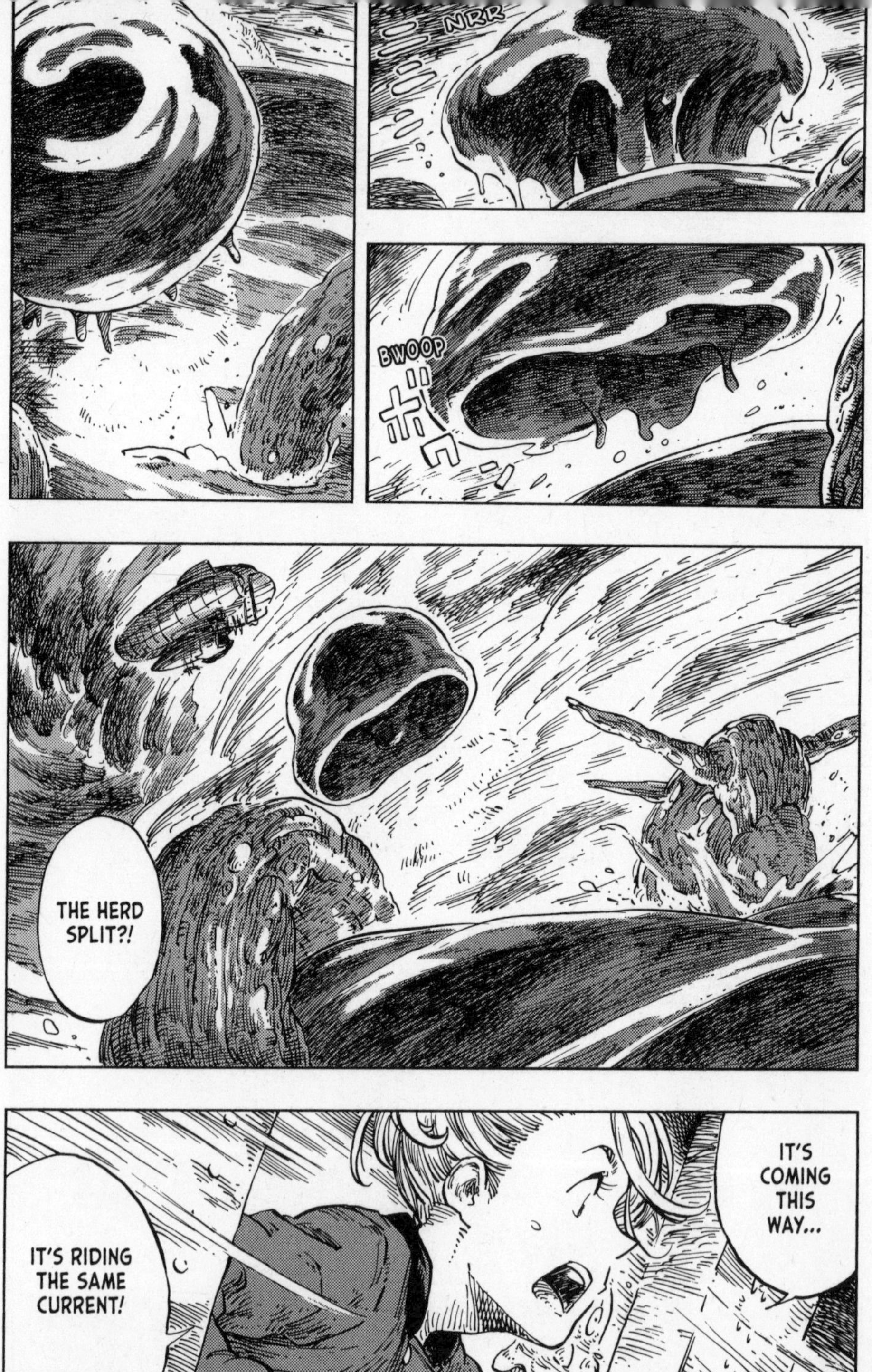
NRR
BWOOP
THE HERD SPLIT?!
IT'S COMING THIS WAY...
IT'S RIDING THE SAME CURRENT!

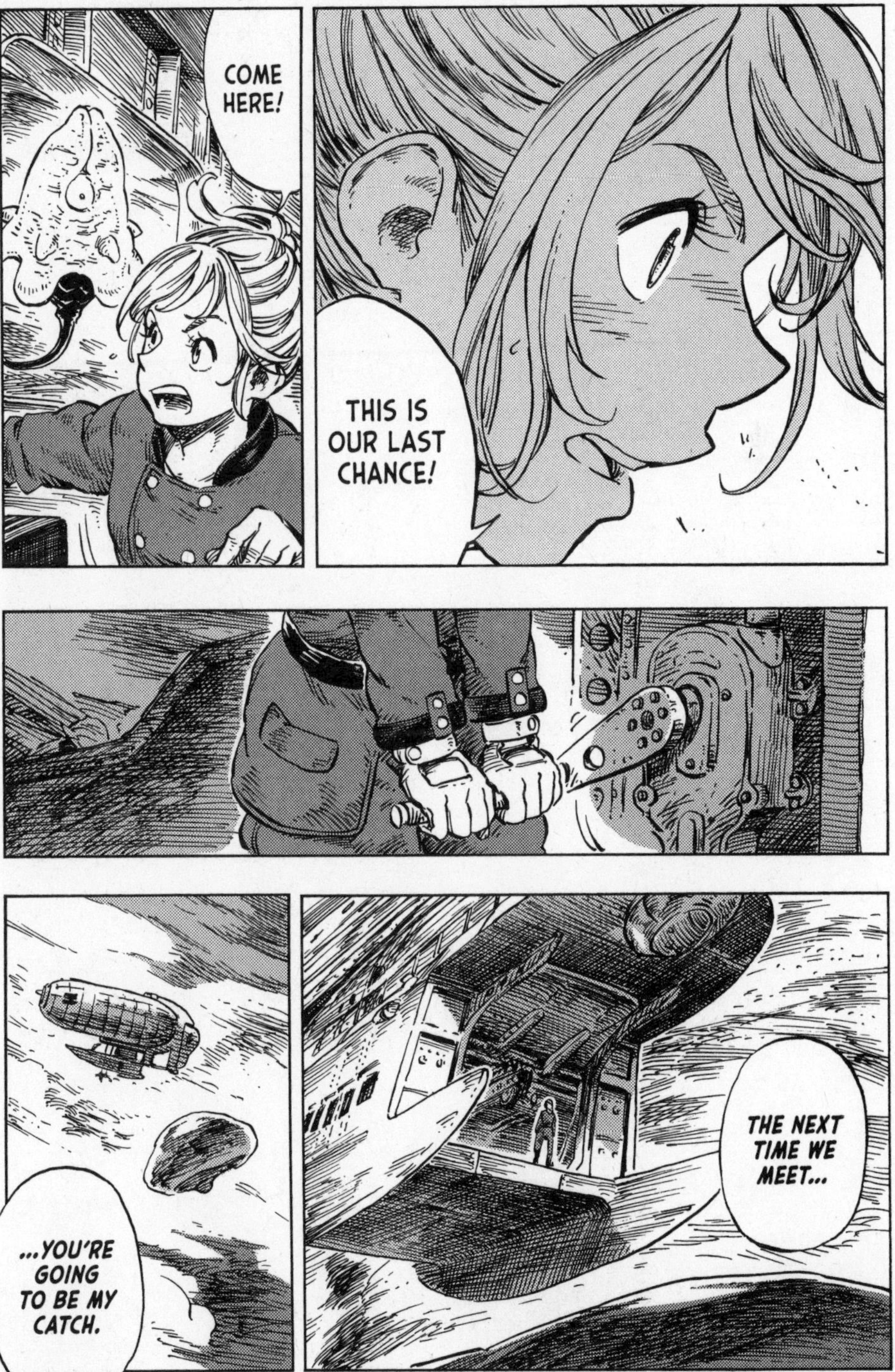
THIS IS OUR LAST CHANCE!
COME HERE!
THE NEXT TIME WE MEET...
...YOU'RE GOING TO BE MY CATCH.

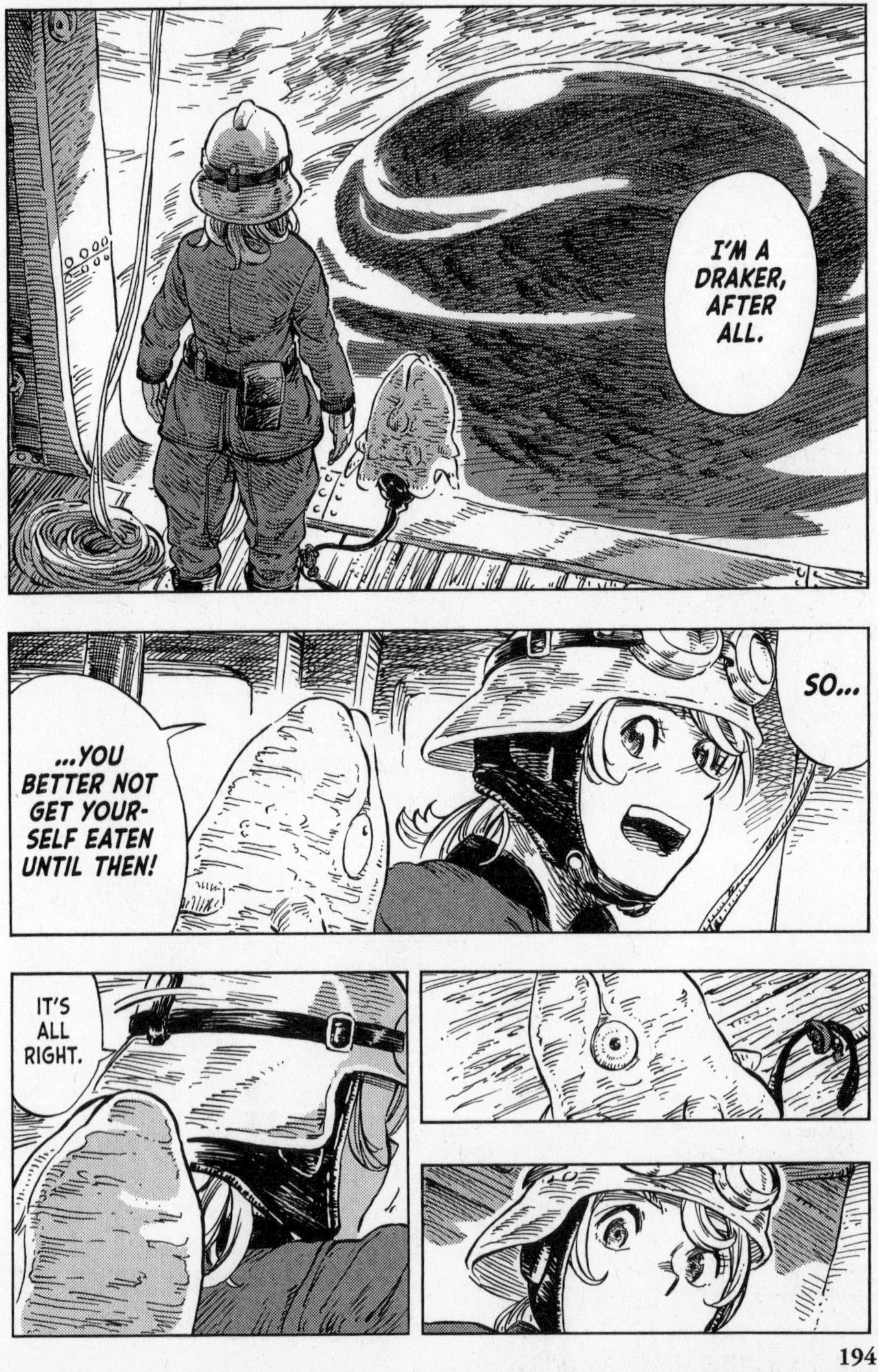
I'M A DRAKER, AFTER ALL.
SO...
...YOU BETTER NOT GET YOUR-SELF EATEN UNTIL THEN!
IT'S ALL RIGHT.

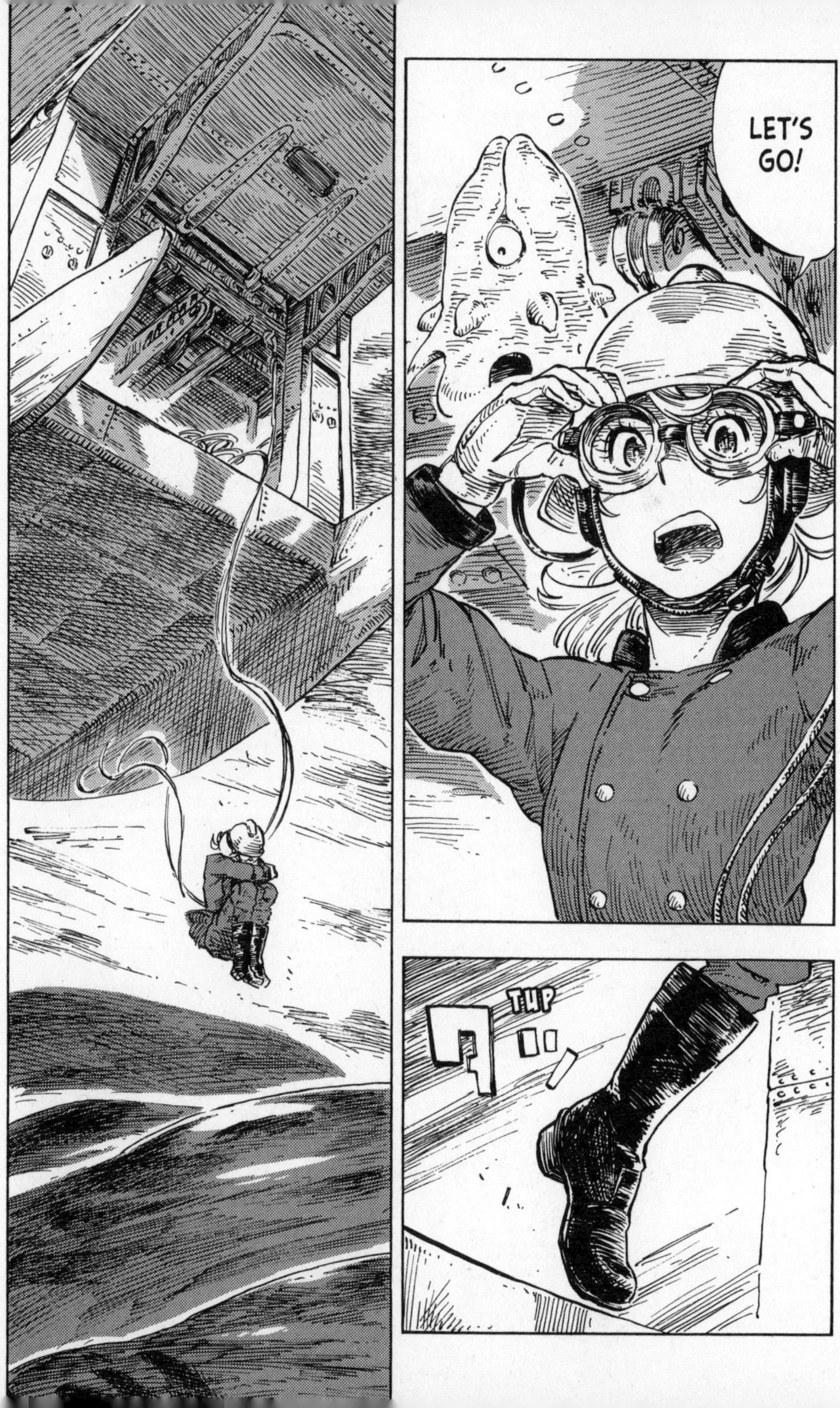
LET'S GO!
TUP

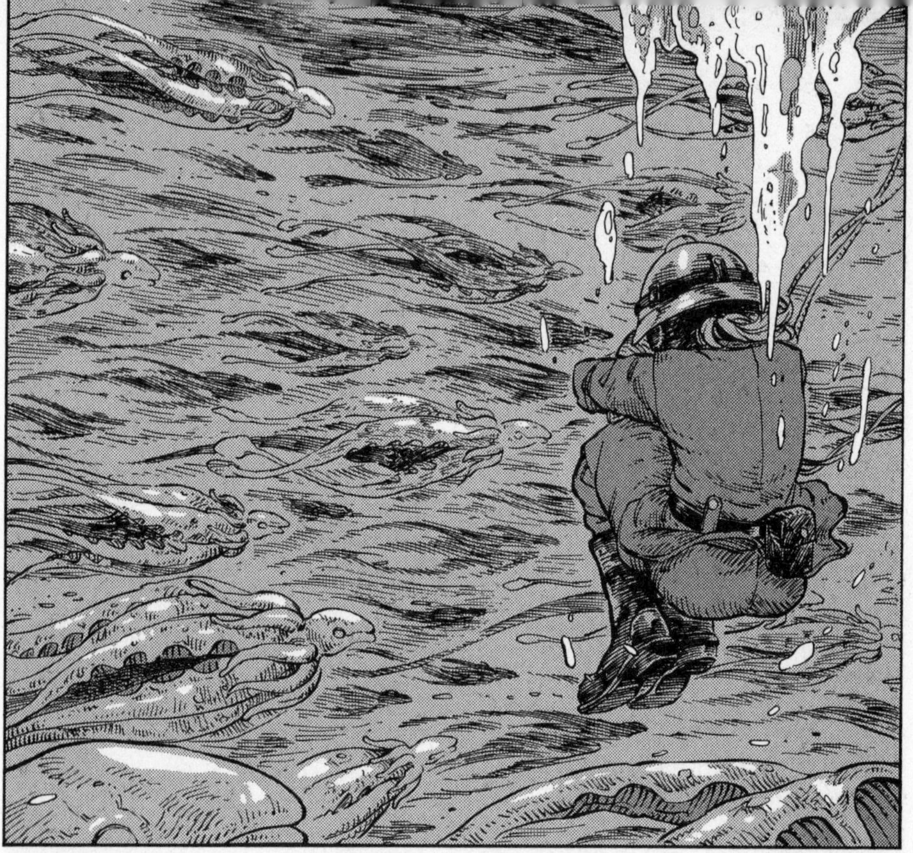
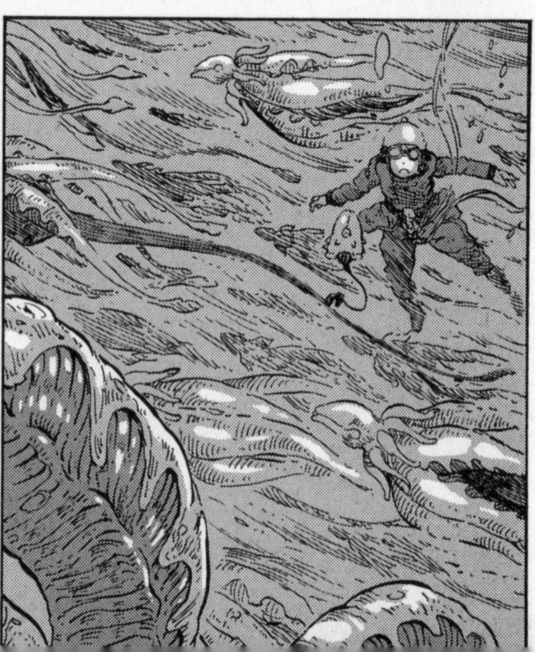
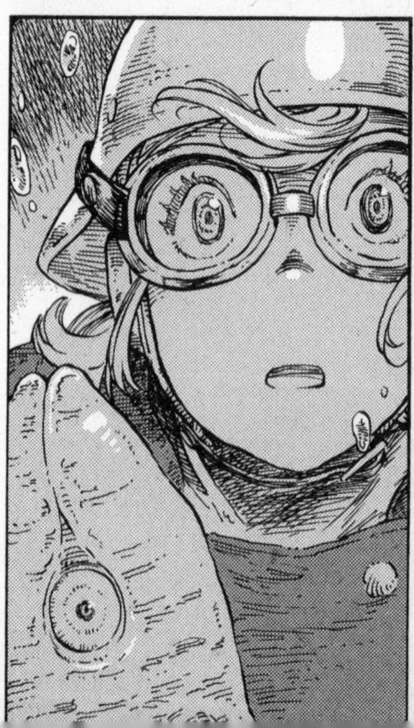

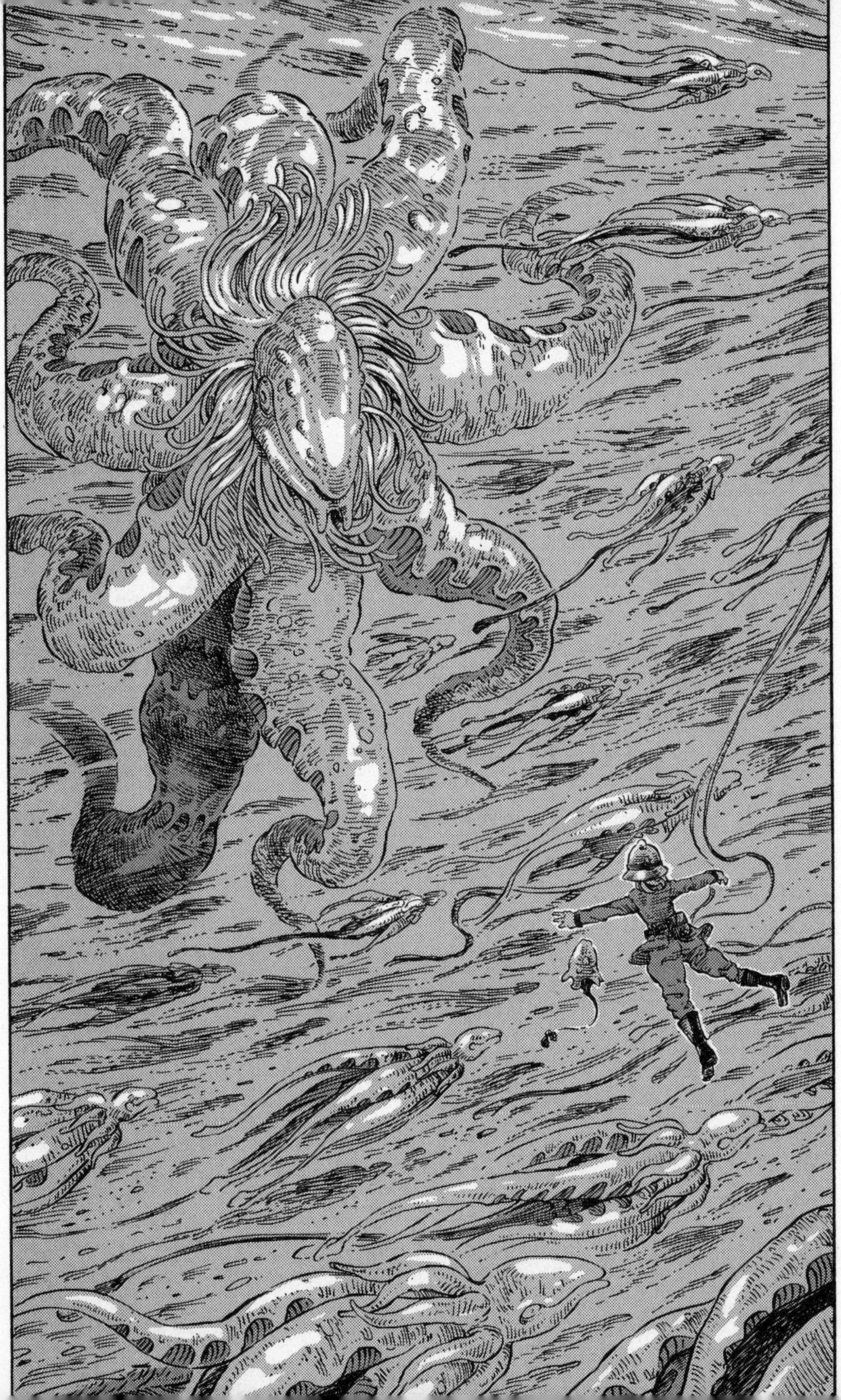

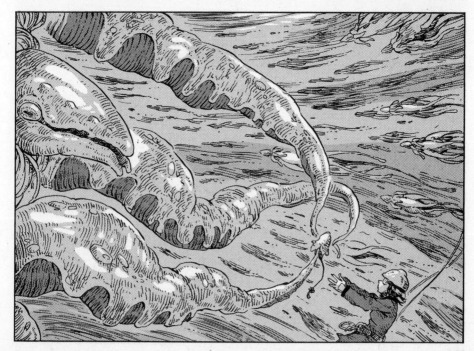

WRIG

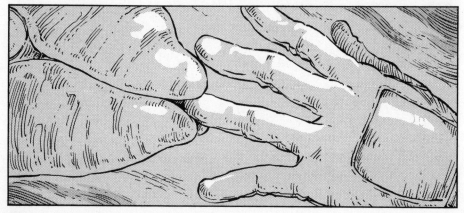

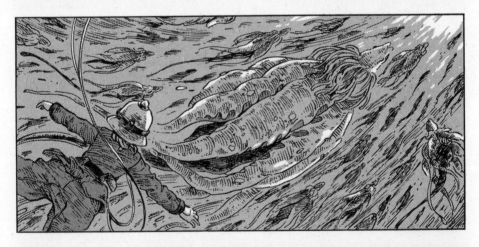

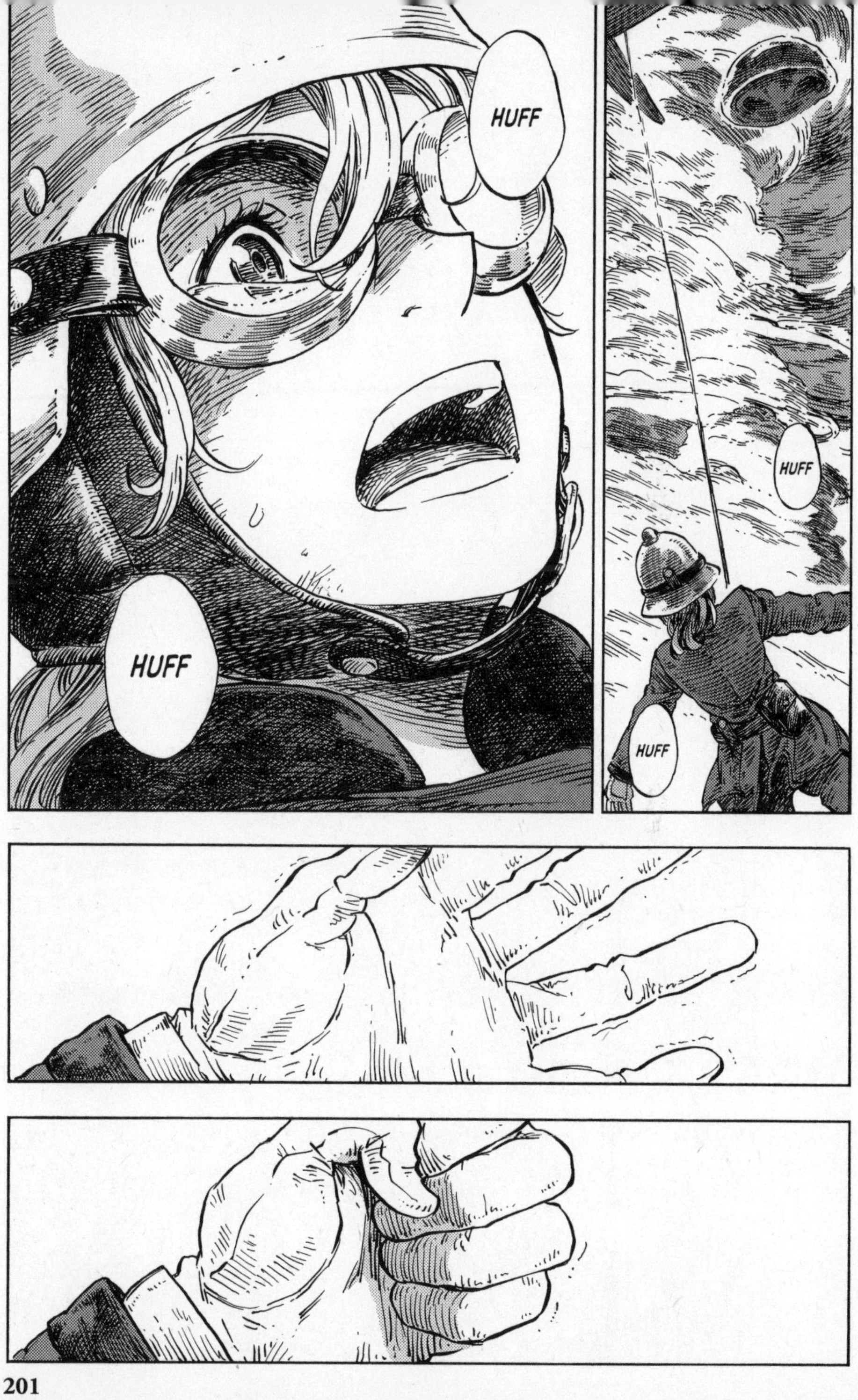
HUFF
HUFF
HUFF
HUFF

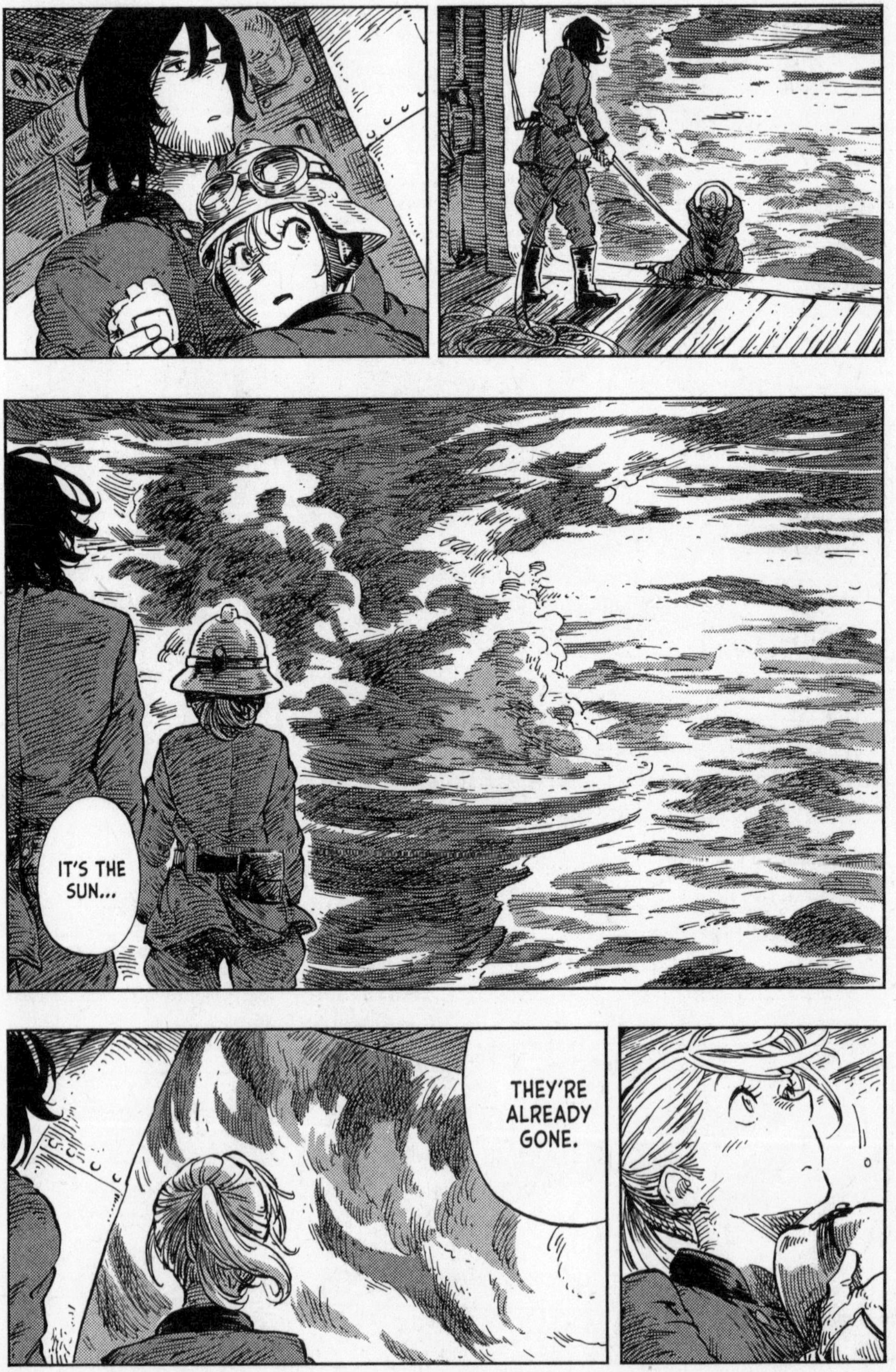
IT'S THE SUN...
THEY'RE ALREADY GONE.

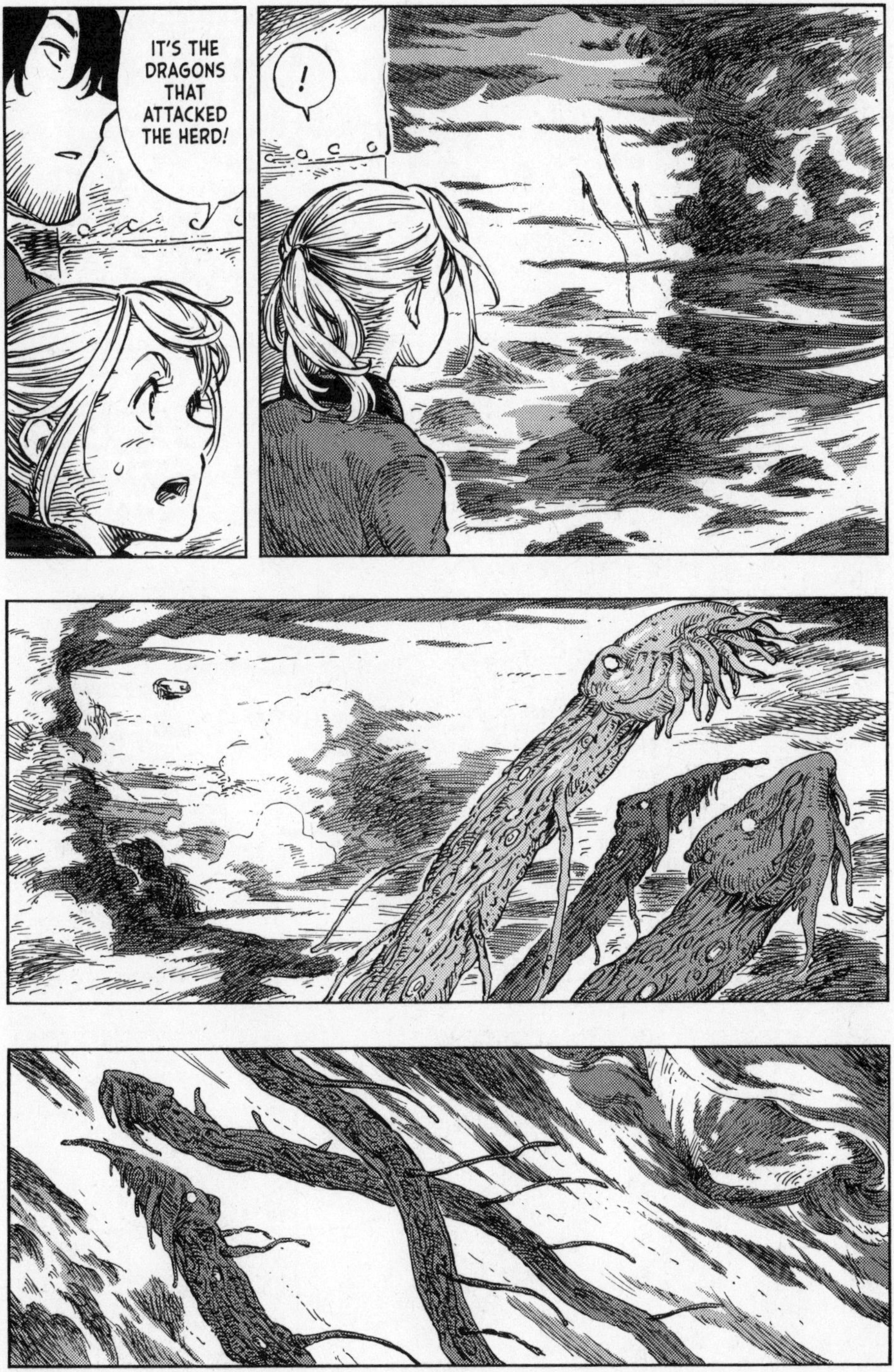
!
IT'S THE DRAGONS THAT ATTACKED THE HERD!

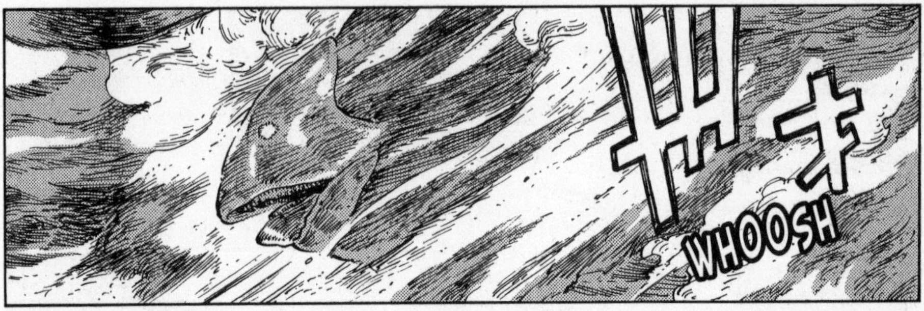
WHOOSH

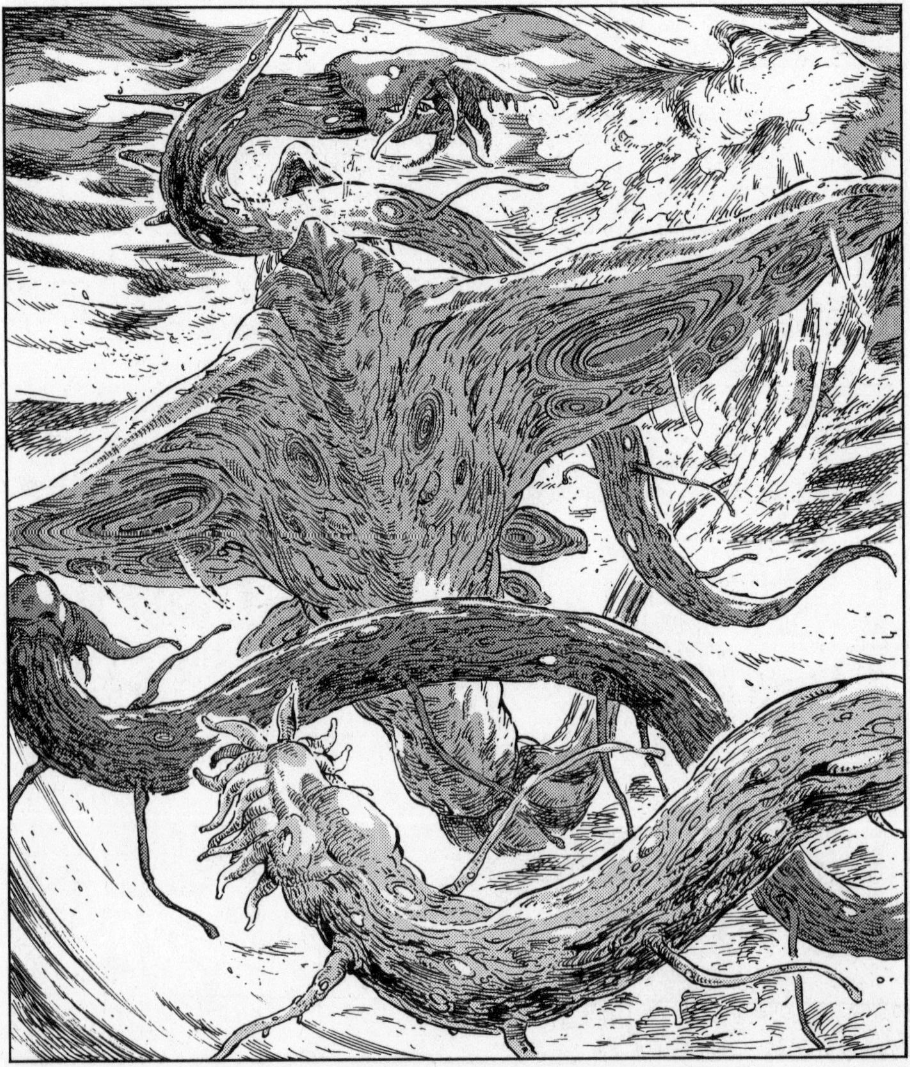

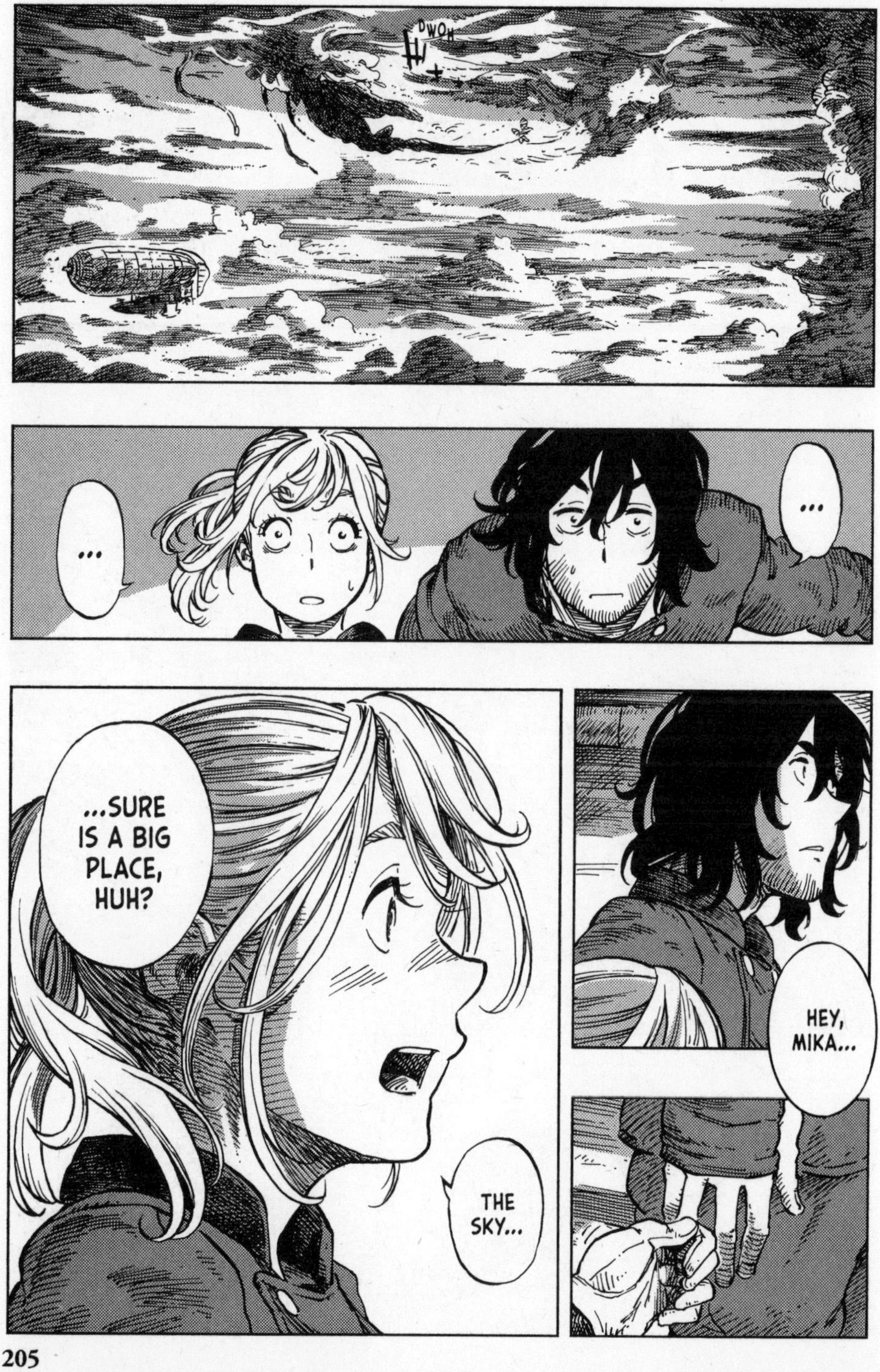
DWOH
...
...
HEY, MIKA...
THE SKY...
...SURE IS A BIG PLACE, HUH?

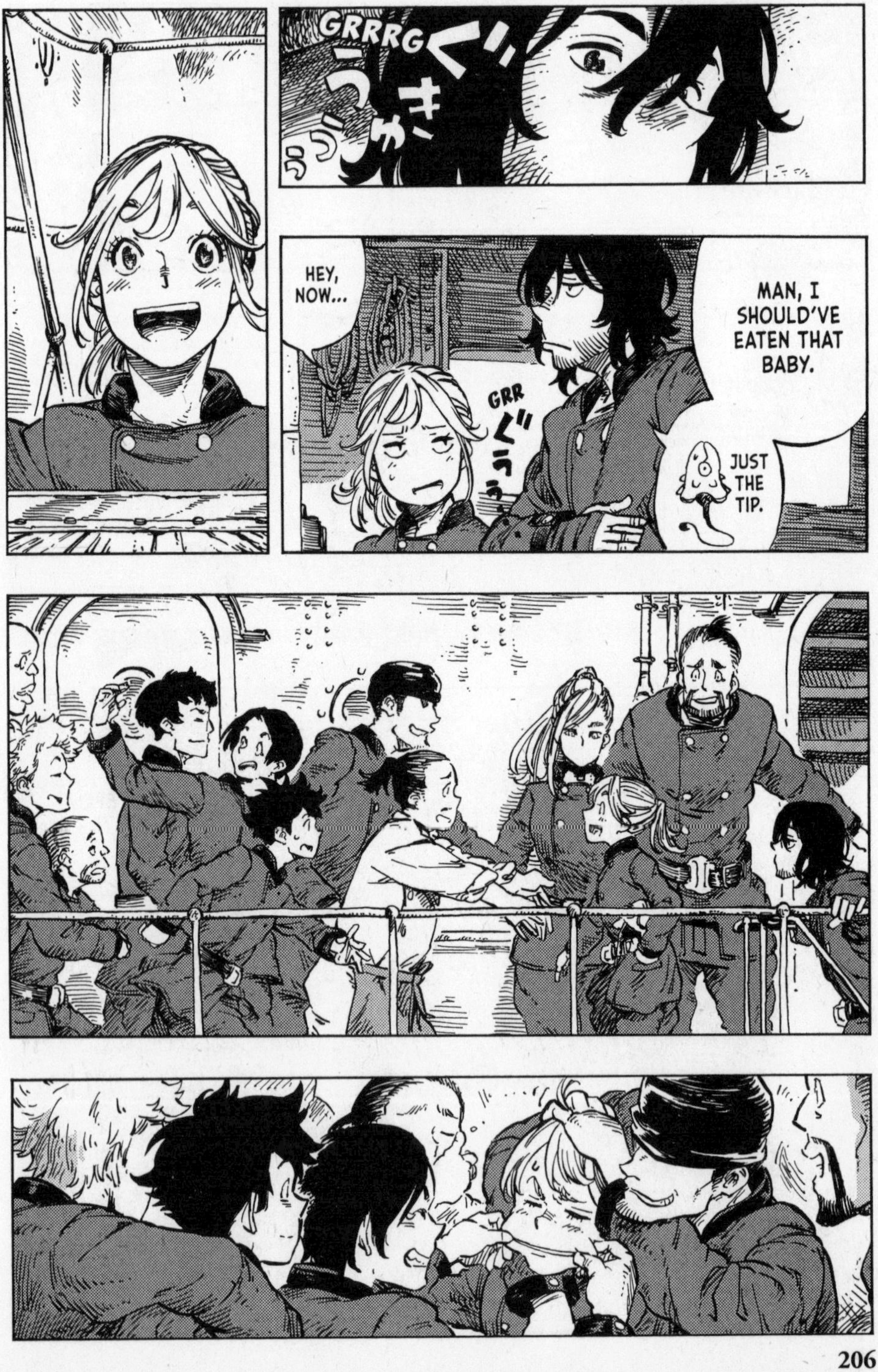
GRRRG
MAN, I SHOULD'VE EATEN THAT BABY.
JUST THE TIP.
GRR
HEY, NOW...

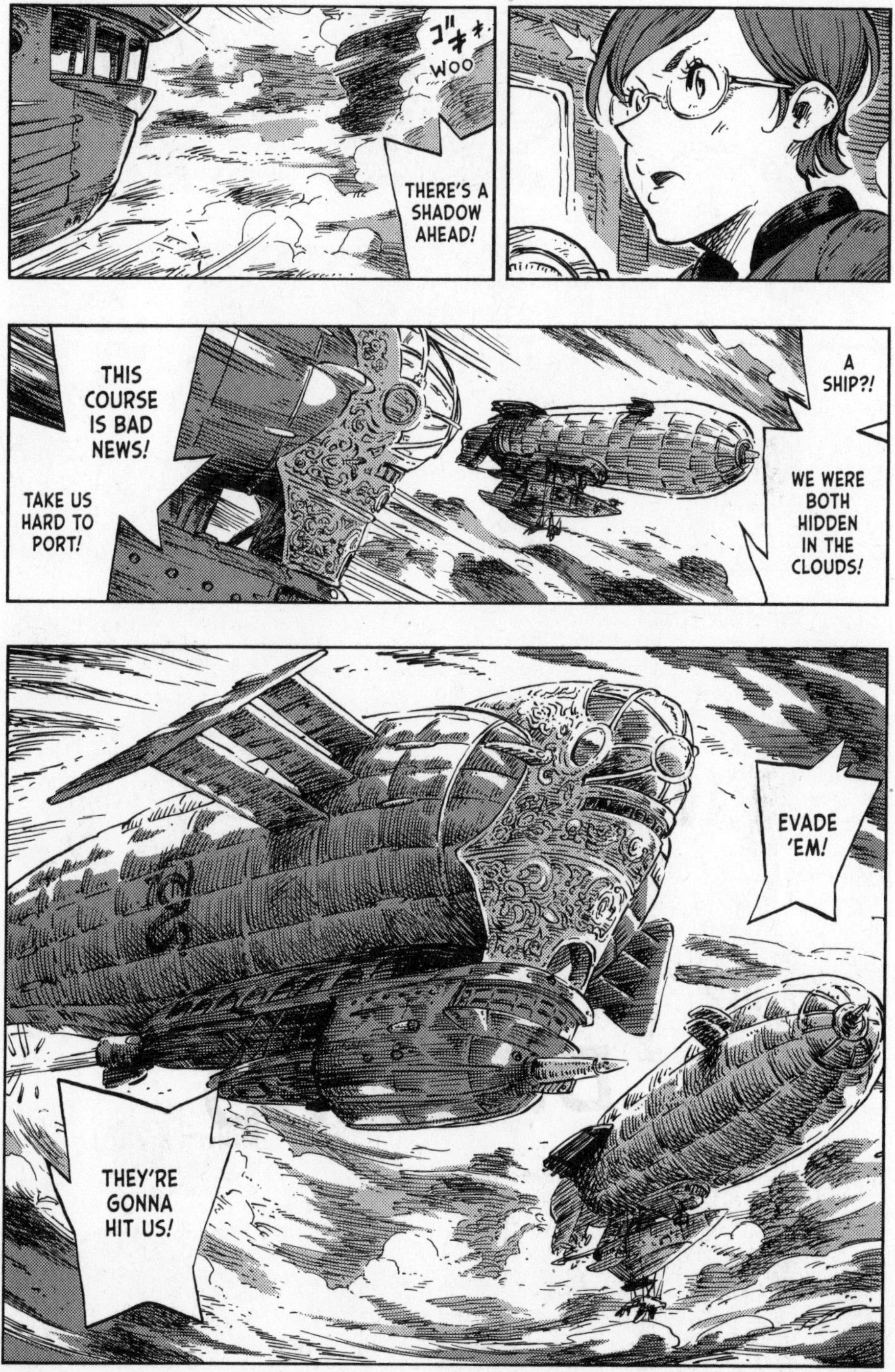
ゴォ
WOO
THERE'S A SHADOW AHEAD!
A SHIP?!
WE WERE BOTH HIDDEN IN THE CLOUDS!
THIS COURSE IS BAD NEWS!
TAKE US HARD TO PORT!
EVADE 'EM!
THEY'RE GONNA HIT US!

A Kodansha Comics Trade Paperback Original
Drifting Dragons 3 copyright © 2017 Taku Kuwabara
English translation copyright © 2020 Taku Kuwabara

Published in the United States by Kodansha Comics, an imprint of Kodansha USA Publishing, LLC, New York.

Publication rights for this English edition arranged through Kodansha Ltd., Tokyo.

First published in Japan in 2017 by Kodansha Ltd., Tokyo as *Kuutei Doragonzu*, volume 3.

ISBN 978-1-63236-945-1

Original cover design by Miki Kawano

Printed in the United States of America.

www.kodanshacomics.com

9 8 7 6 5 4 3 2 1
Translation: Adam Hirsch
Lettering: Thea Willis
Editing: Paul Starr
Kodansha Comics edition cover design by Phil Balsman

Publisher: Kiichiro Sugawara
Managing editor: Maya Rosewood
Vice president of marketing & publicity: Naho Yamada

Director of publishing services: Ben Applegate
Associate director of operations: Stephen Pakula
Publishing services managing editor: Noelle Webster
Assistant production manager: Emi Lotto